Endorsement statement

Endorsement indicates that a resource has passed Cambridge International Education's rigorous quality-assurance process and is suitable to support the delivery of their syllabus. However, endorsed resources are not the only suitable materials available to support teaching and learning, and are not essential to achieve the qualification. For the full list of endorsed resources to support this syllabus, visit www.cambridgeinternational.org/endorsed-resources

Any example answers to questions taken from past question papers, practice questions, accompanying marks and mark schemes included in this resource have been written by the authors and are for guidance only. They do not replicate examination papers. In examinations the way marks are awarded may be different. Any references to assessment and/or assessment preparation are the publisher's interpretation of the syllabus requirements. Examiners will not use endorsed resources as a source of material for any assessment set by Cambridge International Education.

While the publishers have made every attempt to ensure that advice on the qualification and its assessment is accurate, the official syllabus, specimen assessment materials and any associated assessment guidance materials produced by the awarding body are the only authoritative source of information and should always be referred to for definitive guidance.

Our approach is to provide teachers with access to a wide range of high-quality resources that suit different styles and types of teaching and learning.

For more information about the endorsement process, please visit www.cambridgeinternational.org/endorsed-resources

Cambridge International Education material in this publication is reproduced under licence and remains the intellectual property of Cambridge University Press & Assessment.

Third-party websites and resources referred to in this publication are not endorsed.

CAMBRIDGE

Modern Europe, 1774–1924

for Cambridge International AS Level History

COURSEBOOK

Graham Goodlad & Patrick Walsh-Atkins

Third edition with Digital access

CAMBRIDGE
UNIVERSITY PRESS & ASSESSMENT

Shaftesbury Road, Cambridge CB2 8EA, United Kingdom

One Liberty Plaza, 20th Floor, New York, NY 10006, USA

477 Williamstown Road, Port Melbourne, VIC 3207, Australia

314–321, 3rd Floor, Plot 3, Splendor Forum, Jasola District Centre, New Delhi – 110025, India

103 Penang Road, #05–06/07, Visioncrest Commercial, Singapore 238467

Cambridge University Press & Assessment is a department of the University of Cambridge.

We share the University's mission to contribute to society through the pursuit of education, learning and research at the highest international levels of excellence.

www.cambridge.org
Information on this title: www.cambridge.org/9781009556200

First published 2013
Second edition 2019
Third edition 2025

20 19 18 17 16 15 14 13 12 11 10 9 8 7 6 5 4 3 2 1

Printed in Poland by Opolgraf

A catalogue record for this publication is available from the British Library

ISBN 978-1-00-955620-0 Paperback with Digital Access

ISBN 978-1-00-955621-7 Digital Coursebook

ISBN 978-1-00-955622-4 Coursebook eBook

Additional resources for this publication at www.cambridge.org/9781009556200

Contents

How to use this series

This suite of resources supports learners and teachers following the Cambridge International AS Level History syllabuses (9489/9981/9982). The components in the series are designed to work together and help learners develop the necessary knowledge and skills for studying History.

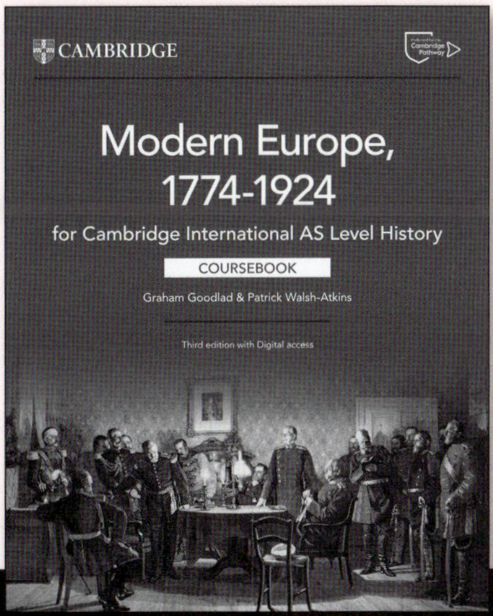

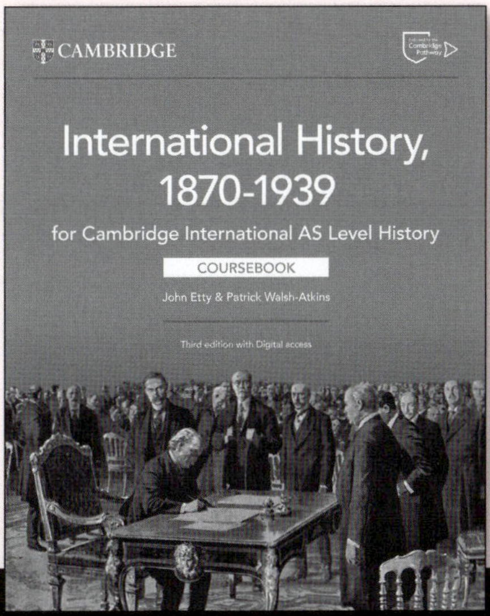

The Coursebooks are designed for learners to use in class with guidance from the teacher. One of the Coursebooks offers coverage of European option: Modern Europe, 1774–1924 and the other offers coverage of International option: International history, 1870–1939 of the Cambridge International AS Level History syllabus. Each chapter contains in-depth explanations, definitions and a variety of activities and questions to engage learners and develop their historical skills.

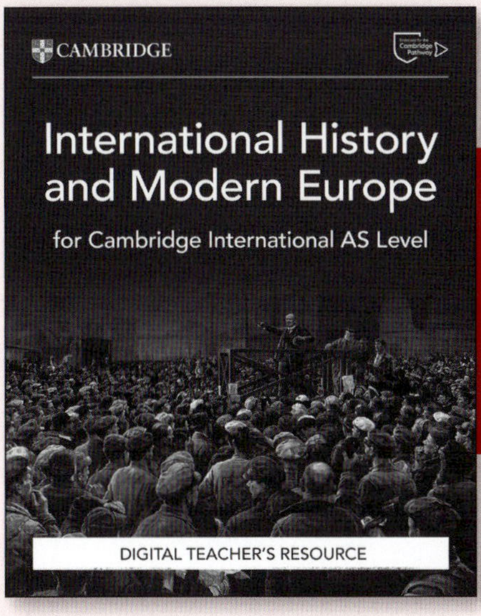

The Teacher's Resource is the foundation of this series. It offers inspiring ideas about how to teach this course including teaching notes, how to avoid common misconceptions, suggestions for differentiation, formative assessment and language support, answers and extra materials such as worksheets and historical sources.

How to use this book

This book contains a number of features to help you in your study.

KEY QUESTIONS

Each chapter begins with Key questions that briefly set out the topics you should understand once you have completed the chapter.

Timeline

The timeline at the start of each chapter provides a visual guide to the key events which happened during the years covered by the topic.

GETTING STARTED

Getting started activities will help you think about what you already know about the topic of the chapter.

ACTIVITY

Activities are a mixture of individual, pair and group tasks to help you develop your skills and practise applying your understanding of a topic. Some activities use sources to help you practise your skills in analysis. Please note, some sources have been abridged or adapted.

KEY CONCEPT

Key concept boxes contain questions that help you develop a conceptual understanding of History, start to make judgements based on your knowledge and understanding, and think about how the different topics you study are connected.

KEY TERM

Key terms are important terms in the topic you are learning. They are highlighted in bold where they first appear in the text, and definitions are given in the Key terms boxes. All of the key terms are included in the glossary at the end of the book.

KEY FIGURE

Key figure boxes highlight important historical figures that you need to remember, and briefly explain what makes them a key figure.

Reflection

Reflection boxes give you the opportunity to think about how you approach certain activities, and how you might improve this in the future.

Practice questions

These questions, written by the authors, help you prepare for assessment by writing longer answers.

Improve this answer

These sample answers to some of the practice questions are accompanied by notes on what works well and how they could be improved. After reading the comments, you are challenged to write a better answer to the question.

The answers and the commentary are written by the authors.

TIP

Tips are included in the Preparing for assessment chapter. These give advice on important things to remember and what to avoid doing when revising.

SELF-EVALUATION CHECKLIST

Each chapter ends with a checklist of the main points covered in that topic, and gives you space to think about how confident you are with these points. Take time to fully reflect on your current level of understanding before you select an option. If you select 'Needs more work' or 'Almost there' for any of the points, revisit the relevant content and make a clear action plan for increasing your confidence in that area. It is worth revisiting the checklists when preparing for assessment.

You should be able to:	Needs more work	Almost there	Ready to move on

Please be aware that this book contains some historical texts and images that may distress the reader. This material reflects the language and attitudes of the period in which they were created, but does not align with the current values and practices of Cambridge University Press & Assessment. Teacher support is advised.

The maps included in this book are historical and are not intended to represent current border and country agreements. They are provided for educational and illustrative purposes only.

Getting started with Cambridge International AS Level History

Introduction

Congratulations on choosing to study Cambridge International AS Level History – a subject that is highly regarded by universities and employers. AS Level History helps students to understand why the modern world is the way it is and how it has changed over time.

Aside from studying fascinating information about extremely important events that have had an impact on the way many people live today, students of history also get lots of practice at analysing large amounts of information, prioritising and extracting the most relevant information, synthesising and comparing different information, and constructing and assessing arguments. These skills are essential in careers such as law, administration, politics and government, TV research and journalism.

History students spend time enquiring and searching for information, learning where to look and what questions to ask. These skills are essential in careers such as policing, investigative reporting and market research.

Historians communicate their ideas in an organised, structured and logical fashion. History requires extended, logical, reasoned debate in writing. These skills are essential in careers that require writing reports, including academia, the civil service and journalism.

History teaches you to understand individuals and groups – their feelings, attitudes, prejudices and motivations. These skills are essential in careers such as personnel, law, teaching and social work.

AS Level History introduces you to historical skills such as explaining cause and consequence, change and continuity, which are essential in any career that requires analysis and strategy, such as the armed forces, teaching, advertising, medicine, banking and accountancy.

History helps you to develop skills of problem solving and evaluating solutions, information handling, communicating ideas, flexibility and tolerance – skills that are essential in problem solving in industry, and in research and development teams in science and engineering.

While studying AS Level History, you will work independently and participate in discussion, which is essential for developing your own ideas and judgement. Your teacher cannot tell you what to think or what opinions to have, although they can help you learn how to think and how to form opinions. To be successful in this course, you will have to put forward your own views on a subject and explain your reasons for coming to those views.

History is not a series of universally accepted facts, which once learned, will provide you with a detailed and accurate understanding of the past. Just as historical events were perceived in many different (and often contradictory) ways by people who experienced them at the time, so they have been interpreted in many different (and often contradictory) ways by historians who have studied them subsequently. Historical debates rage all the time, which makes it very clear that historians often disagree fundamentally about the reasons for, or the significance of, certain key events.

You need to understand, for example, that there is no right answer to why the French Revolution broke out in 1789. Many historians have researched this topic in depth and have come to very different conclusions. You will need to learn to reflect on those conclusions and to reach your own judgement. This process of reflection will also give you an insight into the methods historians use to put across their ideas; you will be able to adapt these methods for your own use when answering historical questions.

You will be asked for your opinion or judgement on an issue like this and will have to make up your own mind. You need to study the evidence, reflect on what kind of evidence it is and then analyse what it proves. This will allow you to form an opinion. When asked for an opinion or judgement, you will need to back up what you offer with reasons and evidence. In this way, historians are like lawyers in court. You are making a case and then proving it.

Sometimes your fellow learners and teachers might disagree with your opinion and be able to provide compelling evidence to demonstrate why. Sometimes they might convince you to change your mind. Sometimes you will be able to convince them to change or refine their opinions. Sometimes you might just agree to differ. It is this ability to see things in different ways, and to have the confidence to use your own knowledge and understanding to make judgements, form opinions and develop arguments, that makes studying history so interesting and challenging.

The information in this section is based on the Cambridge International Education syllabus. You should always refer to the appropriate syllabus document for the year of examination to confirm the details and for more information. The syllabus document is available on the website: www.cambridgeinternational.org.

How does Cambridge International AS Level History differ from Cambridge IGCSE™ History?

If you have studied Cambridge IGCSE or O Level History, it is likely that you will have encountered some parts of your AS Level topics before, but you will also encounter interesting new topics. The topics you will study are covered in more depth at AS Level than at Cambridge IGCSE and O Level.

When studying Cambridge IGCSE History, students consider how attitudes to events differed, but the differences are often quite obvious. At AS Level, you will continue to investigate how historical events were perceived in many different (and often contradictory) ways by people who experienced them at the time, but you will consider in more depth why these differences arose. Study at AS Level requires you to engage much more carefully with the sometimes-subtle differences of opinion, to think really deeply about the different attitudes that underpinned people's positions, and to explain the complex relationships between different ideas that motivated people in the past.

The skills you will develop at AS Level are the same as those required at Cambridge IGCSE History. You will need to recall, select and use historical knowledge appropriately and effectively. At AS Level, however, you will need a much greater depth of knowledge, a much higher level of sophistication in the responses you write, and a much bigger emphasis on:

- analysis and substantiated judgements (judgements backed up evidence) about causation, changes and continuities, consequences and significance, and the relationships between key features and characteristics of the periods studied
- analysis and interpretation of a range of source materials
- evaluation of source materials.

What are the key concepts?

The syllabus identifies key concepts for AS and A Level History. Considering these concepts and keeping them in mind as you work through the course will help you see patterns, make connections, develop a deeper understanding and gain new perspectives. You will also come across Key concept boxes as you work through this book where we draw your attention to particular links, patterns and ideas. The key concepts for this course are as follows.

Cause and consequence

Causation (the study of causes) relates to the major events you will study. Its focus is not on the events themselves, but on:

- the circumstances and conditions that shaped the events
- the things that led directly or indirectly to the events
- the actions people took (and the beliefs that motivated them) to bring about the events.

Consequences are the effects, results and outcomes of events. They can be direct or indirect.

Change and continuity

When you study the history of a given period and/or place, you will almost always investigate how and why things changed. These changes may be big or small, and they may have profound or relatively trivial impacts. Just as history involves the study of these patterns and processes of change, it can also involve analysis of how some other things remained the same. Continuities can be just as important for historians as changes.

Similarity and difference

Despite living in different periods and places, people can have quite similar experiences. Despite having similar causes, comparable events can have remarkably different outcomes. Despite experiencing the same circumstances and having access to the same information, people can adopt profoundly different attitudes and form totally different opinions on certain issues. History involves study of the similarities and the differences in each case.

Significance

History is not a set of facts that everyone accepts. Some aspects of the past are considered more important by some people than others. People make judgements about significance at the time, and historians continue to make these judgements as time goes by. Studying history involves understanding that people think that different things are significant depending on their own context, values, interests and concerns.

Interpretations

The work of historians involves researching, reconstructing and explaining events in the past. There is no single correct way to do this work, so historians go about their work in different ways. One consequence of these different approaches is that historians present different interpretations of the past, and historians can disagree with each other. Especially at A Level and beyond, study of history involves investigation of historical interpretations and the methods that created them. This key concept is not assessed at AS Level.

What topics will I study?

You may be studying Cambridge International AS Level History (9489). In this syllabus, there are three content options. You are studying the European option: Modern Europe, 1774–1924.

Alternatively you may be studying Cambridge International AS & A Level European History (9981). Both syllabuses have the same content and assessment structure.

You will study three topics. These topics match the content chapters in this coursebook:

1. France, 1774–1814
2. Liberalism and nationalism in Germany, 1815–71
3. Russia from autocracy to revolution, 1881–1924

Out of the many thousand historical topics that could be chosen for study, these three are strong candidates. All are interlinked. All had a profound influence on both contemporary events in the world and later decades. We can still see now in the 21st century very clearly why all three are so significant. The ideas behind the French Revolution of liberty and nationalism are still present and played an important role in the rise of Germany. The growth of a powerful and strongly nationalist nation in central Europe played a key role in causing the two World Wars of the 20th century. Some of the more radical ideas behind the French Revolution influenced the communist ideas behind the Russian Revolution, which of course still has a profound influence today. All three topics provide us with opportunities to study why things happen, what influences the course of events and how significant are individuals in changing the course of history. All have aroused great controversy and great historians are still arguing about them. You'll have an opportunity to see why.

You must study all three topics. Each topic is divided into four key questions and each key question contains different historical content. For instance, the first key question you will look at is 'What were the causes and immediate consequences of the 1789 Revolution?'.

You could be assessed on any of the content that is specified under the key questions, so make sure you have studied it all. This coursebook covers all of the key questions and syllabus content for the European option.

How will I be assessed?

Assessment for Cambridge International AS Level History is via two papers, often known as Historical Sources (Paper 1) and Outline Study (Paper 2).

Historical Sources (Paper 1)

In this paper you will answer one question which is based on historical sources.
This question will always have part **a** and part **b**, and you must answer both parts.

Paper 1 will examine one of the three topics, but

- you cannot choose which topics you write about on Paper 1
- the topics will rotate from year to year
- no topic will appear on both Paper 1 and Paper 2 at the same time.

Outline Study (Paper 2)

Whichever topics were **not** assessed on Paper 1 will be examined on Paper 2.
The examination paper will contain two essay-based questions: one on each of the remaining two topics. These questions will always have part **a** and part **b**, and you must answer both parts of both questions.

Your teacher will confirm which topics will be assessed on which paper. The information is also included in the syllabus. Make sure you know the allocation for your year of examination.

What types of questions will test my skills?

As discussed in the paper descriptions, there are two broad types of question: source-based questions and essay-based questions. You will look at these in more detail in the Preparing for assessment chapter at the end of the book.

There are certain key words that appear in many AS Level History questions. These 'command words' are the instructions that specify what you need to do. They make it clear what is expected from a response in terms of skills, knowledge and understanding.

The guidance and suggested approach that appear in Table 0.1 have been written by the authors.

Command word	Meaning	Guidance	How to approach these questions
Compare	Identify/comment on similarities and/or differences.	You should identify at least one point where the sources differ in relation to the prompt and at least one where they agree, as well as providing good evidence from the sources to explain those similarities and differences. You should also comment on the sources' provenance (the term used for a source's background) using contextual knowledge.	Ensure that you fully demonstrate your grasp of the sources. Do not just describe the contents – make sure you use the information in the sources to compare them. Also demonstrate that you have carefully evaluated the sources.
Explain	Set out purposes or reasons / make the relationships between things clear / say why and/or how and support with relevant evidence.	You should give about three clear points explaining why something happened. Each point should be backed up by a relevant and accurate detail.	Try to prioritise those points making it evident why you thought one of those points was more important that the others.
To what extent ...? How far do you agree ...? How far was ... successful? How far was ... unsuccessful? How far was ... the key factor? How far was ... the main reason? How important was ...? How successful was ...?		You should develop a clear case both for and against the view stated, demonstrating not only your knowledge and understanding of the topic, but also your ability to analyse the question and come to a reasoned conclusion.	You should make a firm judgement on the issue of extent.

Table 0.1: Syllabus command words and meanings with additional guidance from the authors

Working with sources

Source-based questions are testing your ability to read, contrast, evaluate and judge a range of sources.

In order to make judgements about past events, historians usually gather a lot of information and evidence. They can use a wide variety of sources for this, including written extracts, speeches, photographs, cartoons, posters, film footage, oral records and archaeological finds.

Often, the evidence contains conflicting views and even contradictory or incomplete information. This does not necessarily mean that the historian cannot use the information. In fact, historians have to use this kind of evidence, because no source is perfectly complete, trustworthy and useful for any purpose. Historians just have to use what they can find and make wise decisions about how to use the different pieces of evidence they have available.

Writing history involves careful analysis of the evidence, while considering the limitations of the sources from which the evidence derives. Sometimes the limitations come from the people who created the records in the first place. All sources reflect the perspectives and opinions of the people who produced them, but some sources are so one-sided or narrow in their viewpoint that they have to be used with great caution.

A note on bias

The word 'bias' is often misused in history essays. A dictionary definition of bias is 'the action of supporting a particular person or thing in an unfair way by allowing personal opinions to influence your judgement'. Bias can be explicit and conscious, for example, politicians seeking election will naturally emphasise the good points about their record and emphasise the bad points about their opponent's. Bias can also be implicit and unconscious.

Take the example of a photograph: you can easily imagine how a photographer can choose what to include in an image and what to leave out. The photograph can turn out quite differently, depending on what the photographer wanted to capture. Written documents are the same.

Historians must remember that any source of evidence can be created (or altered later) by those wishing to present a particular picture. Historians, therefore, need to analyse their sources very carefully in order to form their own opinions and judgements about the past while avoiding a one-sided or very biased study of an event or person. Learning how to reflect on and evaluate information before you make up your own mind on a subject – whether this is who you might vote for or which mobile phone you might buy – is an important skill to acquire.

You will meet a variety of different historical sources during your course. You will need to be able to analyse those sources in the light of your own subject knowledge. The key word here is *analyse*. This means going far beyond just a basic *comprehension* of what a source is saying or showing. A mistake to avoid in answering source-based questions is just describing or summarising the source. You need to ask yourself questions about how reliable the source is and why it appears to contradict what some other sources seem to suggest.

Primary sources

A primary source is one that was written, spoken, drawn or photographed at, or very near, the time. It could also be a recollection some years later of an event or person. It was usually produced by someone who was directly involved in the event, or who was an eyewitness to it.

Different types of primary source you might be asked to use include:

- a speech
- a private letter
- a diary
- an official document, such as an Act of Parliament, an order from a minister to a civil servant, a report from an ambassador to their foreign secretary, a secret memorandum by an official, a legal judgement
- an autobiography
- a cartoon
- a photograph
- a newspaper report
- an interview.

Primary sources often reflect the customs and beliefs of their creator as well as the time and place in which they were created, which is called their historical context. You must remember that primary sources must be studied and understood within the context in which they were written. You should not disregard the usefulness of a primary source just because it does not reflect your own values. For instance, opinions about human rights today are very different from those held by many people 150 years ago.

A primary source has many advantages to a historian:

- It provides a first-hand, contemporary account.
- It can offer an insight into the author's perceptions and emotions at the time.
- A source created by someone directly involved in an event might give detailed 'inside information' that other people could not know.

A primary source is not necessarily a better source of information, however. Disadvantages of a primary source might be:

- The source only gives the reader the opinions of the person who created it. These opinions might not be typical of opinions at the time.
- A source created by someone directly involved might contain bias – for example, in trying to convince an audience to agree with a particular line of argument.
- Eyewitnesses might not always be completely reliable. They might not have access to the full details of an event, and they might be reporting an incomplete or an inaccurate version of events.
- The source might be based on the memory of an event or meeting which happened many years before, or it could be over-reliant on the recollections of another person.

A note on hindsight

Hindsight is the ability to look back at an event some time after it has occurred, with a fuller appreciation of the facts, consequences and effects. With hindsight, it is easier to understand the reasons why an event took place, its significance and the impact it had. Historians are fortunate to have hindsight, but it is vital to remember that people living at the time of the event did not have the advantage of hindsight!

Assessing the reliability of sources

It should now be clear that historians have to be extremely careful when using sources. They cannot just accept that everything a source tells them is completely reliable or true. People exaggerate. People tell lies. People might not have seen everything there was to see. People have opinions that others do not share. People simply make mistakes.

Imagine you are out walking, lost in your own thoughts, when you hear a screeching of brakes and a thud behind you. As you turn in the direction of the sounds, you see a pedestrian fall to the ground, clearly having been hit by a car that you see driving quickly away. You are the only person around. Your first priority is to try to assist the pedestrian and call the emergency services. The police, when they arrive, see you as a vital eyewitness to the accident, and they want to take a statement from you.

But were you really an eyewitness? Did you see the accident, or just hear it and see the result? You saw the car drive quickly away, but does that mean the driver was speeding or driving dangerously at the time? How might your sense of pity for the pedestrian affect your idea of what actually happened? Could you be certain the pedestrian was not to blame for the accident? Could the pedestrian have stumbled into the path of the car?

Deliberately jumped? Could you describe the car in detail, or the driver? How far might your own shock influence your recollection of the event? How and why might the statements of the car driver and the pedestrian differ from your own?

So, as historians, what can we do to minimise the risk of drawing inaccurate conclusions from sources? There are several questions that might be asked in order to determine how reliable a source is, and to evaluate its provenance. Here are some factors that you might consider when evaluating a source. These apply to all types of sources, not just written ones:

- Who wrote/spoke/produced the source?
- When was it written/produced?
- What does the source actually say? What is its message?
- What is the context?
- Who was the intended audience?
- Why was it written/produced? What was the author's motive?
- How does it compare with other sources?
- How reliable is it likely to be?

Suppose, for example, that the driver of the car involved in the accident later gave this statement to the police:

> I was driving carefully along the road, well within the speed limit. Suddenly, and without warning, a pedestrian jumped out in front of me from behind a parked vehicle. I did not see him until it was far too late, and it was impossible for me to stop in time and avoid hitting the pedestrian. In a state of panic, I did not stop. I drove away, in shock, but within minutes I calmed down and realised that I had to go and report the issue to the police. I had my children in the car, so once I had taken them home, I reported the incident to the police.

Who wrote the source?

The driver of the car involved in the accident. If the driver was anxious not to be blamed for the accident, they might have a very good reason for being less than honest.

When was it written?

Later on the same day as the accident. By this time, the driver would have recovered from the initial shock and understood that there was probably no option but to report the incident to the police. The driver might well have seen the witness and believed that they had the car's details and description. However, there would have been time for the driver to reflect on the incident and develop a version of events so that the responsibility for the incident could be placed on the pedestrian. Considering how quickly the event took place, the shock caused by what happened and what might have happened since, can we be sure that the driver's memory is completely accurate? Some details might accurate, but not others – how can we tell which bits to believe?

What does it actually say?

The driver claims not to have been driving too fast or dangerously. The driver says that the accident was entirely the pedestrian's fault for jumping out suddenly into the road from behind a vehicle, without checking for traffic. The driver admits to leaving the scene of the accident out of panic.

What is the context?

The driver reporting to the police to admit involvement in the accident. The police would take this statement if the case went to court. Does the seriousness of the context make people more or less likely to be completely truthful?

Who was the intended audience?

Initially the police, but also, possibly, a lawyer who might have to decide whether or not to take the driver to court, and, therefore, a judge and a jury.

Why was it written? What was the author's motive?

The statement had to be written as it was the law. It is possible that the driver accepted the need to report their involvement in the accident. It is also possible that the driver realised that the police would probably catch up with them, and so was anxious to report the incident to clear their name by blaming the pedestrian.

How might it compare with what other sources say?

The police are in a difficult position here.

- The driver might well be telling the whole truth and giving a perfectly accurate description.
- The driver might also have made up the entire story, if they were driving too fast or using their phone.
- Other witnesses might be able to comment on how fast the car was going at the time.
- There might be some CCTV footage of the accident (though the quality of the footage might not be good).
- Mobile phone records can be checked.
- Marks on the road can be assessed.
- The driver mentions 'children' in the car. Would they be able to give a version of events? But, if so, would they just support their parent?
- If the parked vehicle that hid the pedestrian from view was no longer there, can an accurate picture of the whole event be made?
- The pedestrian might be concussed and not have an accurate recollection of events.
- If the police discover that the pedestrian suffered from depression, might that make it more likely that he had 'jumped out' as the driver's statement alleges?

How reliable is it likely to be?

This source is not reliable on its own. It is somewhat reliable if we were studying the perspective of the driver, but we must consider their possible purposes for their statements in the source. The driver would not want to be blamed for the accident, as previously mentioned, which reduces the reliability of this source. We must also consider when the source was written when thinking about its reliability. This source was written after the driver had time to think about what they would say to the police, rather than on the scene of the accident. This also makes the contents of the source questionable. We would need to look at a variety of other sources to find out what actually happened in the accident.

Finding the truth can be a very challenging task. Your analysis skills will develop as you work through the source-based activities and questions in this coursebook.

When answering questions on sources, remember:

- You do not need to provide a summary of the sources or copy out large parts of them. You might need, however, to quote just a phrase or two to back up your points.
- To evaluate the sources. You must show clearly that you have really thought about their value, which is partly based on their provenance (where, when and whom they come from) and validity (whether the evidence is valid and trustworthy).
- To include relevant contextual knowledge.
- To reach a focused and balanced judgement based on evidence. A balanced judgement is one that is one that considers several different points of view.

Essay-writing skills

Essay-based questions test your knowledge, understanding and skills of analysis. The activities and practice questions in this coursebook will help you to develop your essay-writing skills. To write a strong answer, you should:

Plan your answer

You do not need to write a plan to impress anyone else – your plan only has to be useful for you, so it does not have to go into the same level of detail as your essay. You should include just enough information about your ideas to help you structure your answer and to ensure that you do not forget key points and that you focus on the specific question set.

One of the best ways to understand how to approach essay-writing is to write some detailed plans. The other chapters in this book provide practice questions and there are several examples in the Preparing for assessment chapter at the end of the book. You should work through as many as you can, to ensure that you fully understand what essay-based questions require.

Stay focused on the question

Take time to make sure you understand the question and what is required. It is important to keep a clear and fixed focus on this question alone. Make sure that you are not just trying to repeat a question that looks similar to one that you may have answered before but that is, in fact, very different. If the question is on Bismarck's domestic policies–and only his domestic policies–then do not list his foreign policy achievements simply because you have happened to have revised them in great detail!

Be clear and precise in your writing

Use words you understand and select key words carefully in order to convey the meaning you want to communicate. History essays are generally written in formal, academic language, so:

- Write impersonally: in other words, do not use 'I' or 'we' in your essays. This applies particularly when you are asked to reach a judgement or a conclusion.
- Take care with sentences and punctuation: in general, try to write in short sentences. Stick to the point and use words you fully understand.

- Write one idea in each paragraph and fully develop it. Begin the paragraph by clearly stating the point that you are making; the detail that follows should directly support this point.
- Support the statements you make: provide developed arguments and support your ideas with evidence. Do not miss out stages in your logic. For example, do not just write that something was a consequence of a person's beliefs – explain the connection fully and include evidence of it.
- When you are asked to reach a judgement on an issue, you must make sure that your judgement is based on analysis you have provided in your essay. It is always worth emphasising what you feel is the most important factor in reaching your judgement.

How can I be successful in this course?

To achieve to the best of your abilities when studying Cambridge International AS Level History, you can focus on:

Acquiring in-depth subject knowledge

Acquire the required knowledge and learn it as you go along. Do not wait until the end of the course before you attempt to learn the content because your ability to analyse the content during the course depends on what you can recall. Space out your study sessions so that you have short breaks between sessions, revisit previously learned material so that you remind yourself of the content and ask your teacher for help if you get confused. When you study, use a combination of quizzing, self-testing, reading and noting, listening, writing answers to questions and discussing your ideas.

The notes you make during the course are very important, and it is essential that you present your notes effectively. Copying lists of facts from a book can be a pointless exercise. You need to think about what you are writing, understand it and learn to analyse it. Make your notes in such a way that you are answering a simple question. For example: 'What were the most important causes of the 1905 Revolution in Russia?' Do not just write a list of the causes. Prioritise them with reasons. This will prompt you to study all the various things that happened in Russia in the build-up to the events of 1905. You will think about which issues were the most important and why. Once you have identified the key points, make sure there are two or three relevant factors which show that you understand why they were key points. Doing this will then help you deal with a variety of questions on the causes of the 1905 Revolution. Good notes will help you to revise effectively later.

Selecting and using that knowledge effectively

Once you have acquired the appropriate subject knowledge, you must practise using it effectively. If you are asked a question on why Napoleon fell from power, do not write about his military victories: focus on his defeats.

Developing independent thinking skills

You must learn how to think for yourself and be able to challenge ideas. You will be asked for your view on a subject, for example, whether it was Lenin's skills or the failings of his opponents that led to his success in 1917. Think carefully about both sides of the argument implied by the question, and about whether there is actually a third possibility that could overlap with both of the opposing points of view. Consider whether they might both have been true at different points in time, or whether it was the interplay of both factors that was critical. You will have to consider both sides of the argument and come to a judgement.

Handling and evaluating different sources

You need to look at different sources and assess how accurate they are, how much you can trust them as evidence, how valuable they might be for a historian and what they contribute to your own knowledge and understanding of a topic. For example, you may need to put yourself in the position of a historian who is writing about the 1848 revolutions in Germany. Some contemporary sources were very optimistic about the chances of success in these revolutions in Germany; some were very pessimistic. Some sources are obviously from writers or cartoonists with a strong bias; others may have been produced by people who are more balanced in their views. Which is the most reliable and useful? Why? This is the sort of skill that might be useful in the present day, for example, if you are deciding which way to vote in an election after you have been presented with arguments from all sides.

Analysing and making judgements

This combination is an essential skill. You might be asked for a judgement on, for example, whether the rule of the Directory between 1795 and 1799 was successful – or not. First, you will have to work out for yourself what the criteria for 'success' are in this context. Then you will need to consider the grounds on which historians might see the Directory and the Directors as a success – you may like to imagine yourself as the defence lawyer in a trial. Next, you should consider the grounds on which historians might not see this period and its rulers as a success. Finally, in the most difficult part, you will have to weigh up the two sides and come to a conclusion. You must reach a clear judgement on which factor was most important and be prepared to give clear reasons to defend your decision.

Explaining

You will need to explain quite complex issues clearly. For example, you could be asked to explain why Bismarck went to war with France in 1870 and have ten minutes in which to do it. You will have to briefly explain why this war was important to German unification then in three or four sentences explain why his actions were designed to overcome all the main obstacles to German unification. Try to identify what you think was the most important reason and explain why. Always stress what you feel is the most important point and provide factual evidence to back this up. Suggest also what other factors are less important and why – but always make sure you keep the links between them clear. The key is to show that you have really thought about it.

You are now ready to start the course! While it may be challenging at points, we are confident that you will also find it interesting and enjoyable. We hope you find the course as rewarding as we found writing this book for you.

Graham Goodlad and Patrick Walsh-Atkins

› Chapter 1

France, 1774–1814

KEY QUESTIONS

This chapter will help you to answer these questions:

- What were the causes and immediate consequences of the 1789 Revolution?
- How and why did France become a republic by 1792?
- How well was France governed in the period 1793–99?
- What caused the rise and fall of Napoleon Bonaparte?

Timeline

Aug 1786 Finance Minister Charles Calonne submits plan for major financial reforms

Apr 1787 Calonne is dismissed and financial crisis grows

May 1789 Estates-General meets

Jun 1789 National Assembly is announced

Jul 1789 Storming of the Bastille

Aug 1789 Declaration of the Rights of Man

Jul 1790 Civil Constitution of the Clergy

Jun 1791 Royal Flight to Varennes

Oct 1791 Legislative Assembly meets

Sep 1792 Overthrow of the monarchy

Jan 1793 Execution of the king

Sep 1793 The Terror starts

Jul 1794 Fall of Maximilien Robespierre

Nov 1795 Directory established

Nov 1799 Directory overthrown by Napoleon and Consulate established

Mar 1804 Civil Code published (later to become Code Napoléon)

Dec 1804 Napoleon becomes Emperor of France

Jun 1812 Napoleon invades Russia

1814–15 Napoleon defeated and forced into exile; Bourbon monarchy restored

GETTING STARTED

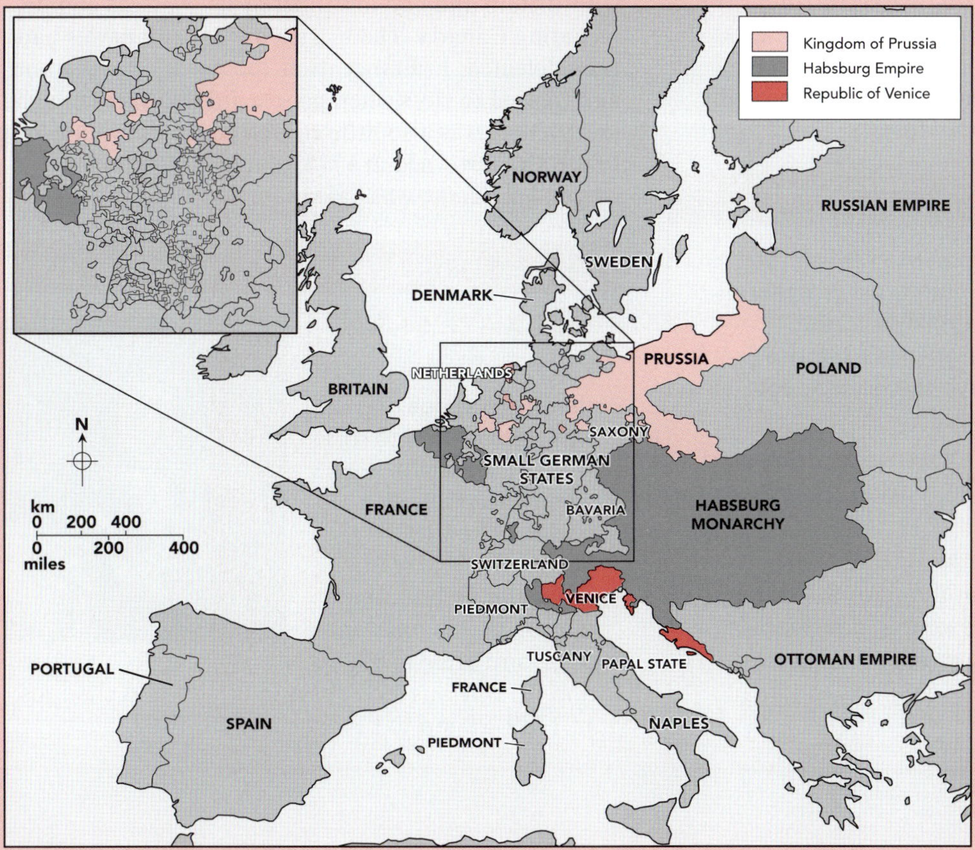

Figure 1.1: The political divisions of Europe in 1789.

Using the resources available to you, research the questions:

a France was involved in two major wars, one between 1756 and 1763 and one between 1778 and 1783. What was the outcome of those two wars for France?

b Was France a rich or a poor country in 1789?

c Look at the countries surrounding France in 1789–including Britain. What sort of relationship did France have with them? Was it always peaceful?

Introduction

In 1789, the French king ran into major economic difficulties and badly needed to raise a great deal of money. He had experienced these difficulties before and they had not been solved. The king decided to call a meeting of France's only elected Assembly, which had not met for over 170 years, to help him solve his problems. This decision ultimately resulted in his execution. It also led to the end of the monarchy in France and the creation of a **republic** which was remarkably **democratic** by the standards of the 18th century. In addition to this political and **constitutional revolution**, there was a religious and social revolution – and all these changes happened in just four years.

This new republic lasted only until 1799, when it was replaced by a **dictatorship**. However, the events that started in 1789 in the royal palace of Versailles, near Paris, had a major impact on France and on the rest of Europe. The ideas of 'liberty, equality and fraternity' for all have lasted in France to this day. Those ideas followed the armies of the French dictator, Napoleon, into the rest of Europe, and played a major role in the events described in the two later chapters in this book, on Germany and Russia. The French Revolution brought in the start of 'modern' European history.

KEY TERMS

Republic: A form of government in which the head of state is not a hereditary ruler (someone who rules because they are related to the previous ruler) such as a king. Instead, those people in the state who have the right to vote choose the leader.

Democratic: When citizens have equal rights and take part in political decision-making. This system is known as a democracy.

Constitutional revolution: A constitutional revolution takes place when the rules about how a country is governed–for example how leaders are chosen–are completely changed.

Dictatorship: Rule by one individual without any limits to their power.

1.1 What were the causes and immediate consequences of the 1789 Revolution?

Many factors led to the crisis of 1789 and the revolution which followed. One factor was the reluctance of French monarchs to change the way they ruled France. Other factors resulted from social and economic changes in previous decades, or from unwise decisions, such as going to war without the money to pay for it. All these factors played a major role in the events of 1789.

The Ancien Régime and pressure for change

The system of government in France before 1789 was known as the **Ancien Régime**. This system had not changed much for nearly 200 years. However, by 1788, France was facing an increasing number of difficulties. In 1763, France had been humiliated in a major war with Britain and had lost most of its overseas empire, including Canada. The French armies and navies had been defeated. In France itself there was often famine, and this led to riots when people did not have enough food. There was also little confidence in the young king, **Louis XVI**, crowned in 1775, and his Austrian wife, **Marie Antoinette**, was hated.

KEY FIGURE

Louis XVI (1754–93)

King Louis XVI was deeply religious and was determined to rule well. However, he was weak and indecisive, and reluctant to accept the reality of the situation he found himself in. His resistance to reform after 1789 and his obvious lack of sympathy for the changes of 1789–90 led to his execution in 1793.

KEY TERM

Ancien Régime: This means 'the old system of government' and describes how France was governed before 1789. It covers not only the government and administration, but also the structure of society and the role of the Church.

KEY FIGURE

Marie Antoinette (1755–93)

Marie Antoinette was an Austrian princess who married Louis XVI and became very unpopular in France. She was disliked partly because she was from Austria (a traditional enemy of France), and because she spent so much money on clothes and jewellery when so many in France were hungry.

A major cause of the crisis of 1789 was the inability of the king of France and his government to manage a series of social, economic and political problems that all became serious during the course of 1788. None of these problems on its own was impossible to solve, but when they all became urgent at the same time it was too much for the old system of government to handle.

Absolute monarchy and the structure of royal government

France in the late 18th century was ruled by an **absolute monarch**, Louis XVI, who had no official limits to his power. However, it was a difficult country to govern. It had a population of about 27 million. There were significant regional differences across the country, along with a strong tradition that each part of France was allowed to deal with local issues in its own way.

There were also different legal systems in different parts of France, which dated back for centuries, and many local lawyers were resistant to any change. The regions had different systems of taxation and there were also customs barriers between some parts of France, meaning that it was impossible to trade goods freely around the country.

As an absolute monarch, Louis could appoint and dismiss ministers and generals and take decisions such as going to war on another country. He could imprison a subject without trial. In practice, however, his power was limited by the old-fashioned and often corrupt structure of government in France. The nature of government meant that the king's orders were often ignored or too difficult to carry out. The king often chose ministers simply because he liked them, not on the grounds of their ability. Many officials were badly paid, so they took bribes to increase their income. The structure of French government was ill-equipped to deal with challenges and needed fundamental change.

Despite this, people who hoped to change how France was governed faced major challenges. While many people wanted **reform** and efficiency, there were also many whose income depended on keeping the old system.

KEY TERMS

Absolute monarch: A king or queen who has complete power in a state. They can make laws and there are no limits to their power.

Reform: Change for the better; in this context, improvement in the system of government.

King Louis XVI and the parlements

The king was at the top of the social and political hierarchy. Louis XVI was crowned in 1775, when he was young and inexperienced. He had a great sense of duty and many good intentions of ruling well. He inherited a system in which the king had (in theory at least) absolute power, and he wanted not just to keep that power, but to increase it in practice too.

However, in reality there were some limitations on the power that Louis held. Traditionally, laws made by the king could not be carried out unless they were published by local **parlements** (courts of appeal). So, the lawyers who were members of the parlements were in a position to delay or prevent the implementation of royal wishes. Only lawyers from the **nobility** could be members, and they were usually more interested in preserving their own privileges than anything else.

The king's courtiers and ministers disagreed on the issue of the role of the monarch. Some wanted to give the monarch greater powers, to enable him to control every part of French life and stop any local autonomy (the right for a region to govern itself). These people wished to end the ability of the parlements to block the king's orders.

Other ministers and courtiers wanted a system in which the king had to consult the nobility on matters of policy and administration, thus reducing his power. A few wished to reform the whole system and make it both more efficient and more inclusive, removing its most obvious weaknesses. For example, the king appointed officials known as intendants to administer the localities (called 'departments') in France. The intendants were royal agents, and their job was to carry out royal wishes in their departments. They were often hated by local parlements, who did their best to ignore and resist them. Local nobles also disliked and did not support the authority and influence given to the intendants because they considered that the intendants were of a lower social rank. Inefficiency seemed to be built in to the French system of government.

KEY TERMS

Parlements: Courts of appeal in the justice system. There were 13 local parlements in France at this time, and the one in Paris was the most powerful. They were not elected bodies and did not represent all French people.

Nobility: The highest class in society, also known as the aristocracy. A nobleman/aristocrat usually had a title (for example, duke or count), and when he died his eldest son inherited the title. Other members of the noble family, such as wives and younger sons, also had noble rank. (The terms nobility and aristocracy can be singular – when referring to the class as a whole, or plural – when referring to the members of the class.)

French society: the Estate system

French society had traditionally been divided into three separate social classes, known as 'Estates'. The First Estate consisted of all the bishops and priests, monks and nuns of the Roman Catholic Church. The Second Estate contained all the nobility, who gained their position in this Estate either by birth or by being awarded this status by the king. The Third Estate included everyone else in France. It was assumed that members of each Estate shared the same values and had similar interests, but events showed that this was not the case. There were huge divisions within all three Estates, and this was to play a major part in the events which followed.

The First Estate: the Church

The Roman Catholic Church, with about 170 000 clergy, monks and nuns, was a very wealthy organisation. It owned 10% of the land across the country and paid no taxes. It controlled most of the education in France and also approved or banned all publications. The Church was determined to maintain its control over as many aspects of French life as possible, and to keep hold of its wealth and privileges. The peasantry had to pay taxes to support the Church, which caused bitter resentment in many areas. Often, the poor supported the rich.

Members of the nobility nearly always held the most senior posts in the Church. These were often inexperienced young men with little interest in performing their religious duties. Birth was more important than ability or suitability for such a role. The ordinary clergy who came from the lower classes were often hardworking and devout men who wanted to help their parishioners. But, because they were commoners, they very rarely progressed to senior roles where they might reform the way the Church was managed and the way it contributed to French society. Also, although the Church did not pay taxes, it did sometimes pay a contribution to the government. However, it was the lower clergy, not the wealthy bishops, who paid this contribution.

These factors led to a growing division within the clergy between the rich noblemen and the poor commoners. This was one of the reasons why the Church was not able to present a united front to the revolutionary forces that later set out to destroy it. The Church and its role and position in France provided more reasons why change was needed for France. Dissatisfied clergy played an important part in the events of the French Revolution.

The Second Estate: the nobility

The nobility dominated France. This tiny minority of the population owned around 30% of the land and most of the wealth. There were about 140 000 members of the most senior nobility. They paid almost no taxes. They were also exempt from things like **conscription** to the army and responsibility for road repairs. Instead, they enjoyed a range of benefits, often created centuries earlier, such as being able to hunt wherever they wished. The nobility dominated all the key posts in the royal court, in the government, the Church, the **judiciary** and the army. One of the reasons why the French army often performed badly was that the officers were noblemen and promotion was based on noble rank rather than on ability or experience.

The French nobility were mostly hostile to people involved in trade and commerce, seeing such activities as beneath them. Unlike the British nobility during the same period, who were deeply involved in innovation in agriculture, industry and commerce, and who sometimes accepted their sons marrying the rich daughters of manufacturers from the **middle class**, the French nobility tended to remain a group apart. Generally, they did not wish to associate with the lower classes in such matters as industry and commerce.

KEY TERMS

Conscription: Compulsory entry into the army as a service to the state.

Judiciary: The justice system, including the judges who enforce a country's laws.

Middle class: The social class between the nobility/aristocracy at the top of the social structure, and the labouring working class and rural peasants at the bottom. Its members were usually educated: either small rural landowners or professionals such as lawyers, doctors, local government officials and successful business owners in the towns and cities. They usually owned property and had to pay taxes.

As in the clergy, there was a division between the 'higher' and 'lower' nobility. The highest nobles lived at Versailles, the court of the French king near Paris. Here, in this vast and splendid palace, they were able to gain power, influence and the top jobs and pensions, which the king awarded. They lived in an isolated and privileged environment and were determined to keep it that way. A talent for court politics was important for achieving the most important jobs, and frequently senior noblemen did not need administrative ability to be successful. The 'poorer' or 'lower' nobles were anxious to retain (keep) their privileges, but often resented the power and wealth of the 'higher' nobility at Versailles. The members of the lower nobility were a reason why the nobility did not act together to defend their power during the years of the revolution.

Figure 1.2: An illustration of French nobility under the Ancien Régime.

The Third Estate: the commoners

The Third Estate contained everyone who was not a member of the clergy or a noble. Some members of the Third Estate were wealthy merchants or landowners, and in French towns, a middle class was growing. Increasingly, these people were well educated, buying property and growing richer. By 1780, this class owned around 20% of the land in France. They were involved in either commerce or industry, or professions such as law and medicine. Some were successful lawyers and others were shopkeepers or skilled workers.

However, the vast majority of the Third Estate at this time were poor rural peasants or the urban working class, often living in serious poverty. The members of the Third Estate often had very different priorities and hopes, even though they were seen to be in the same class. The richer members wanted involvement in the political life of the nation, but the poorer members were more concerned with feeding themselves and their families.

The discontent of the Third Estate

The majority of France's future revolutionary leaders came from the growing middle class. Many of them were originally lawyers. Some were involved in aspects of local government and administration. These men became frustrated that they had no power or influence over national issues and could not join the top levels of government, the military or the legal profession. Only the higher nobility could expect to take up those jobs. Also, although people in the middle class were not as heavily taxed as the peasantry, they did pay some taxes, and resented a system where they had no say in how their money was spent. Another problem was that it became possible in some regions to pass many traditional middle-class posts, such as local judges and tax collectors, from father to son, or to buy them for cash. People were not appointed to these posts for their ability or honesty. People who had paid large sums of money to become a tax collector were often more interested in gaining a return on their investment than in doing an honest job. As a result, money influenced local administration and the law, and corruption grew. Educated and increasingly angry members of the middle class, who were determined to bring about reform, would play a decisive role in the coming events.

Discontent was also growing among the peasantry and among the population of the towns and cities. Agriculture was not highly developed and was inefficient. Peasants farmed tiny plots of land, and their main aim was to grow enough food to survive. They were heavily taxed by the government, by their noble landlords and by the Church. In addition, they had to maintain the roads for their landlords and their local community, although they were not paid for this work. Landlords had the right to hunt on the peasants' land and damage their crops. The peasants were also forced to use their landlords' wine presses to make their wine and flour mills to grind their corn, and to pay their landlords to do so.

There were only three good harvests between 1770 and 1789, and this caused real poverty and hunger in both towns and the countryside. France's agricultural economy could not provide an adequate living for those who lived in the countryside, so many peasants were forced to move to the towns. This growing urban population, poor and unskilled, found there was little or no chance of quality employment. Unlike Britain, which was developing many new industries, for example, in textiles (woven cloths), that were creating jobs and wealth, France had few factories to absorb this migration of workers. A trade treaty with Britain in 1786 had the unintended consequence of seriously damaging the limited French textile industry in several major cities. This caused much unemployment and poverty in 1788–89.

Meanwhile, the existing urban working class saw their standard of living decline as food prices rose. Bread usually formed about 75% of the diet of most of the French population. In normal times, a family would spend between 35% and 50% of its income on bread. After a bad harvest, when prices rose, fear of starvation took hold, and there was no money for heating and clothing. Increasing poverty, worsened by a decline in wages, led to growing urban and rural unrest, including bread riots, such as the Flour Wars of April and May 1775. The police force had only limited numbers and found it difficult to maintain order.

There was, therefore, a hungry, highly taxed, lower class in both town and countryside, whose members had no way of changing their situation. This was an important factor in the events that followed 1789. The division between the rich and the poor in France grew towards the end of the century. The poor saw the people they had to pay taxes to–especially the nobility and the Church–enjoying lives of luxury. Peasants and urban workers had no means of finding solutions to their **grievances**. The legal system offered them no support and often worked against them. It was, in fact, another means of control as it upheld the rights of the rich and often denied them to the poor.

KEY TERM

Grievances: Causes for complaint, usually over unfair treatment. For example, the complaint that the poor had to pay taxes, while the nobility did not.

Figure 1.3: Cartoon published in France in 1789. The caption says, 'Your game will soon be over'. It shows a peasant carrying a nobleman and a priest. How accurately does the cartoon represent the situation in France in 1789? What point is the cartoonist making?

Divisions in society

The king's closest advisors disagreed about how France should be governed. There were divisions within the nobility and the clergy about their roles and influence. There were often bitter local rivalries within the regions of France about how that region should be administered. France was an extremely difficult country to govern and needed serious reform. However, there had been little, if any, change in how it was governed for more than a century. While there was an obvious and strong need for change, there was little agreement on what was actually needed. There was also great resistance to any changes at all by some important sectors of French society.

ACTIVITY 1.1

a Work with another student to identify the principal social, economic and political problems which faced Louis XVI in 1789. Copy and complete the table to help you categorise the problems you have identified. Aim to provide about three points in each column.

Social	Economic	Political

b Now, explain why each set of problems was leading to a serious situation.

The influence of the Enlightenment

In the 18th century, France was home to some of the greatest European thinkers and writers of the period. They became part of an intellectual and philosophical movement known as the 'Enlightenment', and they had a major influence on the revolutionary process in France. It can be difficult to assess the importance of abstract ideas for actual events, but it is known that many of the revolutionary leaders, and also Napoleon Bonaparte (see Section 1.4), were familiar with, and strongly influenced by, the ideas of these thinkers.

Many of these writers did not just criticise what they saw in France; they also supported practical improvements. Some of the most important figures of the Enlightenment were:

- **Voltaire**, who was very critical of the role, wealth and influence of the Roman Catholic Church, and attacked religious intolerance. He also criticised the French legal system and its frequent miscarriages of justice.
- **Montesquieu**, who was critical of **autocratic** power. He wanted a system of checks and balances, where one part of a system of government could check the actions of ministers and the king. He was impressed by the British system, where an elected **parliament** controlled law-making and could check the king's government. Montesquieu also promoted the idea of the 'rule of law': that everyone, whatever their rank in society, should be equal before the law and subject to the law of the land. No one should be above the law, even a king.

- **Diderot**, author of an encyclopaedia of 'sciences, arts and crafts', who was determined to advance knowledge. He strongly supported independent thinking and wanted to promote a critical and questioning attitude to everything, including government.
- **Rousseau**, who argued for more, and better, education. Rousseau was a great political thinker who wrote about power and liberty. He proposed many ideas on how there could be both authority and order in a society, as well as human freedom.
- **Quesnay**, who wrote on economics and argued against the restrictions on the free production and movement of goods within France. He was keen to modernise the French economy.

KEY TERMS

Autocratic: Where all power in a state belongs to a single monarch (the autocrat), whose authority is unlimited.

Parliament: A group of (usually) elected politicians or other people who make laws for their country.

These men challenged established ideas, institutions and social structures. They encouraged argument and debate on a wide range of major public issues. They argued that there could be improvement in all areas of public life. Ideas were spreading throughout France, such as religious toleration, legal equality, the right of men to participate in politics and national decision making, and the ending of **censorship** by the Church and the Church's control over education. There was a real debate on these issues in France at the time.

Many of the future leaders who emerged during the revolution had read, thought about and debated the ideas of these great writers of the Enlightenment. When the Ancien Régime collapsed after 1789, these thinkers provided ideas that suggested a way forward for the new governors of France. However, when ministers adopted some of these new ideas, such as Quesnay's economics, many **conservatives** were worried by such change and this contributed to the unsettled atmosphere in France before 1789. These thinkers did not cause the revolutionary process which started in 1789, but many of the ideas which they **advocated** had a strong influence on the process itself. After the revolution, France showed plenty of evidence that the ideas of these men had an impact on events between 1789 and 1815.

KEY TERMS

Censorship: The suppression of ideas which challenge authority, whether expressed in speech, writing or other media.

Conservative: Generally opposed to change, or someone who wants to uphold traditional ideas and institutions in government and society.

Advocate: To support something in public, or someone who publicly supports something.

ACTIVITY 1.2

Either on your own or in pairs, look at the thinkers and writers associated with the Enlightenment.

a What aspects of French life before 1789 would they have wanted to change?

Specifically, what aspects would each of the five Enlightenment thinkers listed here have found unsatisfactory? Consider each thinker in turn.

b Then, working with a partner, consider:

i At the time, what impact might Enlightenment ideas have had on society?

ii How much can writers of abstract ideas influence politicians or political events?

The American War of Independence

Social and **ideological** factors were very important in the start of the revolutionary process in 1789, but politics and economics also played a key role. In 1778, the French government decided to form an alliance with the colonists in America who were fighting for independence from France's old enemy, Britain. France had fought against Britain between 1756 and 1763 (the Seven Years' War) and had suffered several military defeats. France wanted to recover the colonies (such as Canada) that Britain had taken in 1763, and also to regain the military reputation it had lost. So, France allied with the American colonists and declared war against Britain. It was a war for revenge.

Many of the **principles** for which the Americans fought their former colonial rulers, the British, such as 'no taxation without representation', and 'the rule of law', were inspired by Enlightenment ideas and reappeared in France during the revolutionary period. Some of the French soldiers and sailors who fought alongside the Americans for American freedom and 'rights' realised that they did not have that 'freedom' or those 'rights' themselves in France. Some of the French who fought in America became significant personalities in the revolutionary period.

KEY TERMS

Ideological: Based on a set of political ideas and beliefs (an ideology).

Principles: Basic or fundamental rules or beliefs which act as a guide for action. For example, a principle that developed during the American War of Independence was that 'all men are equal'.

National debt: The amount of money borrowed by a state or country, often at very high rates of interest.

Economic problems and attempts to deal with them up to 1787

The American War of Independence was one of many economic problems that faced France in the 1770s and 1780s (see Figure 1.4). These problems included:

- an inefficient and corrupt tax collection system
- the problem that government spending always exceeded income
- the high cost of government borrowing
- a growing population that did not have adequate supplies of food
- unemployment in both towns and the countryside.

Many finance ministers attempted to address these problems. Louis knew that France faced serious economic problems, but he lacked the ability to understand how complicated these problems were and was reluctant to deal with them. When able ministers offered solutions or sensible advice (such as avoiding costly wars), Louis often ignored them.

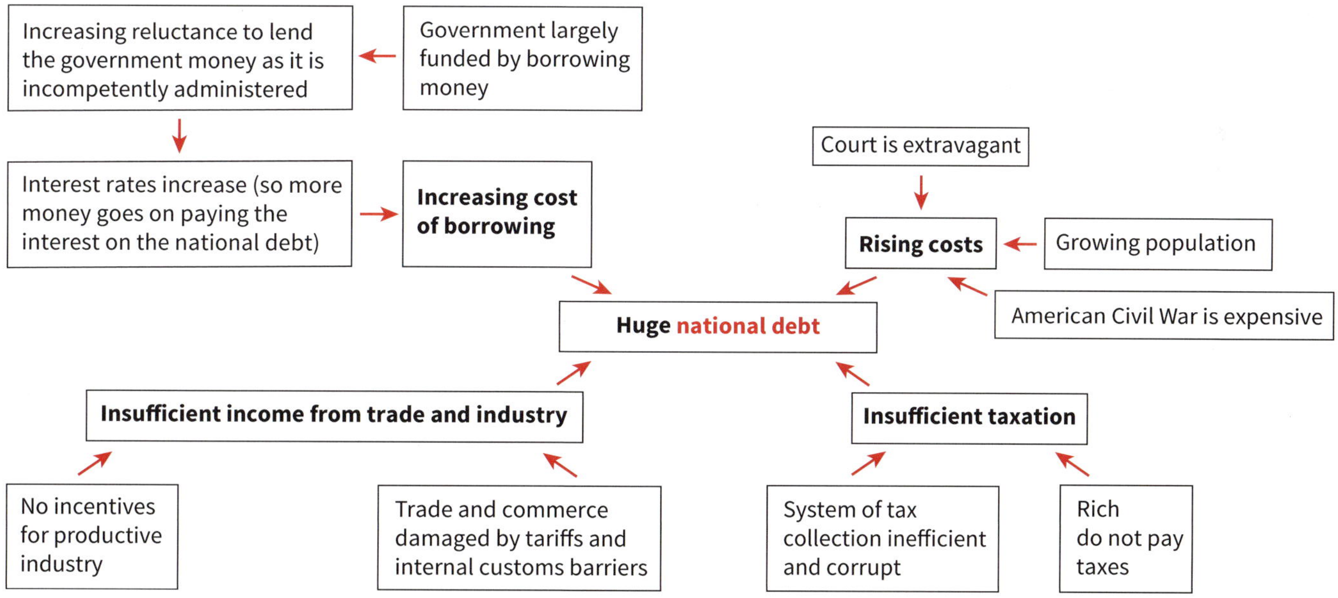

Figure 1.4: France's economic problems before the revolution. The figure shows clearly that there was not just one economic problem facing the French monarchy in the 1780s, but a whole series of problems which kept on making the situation worse.

Turgot

Anne Robert Jacques Turgot, an admirer of the economist Quesnay, was the finance minister when Louis became king in 1775. Turgot tried to end the many restrictions on trade and commerce in France, but this upset the middle-class who benefited from these restrictions. Turgot also attempted to end the system known as the *corvée* that meant peasants had to work for a number of days, without pay, for the nobility. That attempt made him powerful enemies.

Turgot warned against further involvement in wars, arguing that 'the first gunshot will drive the state to bankruptcy'. He predicted that a war would do little harm to Britain in the long term, and instead would both prevent the vital financial reforms that France needed, and also risk national bankruptcy in France. (His prediction was correct–fighting a major war later led to national bankruptcy for France and little gain.)

However, the king ignored Turgot, and took advice from the Count of Vergennes, his foreign minister, who was interested in France's (and his own) prestige, and did not worry about the cost. The cautious and sensible Turgot was dismissed in 1776. He was the first of several finance ministers that Louis dismissed.

KEY FIGURE

Anne Robert Jacques Turgot (1727–81)

Turgot trained as a lawyer, but he was interested in economics. He gained a reputation as a fine administrator and reformer under Louis XV and was put in charge of royal finances by Louis XVI. However, his attempted national reforms would have meant a loss of income for the nobility. This led to his removal from office in 1776.

Necker

In 1777, a new finance minister was appointed. This was **Jacques Necker**. He was an unusual choice because he was not a French nobleman, but a middle-class banker of Swiss origin, and also a Protestant in a strongly Roman Catholic country. This meant that many people at the king's court disliked him, notably the influential queen.

KEY FIGURE

Jacques Necker (1732–1804)

Jacques Necker was born in Switzerland and trained as a banker. He was finance minister three times: 1777–81, 1788–89 and 1789–90. Some historians argue that in his first period as minister he caused many of the problems which faced France in later years. When he was recalled to office in 1788, he was seen as the man able to solve France's economic problems. He was, however, unable to provide either an accurate picture of the royal finances or solutions to the financial problems facing France. In 1789, he advised the king to call the Estates-General.

The appointment of an outsider like Necker indicates that there was a growing awareness that French state finances were in a dreadful state. The American war had led to a national debt of 3315 million livres, while the government's annual income from a very inefficient and corrupt tax system was 585 million livres. Over 40% of government income was spent on interest payments for that debt. It was an unsustainable position, and lenders became reluctant to lend money to the government or charged very high rates of interest.

Necker promised to reform the financial system. Many people (unwisely, as it turned out) had great confidence in him. He investigated and analysed the state of France's finances, but he did not deliver any real reform. He funded the expensive war with Britain through borrowing at increasingly high interest rates. He did not increase taxes or require the wealthy to contribute more.

In 1781, Necker published a public account of the royal finances. This was the first time that this had happened in France. However, in this report Necker claimed that these finances were in a good condition. They were not, but many believed him and felt there was no need for any change. Necker also hid the huge cost of the war with Britain. Necker was dismissed four months after the report was published. Government borrowing at high interest rates continued to increase. This meant that more and more of the state's income from taxes had to be spent on paying interest on the growing national debt.

The war with Britain ended in 1783. The United States became independent, but France had gained nothing from the war except greater national debt and the gratitude of the Americans.

Calonne

As there was growing concern about the state of royal finances, another finance minister, **Charles Calonne**, was appointed in 1783. Initially, Calonne did not cut royal spending and simply borrowed yet more money to keep the government running. However, he did start to plan important changes. He was aware that without fundamental change France would go bankrupt, and no one would lend it money, even at very high rates of interest.

KEY FIGURE

Charles Calonne (1734–1802)

Charles Calonne was finance minister from 1783 to 1787. After his appointment, he realised the disastrous state of France's finances. In 1786, he suggested major reforms to the king; these reforms included taxing both the nobles and the clergy. The king dismissed him in 1787.

In 1786, with the cost of servicing the state's debts becoming too high, Calonne submitted a series of reforms to the king. He made three main proposals:

- Reform the system of taxation by increasing taxes for the wealthy and making the system more efficient.
- Stimulate the economy generally and encourage commerce and industry.
- Create confidence in France and its economy so that France could borrow more money at lower rates of interest.

The king, who was prepared from time to time to take an interest in financial matters, approved the plans. There was growing public concern and interest in the economy, so these proposals were submitted to the **Assembly of Notables** in the hope of gaining support for the measures. French kings had only summoned this Assembly four times in the past, to deal with emergencies. It could not pass any reforms of its own, but it could give opinions on proposals by the king or his ministers. Calonne hoped that this Assembly would help him to gain some support for much-needed financial reform.

KEY TERM

Assembly of Notables: A group of noblemen and senior members of the Church. The Assembly had no authority – it could only consult, but not actually do anything.

The financial and political crisis 1787–89

The two years between 1787 and 1789 were dominated by a growing sense of crisis. It was becoming increasingly clear that a solution to the financial problems facing the government was needed. The government was collecting too little money, and the national debt was rising. Increasingly, bankers were reluctant to lend to the government. The first attempt at a solution came in early 1787.

The Assembly of Notables

The Assembly of Notables met in February 1787, for the first time since 1626. The Assembly was made up of nobles and clergy (only ten of the 144 members were not nobles). Calonne was expected to manage it.

The failure of Calonne's reforms

Calonne was in an impossible position. The vast majority of the Notables disliked him. He had little serious support from the king and the rest of the government for any of his reforms. Many of those in a position of influence believed Necker's earlier statement that all was well with the royal finances. In addition, the expensive war was over, so many thought the crisis was also ended. Calonne had no idea how to manage the Notables, and, in fact, no one really knew what the Notables' role was. Was the Assembly of Notables just there to be consulted? Was it there just to support changes? Did it have any authority? Most Notables recognised a need for some reforms, but they wanted to make sure that they, and the class that they represented, did not suffer from those reforms. For example, they did not wish to pay any taxes. There was no representation in the Assembly of the peasantry (the people who had to actually pay the taxes), or even of the growing middle class. Calonne attempted to put forward his reforms, but as these reforms involved reducing noble privileges and making the nobility pay taxes, they were ignored.

The king was faced with a challenging situation. Again, he demonstrated little skill and tried to solve the problem by dismissing Calonne in April 1787.

Brienne and the involvement of the Parlement of Paris

The king replaced Calonne with a new finance minister, Étienne Loménie de Brienne, thinking that, as president of the Assembly of Notables, Brienne would have some influence over its members. However, the king disliked and distrusted Brienne, and with limited royal support Brienne could achieve little. When the Notables demanded an accurate account of the royal finances, the king refused and instead dismissed the Assembly in May 1787.

The meeting and subsequent dismissal of the Assembly of Notables showed:

- how deep France's financial crisis was
- the failings of the king and his court and government
- that the public had not been given a true picture of the state of the royal finances
- that there was growing opposition in the country to the king and his government
- that the public was beginning to demand change and greater involvement in government.

The king's failure to grasp either the nature and extent of France's financial problems or the impact it was having on his people, proved highly damaging to him and his government. His frequent dismissal of his finance ministers did not create confidence in royal government either. The dismissal of the Assembly caused great anxiety and protest among the educated public and marked the start of the financial and political crisis that eventually led to the crisis of 1789 and the fall of the monarchy itself.

Brienne had to raise money, so he increased taxation in the areas under his control in 1788. However, he did not increase taxes for the rich, so the extra taxation largely affected the poor. He then borrowed even more money. He found it very difficult to persuade bankers to lend to a state which many felt was near breakdown, so high rates of interest had to be paid.

Brienne also attempted to gain support for increased taxes from the Parlement of Paris–the most powerful of the country's parlements–but failed. The Parlement refused to support tax increases until it was given an accurate picture of the royal accounts. The king again refused to allow this, seeing such demands as an attack on his royal powers. Instead, he banished the Parlement members to the provinces. The people of Paris were so angry at the king's action that huge crowds, including members of both middle and lower classes, took to the streets in protest. This was the first sign of a potential alliance between the middle and lower classes against the king and the nobility. It was also the first indication of the ability of Parisians to influence events.

The financial and political crisis continued to grow throughout 1787 and 1788. The king recalled the Paris Parlement and met with it in November 1787, but he mismanaged it. He still did not realise why there was so much concern about the state's finances. Isolated in Versailles, he remained unaware of French public opinion.

The king, therefore, undermined his ministers who were trying to negotiate with, and manage, the Parlement. When the Parlement refused to support new taxes, the men who led the opposition to new taxation were arrested and imprisoned in the Bastille, a royal fortress in Paris. The arrests led to protests across the whole country, demonstrating the wide level of public interest and support for reform. However, the king still did not see that a major political and economic crisis was developing in France, and that his power and authority were at risk.

Meanwhile, divisions were emerging among the nobility and clergy over whether to support any change to their privileged and untaxed status. It was clear, too, that the growing middle class was becoming increasingly angry about the privileges given to the nobility and clergy over taxation.

The atmosphere of crisis worsened throughout 1788 as there was widespread anger at the king's refusal to become involved in a civil war in the Netherlands (now Belgium and Holland), to the north of France. Many French people felt that France had an interest in this area and worried that Austria might increase its power there. Despite the reality that there was no money to pay for any military intervention in the Netherlands, there was a sense of national humiliation. France no longer seemed to be one of the great powers of Europe. Also, the lack of money, and the incompetence of the

Figure 1.5: The Paris Parlement meeting in the early 18th century.

(noble) officer corps, meant that the army was viewed as potentially unreliable, even though it was the only way of keeping order in France.

By now, thousands of **pamphlets** were being published throughout France, demanding social, economic and political change. Public anxiety was rising. The Paris Parlement demanded complete constitutional change and was widely supported nationally in this demand.

KEY TERM

Pamphlet: A small booklet or leaflet.

Economic problems

By August 1788, it was clear that the state was virtually bankrupt, and this situation began to be publicly admitted. Brienne was aware of the scale of the problem, and had some solutions, but the king dismissed him. His dismissal further reduced public confidence in the king and his court. Instead of resolving the crisis, the king was making it worse.

Bad harvests and food shortage

In 1788, a severe drought meant that little wheat was grown, and then a series of heavy hailstorms badly damaged the crop before it could be harvested. The harvest was one of the worst harvests of the century – about 40% less wheat was harvested than the average for the previous decade. Everyone knew that this would lead to a shortage of bread, the principal diet of the poor. The winter of 1788–89 was hard and many people went hungry in the spring of 1789.

Unemployment and price rises

Two factors combined to accelerate the problems facing France in 1788. The first was increasing unemployment in both rural and urban areas. A growing population in the countryside together with stagnation (lack of change) in agricultural output meant that an increasing number of peasants moved to the towns in search of work in the late 1780s. However, the largest employers in the towns, the textile manufacturers, were making workers jobless as a result of competition from cheaper and better-quality imports from Britain. In the town of Troyes, over 10 000 workers were dismissed in 1788. By 1788 it was estimated that over 30% of the population of France were living in poverty – about 8 million people. The terrible harvest of 1788 led not just to a shortage of bread but also to rapidly rising prices. In 1786, buying the essential bread for a family could require 40–50% of a worker's income; by early 1789 it could require 80%. That left little money for rent or heating or for any other goods. This situation further reduced demand for goods such as textiles.

Necker reappointed as finance minister

The king's next attempt at a solution was to recall Necker as finance minister. Necker took office in August 1788 facing a very challenging financial situation. It was impossible for him to meet the huge expectations placed on him by both the king and the public. The king was unwilling to make the changes needed, the public wanted more change than the Court did and the nobility and the clergy were not willing to give up their privileges. Necker's own analysis of the problems and necessary solutions was flawed as well. His earlier belief that the American war could be paid for by borrowing had contributed to the present crisis: great hopes were being placed on a man who was not as able as many people thought.

The king's decision to call the Estates-General

Necker recommended that the king should call the **Estates-General**, to solve France's problems. The Estates-General was an assembly that represented all three Estates, but had not met since 1614. The king agreed to this proposal.

> **KEY TERM**
>
> **Estates-General:** An assembly that represented the three social classes (Estates) of France under the Ancien Régime: the nobility, the clergy and the Third Estate, who represented the majority of the French people. The Estates-General of 1789 was the first to be called since 1614.

The cahiers de doléances

Before the Estates-General met, the districts of France were asked to put forward a list of issues they wanted the Estates-General to consider when it met (as had been done in the past). These lists were known as cahiers de doléances. They were requests for change and grievances that needed to be addressed. Each of the three Estates submitted their own list. In March 1789, the cahier from Dourdan, in northern France, contained the following, quite typical, demands. Each of the three Estates submitted their own lists.

The clergy–**the First Estate**–asked:

- to retain all the rights and privileges of the Roman Catholic Church
- to ban the practice of any other religion in France
- to give the Church complete control of all education
- to ban all publications attacking the Church and give the Church full control over all publications
- to retain freedom from any taxation unless it decided to contribute
- for a reform of local legal systems to ensure fairer justice for all
- that care should be taken to ensure adequate food supplies for all
- that landlords should be prevented from imposing high charges on peasants and hunting on their lands.

The nobility–**the Second Estate**–asked that:

- only the king should have power to make laws
- there should be no change in the system of taxation without the consent of the Estates-General
- the distinction between the three orders of the Estates-General should be strengthened
- the system of voting by Estates should remain – each Estate should have only one vote
- care should be taken to ensure the supply of grain
- fewer restrictions should be placed on agriculture and industry
- there should be reform of the many legal systems.

The Third Estate–in theory the rest of the French people, but in practice the middle class–asked that:

- the national debt should be paid off
- all taxes should be shared equally
- the system of compulsory work for a landlord should be ended
- the administration of justice should be reformed
- there should be regulations to ensure the supply of affordable corn for everyone
- the much-hated salt tax, known as the *gabelle*, should be abolished
- the privilege of hunting by the nobility on tenants' land should be abolished

- the many regulations restricting trade should be abolished
- there should be a school in every town
- the Church should be reformed
- there should be local elections for local assemblies to deal with local issues.

However, different regions produced different requests, some more **radical** and some more conservative. There were over 40 000 cahiers overall. It should be noted that while there were plenty of requests for change, there were also many requests for no change at all.

KEY TERM

Radical: Far-reaching or extreme. A radical (or a radical person or organisation) is someone who supports extreme social or political change.

ACTIVITY 1.3

Working on your own or in pairs, make three separate lists:

a The concerns that **all three** Estates agreed on

b The concerns that **only** the First and Second Estates agreed on

c The concerns of the Third Estate that differed from those of the First and Second Estates.

The meeting of the Estates-General

On 5 May 1789, members of the Estates-General of France gathered at the royal palace of Versailles, just outside Paris. In the background there was widespread social, economic and political unrest, as well as the prospect of national bankruptcy. There was also the feeling that France had been humiliated by not

Figure 1.6: The opening assembly of the Estates-General in Versailles, engraved by Isidore Stanislas Helman after a drawing by Charles Monnet, painter to Louis XVI. At this assembly, the Estates were seated quite separately and the proceedings were dominated by the king.

intervening in the Netherlands civil war. It was a tense and worrying atmosphere. Solutions to major problems were needed.

The Estates-General was the nearest thing that France had to a national law-making and **representative** body, although its precise role had never been clearly determined. Louis XVI's immediate predecessors had not called it to meet, as they saw it as a potential threat to their absolute power. Both the monarch and court on one side and the mass of the French people on the other had great hopes for the outcomes of this meeting. There had been immense interest in choosing its members, particularly from the middle class. The three Estates met in different parts of the palace of Versailles, but each Estate had one vote when it came to making decisions. The king and his ministers expected the First and Second Estates, the clergy and the nobility, to support them and outvote the Third Estate if it tried to make any radical changes they disliked.

Problems soon arose because the representatives elected for the Estates-General represented many different views, and many of their aims were conflicting:

- **The First Estate** (the clergy) was less dominated by the more noble bishops than expected, with many ordinary parish priests present. However, the representatives of the First Estate did not demonstrate any clear or united views on the current crisis.
- **The Second Estate** (the nobility) had a few **liberal** members, but the majority were conservative and were determined to uphold their noble privileges. They were prepared to consider some changes, such as more regular meetings of the Estates-General, which they could dominate. Most accepted the need to reform the nation's finances but were unwilling to agree to changes at their own expense.
- **The Third Estate** represented everyone else! While the rural peasant and the urban working class (the vast majority of the population) had no actual representatives, many of the middle-class deputies were aware of their grievances such as the taxes on food and other essentials (and high taxation generally) and noble privileges. The majority of these deputies were middle-class lawyers, small landowners, and merchants and bankers. They were also concerned about taxation and noble privilege, but many wanted much greater participation in the political process, with more power given to the Third Estate. Like the American colonists France had supported, these deputies wanted 'no taxation without representation'. Some were also deeply concerned about more abstract issues, such as the right of all to be represented, where power should lie in the country and the equality of all men.

The opening meetings did not go well either for the king or for the reformers. In nearby Paris public tension was rising. In April 1789 the price of bread was 75% higher than it had been in 1787 and there had been serious riots in Paris over rumours of wage cuts for workers. Soldiers had fired on crowds killing over 200 people to try and restore order.

The king's main concern was to find a solution to his financial problems. Many of the Third Estate wanted a more extensive overhaul of government, politics, society and the economy. Some clergy and noblemen were prepared to accept a few major changes. Many more, unrepresented, people just wanted basic improvements to their lives, such as lower taxes, lower rents and cheaper bread. In the background, an increasingly radical and uncensored press was arguing for major reforms.

KEY TERMS

Representative: Typical of a class or group of people or speaking and acting on behalf of other people. A representative body is an organisation whose members are elected or appointed to speak and act on behalf of different groups of people.

Liberal: Believing that government should allow as much personal and economic freedom as possible. A liberal (or a liberal person) is someone who believes that government should allow personal and economic freedom.

The National Assembly and the Tennis Court Oath

In May 1789, it was clear from the start that the first two Estates were refusing to support any of the demands for radical reform made by the Third Estate. They were more concerned with protecting their privileges than with dealing with the problems the country was facing. There was also the further complication that the First and Second Estates were divided among themselves over whether or not to cooperate with the Third Estate. Some clergy and noblemen were aware that, unless there was reform, the anger boiling up from the Estate below might have dangerous consequences. However, there was no clear leadership from the court and king on any issue and this was a critical factor in the developing crisis. In calling the meeting, the king had lit a fire which he was unable to put out.

ACTIVITY 1.4

Your Majesty, you have just received the demands of the Third Estate and you know you must respond to them. If you remain silent you will risk seeing the rights of the Crown compromised and your authority destroyed. If you dissolve the Estates-General, it will create even greater danger and misfortune. The nobility is determined to retain all its powers and privileges and insists on voting by order. It is in no mood to accept any compromise towards the Third Estate. The clergy, naturally inclined to try and conciliate and compromise between the King and the other two Estates, is in no position to act. Many of the lower clergy are prepared to side with the Third Estate to improve their own positions. The Third Estate is now raising the most unreasonable pretensions and are advocating opinions which are incompatible with the power of the King. There is real overexcitement there. We have much public anger, and the people of Paris are putting forward democratic opinions that are destructive of the principles of the Monarchy. Everything thus calls upon Your Majesty to act and prevent the terrible disorders which might follow if you do not.

From a memorandum of 16 June 1789, by a senior minister, Barentin, to the king. The king had asked him for advice on 14 June.

a Why was Barentin so anxious for the king to act quickly to deal with the crisis of the summer of 1789?

b When you have finished studying this chapter, return to this question. Using contextual knowledge, comment on how perceptive Barentin's advice proved to be.

Many of the Third Estate were influenced by a pamphlet written by a clergyman, the **Abbé Sieyès**, which sold over 300 000 copies. This pamphlet argued that political power should lie with the people of France, and not with the monarchy or nobility.

KEY FIGURE

Abbé Emmanuel Joseph Sieyès (1748–1836)

Sieyès was a member of the clergy, but he was strongly influenced by Enlightenment thinking on politics and law. In January 1789 he published a pamphlet called 'What is the Third Estate?'. This pamphlet attacked the monarchy and argued passionately for power to lie with the Third Estate, the real representatives of the French people.

On 17 June 1789, the Third Estate, tired of royal indecision and the selfish attitude of the other two Estates, made a decisive move. The members agreed to change the name of their Estate to the 'National Assembly'. By this action, they were saying that **sovereignty**, the supreme or final power within France, now lay with the people of France, represented by this new Assembly. Sovereign power no longer lay with the monarchy. The Assembly was, in effect, announcing that it was now in charge of France. As an example of this newly acquired power, it decided to assume control of the system of national taxation. Louis tried to stop the Assembly's radical plans by shutting it down and closing its meeting room, using soldiers to keep the members of the Third Estate out. The members simply moved to a nearby building, a covered tennis court. There, in what became known as the 'Tennis Court Oath', they decided to continue meeting until they had established a new, reformed **constitution** for France that would deal with all their grievances. This was the first, critical, step on the road to the French Revolution, although no one then expected it to lead to the execution of the king, the end of monarchy in France and the creation of a republic within four years.

KEY TERMS

Sovereignty: Ultimate political authority within a state.

Constitution: A written document which sets out the rules by which a country is governed; for example, how much power the government should have and what limits there should be on that power.

Figure 1.7: *The Oath of the Tennis Court*, ink drawing by Jacques-Louis David, 1790.

ACTIVITY 1.5

Look at the drawings in Figures 1.6 and 1.7.

- a How accurately do you think the artists conveyed the two events?
- b How might the seating arrangements seen in Figure 1.6 explain why the Estates-General failed?
- c Why do you think the Figure 1.7 artist put the two clergymen at the very front of his painting?
- d What value, if any, do you think images such as these have for a historian?

Louis' refusal to carry out reform

During the spring and summer of 1789, a series of events across France drove the process in an even more revolutionary direction. In the countryside and towns, there was serious hunger because of the poor harvest of the previous year, adding to a tense situation. Although Necker warned him to be cautious, the king still failed to understand the extent of his people's grievances, and continued to make unwise and provocative decisions:

- He refused to give any power to the National Assembly and insisted that the Estates-General should continue to act in the way he expected, with the First and Second Estates being able to outvote the Third and prevent any change he disliked.
- He moved troops into both Paris and Versailles. Many people saw this as an attempt to stop any reforms by force.
- He dismissed Necker, again. Many people had felt that Necker was the one man capable of bringing in sensible reforms and solving France's economic problems.

As a result, even previously **moderate** members of all three Estates began to believe that Louis himself was the problem. It was becoming clear that the king would never reform French government unless he was forced to do so.

KEY TERM

Moderate: In a political context, a moderate person is one who does not hold extreme or radical views.

ACTIVITY 1.6

> We come to place before your Majesty our greatest fears. We are patriots concerned for the welfare of our electors, public peace and for the happiness of our beloved country. But we see your troops approaching us from all directions, armed camps being set up around us, Paris is besieged. Does the King distrust the loyalty of his people? What does this display of force mean? We are not rebels who need to be crushed. We do not blame your Majesty for the ills which affect us, but we fear that the people in the provinces will be alarmed for our liberty. The danger is for Paris – how will a hungry people denied so much react to the presence of armed troops eating their food? The presence of these troops will cause riots and anger and lead to great violence. Those troops might also remember they are men like us. The danger is great – great revolutions have been sparked off by less trivial causes than these.
>
> **Petition (request) from the Third Estate of the Estates-General to the King, 10 July 1789. From a report in a newspaper *Le Journal de Paris*, 12 July 1789.**

Read the extract from a Paris newspaper and then answer the following questions:

a What is the attitude of the petitioners (requesters) towards the king?

b What threats to peace are identified in the source?

c What do the petitioners see as the greatest threat to peace? Explain why.

ACTIVITY 1.7

Working in pairs or small groups, prepare for a class debate on responsibility for the crisis in France of 1789. Each pair/group should prepare to argue that a specific factor was most responsible. Factors could include:

- the king
- the Ancien Régime as a whole

CONTINUED

- Necker
- the Church and the nobility
- the French economy
- any others you can think of.

Focus on why your factor should be seen as the most important, but also take care to point out why the other factors are less important.

The outbreak of revolution

No one in France in the summer of 1789 anticipated the revolution that was to come. Most expected there to be some changes that would deal with France's problems. However, seemingly unconnected events, and the way in which individuals reacted to them, led to a process that no one seemed to be able to control.

The Storming of the Bastille

The turning point, when the reform movement became increasingly revolutionary, occurred on 14 July 1789. Angered by rising bread prices and fearing that the reforms they had hoped would emerge from the meeting of the Estates-General were not going to happen, the people of Paris acted. A violent Parisian crowd, known as a 'mob', attacked the old royal fortress in Paris – the Bastille. The Bastille was seen as a symbol of royal power and tyranny, although it actually contained few prisoners, troops or arms. During the attack, the Bastille was destroyed, and its royal governor was killed and his body dragged through the streets of Paris. The event was highly significant – an attack on a royal fortress demonstrated the anger of the Parisian working class towards the monarchy and their determination to achieve change. While the King and his court failed to grasp the significance of the assault on the Bastille, it had a huge impact on France as a whole. Never before had there been such an attack on royal authority which had gone unpunished. It encouraged radical reformers to demand even more change and other groups of the working class to use violence to achieve their aims. It was the first of many occasions in the following years, when the working class of Paris, often hungry and encouraged by extreme ideas in the press, drove the revolutionary process forward.

ACTIVITY 1.8

Figure 1.8: *Prise de la Bastille* (Storming of the Bastille) by Jean-Pierre Houël, 1789. Houël was a famous painter and artist who was in Paris during the summer of 1789.

Look at the painting in Figure 1.8.

a Do you think the painting is an accurate representation of the 'Storming of the Bastille' on 14 July 1789? Use your contextual knowledge about the events to support your judgement.

b Consider whether the 'Storming of the Bastille' was just an act that showed the people's feelings but had limited impact.

The Great Fear

The Storming of the Bastille inspired an even greater breakdown of law and order throughout France. This became known as the 'Great Fear' of the summer of 1789. It took many forms. There was a mass refusal to pay taxes by most people who had to pay them, both middle and working class. Without an income, government could not function. Grain shipments to cities were attacked and the grain stolen, which worsened food shortages in those cities. The homes of many nobles were looted, and their owners were attacked. Town leaders who opposed reform were killed. There were attacks on some of the wealthier bishops and their property was stolen. Law and order collapsed throughout France. Every region was affected.

The king seemed reluctant to act decisively, either to support reform or to stop it, or to restore order. Many of his noble courtiers fled both the court and the country, fearing for their lives, because so much anger was being directed towards the rich and privileged. In the middle of this chaos the representatives of the Third Estate at Versailles again seized the initiative and acted. What followed was a revolutionary change in how France was governed.

KEY TERM

Feudalism: A social system in medieval Europe, in which the nobility held lands from the Crown in exchange for military service, and the lower classes were tenants of the nobles. These tenants had to live on their lord's land and serve him with their labour and a share of their crops (or other taxes).

The August Decrees

In what became known as the 'August Decrees', the National Assembly abolished what was left of **feudalism** in France.

Figure 1.9: 'The Awakening of the Third Estate'. In this cartoon, the nobleman and the cleric on the left are showing fear at the sight of the member of the Third Estate on the right, breaking free from his chains and reaching for weapons. In the background is the Bastille and the head of its governor on a spike. How reliable is this image in describing the events in France during 1789?

The Assembly:

- ended all the privileges of the nobles, such as their exemption from taxes
- ended the duties that a peasant owed to his noble landlord, such as paying taxes to him and having to work his land unpaid
- abolished the parlements and their old-fashioned legal processes
- abolished the provincial estates, which had been created in the Middle Ages and had largely fallen into disuse
- radically reduced the status of the Roman Catholic Church in France and stopped peasants from having to pay a tax to the church
- ended the practice of being able to buy a government job; they stated that such posts must be awarded on merit alone.

So, in a matter of days, influenced by the growing demand for change across France and the absence of any solutions or leadership from the king and his ministers, the Assembly introduced the most radical reforms seen in France for centuries. Through the August Decrees, the Assembly ended much of the Ancien Régime, and attempted to be seen as the centre of authority in France.

ACTIVITY 1.9

The Decrees stated that:

- all power came essentially from the nation and should come only from the nation
- the French government was monarchical but there was no authority superior to the law; the king reigned only in the name of the law and was, therefore, under the law
- the National Assembly should be permanent and composed of a single chamber of members, elected by the people every two years
- the National Assembly had legislative power
- the king could veto (prevent) a law

CONTINUED

- no taxes of any kind could be raised except by the express permission of the National Assembly
- executive power resided with the king, but he could not make laws and would be under the law and accountable under the law
- justice would be administered only by courts established by law, following the principles of the constitution and according to the forms determined by law.

---

a Identify the principal differences between government under the Ancien Régime and the principles of government set out in the Decrees.

b In your opinion, how far do you think these changes represent a revolutionary change? Make a list of three reasons, with supporting examples as evidence, to justify your answer.

Reflection

How did you decide on a definition of a 'revolution'? In pairs, explain your method to each other. How are your methods different? Would you change your method for defining a 'revolution' following your discussion?

The Declaration of the Rights of Man and of the Citizen

The August Decrees were soon followed by an equally important statement of principles that the National Assembly intended as the basis of government in France in the future. Later in August 1789, the Assembly passed what would become one of the key statements of the whole revolutionary period – the Declaration of the Rights of Man and of the Citizen. The influence of several Enlightenment thinkers can be clearly seen in this famous document. The articles of the declaration established the principles on which to base the new system of government in France.

The declaration was a remarkable, and genuinely revolutionary, document for its time.

The representatives of the French people, organised as a National Assembly, believing that the ignorance, neglect, or contempt of the rights of man are the sole cause of public calamities and of the corruption of governments, have determined to set forth in a solemn declaration the natural, unalienable, and sacred rights of man, in order that this declaration, being constantly before all the members of the Social body, shall remind them continually of their rights and duties … Therefore, the National Assembly recognises and proclaims, in the presence and under the auspices of the Supreme Being, the following rights of man and of the citizen:

Articles:

1 Men are born and remain free and equal in rights.

2 The aim of all political association is the preservation of the natural rights of man, which cannot be taken away. These rights are liberty, property, security and resistance to oppression.

3 The principle of all sovereignty resides essentially in the nation. No body nor individual may exercise any authority which does not proceed directly from the nation.

4 Liberty consists in the freedom to do everything which injures no one else; hence the exercise of the natural rights of each man has no limits except those which assure to the other members of the society the enjoyment of the same rights. These limits can only be determined by law.

5 Law can only prohibit such actions as are hurtful to society. Nothing may be prevented which is not forbidden by law, and no one may be forced to do anything not provided for by law.

6 Law is the expression of the general will. Every citizen has a right to participate personally, or through his representative, in its foundation. It must be the same for all, whether it protects or punishes. All citizens, being equal in the eyes of the law.

7 No person shall be accused, arrested, or imprisoned except in the cases and according to the forms prescribed by law.

8 The law shall provide for such punishments only as are strictly and obviously necessary.

9 All persons are held innocent until they shall have been declared guilty.

10 No one shall be punished on account of his opinions, including his religious views.

11 The free communication of ideas and opinions is one of the most precious of the rights of man. Every citizen may, accordingly, speak, write, and print with freedom, but shall be responsible for such abuses of this freedom as shall be defined by law.

12 The security of the rights of man and of the citizen requires public military forces. These forces are, therefore, established for the good of all and not for the personal advantage of those to whom they shall be entrusted.

13 A common contribution is essential for the maintenance of the public forces and for the cost of administration. This should be equitably distributed among all the citizens in proportion to their means.

14 All the citizens have a right to decide, either personally or by their representatives, as to the necessity of the public contribution; to grant this freely; to know to what uses it is put; and to fix the proportion, the mode of assessment and of collection and the duration of the taxes.

15 Society has the right to require of every public official an account of his administration.

16 A society in which the observance of the law is not assured, nor the separation of powers defined, has no constitution at all.

17 Since property is an inviolable and sacred right, no one shall be deprived thereof except where public necessity, legally determined, shall clearly demand it, and then only on condition that the owner shall have been previously and equitably indemnified.

From the Declaration of the Rights of Man and of the Citizen. Approved by the National Assembly of France, 26 August 1789.

ACTIVITY 1.10

Read the 17 key points of the Declaration of the Rights of Man and of the Citizen. Working on your own:

a Identify which you feel are the five most important rights. Using no more than ten words, explain your choice.

b Explain why this was such a revolutionary document in France in 1789.

The king and his courtiers did not react to the Declaration and made no attempt to influence events. Therefore, having set out the basic principles of government in the Declaration, the Assembly started to make fundamental changes to the way in which France was governed. At this stage of the revolutionary process, though, there was no direct attack on the monarchy itself.

In October 1789, the Assembly started to design a new constitution. It began a series of debates on what type of government would be best for France. Many of the ideas suggested by the Enlightenment thinkers can be seen in the Assembly's debates.

Initially, the king was unwilling to accept any radical change to the system of government or any limit to his powers and was not prepared to allow ordinary subjects to debate his role. However, in October 1789, food prices started to rise again and there was a serious shortage of bread in Paris. Rumours spread that troops known for their loyalty to the king had arrived at Versailles, and the king was extravagantly entertaining them to ensure their loyalty. Fears grew that these troops would be used to restore royal power, abolish the National Assembly and destroy all that had been achieved. Many cheap, radical newspapers in Paris demanded that the king should not close the Assembly and that he should reform the system of government. Tension in Paris was again growing.

The March of the Women

On the morning of 5 October, alarm bells sounded in Paris and crowds of women began the 20 km march from Paris to the royal palace at Versailles. Initially there were about 7000 women, and some were armed. They were not just concerned about the price of bread. They wanted an end to the king's indecision and royal agreement to the August Decrees. Arriving at Versailles, they invaded the meeting of the National Assembly, which was debating its reaction to the king's

Figure 1.10: The women of Paris march on Versailles, October 1789.

unwillingness to accept constitutional change. To pacify this angry mob, the Assembly sent some of its members, and a number of women nominated by the marchers, to meet the king. They persuaded him to accept the August Decrees. Public anger and direct pressure had worked again.

This **concession** did not satisfy the women protesters, however. Joined by many other Parisians, they demanded that the king and the royal family return with them to Paris. When the king did not reply immediately, the crowd broke into the Palace of Versailles. The king and his family were escorted to Paris by a crowd of 60 000 and remained there. One commentator said, 'they came more like prisoners than princes'.

The king had been forcibly removed to Paris, where radical influences were very strong. The National Assembly followed him there. The people of Paris were increasingly prepared to use violence to protect the revolutionary changes. They had set up a citizens' militia, known as the **National Guard**, to protect the reforms that had taken place. Paris was emerging as an increasingly radical force dominating events. The fact that the new, self-appointed, decision-maker in France, the National Assembly, met in Paris from then on was highly significant. It had a major influence on subsequent events.

The march ended decades of royal government at Versailles. Government in France was now removed forcibly to Paris and open to new and radical pressures. Royal authority and the whole Ancien Régime had clearly come to a sudden end. What made it so remarkable was that not only was it the French working class that had achieved it, but it had been inspired by women.

KEY TERMS

Concession: A concession is when one person (in this case the king), agrees to the demands of another person or other people.

National Guard: A largely middle-class militia, created in 1789 to act as a national police force. It played a vital role in trying to maintain law and order in France during the revolutionary period.

KEY CONCEPT 1.1

Significance

Historians are likely to regard something as 'significant' if it had important consequences or if it tells us a lot about what was happening in a particular place, at a particular time. For example, they might consider the impact of a single event.

Look back at the events in France from the early 1780s to 1790. How significant do you think the storming of the Bastille was in the development of the revolution in France?

- Was it just an event which got enormous publicity at the time (and is still celebrated today) but had little actual impact on events?
- Was it an event which had a great influence on many people?
- Did it play a critical part in making a series of events into an actual 'revolution'?
- Were there already enough forces demanding change?

Note the difference between 'significance' and 'importance'.

KEY CONCEPT 1.2

Interpretations

There is little disagreement about the main events which led to the outbreak of the French Revolution. However, many historians disagree over the reasons why a revolution broke out in France in 1789.

Was it caused by:

- poverty, leading to a revolt of the lower classes?
- prosperity, a growing middle class wanting to make more money?
- a national struggle for liberty or democracy or equality or justice?
- a criminal conspiracy against the old social order?

CONTINUED

Historians come to the topic with different perspectives and their perspective influences their evaluation of why something happened.

In the early 19th century, historians of the causes of the revolution were largely liberals who:

- argued that it was the natural part of the progress of a society, with the establishment of representative government
- felt the crimes of the nobility, the Church and an absolute monarchy made it inevitable.

Conservatives suggested that:

- it was a series of crimes by the lower and middle classes against society, the Church and the state which led naturally to the 'Terror' (see Section 1.3) and the killing of the king.

Later, 19th-century historians suggested that:

- famine led to the king promising reform, raising high hopes, and then dashing them, which led to the anger of 1789 onwards
- it was very politically and ideologically driven, some seeing it as a middle-class conspiracy
- it was a desire for equality, followed by a desire for democracy and then a desire for national sovereignty that led to a republic.

Some 20th-century historians argued that:

- it was a struggle between classes rather than ideas or ideologies
- it was largely a clash between the middle class and the nobility and the Church over property
- it was caused by a mix of prosperity and poverty: a more prosperous middle class wanting power, and an urban working class and rural peasantry wanting food and jobs; some argued that the urban working class were the driving force, others that the rural peasants were more important.

From George Rude's *Interpretations of the French Revolution. Historical Pamphlet No. 47*, 1961.

CONTINUED

- Working in small groups, choose one of the suggested causes of the revolution and prepare for a class debate on the issue.
- Make out a case for your cause – pointing out the evidence while at the same time trying to identify the weaknesses in your opponents' cases.
- Finally, try to come to an agreed conclusion as to what the class feels is the most likely cause.

Within months most royal power and authority had gone. Almost overnight, during a few days in October 1789, France had been transformed from a medieval, semi-feudal state into something quite different. No one yet knew how different. The Ancien Régime was no more. It was a remarkable work of destruction. A new system of government and social order now had to be created, and there were many different ideas about what form these might take. Some basic principles on which a new system of government should be based had been laid out. It now remained to put them into practice.

Members of the Assembly had no experience in law making or policy making at a national level. They were heading into the unknown. No one in France, at the beginning of 1789, anticipated the series of events which became known as the 'French Revolution'.

ACTIVITY 1.11

Either on your own or in pairs, consider the question:

'To what extent was Louis XVI responsible for the crisis of 1789?'

a Put yourself in the position of a lawyer prosecuting Louis for causing the crisis:

  i What evidence would you produce?

  ii Which would you see as the most important points to bring up and why?

CONTINUED

b Put yourself in the position of a lawyer defending Louis: What would you see as the most important points in his defence? Why?

Who or what else could be blamed?

c Having weighed up both sides of the argument, do you feel that he was, or was not, the principal cause of this crisis? What are your reasons for this conclusion?

1.2 How and why did France become a republic by 1792?

The destruction of the old system had taken place by the end of 1789, but two major problems remained to be settled. The first was to persuade the king to accept the changes, and the second was the issue of whether the Assembly was capable of making decisions about the future of France.

There was broad agreement amongst the majority of the French people in 1789 that there had to be some change in the system of government. However, the new and inexperienced decision-makers disagreed over who should govern the country and how it should be governed. A deep hostility between Paris and the many regions of France which resented domination by Paris made this even more complicated.

The serious social and economic problems discussed in Section 1.1 continued, and, when war broke out against Austria in 1792, this worsened the situation and created many additional problems. The king's failure to provide any leadership in solving these problems together with the pressure from a hungry mob in Paris and the fear that the First and Second Estates would combine to bring about a return to the Ancien Régime, drove the Assembly towards more radical political and constitutional solutions to those problems.

The years 1790 to 1792 saw a very large number of radical changes in a very short time, including the abolition of the monarchy and nobility, a new republican constitution and major changes to the Roman Catholic Church. A new calendar was introduced, in which 22 September 1792 (the day after the new republican constitution was accepted) became the first day of Year 1. There were still 12 months, but they were given new names, such as Prairial, Brumaire and Thermidor. France returned to the old calendar in January 1806.

Revolutionary and counter-revolutionary groups

The representatives who met in the Assembly in 1790 were mostly men of property, often lawyers. Many were influenced by the ideas of the Enlightenment. They soon realised that an individual member of the Assembly could achieve little on his own, and the only way that decisions could be made and laws passed was by joining a group of like-minded Assembly members. These groups were known as 'clubs', and members would meet separately from the Assembly to discuss political matters. With no leadership from the king or his ministers, it was these groups which produced the ideas and policies that determined the way forward for the revolutionary process. They became the driving force of the revolution. The largest and best-organised clubs dominated the decision-making process.

Figure 1.11: A 19th-century engraving showing discussions in the Jacobin Club.

The principal revolutionary groups and their aims

Three main groups emerged, like modern political parties, representing the conservatives (the Right), moderate reformers (the Centre) and radical reformers (the Left) within the Assembly.

The Jacobins

The best known–and most influential–of these political clubs was the Jacobins. The group, formed in 1789, was open to all citizens and had linked groups across all of France. By the end of 1791 there were over 900 Jacobin groups throughout France. The Jacobins were particularly powerful in Paris and had strong connections with the Parisian working classes, which were always a powerful and radical force in the revolution. The Jacobins sat on the left-hand side of the Assembly. They were the most radical of the three groups, later arguing strongly for the execution of the king, and for the complete end of the nobility and the Roman Catholic Church in France. They also believed in extending the right to vote to more men than the other groups wanted, and they became the strongest supporters of war against Austria. The Jacobins were largely responsible for the events known as '**the Terror**' in 1793–94.

KEY TERM

'The Terror': Also known as the 'Reign of Terror', this was the name given to the period of extreme violence in France in 1793 and 1794 when thousands of French people were either executed after a brief trial by a revolutionary tribunal or murdered by mobs. Those who died were mainly royalists, nobles, clergy or just political opponents of the Jacobins.

One of the leaders of the Jacobins was **Maximilien Robespierre**. He became one of the most important of the revolutionaries between 1792 and 1794 – the years when the revolutionaries carried out the trial and execution of the king and created a republic in France.

KEY FIGURE

Maximilien Robespierre (1758–94)

Robespierre, a lawyer, was elected to the Estates-General in 1789 as a member of the Third Estate. He was strongly critical of the monarchy and was one of the first to suggest that the king should be put on trial and that France should become a republic. Robespierre has become inextricably linked to the period known as the 'Reign of Terror', in which thousands of people were executed for opposing the revolution. He was eventually arrested and executed in July 1794.

The Feuillants

The Feuillants, a group formed in 1791, were also known as the Society of the Friends of the Constitution. They were more conservative than the Jacobins and sat on the right-hand side of the Assembly. They were strong supporters of a **constitutional monarchy** and opposed the decision to go to war with Austria in 1792. They were prepared to keep the king, if he accepted the revolutionary changes that had taken place, such as equality before the law. They were strong opponents of the much more radical Jacobins. Many of the Feuillants were later executed by the Jacobins during the Terror.

KEY TERM

Constitutional monarchy: A system of government in which a monarch's powers are limited by laws and rules. These are set out in a constitution which is usually written down.

The Girondins

The third major club was the Girondins. Led by **Jacques Pierre Brissot**, among others, the Girondins acquired this name as some of the members came from the Gironde region of France. This group was also formed in 1791. Its members were moderate republicans and voted in favour of the war with Austria in 1792. The Girondins were not as radical as the Jacobins and were not so concerned with political, social and economic equality. Some members opposed the execution of the king and felt that the Paris 'mob' was too influential, and that there should be more consideration of the wishes of the people of all of France. Many Girondins were executed in the Terror.

KEY FIGURE

Jacques Pierre Brissot (1754–93)

Brissot was a leading Girondin, although he had led a smaller group called the 'Brissotins'. He strongly supported all attempts to export the revolution to the rest of Europe and wanted to abolish slavery in the French colonies. He was a supporter of the war with Austria and initially opposed the execution of the king. He was executed in 1793 for his views.

The Cordeliers

Another club was the Cordeliers Club, also known as the 'Society of the Friends of the Rights of Man and Citizen'. The Cordeliers Club was another radical club. Unusually, it was open to men who had little or no property (and so were not allowed to vote) and also to women. It played a major part in organising the protest marches in Paris which led to the Champs de Mars incident in 1791. Not only did the Cordeliers provide several of the more radical and inspirational of the revolutionary leaders such as Marat and Danton, but they were one of the first groups to demand the ending of the monarchy and the creation of a republic.

ACTIVITY 1.12

Consider these two questions:

a Explain why political clubs came into existence after 1790 and why they had such an impact.

b Explain why the revolution became increasingly radical after 1790.

For each question, identify about three different reasons and develop them in a little detail.

Explain which you think was the most important and why.

Counter-revolutionary groups and the reasons for their failure

Although many French people opposed both the revolution and the revolutionaries, they were unable to stop their progress. There were several attempts to restore the king to his former powers by 1792, but all these attempts were unsuccessful.

One reason for this was a lack of realism on the part of the people who wished to restore the monarchy. Louis XVI, his wife and courtiers never grasped the depth of feeling in France against the system of government which had existed before 1789. The king could not accept that there had to be major limits to his powers and that in future he would have to rule with the consent of his people. His heir, his son Louis, was a boy, and the next in line to the throne after him (the future Louis XVIII), always insisted that the Ancien Régime should be fully restored, with a return to the Three Estates. None understood that most French people would refuse to accept this.

In addition, bitter internal divisions weakened the royal supporters. Within France, some active opponents of the revolution were more anxious to restore the position of the Church than the king. Regions such as Brittany were willing to fight against the revolution, but their inhabitants did not want to leave their homes and advance on Paris to overthrow it. Some people hated change and feared that 'different' would mean 'worse'.

The 40 000 **émigrés** who fled France could not agree about their aims or about how to achieve them. Some émigrés wanted a restoration of the former monarchy, with all powers and privileges returned to the nobles and clergy. Others felt that concessions had to be made and that there must be a constitutional monarchy which operated within limits. Some proposed killing all the revolutionaries, but others argued for reconciliation. Some émigrés refused to associate with others as they were seen as not 'noble' enough because class divisions were still strong. Like Louis XVI, they underestimated the strength of loyalty to the revolution and assumed that if they returned to France, much of the population would rise up to support them.

KEY TERM

Émigrés: Members of the French population who left France during the first years of the revolution, and later the Terror, in many cases fearing for their lives. Most were nobles, but some were middle-class people who disagreed with the extremism of the Jacobins.

The royalists also lacked effective leadership. There was no charismatic figure, with clear and realistic aims, who could unite all those who opposed the revolution. Louis XVI was incompetent and mistrusted, his son was a child in poor health, and the next heir, the future Louis XVIII, had a talent for alienating people and had no leadership skills.

In addition, the royalists also had little effective foreign support. At different times, Austria, Prussia, the Netherlands and Britain fought against revolutionary France, but none could defeat it. This was partly because, despite initial difficulties after many officers became émigrés, revolutionary France developed one of the best armies in Europe. In the new army, servicemen were promoted because of ability rather than birth, and this proved highly successful.

In 1792, when Prussia and Austria invaded, they were driven back at the Battle of Valmy by the revolutionary army. This victory was a huge boost to revolutionary morale. As one invader wrote: 'The enemy has formidable artillery, and their army is not as contemptible as we thought it would be. Nobody is coming over to join us as we had hoped, and we have not noticed that opinions have changed in the territories we have invaded.' The revolutionary French army proved superior to all, driving the Austrians out of the region that is now Belgium and then successfully invading Italy. Britain proved to be the strongest opponent, but it had no strong army and was probably more interested in weakening France and seizing its remaining colonies than in putting a king back on the throne. There was one major British expedition against France–the Quiberon expedition in 1795–in which British ships landed émigrés on the coast of France, who then joined with some local rebels. However, this attempt was smashed by the republican General Hoche, and nearly 700 royalist supporters were shot.

Ultimately, too many people in France welcomed the revolution and the ending of the Ancien Régime for the counter-revolutionary groups to succeed. In addition, fear of reprisal and the ruthless actions by the revolutionary armies deterred many people from supporting the royalists. After 1793, many counter-revolutionaries were executed, and their property was seized.

Figure 1.12: The revolutionary army attacking the Austrians at Valmy.

ACTIVITY 1.13

Working on your own or in pairs, consider the question 'The counter-revolutionary groups failed as they were too divided.' How far do you agree?

a Copy and complete the table to help you answer this question. In one column, note the various divisions among the counter-revolutionaries. In the other, record other factors which caused them to fail.

Divisions among the counter-revolutionaries	Other causes of failure

b Make out a clear case explaining why one 'side' is more likely to be right than the other. Remember there is no 'right' answer!

Reforms

Initially in 1790 most members of the National Assembly agreed broadly on four important aims:

- France should still have a monarch, who would pass the throne to his eldest son. However, his power should be limited and shared with others. Most Assembly members were hoping for a constitutional monarchy, like the system in Britain. The king would have to obey the laws of the land and an elected assembly or parliament would limit his ability to make laws and decide policies.
- The privileges of the Church and the nobility should be abolished. Important and responsible jobs should go to the most able candidates, not just to a noble.
- There should be a fair system of taxation.
- There should be proper accountability in government and a better system of justice which ensured equality for all.

However, no one had a clear plan of how to achieve these aims. There were no obvious leaders among the Third Estate and no real understanding of what the majority of French people really wanted. Ministers and generals were used to taking orders from a king and government had centred on the royal court. Voting in elections for political leaders was a new concept. Political life like this had not existed in France before 1789 and members of the Assembly were inexperienced in making laws and deciding national policy. They were not helped by the members of the nobility and clergy who opposed change and wished to retain their powers and privileges. Meanwhile, in the background in 1790 were a breakdown of law and order throughout France, hunger for many of the population, and widespread fear and tension.

During 1790, the Assembly started the work of reconstruction and change, focusing on the four aims. Many of the changes that the Assembly introduced in 1790 lasted for years after the revolution. However, they did not address all the problems which concerned the poorest people in France, particularly the high price of food. This failing remained a cause of instability.

Financial reforms

The National Assembly carried out a number of financial reforms in order to restore economic stability.

Sale of Church property and production of assignats

To solve the immediate financial crisis, the Assembly decided to try two policies until a better and fairer system of taxation could be created to ensure that the state had a regular income.

First, to raise money the Assembly agreed to sell off the lands and valuables which had belonged to the Roman Catholic Church. This had the added advantage from the point of view of the revolutionaries that those who bought the church land now had a vested interest in not returning to the days of the Ancien Régime.

Second, to address a shortage of gold and silver coins, the Assembly issued a temporary paper currency called assignats. This paper currency was guaranteed by the government. The real value of this type of currency depended on people's willingness to accept it as payment for goods or their labour.

Both policies worked reasonably well in the short term and brought some financial stability and a degree of economic recovery.

Figure 1.13: A 500-livre assignat. What symbols of royal authority are included on the note? Why do you think this is, and what does this suggest about the National Assembly?

Taxation reform

The Assembly designed a new system of income tax, so that the burden of taxation fell on those best able to pay: the rich. It abolished the hated taxes on essentials, such as the gabelle (the salt tax), and introduced a new tax on land, which, of course, applied to the owners of property. These changes dealt with one of the greatest grievances which existed before 1789. There were no more tax exemptions for the rich. Taxation was now based largely on wealth and property. This principle remained long after the revolution.

Local government

Local government was also in need of reform. The old system had mostly been established centuries earlier and was inadequate for dealing with the problems facing France in 1789. The Assembly abolished this system and instead created 83 new departments (administrative areas), designed to end the old regional differences, and these became the main links between Paris and the localities. Effective local government structures at all levels were set up, from big cities to small villages, with elections for key officials.

Democracy was now being established throughout France. The nobility were no longer in control, and the rich could no longer buy jobs such as tax collectors that enabled them to make money corruptly. This was a significant change to the way in which France was governed, and the system has largely remained the same to this day. The French people, however, were not yet used to having elections and this inexperience later caused major problems and contributed to the increasing political instability.

Justice

The Assembly also changed the system of justice. Now justice had to be open to everyone, free if necessary, and properly accountable. It would no longer be run in the interests of lawyers and the nobility. The people would elect a local administrator of justice, known as the Justice of the Peace, who would also be the keeper of law and order. This was a popular, necessary and long-lasting measure.

Church reforms

Initially there was no attempt to change religious beliefs. However, the Church became largely an agent of the state. For example, the state took over Church lands and sold these for its own uses, and the clergy came under state control. Monasteries and convents were closed, the number of bishops was reduced, and bishops had to be elected. The main focus of the clergy would be on either teaching or charitable work.

The new law which passed these reforms was known as the **Civil Constitution of the Clergy** and the king reluctantly agreed to it. However, there was a major split over whether all the clergy should take a special oath agreeing to the changes in this Civil Constitution. For many people in France, both clergy and ordinary believers, enforcing such an oath was too radical a step, and this caused great divisions and opposition. In several of the more rural areas of France this issue led many of the peasantry to oppose the new 'revolutionary' government. Priests and believers had to choose between obeying the new laws or following their deeply held religious beliefs. This issue also divided the revolutionaries and played a role in the continuing political instability in France.

KEY TERM

Civil Constitution of the Clergy: The law of 1790 in France by which the state took control of the Church and its wealth and lands.

ACTIVITY 1.14

Figure 1.14: A cartoon from 1791 showing Roman Catholic priests and nuns being evicted from a church. The French title says: 'The relocation of the clergy' and the text below says: 'I've lost my profits; nothing can equal my pain'.

Look at the cartoon in Figure 1.14.

a Why were priests being evicted from their churches in 1791?

b What impression of the priests is given by the cartoonist?

c Does the crowd in the background look hostile or friendly?

ACTIVITY 1.15

By the end of 1790 France had undergone numerous fundamental changes.

a Consider the reforms outlined. Do you think the National Assembly can be seen as successful by the end of 1790? Either on your own or in pairs, think about the criteria for 'success' in this context. How well do you think the Assembly met those criteria?

- **i** What points can you put forward to argue that it did?
- **ii** What points can you make to argue it did not?

Have you given a clear answer to the issue of 'extent'? Is the reason why you have come to your conclusion clear?

b What fundamental problems do you think France still faced at the end of 1790? Work in pairs to identify them and put them in order of importance, together with your reasons.

Political instability

By the end of 1790, it appeared that the 'revolution' was over and that the greatest grievances of the French people had been addressed. There were many signs of trouble to come, however. Another bad harvest in the summer of 1790 was likely to lead to hunger, particularly among the poor, and, therefore, more popular unrest in the winter and spring of 1790–91. The lower classes were not the only people to dissent, however. There were growing numbers of nobles and clergy opposed to the changes and determined to keep their privileges. On the other hand, censorship was gone, and there was now a free and increasingly radical press arguing for more extreme measures.

There was deep unrest in many rural areas over taxes and the changes to the Church. There were fears that the 6000 army officers who had fled abroad to Brussels might be plotting to return the Ancien Régime. All these issues together created an atmosphere of uncertainty that led to further rapid political and social changes. So, political instability continued.

Disagreement on the terms of the new constitution

Many problems still faced French politicians. There was an obvious need for an agreed constitution, but no one was sure who should write it. Also, there was no agreement on its basic principles. For example, what should the role of the king be in the future? How much power should he have? Louis was reluctant to agree to any change. Would he try to return to the Ancien Régime? Some members of the Assembly, such as the Jacobins, wanted to end the monarchy and to create a republic. Other members wanted to retain the monarchy but to limit the king's powers. There were divisions about who could vote – should all men have the vote? Or only men who owned property? Some radicals suggested that women might be given the vote. There were also disagreements on what role, if any, the Church should play in French society.

The Assembly was badly divided on many other issues too. In the French colonies in the West Indies, enslaved people had organised a series of revolts, fighting back against their treatment and status. There was serious disagreement in the Assembly about how to deal with these revolts. Some members argued for the ending of enslavement altogether; others (often merchants who made money out of it or who were deputies from the ports which imported West Indian sugar) wanted the rebellions dealt with aggressively so that they would not continue.

The behaviour of the king and the flight to Varennes

One major cause of the instability of this period was Louis' reluctance to try to offer any leadership. He still had no idea of the nature or extent of the problems facing France. Nothing in his training or upbringing had prepared him for managing the situation facing the French monarchy. While he had formally agreed to changes such as the August Decrees, he had done so without showing enthusiasm or commitment. He did not inspire trust. When he finally took an action, he often did not think about it carefully, and it could lead to disastrous consequences.

In June 1791, Louis and his family tried to escape from Paris to the Austrian-controlled Netherlands to the north. Austria was the former home of Queen Marie Antoinette and was seen as an enemy both of France and of the revolution. Supporters of the revolution at the town of Varennes in northern France (east of Paris) captured the royal family before they could reach the Netherlands and returned them, under armed guard, to Paris.

There, the king effectively became a prisoner of the people. His attempted flight increased suspicions that he was determined to reject the changes that had occurred, to appeal for help from the queen's family and to restore the Ancien Régime with military support from Austria. People believed that he was aiming for France to be invaded by foreigners who would destroy the revolution. Many French people now saw him as a traitor to his own country.

Following the king's capture, many more of the nobility escaped France and set up centres of opposition abroad. These émigré nobles were seen as a serious threat to the revolution. Although there were some moderates in the Assembly who still felt they should try to negotiate with the king and keep him as a constitutional monarch, the flight to Varennes had inevitably strengthened the more radical view that the king should be killed, or at least **deposed**. The French people now had to make a decision. Antoine Barnave, a noted contributor to Assembly discussions and friend of Marie Antoinette, asked: 'Are we going to finish the revolution or are we going to begin it afresh?'

KEY TERMS

Depose: To remove someone from power or from their position (for example to remove a king from his throne).

Legitimate: Legally entitled. A legitimate ruler is someone who is legally entitled to govern.

ACTIVITY 1.16

Source A

Few people had a clearer idea than the king himself of the situation in which France found herself: he was convinced that the ills of his kingdom were so glaring that they would correct themselves. He knew France was likely to have a civil war. He knew a foreign war would be useless. He felt the émigrés would become the object of hatred. He believed that only he could erect a barrier against all the misfortunes which must result from all these problems; he was convinced of this. He would help the moderates in the National Assembly against the popular revolutionary current. He would accept the changes he had already agreed to, and he would

CONTINUED

deal with the foreign powers. He would accept reasonable proposals coming from Paris.
He wanted his crossing of the frontier to prevent a civil war, to become a brake on treachery and stupidity. He was resolved that once the **legitimate** rights of royal authority had been restored, and the constitution, freely discussed, should have been approved by him, to proceed to Compiègne, to stay there for a long time, and thus gain respect for this fundamental law of the state, far from the disturbances of Paris, and remain there until the constitution was fully operational.

From the Duc de Choiseul's 'Account of the Flight to Varennes, 20 June 1791'; written in 1822.

Source B

The premier public servant abandons his post; he arms himself with a false passport; after having said, in writing to the foreign powers, that his most dangerous enemies are those who spread alleged doubts about the monarch's intentions. He breaks his word, he leaves the French a declaration, which if not criminal, is against the principles of our liberty. He must have been aware that his flight exposed the nation to the dangers of civil war. He suggests that he only wished to go to Malmédy, but I say he did not intend to make peaceful observations to the National Assembly, but he wished to support his own claims with arms, and it was a conspiracy against liberty.

From a speech by the Abbé Gregoire in the National Assembly's debate on whether to suspend the king, July 1791.

a Either on your own or in pairs, compare the different views on Louis' reasons for the flight to Varennes in the two sources.

b Which source could be seen as the most reliable, and why?

c What contextual knowledge can be used to explain why one of the sources might be more accurate than the other?

The Champ de Mars Massacre

A violent event in Paris worsened the atmosphere. In July 1791 there was a massacre in the Champ de Mars, a large green space near the centre of Paris. The National Guard fired upon a group of citizens trying to **petition** the Assembly to ensure that it dealt firmly with the king after his attempted escape. More than 50 people were killed. Many people saw this as a possible counter-revolutionary action and an attempt by the king to regain power. Several more radical Assembly members fled in fear of a royalist attack, and many people began to support a more extreme solution to the problem of the king.

KEY TERM

Petition: To request something from someone. A petition is a document, usually signed by many people, making a request to those in authority.

From constitutional monarchy to republic

In September 1791, the National Assembly created a new constitution for France. The king, reluctantly, agreed to it. Being a prisoner he had little choice. This new constitution:

- retained the monarchy and allowed the king to veto new laws
- transferred sovereignty and the right to make laws to a new Legislative Assembly, which replaced the National Assembly. This Assembly was to be indirectly elected by the people of France, and two-thirds of the adult male population would now be allowed to participate in local and national elections. This would make France the most democratic country in Europe.
- established the separation of powers. This arrangement was based on an idea of Montesquieu (see Section 1.1) and it meant that

Figure 1.15: The National Guard (on the right) firing at the crowd in the Champs de Mars.

the Legislature (the Assembly), the Executive (the government) and the Judiciary (judges and the legal system) were largely independent of each other. This system was designed to prevent tyranny in the future. One 'power' would be able to check the other.

This constitution made France into a constitutional monarchy and was a significant step towards democracy. However, it survived for only one year. Poor harvests led to widespread unrest. Many people disliked the oath that the clergy had to take agreeing to the Civil Constitution of the Clergy. The king was obviously mistrusted and there was a growing counter-revolutionary movement both inside France and abroad, with the émigrés hoping for another foreign invasion. At the same time, many Assembly members felt that the revolution had only just started and hoped to create a republic with no monarchy. Few had any real faith in this new system.

Legislative Assembly, 1791–92

In October 1791, the National Assembly dissolved itself, feeling that the creation of the new constitution meant that its work was done. It had achieved some remarkable changes since the days of the Tennis Court Oath. The National Assembly was replaced by a new Legislative Assembly and new elections took place across France. None of the 745 newly elected deputies from all over France had been members of the former assembly. A group of men with no experience in making laws or policy for the nation were now to decide France's future. In addition, there was anger as the poorest people were still unable to vote and people did not believe that the new deputies represented the French people as a whole.

Initially the king appeared to support the new constitution and to accept his reduced role in governing France, but this soon changed. The new constitution gave the king two important powers: the right to appoint ministers and the ability to reject any measures passed by the Assembly. However, none of the ministers the king appointed were trusted and, a few weeks after the new Constitution took effect, he rejected a measure attacking émigrés. This action aroused suspicion. The Assembly itself was badly divided: the three main clubs disagreed constantly, with the Jacobin members always demanding much more radical measures.

During the winter of 1791–92, the Legislative Assembly faced several issues.

- The issue of slavery continued to cause divisions within the Assembly.
- Another poor harvest in 1791 meant that there was a shortage of bread, and prices of basic foods were rising.
- The refusal of some clergy to take the oath agreeing to the Civil Constitution of the Clergy was causing anger in many parts of France and leading to armed rebellion.

However, the issue which dominated the Assembly almost from the start was war – and this issue led to the Assembly's collapse. Émigré nobles who had fled abroad appealed for help to restore what they regarded as law and order in France. Meanwhile, some nobles who remained behind, including the queen, were in contact with influential friends and family abroad, seeking allies in the struggle to overturn the revolution.

Absolute monarchs across Europe were sympathetic to these appeals as they were terrified of revolutionary and democratic ideas spreading to their countries. In particular, there was real fear in France that Austria and Prussia would intervene to support Louis and destroy the revolution. These countries were both major European powers ruled by absolute monarchs, and the emperor of Austria was the queen's brother. In the Declaration of Pillnitz in 1791, Austria and Prussia had made a public statement supporting Louis and opposing the revolution.

Declaration of war on Austria, April 1792

Many of the new radical and inexperienced members of the Assembly began to demand a war against Austria and Prussia, even though neither country wished to actually invade France. These radicals hoped that war would force the king to take sides and either support the revolution enthusiastically or **abdicate** or emigrate. They also hoped a war of 'liberation' would play a major part in ensuring the end of feudalism and absolutism in both France and in the rest of Europe. The radicals aimed to export their republican, egalitarian and democratic ideas to other countries. They also thought that war would improve the French economy. They were unaware of the negative impact of the American war on the events of 1789. Their inexperience in governing a country was a serious problem for France.

KEY TERM

Abdicate: To give up a public office (for example, for a king to give up his throne).

Encouraged by popular opinion, and with the apparent support of the king, the Assembly declared war on Austria in April 1792. France was unprepared for war, and many experienced officers had left the country. When the campaign began in what is now Belgium, the French army suffered several military defeats, and the Austrians advanced into France. However, the war had a decisive effect on the progress of the revolution: it put many Frenchmen in the position of having to make up their minds who and what to fight for. The many people who disliked the idea of a possible foreign invasion of their country had to support the revolution.

At the same time, many nobles and army officers joined the Austrian enemy. There was evidence that the queen, Marie Antoinette, was trying to help the Austrians. The king made it increasingly clear that he would like the enemy invasion to succeed, and his refusal to support the Assembly over the clergy's Civil Constitution oath made it clear where his sympathies lay. The war meant that people had to take sides. It forced people to make decisions and led to an alliance of the middle and working classes against the monarch and nobility.

ACTIVITY 1.17

Source A

One of the most stupid ideas that can come into the head of a politician is to believe that it makes sense for a nation to send armies against a foreign people to make them adopt its laws and its constitution. No one loves armed missionaries, and the first reaction that natural instincts and commonsense gives is to see them as enemies and get rid of them. Movements which would be supported are those which are directed against real tyrants, like the American revolt against the English or the events here of 14 July 1789. A foreign war, provoked and directed by a government in the sort of circumstances that we are in, is a nonsensical movement which will lead to the collapse of our state. Such a war will distract public opinion, create a diversion from the real fears of our nation and give the enemies of our liberty an advantage. War will mean our constitution will be subverted and is part of a conspiracy to destroy liberty in France.

From Robespierre's speech in the Jacobin Club, 11 January 1792.

CONTINUED

Source B

What divides Robespierre and me is, 'What position should we take on the possibility of war?' If we are in danger, then while I think it is not necessary to attack, we must defend ourselves. It is much better to fight in our enemy's country than in our own. We must carry the war beyond the Rhine. The émigrés have succeeded in collecting soldiers in Worms and Coblenz and are both arming and providing them with supplies. The German princes have helped them. Therefore, it is necessary that France uses its army to crush its impudent neighbours and prevent attacks. We know that the king and his court want war and may have secret intentions against us. We know that we are correct in suspecting the king's government, but we must use a great military force to compel the Austrian emperor to recognise our new rights and deprive the émigrés of any support.

From Jacques-Pierre Brissot's speech in reply to Robespierre in the Jacobin Club, 20 January 1792.

a Working on your own or in pairs, compare the views of Robespierre and Brissot on the possible outcomes of going to war. To help with your analysis, copy and complete the table.

Robespierre	Brissot

b When you have studied Section 1.3, return to these sources. In the light of later events, which of the two do you think had the more perceptive argument?

The September Massacres

In the summer of 1792 the revolutionary process accelerated. There were two significant events, both inspired by the Paris mob. In the background there were bitter divisions within the Assembly, with little or no agreement on how France should be governed. Invading armies were threatening France from the north and the east. Parisians believed that the king and queen

Figure 1.16: The people entering the Château des Tuileries during the French Revolution.

were secretly trying to encourage the foreign invasions and destroy the revolution and felt that the Assembly was providing no leadership to protect it. Public tension was rising in Paris. On 10 August, fearing that the king was assembling troops in the Tuileries Palace, the Paris mob attacked the palace. The king was taken prisoner and over 700 of his armed supporters were killed. About 400 attackers died. The palace was set on fire and many of the defenders were taken prisoner. Within days the Assembly decided that the king should be suspended, and the future of the monarchy decided by a National Convention that was to be elected by the majority of French men. This was a major step towards creating a democracy: once again, the Paris mob had driven the revolution forward. This attack was also known as the 'Journée' and is referred to as the 'Second Revolution' because of its impact on the course of events.

The attack on the Tuileries was followed in early September by what became known as the 'September Massacres'. There was still anger that royal supporters had resisted the attack on the Tuileries and that Parisians had died. On 2 September, news arrived in Paris that the invading armies had taken the French fortress of Verdun, seen as vital for the defence of northern France and Paris itself. This created a panic in Paris. Encouraged by leading members of the Assembly, the mob stormed the prisons of Paris and murdered over 1100 prisoners without considering their gender, crimes or beliefs. Law and order broke down, and the revolution moved into a very different phase. There were similar, smaller attacks in other French towns. The revolution was becoming increasingly violent.

ACTIVITY 1.18

- **a** Identify the principal reasons, why, by the end of 1792, France was almost certain to become a republic. Working as a group, initially identify six to seven reasons.
- **b** In smaller groups, take one of those reasons and research it in depth.
- **c** Each group should present their research to the class. See if you can agree on which reason was the most important and why.

The National Convention and the abolition of the monarchy

The National Convention was elected by all French men, unless they were servants or unemployed. It was the most democratic electoral system in Europe, although fewer than 25% of people entitled to vote actually did so. The membership of the Convention was young and middle class and many were lawyers or businessmen. Some working-class men were elected, however. They were much more politically experienced than the men who had first met at Versailles in 1789, and they were strongly influenced by the king's clear opposition to reform and his links with France's enemy, Austria.

At the end of 1792, the newly elected National Convention decided to abolish the monarchy and make France a republic. Louis' actions seemed to give them no alternative. He obviously lacked commitment to the constitutional changes that had been made and there were many émigrés outside France determined to restore the Ancien Régime. Few people still trusted the king to accept his role under the constitution. He seemed determined to undermine or destroy the revolution at every opportunity. He had few supporters in the Convention. Louis was put on trial, but there was considerable debate on what he could be charged with. In the end he was tried for treason – the crime of either supporting your country's enemies in wartime or trying to destroy the government of your country. Some felt that Louis had committed both of these offences. The king was condemned to death. His opposition to any change, the distrust he generated, the fear that he was betraying France to the Austrians, the background of war and the memory of the Journée all contributed to the feeling that the revolution would only survive if he was killed. Many felt he had given the Assembly little choice but to kill him.

In three short years France had gone from an absolute monarchy which had governed France to the point of becoming a democratic republic. This outcome had not been seen as even a remote possibility in the summer of 1789. But a movement that had started in 1789 as an attempt to solve France's problems had caused much greater ones.

ACTIVITY 1.19

Louis, the French people accuse you of having committed many crimes in order to establish your tyranny by destroying liberty in France.

You attacked the sovereignty of the people by suspending the assemblies of its representatives and by driving them by violence by their sessions.

You caused an army to march against the citizens of Paris and caused their blood to flow.

You withdrew this army only when the capture of the Bastille and the general uprising showed you that the people were victorious.

For a long time you contemplated flight and made your escape as far as Varennes with a false passport.

You apparently accepted the new Constitution. Your speeches announced a desire to maintain it, but you worked to overthrow it before it was achieved.

Your brothers, enemies of the state, have rallied the émigrés. They have raised regiments, borrowed money and formed alliances against us in your name.

You allowed the French nation to be disgraced in Germany, in Italy and in Spain.

You caused the blood of Frenchmen to flow.

From accusations made against King Louis XVI at his trial in December 1792.

a What crimes does this source accuse the king of committing? Looking back on what you have learned so far, how far do you agree that the king is guilty of them?

b How does this source help you assess the significance of the king's death in the history of the revolution? (Note that 'significance' is not the same as 'importance'.)

ACTIVITY 1.20

Consider the question: 'To what extent was the Parisian mob the driving force behind the French Revolution between 1789 and the end of 1792?'.

a Work out first what you understand by the 'driving force'. Then consider events in which the Parisian mob played a role – note down some examples.

b What other factors might be a 'driving force'? Did they include hunger? Or the actions of the Assembly and the Convention? Were any leaders demanding change? How about the fear of the possible revenge of the king, the émigrés and the invading armies? Take care to weigh up these and any other factors you can think of before deciding.

1.3 How well was France governed in the period 1793–99?

Louis was publicly executed by **guillotine** in early 1793. However, the king's death solved little and in fact created even more problems. It also increased the number of enemies of the revolution both in France and abroad, as the execution of a king horrified the other kings of Europe.

KEY TERM

Guillotine: A method of execution invented by a French doctor, Guillotin, in 1789 to replace other, often cruel and inefficient, methods of execution. It was designed to behead quickly and cause no suffering in the process. The weighted blade dropped and killed instantly. Thousands died this way during the French Revolution.

The years of instability, 1793–95

After the execution of the king, chaos and instability descended on France until 1795. This situation was caused by various factors. France had been ruled by a single monarch for centuries and the transition from a monarchical system of government to a new democratic one was not easy. Many ordinary people doubted the right of this new form of government to exist and to govern France.

Problems facing France after the execution of Louis XVI

A central problem was the need to find a new form of government that was acceptable to a large enough proportion of the French people to make it work. This was difficult as there were not many experienced lawmakers and administrators. In addition, a range of serious social, economic and religious problems needed to be managed. Serious hunger continued throughout France and there were regular food riots, while a radical and uncensored press encouraged extreme ideas.

Several provinces, especially the Vendée and Brittany (see Figure 1.18), had opposed the death of the king. People in these provinces hated the attacks on the Church and resented having to take orders from Paris. This led to open armed rebellion in both provinces which an army was needed to suppress. Major cities such as Lyon and Marseille also resented the dominance of Paris and its mob. Meanwhile, the government faced a risk of foreign invasion supported by émigrés who were determined to restore the Ancien Régime.

The influence of the sans-culottes

The Paris mob, the **sans-culottes**, was a major and disruptive influence between 1793 and 1795.
The sans-culottes had already demonstrated their power and influence in the storming of the Bastille, the attack on the Tuileries and the September Massacres. Before 1793 the sans-culottes had usually been supportive of the Assemblies and Legislature in their demands for change; however, they now came into conflict with the Legislature over the future of the revolutionary process.

KEY TERM

Sans-culottes: Working-class radicals of Paris and other French cities. They were named after the type of clothes usually worn by the urban working class, that is, trousers, rather than the expensive culottes (knee breeches) usually worn by the rich. 'Sans' in French means 'without'.

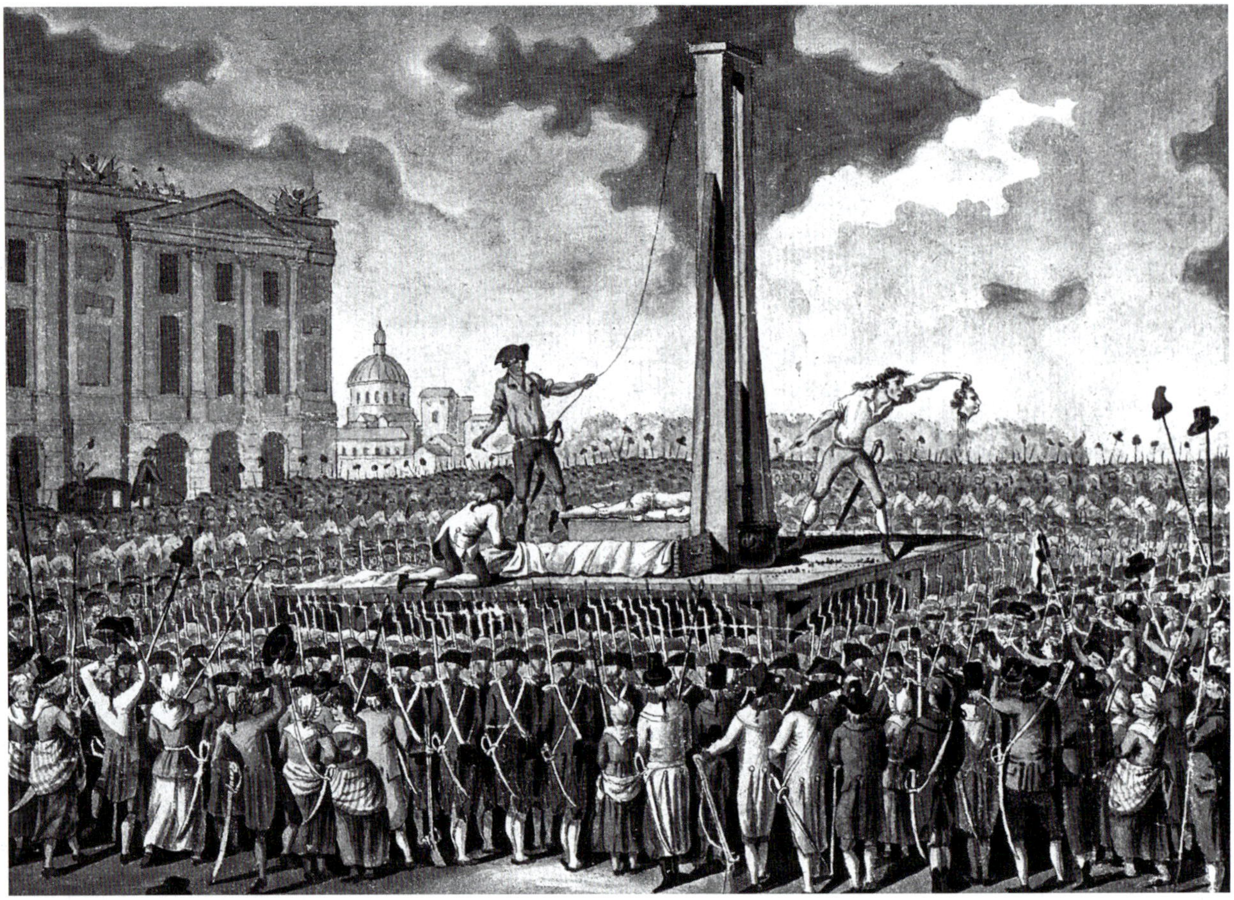

Figure 1.17: The execution of Louis XVI, January 1793.

The sans-culottes had no clear leaders and often no specific demands, but their principal aims were usually much more radical than the objectives of the more middle-class members of the Legislature. They wanted price controls on basic foodstuffs, strong action against those suspected of hoarding (secretly storing) or speculating in grain (buying grain and keeping it to sell at a profit when its value increases), and votes for all the working class, regardless of wealth – issues which affected the poor. They were less concerned with more abstract issues such as the 'Rights of Man'. Often the leaders of the political clubs such as the Jacobins and Girondins, struggling for power within the Legislature, were prepared to use the Paris mob against their opponents.

Disagreement within the Convention

There was a wide split within the Convention between those who wanted further radical reform (the Jacobins) and those who did not (the Girondins). Some deputies wished to destroy the Roman Catholic church in France; others wanted religious tolerance. Some wanted to abolish slavery in the sugar plantations in the French West Indian colonies; others felt that this would damage the economy. These disagreements made it difficult for the 750 deputies who made up the Convention to make decisions, because there was no established executive government across France. Making a law was easier than ensuring that it was carried out. There was no established system for appointing ministers and holding them accountable.

The effects of war on France in 1793

Throughout this period France was at war with all the major European powers and was threatened with invasion from both the north and the east, as well as facing possible threats from Spain in the south and Britain in the west.

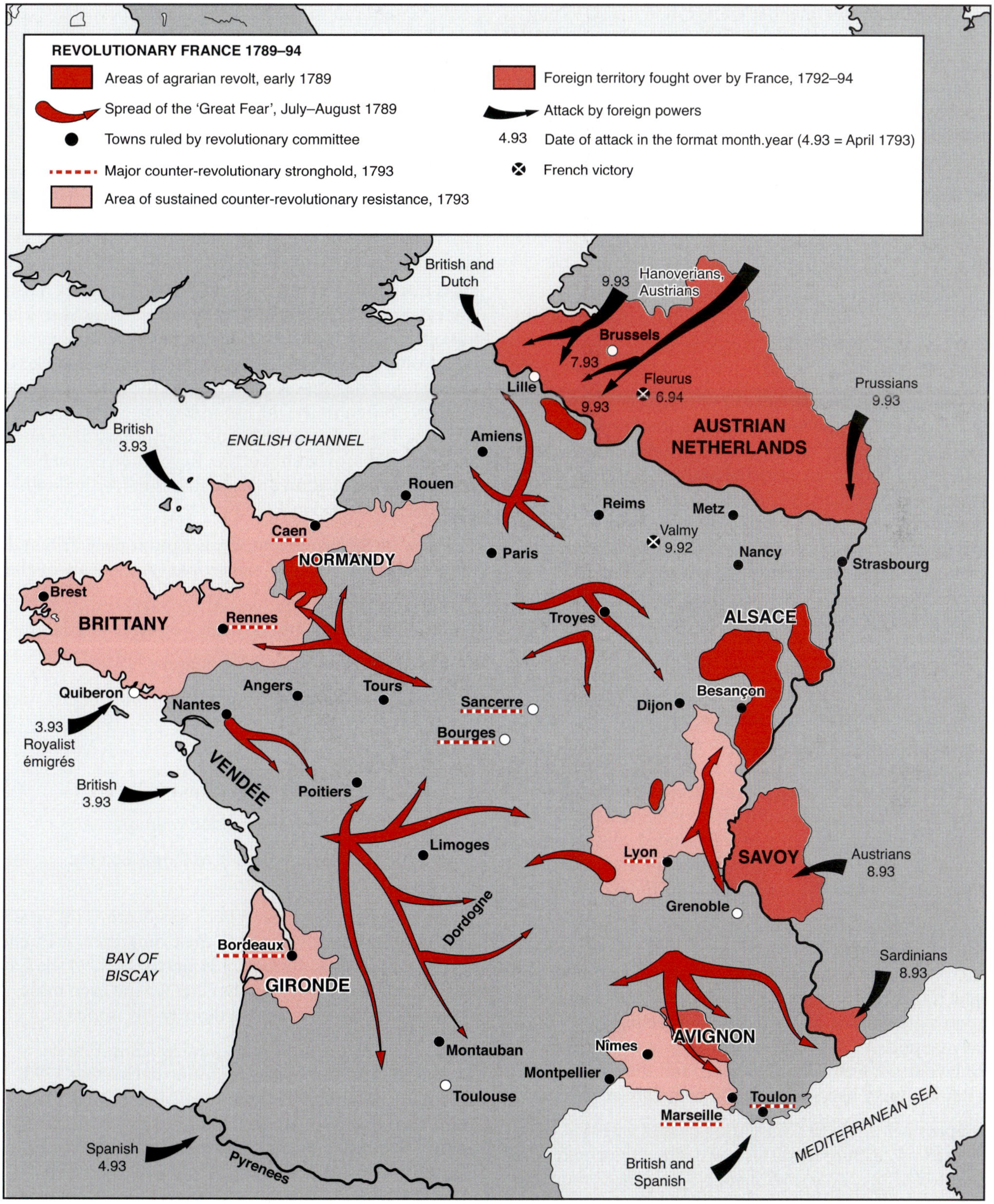

Figure 1.18: A map of France at the time of the revolution. The map shows the invasions made by the foreign armies. It also highlights the main areas of opposition to the revolution, and support for the royalists, such as the Vendée and Brittany.

The war caused resentment at the taxation raised to pay for the army, and even greater resentment at increased conscription (which the rich avoided if they paid a fine). In March 1793 there were riots across France and this led to the middle-class National Guard fighting the working class who had to join the army.

Remarkably, when a demand for all men in France to fight was ordered in August 1793, over 750 000 men joined the army. In addition, the organisation and leadership of this new army was excellent, enabling it not only to force back the invading armies by the end of 1793, but also to start a counter-offensive.

New constitution, 1793, and the Committee of Public Safety

The Convention's inexperienced politicians did their best to govern the new republic of France. In early 1793, after the execution of the king, they wrote another new constitution. Most men, regardless of wealth, were able to vote, but fewer than 25% actually did vote. All power in France now lay with a single elected chamber of about 750 deputies. It was a remarkably democratic structure for its time. However, the constitution made no provision for any executive power. Decision-making proved challenging for the republic as there was no chief executive or prime minister, or any formal way of appointing ministers. With a possible civil war looming, soaring food prices, pressure from the Paris mob and the threat of foreign invasion, the Convention needed to take major decisions. To create an Executive for decision making, in April 1793 the Convention set up a Committee of Public Safety. This was a small group of ministers, all elected deputies, who were given substantial executive powers to deal with the crises facing France. Their powers included control over the military and the judiciary and over law and order, as well as taxation and the management of the economy.

This Committee acted decisively. By the autumn of 1793, Austria had been defeated and the fear of invasion eased. Food prices started to drop, and the new government began to get control of the economy. The Committee imposed a degree of law and order on the regions and heavy taxation of the rich was bringing in money. The revolution seemed more secure, and the Committee of Public Safety had shown that it could govern France.

In September 1793 the Convention passed a new law, the Law of Suspects. This law dealt with people suspected of hoarding food, but also gave the Committee wide-ranging powers to deal with any opponents or suspected opponents of the revolution. They could be arrested, tried and executed on the same day. Deputies could be sent out to the regions with the power to try and execute opponents, dismiss local officials and simply seize any supplies they felt the army needed. The Committee was prepared to use extreme force to protect the revolution and destroy its enemies.

Robespierre and the Reign of Terror

The passing of the Law of Suspects led to what became known as the 'Reign of Terror' (or just 'the Terror') during late 1793 and 1794, when the law got out of control. The law was passed to preserve the revolution by using harsh measures against its internal and external enemies. Then some deputies argued that the law should be used to kill not only actual opponents but also *potential* opponents of the revolution. This included all nobles and senior clerics. Then radical deputies who supported the use of extreme measures began to use the law to execute more moderate thinkers. This led to more deaths. One radical Jacobin argued in 1793, 'The ship of the Revolution can only arrive at its destination on a sea that is red with blood.' (He was guillotined in 1794.)

The Law of Suspects created a Revolutionary Tribunal to punish all 'enemies of the people'. An 'enemy of the people' was anyone who:

- tried to destroy public liberty by force or cunning
- tried to re-establish the monarchy
- tried to oppose the National Assembly in any way
- prevented the army's success or helped the enemies of the republic
- prevented the bringing of food to Paris
- spread false news and misled opinion
- supported the aristocracy and opposed the principles of the Republic.

The punishment for these crimes was death. This gave a terrifying amount of power to the Committee of Public Safety and the Revolutionary Tribunal. In 1794 the Law of Suspects was made even harsher, giving even more powers to the government to destroy any opposition.

During the Terror thousands were killed in France. The queen was sent to the guillotine in October 1793, and many nobles, priests and royalists followed. Over 500 000 people were arrested, and it is estimated that about 16 000 were executed by order of the various Committees of Public Safety, many without a trial. Over 10 000 died of ill treatment in prison. In addition, possibly over 400 000 died in the savage civil wars across France in areas such as the Vendée, when the army

Figure 1.19: The public execution of Marie Antoinette, October 1793.

ruthlessly restored order in the provinces. In Nantes, for example, local revolutionaries executed over 1000 'enemies of the revolution' by firing squad and then drowned over 2000 in a river. The port of Toulon had become a royalist stronghold, but it was retaken by a republican army led by a keen young Jacobin supporter named Napoleon Bonaparte, and over 1000 were executed. As one writer commented, 'the revolution has started to devour its own'. The attempt to defend and build on the gains of 1789 had got out of control.

ACTIVITY 1.21

The great purity of the principles of the French Revolution gives it not only its strength, but also its weaknesses. Its strength gives us the power of truth over lies, the rights of the public interest over private interests. Our weakness is that it places against us evil men who wish to plunder the people and destroy the republic and our country. Unless we punish both the internal and

CONTINUED

external enemies of our republic, we will perish, and dreadful tyranny will return. The driving force of our popular government in peacetime is virtue, bringing goodness and justice to all, but during a revolution and a war it must be both virtue and terror. Terror is the only justice that is prompt, severe and inflexible – it is actually virtue. It is both democratic and just and must be adopted to meeting the pressing needs of our country. It is the only defence of our liberty against tyranny.

From Robespierre's Report to the Committee of Public Safety, 5 February 1794.

a Explain how Robespierre tries to justify the Terror.

b Why do you think he put forward this argument in February 1794?

Dominating the period of the Terror was the Jacobin leader Robespierre. He saw himself as a man of high principles and believed that power belonged to the people and not to governments. He called for the replacement of Roman Catholicism with a 'Republic of Virtue', which emphasised duty, the need for all citizens to help each other, and a loyalty to democracy. Previous revolutionary leaders had limited the power of the Church, but few had attacked Christianity itself. In May 1794, Robespierre introduced the Cult of the Supreme Being to replace the worship of the Christian God. This cult was a new religion based on a mixture of republican values, patriotism and the belief that although a God existed, he did not interfere with men's normal lives. Robespierre himself led one of the ceremonial processions to introduce the cult.

Robespierre was determined to remove all the enemies of his version of the 'correct' revolution from France. He had opponents and potential opponents such as **Georges Jacques Danton** arrested and executed.

KEY FIGURE

Georges Jacques Danton (1759–94)

Danton was a Parisian lawyer who had strong connections with the working class in Paris. A Jacobin, a powerful speaker and a member of the Assembly, he had been a strong advocate of the overthrow of the monarchy. Always a moderate, he opposed the extremes of the Terror, and, in the end, was executed for holding those moderate views.

Committees of Public Safety throughout France continued to use the guillotine ruthlessly. Unless a deputy followed Robespierre's own idealistic principles, he was seen as an enemy to be destroyed. Disagreement could lead to the guillotine. As a result, many revolutionary figures began to fear that Robespierre was hoping to become a dictator with a police state, and that he would undo the work of the revolution. Frightened that he might guillotine them, and assume absolute power, deputies in the Convention managed to get Robespierre arrested. Robespierre attempted suicide but failed. He was quickly executed in July 1794, along with 80 of his supporters, before they could organise his release or escape. Many people felt safer once he was dead.

Figure 1.20: A 19th-century engraving showing Danton defending himself before the Revolutionary Tribunal.

Robespierre remains a controversial historical figure. Some historians argue that he saved the revolution from defeat at a critical time. Others criticise the dictatorial nature of his rule and the executions that took place under his leadership. On a personal level, Robespierre was also a man of contradictions. He was known as 'The Incorruptible' and was highly principled, but he was also a ruthless politician and would not tolerate rivals even among his fellow Jacobins. He sent many of them to the guillotine.

The death of Robespierre brought an end to one part of the revolution. There was a positive reaction to his execution, almost a national sigh of relief that a terrible period was over. A few of his strongest supporters were executed, but others just retired from politics or left the country. The powers of the Committee of Public Safety were reduced, and prisons were emptied of thousands of suspects who had been imprisoned because they were suspected of being 'enemies of the people'. The Jacobin Club was closed. However, France still faced major problems, and it lacked the leadership it needed to address them.

Economic problems

Economic issues continued throughout 1794–95. A poor harvest in 1794 led to another hard winter with food shortages and high prices. The abolition of feudal dues in 1790–91 had led to a serious loss of income by many landowners. They retaliated by raising rents, which was still legal, and this hit small farmers hard and drove many people into poverty. Attacks on noble estates and the seizure of church lands had damaged agricultural productivity. Industries which specialised in the luxury goods demanded by the nobility suffered badly – for example the great silk industry in Lyon. The growing reliance on paper money, the assignats, caused rapid **inflation** throughout the period.

War with Britain led to the British blockading (preventing entry to) all the major French ports. This blockade stopped all goods coming in and out of France and devasted France's overseas trade. The British navy was the most powerful in the world at the time, and its warships permanently patrolled just outside French ports. These ships prevented merchant ships from leaving and captured those trying to enter port. The great ports of Bordeaux and Marseilles were paralysed and there was mass unemployment there.

Meanwhile, the army's demands for food and horses disrupted agriculture, and conscription caused a shortage of men to work the harvests. By 1795 there was a growing desire to end the instability caused by the revolution and find solutions to these economic problems.

The White Terror, 1794–95

Although the foreign threat lifted after French military successes against Austria, French citizens who had suffered under the Jacobin Terror of 1793–94 sought their revenge in what became known as the White Terror of 1794–95. (It was called the 'White Terror' because the leaders had white cockades (bunches of ribbons or feathers) in their hats.) After the closure of the Jacobin Club, people linked with the earlier Reign of Terror were themselves hunted down, arrested and killed. Over 2000 Jacobins were murdered in one area of the south of France alone.

Many people took revenge for damage done to them in local issues which had little to do with the revolution. Royalists who wanted their land back and clergy who hated the Civil Constitution of the Clergy and Robespierre's Cult organised local attacks on local leaders of the revolution. The winter of 1794–95 saw a serious breakdown of order across France which the Convention struggled to manage. There was an increasing demand for a more **authoritarian** government in France which would end the disorder and still defend the gains of the revolution.

KEY TERMS

Inflation: Inflation happens when prices rise rapidly. This means that a worker on a fixed income has to pay more for food or other items, while not earning any more money.

Authoritarian: Preferring to enforce obedience to authority and to limit personal freedom.

The Parisian risings, 1795

By early 1795, Paris had run out of food and on 1 April the mob, or sans-culottes, attacked the Convention again, demanding 'Bread and the Constitution of 1793' and calling for power to be transferred to the local communities in Paris. The sans-culottes also wanted greater democracy and radical measures, such as compulsory seizures of food and the death of the people who had brought down Robespierre. This time, however, the Convention did not respond to pressure from the hungry mob outside their doors. Its middle-class members were tired of what they saw as the excesses of the working class and the continuing chaos in France. They called in troops from the increasingly competent and powerful army and arrested and executed the leaders of the sans-culottes.

When a deputy was killed in May by a mob invading the Convention, the attack was driven out by the army and many of the mob were killed. In the early years of the revolution the working class of Paris had helped drive the revolution forward but now they were provoking a strong reaction to it. One of the soldiers who played an important part in firing on the Paris mob and defeating the insurrection, was the Corsican artillery officer **Napoleon Bonaparte**. (He similarly fired on a Parisian mob four years later.)

KEY FIGURE

Napoleon Bonaparte (1769–1821)

Napoleon was born in Corsica to a family of minor nobility of Italian origin. His family supported Corsican independence, and Napoleon himself did not speak French until learning it in school. After military training on mainland France, he served as an artillery officer first under Louis XVI and then in the revolutionary armies, where the departure of the nobility opened up careers for men of talent. He was a general by the age of 24. Military success led to a political career. With the army as the only dependable basis of power in a country in political turmoil, he seized control, and later declared himself emperor. Numerous military victories followed, as his armies caused destruction across Europe. However, a series of subsequent defeats saw him driven back into France and removed from power.

In the summer of 1795, the ten-year-old uncrowned Louis XVII fell ill and died, and the royalist émigrés living abroad proclaimed his uncle (the Count of Provence), King Louis XVIII. However, the so-called king was in exile in Italy and there seemed little chance of a restoration of the Ancien Régime. Together, the actions of the Paris mob in the spring of 1795 and the White Terror led many to realise that the Constitution of 1793 had failed to deliver stable government. It was time to try again to find a workable system of government for France that would find a middle way between the excesses of the Terror and a return to the Ancien Régime.

ACTIVITY 1.22

Either on your own or in pairs:

a Explain both the rise and fall of the Terror.

b Explain why there was so much political change in the years 1793–95.

For each question identify about three major reasons. Explain each reason clearly, and suggest which is the most important and why.

Figure 1.21: The young artillery officer Napoleon Bonaparte giving the orders to fire on the crowd.

ACTIVITY 1.23

Some historians view the actions of individuals as the reasons why major events such as the French Revolution occur and develop. Others look for answers elsewhere, in the prevailing economic or social conditions, or in the actions of other countries, for example.

Working as a small group, reflect on the events in France between 1788 and 1795.

a Copy and complete the table to help you analyse the reasons why the system of government in France changed so dramatically in such a short time. Add any other headings that you think are appropriate – for example, you might like to assess the part played by religion. Try to identify three or four factors in each column.

Actions of individuals	Economic conditions	Social conditions	Actions of other countries

b To what extent does this exercise help you understand why there is often no simple, or 'right' answer to explaining why such major events took place?

The Directory, 1795–99

The death of Robespierre marked the end of the most bloodthirsty period of the revolution and the start of a move away from the extremism that had characterised Jacobin rule. The public were desperate for stability and good government, but also wished to hold on to the gains of the revolution. Only a small minority of people supported a return of the monarchy, or more radical political changes.

The Constitution of the Year III

The Convention drew up yet another constitution in August 1795. In order to achieve a balance between rule by the masses and dictatorship of one man or one group, it established a system of government that became known as the 'Directory'. Using the new calendar, the constitution was called 'The Constitution of the Year III'. Under the new constitution:

- The Council of Five Hundred (with 500 elected members) proposed new laws.
- The Council of Ancients (with 250 members) accepted or rejected the proposed laws. Its members had to be over 40 years of age and were chosen from the 500.
- Five 'directors', or senior ministers were selected by the Ancients from a list drawn up by the Five Hundred. They were responsible for choosing junior ministers, army leaders, tax collectors and other officials. They ran the country and were responsible to the two Councils. It was a similar system, in theory at least, to the systems of government used in the new United States and in Britain.

The first five directors were all supporters of the revolution and survivors of the Terror:

- **Barras** was a former nobleman and an enthusiastic supporter of the revolution. He had played an important part in Robespierre's downfall. He was initially the most dominant director.
- **La Révellière-Lépeaux** was a strong republican and opponent of the monarchy. He hated the Roman Catholic Church and was determined to prevent the Church from re-establishing any role in French society.
- **Reubell** was very knowledgeable on foreign affairs. He was a more moderate republican than the others, although he had voted for the execution of the king. He had been an opponent of Robespierre and disliked the extremism of the Jacobins.
- **Le Tourneur** was an engineer and military expert.
- **Carnot** was another member with a military background. He was an opponent of Jacobin extremism and an able organiser.

The directors appeared to be a balanced group whose members reflected most contemporary views and who also had some experience of politics and government. There were some claims by their opponents that they were corrupt, however, these seem to have been mainly

Figure 1.22: The five directors of the Directory. The uniform they wore aroused some amusement!

unfounded. Although they made money from their positions in the new government, by the standards of the time they were both honest and competent.

The constitution survived for four years. This was partly because the Directory had the support of the army. The army was beginning to play an increasingly important part in political life in France and, in a way, it was replacing the Paris mob in terms of influencing events. The army supported the Directory because if the royalists won back control of France, the war against Austria would end and many soldiers would be unemployed. The Directory needed the army to put down uprisings by counter-revolutionary groups and to suppress opposition from the Jacobins and other radicals, who believed that members of the Directory had betrayed the revolution. (Although the Jacobin Club had been formally closed, supporters of Jacobin ideas still called themselves, and were referred to as, Jacobins.)

Aims of the Directory

The men who designed the new constitution aimed to restore stability, promote law and order and keep the most important achievements of the revolution. They wanted it to be a middle way between the extremes of the Terror and the failings of the Ancien Régime.

The directors and their supporters came from the middle class, which had gained from the revolution, acquiring land, status and, above all, political power. They were anxious to prevent a more radical democracy and wanted power to remain in the hands of middle-class property owners like themselves. The revolutionaries had ended the abuses of the Ancien Régime. Now these men wanted to make sure they did not lose what had been won at the cost of so much blood and hard work.

Problems facing the Directory

The directors were frequently divided over policy. In addition, there was little continuity of policy, as the new constitution required that directors should only hold office for a short period of time. There were also frequent changes of ministers in key departments: in the four years of the Directory, there were six war ministers and nine police ministers.

Financial problems

The treasury was empty, and the government was almost bankrupt. The revolutionary experiment with paper money was failing and inflation was out of control. A barter economy was growing where people did not use money and instead exchanged goods or services. The continuing war was expensive, and people resented conscription. Prices were rising, and there was a shortage of currency. One Parisian wrote in 1795, 'the price of everything is excessive, there is no more order, there is no authority, everybody is free to sell whatever he has for whatever he wants. It seems as if the time has come at last to die of hunger and cold, lacking everything. What a Republic!'.

The public expected the Directory to stabilise the currency and ensure a sound system of taxation which would enable government to function effectively and maintain law and order.

Continuing political factions

Although the Reign of Terror was over, political divisions and **factions** still remained. Royalists, Jacobins and moderate republicans continued to fight for their own purposes. The press remained uncensored, so both monarchists and radicals were able to express extreme views. In fact, these internal divisions helped the Directory to survive, as the lack of cooperation between the many political groups meant that none was strong enough to challenge the new government.

KEY TERM

Faction: A group within a larger group, where members of the larger group share a common objective but different smaller groups (factions) within it disagree on how best to achieve that objective.

Continuing popular discontent

Anger against the government increased after a severe winter in 1795–96 led to a shortage of food. Riots broke out and there were calls to abolish the 1795 Constitution by which the Directory ruled. The Directory called on the army to suppress the revolts, and the National Guard was re-formed to bring it firmly under government control. The regime gradually became more authoritarian and prepared to use force to stay in power.

Threats from the Jacobins

The Directory came under pressure from the radicals. Some radicals were inspired by Jacobin ideas. They had strong support among the urban working class. They wanted:

- a highly democratic form of government
- compulsory loans from the wealthy
- conscription for all, with no exemptions for the rich
- an end to the system of assignats, which they felt led to speculation and benefited the rich.

Such demands represented a strong attack on the wealthy middle class and the Directory itself.

In 1796 the Jacobins launched a plot to overthrow the Directory and replace it with a 'Republic of Equals'. This was named the Babeuf Plot (after one of its leaders, **Gracchus Babeuf**). The plot was well organised. The rebels issued a newspaper to spread their ideas and gather support and began stockpiling weapons in preparation for the fight ahead. Police spies uncovered the plot, however. The Jacobin leaders were arrested, and Babeuf was executed.

KEY FIGURE

François-Noël 'Gracchus' Babeuf (1760–97)

Considered an extreme radical at the time, Babeuf was a brilliant agitator and journalist. He believed in the vote for all men and women and in the creation of a genuine democracy. He argued for the abolition of all private property and for equality for all. After the failed plot to overthrow the Directory, he was arrested and executed.

Threats from the royalists

Inspired by the failure of the Jacobins in 1796, the royalists put a great deal of effort into their campaign for the elections which were to be held in 1797. Helped by an uncensored press and an angry clergy preaching to their supporters, they mounted a determined attack against the Directory and the whole system of government it represented. They particularly emphasised the poor state of the economy and the failure of the Directory to deal with finance successfully. They argued passionately for the return of the monarchy as the solution to all of France's problems. The royalists achieved some success in the elections, so, fearing a royalist **coup d'état** that would lead to a restoration of the monarchy, the more radical directors acted swiftly. In what became known as the Coup of Fructidor, the directors ignored the election results of 1797, suppressed royalists by force, imposed strict censorship on the press and removed the more moderate (potentially pro-royalist) directors. This left the more radical, pro-Jacobin element of the Directory in charge, which angered many of the Directory's middle-class supporters.

KEY TERM

Coup d'état: The sudden, and often violent, overthrow of government power by a group of citizens or military personnel.

Growing insecurity and resentment among the middle classes

The Coup of Fructidor might have saved the revolution but the actions of the directors increased the feeling of insecurity and uncertainty in France and encouraged a growing desire for stronger government. The middle class had been the greatest beneficiaries of the revolution to date, but they now saw themselves, their position and their property threatened by royalist plots on the one side and radical revolts on the other. The Directory was becoming increasingly unpopular by 1797, but no obvious alternative which might provide better government seemed available.

Successes and failures of the Directory

Apart from the fact that its many enemies were badly divided, there were other reasons why Directory survived until 1799. Although there were failures, the Directory achieved success in many areas. These successes allowed it to hold off its enemies and gave it sufficient support to survive until 1799 – longer than the other constitutional systems created since 1789.

Financial

The economy improved by 1797. Better harvests allowed the directors to take firm control of food prices, which reduced threats from the poor. In addition, the Directory created a fairer and more efficient tax system. There were no exemptions for nobles or the clergy and there were no taxes on essentials, which had always hit the poor hardest. Corruption was largely removed from the collection system.

However, taxes fell mainly on property owners and upset this influential section of the population. The Directory sometimes had to refuse to pay public debts. Key public services were neglected because money was needed to pay for the continuing war. Bankers were still reluctant to lend the government money, except at very high rates of interest. War also damaged trade, as the British continued to stop goods entering and leaving French ports, which caused unemployment.

The cost and economic impact of the war and the effects of the new taxation meant that the now dominant middle class did not believe that the directors were managing the economy successfully. Nevertheless, the system of taxation worked well and lasted long after the Directory ended.

Political

The directors ensured effective government at both the national and local levels and did their best to put the ideas of 1789 into practice. No class had any privileges and there was a focus on equality. The constitution required the directors to hold frequent elections, and the directors did their best to manage these elections. However, there were always fundamental political and ideological differences in the Council and by 1797 the elections were producing many Council members who were hostile to the Directory, as well as members who hated the Jacobins and wanted a restoration of the monarchy. The directors attempted to manage the elections so that favoured candidates won, but these actions discredited the system. In addition to actually surviving for nearly five years after the chaos of the revolutionary years, there were successes. The Directory did consolidate many of the liberal and democratic gains of the early revolutionary years – and they have remained. It did make peace with Spain and Prussia and it was strongly supported by 95% of those who voted in the constitutional plebiscite of 1795. By defeating Babeuf and his radical socialists, the Directors kept the middle class of France as supporters of the revolution and prevented any possible return of the Ancien Régime.

The Directory had always found it difficult to appear legitimate, in spite of the fact that it was sustained by elections. Too many in France felt it was not the right government for them. It had never really solved the issue of a working relationship between the Executive and the Legislature, and many people were reluctant to accept this form of democratic government. The wealthy minority were unhappy with the heavy taxation imposed on them by the majority. The forced loans and conscription required by war were unpopular. Few people liked the constitution and this created an opportunity for both royalists and radicals to put forward their views, which added to a feeling of insecurity.

KEY CONCEPT 1.3

Similarity and difference

Compare the problems facing those who were attempting to govern France between 1792 and 1794 with those facing the Directors between 1795 and 1799.

- Did they face similar challenges such as fighting a war, dealing with hunger and trying to find a type of constitution which would actually work?
- Did very different problems arise, such as the desire for stability, the strength of the émigrés and the demands of radicals like Babeuf?

Anxious to avoid the criticism of being too similar to the Ancien Régime, the Directory devolved power to the towns and regions. In many cases, these did not have the resources to keep control, so disorder grew. The Church retained strong loyalties in many rural areas and some clergy preached disloyalty to the Directory. Many people in France saw their religious faith as more important than support for the revolution. The inability to deal with this conflict between Church and state was a major failure of the Directory.

It was becoming obvious that France lacked a strong, central and inspirational government capable of dealing with the problems and showing its people a clear sense of direction. A powerful and permanent executive branch of government was needed. The French people wanted someone to blame for all that had gone wrong, and an individual they could look to for leadership. They wanted the gains of the revolution as well as social, economic and political stability. (Napoleon was able to sense this, and he capitalised on it – see Section 1.4).

In the elections of 1798, both radicals and royalists were elected to the Council of Five Hundred – this showed how politically divided France was. The new '500' attacked the directors, accusing them of corruption and incompetence, and this added to the uncertainty. By November 1799, France was ready for another coup, particularly one which promised to bring the wars to a close, end the political uncertainty, retain the achievements of the revolution and, above all, bring stability to France.

Military

For most of the period of the Directory, France was at war with other European countries. The directors had inherited the war from the previous government. They held fundamentally different views on whether the war should continue at all and (if it should) what the objectives should be. Directors and ministers of war were in office for a very limited period, so there was no continuity of policy or effective control over the army and its generals. The armies achieved great successes which brought credit, prestige and money to France and its rulers, but these victories came at a cost.

France made significant gains of territory in Italy, Belgium and Germany. The French army, particularly under Napoleon, achieved remarkable military victories over the Austrians in 1797. Large sums of money were looted from Italy, Belgium and Germany and sent to France. Revolutionary ideas were spread to Italy and Belgium.

However, there were also costly failures. The Directory sent troops and ships to support a rebellion in Ireland against its British rulers in 1798. That rebellion failed and the efforts were wasted. Inspired by his successes in Italy, Napoleon set out to conquer Egypt in 1798, aiming to go on to destroy the British Empire in the Middle East and Asia. The Egyptian expedition ended in disaster: by 1799 the British had destroyed both the French fleet and army. The army gained no glory or loot and the cost to the Directory in both money and prestige was considerable (although Napoleon successfully covered up his own failure).

The Directory also prepared the way for its own downfall by allowing Napoleon a free hand both in managing the Italian territories he had conquered and in deciding military strategy. Napoleon gained enormous national prestige, great support from the army, enormous confidence in himself and a taste for power.

Figure 1.23: Napoleon personally leading his troops into battle in the Italian campaign, 1796.

ACTIVITY 1.24

The Directory has often been given a bad press and criticised for achieving little and being easily overthrown. How fair do you think this is?

a Divide into two groups. One group should defend the record of the Directory and the other should criticise it. You could give individual members of each group specific factors to research – for example, the Directory's economic and foreign policies or the challenging legacy of the Terror and the opposition from the royalists and the Jacobins.

b Hold a whole class debate on the issue and see if you can come to a conclusion.

ACTIVITY 1.25

The local peasants are not fond of royalty, they have bad memories of titles and high rents. Their harvests are now better as the aristocrats are gone. They like the idea of equality. They are richer. They have forgotten many of the other evils of the Ancien Régime and only remember those of the Terror. They quite like our military victories abroad but dislike the taxes and conscription that go with them. They are exhausted by endless elections and arguments. They do like their old clergy. This picture proves it only requires peace and a period of calm to make them quite like the Revolution again.

From a local official's report to the Directory in Paris, January 1799.

How well does this source reveal the problems facing the Directory?

1.4 What caused the rise and fall of Napoleon Bonaparte?

Although the system of government created in 1795 was growing increasingly unpopular from 1797 onwards, it remained reasonably secure until 1799 as there seemed to be no alternative. Many people opposed the constitution, ranging from monarchists to extreme Jacobins, from committed Roman Catholics to supporters of full religious toleration, from the very rich to the very poor, but these opponents were too divided to be able to bring it down. This changed suddenly in 1799. An ambitious young general, Napoleon Bonaparte, who had risen rapidly in rank and fame since 1795, decided he could govern France better.

Napoleon Bonaparte's military reputation and political ambitions

By 1799 Napoleon had gained a superb reputation as a successful general. He had also helped create a fine army which was very loyal to him. Initially a supporter of Robespierre and the Jacobins, Napoleon gradually distanced himself from them and became a supporter of the Directory in 1795. He played an important role in suppressing counter-revolutionary forces in Paris in 1795 and helped secure the Directory in office.

The Directory rewarded Napoleon for his support by putting him in command of the army of the interior of France while he was still in his twenties. From this key position he had great control over the future of the revolution. In 1796, Napoleon was put in command of the French army which had invaded northern Italy. With 30 000 poorly fed, badly paid, ill-equipped and demoralised men, he achieved astonishing success. He defeated the Austrian armies by his superb leadership, and was then left in control of the wealthiest and most productive part of Italy.

As a result of his successes in Italy, and a subsequent attack on Austria itself, Napoleon managed to impose a peace treaty on Austria in 1798. This treaty formally gave France control of much of northern Italy and territory in present-day Belgium.

Political ambitions

Napoleon's military successes allowed him to develop political ambitions. As well as defeating national armies, he negotiated with defeated monarchs and dictated peace terms. He became the effective ruler of much of northern Italy and enjoyed the power it gave him.

The weaknesses of the Directory in 1799 gave Napoleon the opportunity to rise from being just *a* leading figure to being *the* leading figure in France. He took every opportunity offered to him to progress. After he was appointed to command all troops in the Paris area in 1799, Napoleon met with the one of the directors, Abbé Sieyès, who had been involved in the making of constitutions since 1789. This meeting gave Napoleon an opportunity to rise further. Sieyès thought that he could use Napoleon to help his own plans to replace the Directory. Napoleon thought the same about using Sieyès but was more careful to conceal it. Napoleon was aiming to become the dictator of France.

The coup of 1799

On 18 November, the 'coup of Brumaire' brought the Directory to an end. A key figure in this coup was the director Abbé Sieyès,. He was helped by the recently appointed minister of police, **Joseph Fouché**.

KEY FIGURE

Joseph Fouché (1759–1820)

Fouché was an extreme Jacobin who had flourished during the unpredictable early years of the revolution. After the Reign of Terror, he survived Robespierre's fall, turning against him just in time. By 1800, Fouché was minister of police, in charge of an extensive policing system, but he kept his contacts with royalists.

Sieyès aimed to create a new system of government which gave more power to the executive process in France and reduced the role of any legislature. It would be a much more authoritarian regime. He knew he had to seize power by a coup: trying to change everything legally through the Council would take too long and would probably fail. To take over, he needed the support of the army and a reliable general. He found such a man in charge of troops in the Paris area – Napoleon Bonaparte.

Napoleon had already laid the groundwork for such an opportunity by his military successes and brilliant public relations skills. He was ready to support Sieyès' plans. He was also clever enough to give the impression that he would not take the opportunity to seize power for himself.

The coup was carefully planned. Sieyès and Napoleon, along with Fouché and another key supporter, **Charles Maurice de Talleyrand**, would attempt to seize power and create a new, more authoritarian, regime. Sieyès and Fouché would organise the coup and Napoleon, with his troops, would provide any force needed to persuade the remaining directors and the Council to give up their powers. A critical success factor in the coup was that Napoleon's brother Lucien had been made President of the Council of Five Hundred just days before the coup.

KEY FIGURE

Charles Maurice de Talleyrand (1754–1838)

Talleyrand was a nobleman and had been a bishop before the revolution. After 1789, he supported the revolutionary governments in their Church reforms. He helped bring Napoleon to power and to form the Consulate. By 1813, however, Talleyrand had lost faith in Napoleon and instead worked for the restoration of the monarchy.

Sieyès persuaded the two legislative Councils to leave Paris and move to St Cloud, about 15 km outside the city, removing them from possible radical supporters. He had spread a false rumour that the Jacobins were about to launch a mob-inspired democratic coup to destroy the Councils, so they would be safer outside Paris. He then arranged the collapse of the Directory by persuading two other directors to resign. This left only two directors, which effectively ended the structure of government created in 1795.

Napoleon nearly destroyed the chances of a successful coup by marching his troops into the Councils' meeting at St Cloud. The meeting broke up in disorder. Some of the Councils' members fled and others demanded the prosecution of Napoleon for his illegal actions. Lucien saved the situation by assembling a few deputies who agreed to end the Directory and place the government of France in the hands of three 'consuls' (including Napoleon). These consuls would administer France until another constitution was written. Lucien used the deputies to give the coup an appearance of legality.

There was remarkably little opposition to the coup anywhere in France. A few Jacobins were exiled or imprisoned, but there were no executions.

The coup succeeded as the Directory had few supporters and the coup aroused little anxiety in France as a whole. The most recent harvests had been good so the hunger and poverty which had played such an important role in the past were less of a problem in 1799. With the Councils out of Paris and away from the possible support of the Paris mob, there was little opportunity for the Councils and the mob to form an alliance to defend the Directory. Both in Paris and at St Cloud there was a large and successful army which was loyal to Napoleon in the background. This discouraged opposition. Napoleon had taken an important step towards total power in France, using means that were as legal as he could make them.

As there were no directors and Napoleon's loyal troops ensured that the Paris sans-culottes would not revolt, power passed to three self-appointed consuls. Sieyès promised another new constitution; in the meantime, France would be governed by the three consuls, who had considerable executive power. Napoleon ensured that he was 'first consul'. This position allowed him to rapidly become the dominant force among them. It was another major step on his path to power in France.

Napoleon had achieved this position because he was an able leader, soldier, administrator and politician and because he had strong support from the army, Sieyès, and his brother Lucien. He also recognised the great desire within France for stability and law and order, and, at the same time, the wish to keep many of the revolution's great reforms. Above all, Napoleon was immensely ambitious.

Figure 1.24: A 19th-century engraving of the coup of the 18th Brumaire which took place on 9 November 1799.

ACTIVITY 1.26

Source A

The Constitution of the Year III was dying. It could neither guarantee your rights, nor assure its own existence. Repeated assaults were robbing it irreparably of the people's respect. Malevolent [evil], greedy factions were dividing up the republic. France was finally approaching the last stage of a general disorganisation. Patriots have come together. All that could harm you has been set aside. All that could serve you, all that remained pure in the national representation has united under the banner of liberty. Frenchmen, the Republic, strengthened and restored to that rank in Europe which it should never have lost, will see the realisation of its citizens' hopes and the fulfilment of its glorious destiny. Swear with us the oath we are taking to be faithful to the Republic, one and indivisible, founded on equality, liberty and the representative system.

From the Proclamation of 21 Brumaire, Year VIII, 12 November 1799.

Source B

On my return to Paris, I found division among all the authorities and agreement on only one truth, that the Constitution was half destroyed and could no longer save liberty. Every faction came to me, confided their plans in me, and asked me for my support. I refused to be the man of one faction. A plan for the restoration of order by men seen as the defenders of liberty, equality and property was created and gave me the responsibility of organising the force necessary. I believed it my duty to my fellow citizens, to the soldiers perishing in our armies and for the national glory to accept their command.

CONTINUED

I then went to the Council of Five Hundred alone and unarmed; twenty assassins threw themselves on me and aimed at my chest ... the grenadiers of the Legislative Body ran to put themselves between me and the assassins ... they carried me out ... cries of 'outlaw' were heard against me ... the grenadiers had the hall evacuated ... The factions dispersed and fled. The majority, freed from these attacks, returned freely and peaceably to the meeting hall, heard the propositions for public safety, deliberated and prepared the resolution which is to become the new and provisional law of the republic. Frenchmen, you will recognise in this conduct the zeal of a soldier of liberty, of a citizen devoted to the republic. Conservative and liberal idea have been restored to their rightful place by the disposal of rebels ...

(Signed) Bonaparte.

From Napoleon's justification of the coup of Brumaire.

a Compare the reasons given in the two sources for the failure of the Directory. You could use a table to list your findings like the one used in Activity 1.23.

b In what ways do the two sources differ on the reasons why the French people should support the new system of government?

Napoleon's initiatives as first consul

When he became first consul in 1799, aged just 30, Napoleon had three broad aims:

- to become, and then remain, the ruler of France
- to end the chaos of the revolutionary years
- to provide effective government in France, maintaining the best of the revolutionary gains while still keeping law and order.

Napoleon believed that France needed firm government and an end to radicalism. He set out to create a middle way, avoiding both Jacobinism and the Terror at one extreme and the Ancien Régime with its privileges at the other. He wanted to offer France political stability, which would in turn create social and economic stability.

Napoleon was well aware that the ideals of 1789 were deeply rooted in France by 1799, and that any attempt to change them radically would be disastrous. He wanted to restore national unity and pride in France. He hated aspects of the Ancien Régime such as feudalism, inequality and religious intolerance. On the other hand, he did not support democracy, and he was determined to break the power and influence of the sans-culottes. These views were shared by many in the middle class.

Napoleon's initiatives as first consul demonstrate how skilfully he moved from being a successful general towards becoming absolute ruler of France. One of his first acts as consul was to release from jail many émigrés and radicals, as well as some priests who had refused to take the oath to support the Civil Constitution of the Clergy. He hoped to create an atmosphere of political and religious tolerance. His message was clear: if people obeyed the law, they would be free to live in peace and follow their own beliefs. In 1802, there was a general amnesty (pardon) for all émigrés. There would be no more executions or revenge. Napoleon created a strong government with two new consuls, the former Jacobin radical Cambacérès and the old royalist sympathiser Lebrun, showing tolerance towards both 'sides'. Both men were known for their strong administrative skills and such skills were important after years of chaos.

Napoleon was aware how much the majority of French people had hated noble privilege, and he did not restore the nobility. Instead, in 1802, he introduced a new 'reward' for service to the state, the Légion d'honneur. This was an award for real achievements which benefited the country, but it carried no special privileges, just status.

Establishing authoritarian control

If Sieyès had been more perceptive, and examined Napoleon's career before 1799, he might have realised that Napoleon was much more than a brilliant general. He had shown strong authoritarian, even dictatorial, tendencies in the management of the lands he had invaded in Italy and Egypt. Napoleon was a rational individual, strongly influenced by Enlightenment ideas and, above all, the idea of a strong unitary state with a powerful central authority.

How Napoleon established authoritarian control

After the coup, Sieyès produced another new constitution, which established the Consulate, with its powerful central Executive. This constitution was a critical stage in Napoleon's rise to power in France. It was made legitimate by a **plebiscite** in order to demonstrate its legality and show that it had popular support.

This new constitution placed the first consul (Napoleon) in the key decision-making role, The first consul appointed ministers. He could also initiate legislation and only limited consultation was required for new legislation. None of the consuls were accountable to the Legislature.

The 'nation' was still sovereign, but in practice it was not going to be consulted. The concept of the need to elect rulers into power was gone. Napoleon said: 'I alone represent the people.' The other two consuls provided an image that power was being shared, but in practice they had none. This was demonstrated in 1800 when Napoleon (but not the other two consuls) moved into the old royal palace in Paris, the Tuileries.

Further steps followed Napoleon's rise to power. In 1802 he was made 'consul for life' (and was allowed to name his successor) and in 1804 he was finally declared Emperor of France. These appointments were also confirmed by plebiscites. In some ways the Ancien Régime had returned.

> **KEY TERM**
>
> **Plebiscite:** Like an election, a plebiscite is a popular vote. Instead of being called to choose a national assembly and a government, however, a plebiscite puts a question to voters about a specific issue and is almost always organised around a 'yes/no' decision. Essentially, it is another word for a referendum.

Setting up new ministries and a Council of State

Napoleon set up new ministries, including the war ministry, and he controlled all major appointments. All ministers reported directly to Napoleon. He also created a Council of State which consisted of all the principal ministers. This council had the authority to govern France if Napoleon was leading military campaigns abroad. Napoleon was good at spotting talent and using it. The Council consisted of a good balance politically and contained many able men who had taken different sides during the revolutionary period. Napoleon also set up the Bank of France under a capable minister. This was a key step towards ending the financial problems that had contributed to chaos during the revolution.

In local government Napoleon imposed major structural reform on the provinces. He created the office of prefect, replacing the old intendants. Prefects were given considerable power and reported directly to Paris. Their role was to ensure law and order locally, collect taxes efficiently and create stability throughout France. Prefects were not elected but Napoleon took considerable care to appoint able men. They were always sent to areas away from their birthplace, where they had no local connections. This was intended to avoid them helping their families or old friends and being open to corruption. This process was an important step in the centralisation of power in France. Like many of Napoleon's reforms, this change has lasted until today.

Reform of the police force and the judiciary

The new regime quickly tackled methods for maintaining law and order. The police force, both local and central, was reformed by Fouché on Napoleon's orders. All the police in France came under central control from Paris. There would be no more government by the sans-culottes. An elaborate system of spies and informers was set up to eliminate any enemies of the state. Mail could be censored as well.

Minor rebellions broke out in Brittany and the west of France in the early 1800s, but they were firmly dealt with. Armed force was used, followed by some executions. 'Never since the time of Robespierre have laws been so severe', one citizen reported, but, once an example had been made, conciliation followed, and calm was restored. In the case of a rebellion in the Vendée, Napoleon personally met with the leaders, granted them an amnesty and left them in peace. However, anyone who continued to rebel was ruthlessly prosecuted. Napoleon also reformed the judiciary. The central government appointed all judges, after checking their loyalty. **Repression** by the government was made easier, but certain key gains of 1789 were kept, such as an insistence on equality before the law. Nonetheless, the interests of the state tended to dominate over those of the individual.

> **KEY TERM**
>
> **Repression:** Repression by a government is when individuals or groups are prevented from expressing their views or acting in a way the government dislikes.

Propaganda and censorship

Napoleon was skilled at using **propaganda** and this skill was important in helping him to retain power. Although he relied on repression to silence opponents, he always tried to show himself and his regime in a positive way. In particular, while Napoleon made it clear in public that he was not responsible for the increasingly unpopular war with Austria and Britain, he strongly publicised his great military victories – such as the battles of Marengo and Hohenlinden in 1800. Both these military successes brought great prestige to France and gained possessions abroad. They allowed Napoleon to enhance his image in the official press, so that he became a national hero.

Just as Napoleon conscripted men to fight in his army, he conscripted painters to portray him in a good way. He told the painters what they should paint and how they should paint it.

His victories were painted and publicised, and his failures were shown as positively as possible. Similarly, he ordered playwrights to write plays which glorified Napoleon and his achievements.

KEY TERM

Propaganda: Communication designed to influence an audience to support a specific action or political agenda. It does so by spreading ideas, information or rumours in ways that appeal to people's beliefs and feelings.

Figure 1.25: A detail from a painting of 1804, showing Napoleon visiting sufferers of the plague in Jaffa in 1799. Napoleon publicised this painting widely. Although the visit occurred during his failed Egyptian expedition, Napoleon took care always to show himself in a good way.

Figure 1.26: *Napoleon Crossing the Alps*, oil painting of 1801. The king of Spain ordered the original version as a gift for Napoleon. Napoleon instructed the artist in how to portray him, and ordered additional copies which he placed on public display at the Louvre Museum in 1801. How does the origin of the painting help to explain the message it contains about Napoleon's image?

The majority of the newspapers before 1800 tended to support radical Jacobin ideas. A major factor behind much of the radicalism of the early stages of the revolution had been the support and spread of extreme views by newspapers and pamphlets. Napoleon's government introduced censorship of the press and shut down over 60 (out of 73) newspapers in 1800 alone. Soon almost the only source for news was the official government newspaper, the *Moniteur*.

Napoleon issued regular news bulletins dealing with all his military campaigns, and these bulletins were the only source of information on his campaigns. The bulletins did not mention the high casualties but did report on the number of captured guns. The censorship system was more effective than it had been before 1789. There was no more freedom for the press and theatres were banned from putting on radical plays. However, Napoleon did not ban all forms of entertainment. That would have offended people of all classes.

Support of the army

Napoleon reviewed all senior military appointments and ensured that only generals loyal to him remained in their posts. He also took great care to ensure his soldiers were well paid and fed, and he did his best to limit the unpopularity of conscription. He was well aware of the important role that the military had played during the revolutionary period; the army ended the revolution and assisted his rise to power.

Control of elections

Napoleon knew that elections had become an expected part of the political process in France since 1789 and that to abolish them would look like a return to the Ancien Régime. He wanted adult males to be involved in the election process and to support him, but he was not keen on giving any institution the power to make policy (and certainly not to replace him). There were frequent elections in the larger towns and regions, but the voters could only select several candidates for possible election to local office. The government made the final choice.

To gain popular support and legitimacy, Napoleon used plebiscites, in which voters were asked a single question and could respond 'yes' or 'no'. The first took place in 1800 when voters were asked to approve the new constitution, which made him first consul. The second happened in 1802 where the voters agreed that Napoleon should become 'consul for life'. The third was in 1804 when voters agreed that he should become emperor (with 99.93% voting 'yes'). All voting was in public, which may have discouraged opponents from participating. There was the appearance, but not the reality, of democracy.

Emperor Napoleon, 1804

By 1804 Napoleon felt secure enough to declare himself Emperor of France. He had established a new dynasty in Europe. He arranged for the Pope, the head of the Roman Catholic Church, to attend his coronation ceremony to demonstrate to the Roman Catholics of France that he had the support of the Church. Napoleon crowned himself as Emperor, and then his wife Josephine

Figure 1.27: The coronation of Napoleon (official title: *Consecration of the Emperor Napoleon I and Coronation of the Empress Josephine in the Cathedral of Notre-Dame de Paris on 2 December 1804*) by Jacques-Louis David, 1807. The painting was ordered by Napoleon after his coronation. It was designed to show Napoleon's support of, and from, the Church.

as Empress. The court that developed at the Tuileries Palace in Paris was similar to Louis XVI's court at Versailles, and many of the courtiers were members of the 'old' nobility.

By the time he became emperor, and had enjoyed further successful military victories and conquests abroad, Napoleon had become increasingly authoritarian. Legislative bodies were marginalised and played little role in government beyond approving the actions of the emperor. Censorship was tightened, and the press had to become enthusiastic about Napoleon and his policies. There was no more popular sovereignty.

As the government had an efficient and centrally controlled police force, Napoleon was able to deal firmly with any opposition. For example, fearing a royalist coup against him in 1804, Napoleon ordered the capture and execution of the Duke of Enghien, who was related to the royal family. This act angered many in Europe, but it sent a clear message to potential opponents.

There was little or no serious opposition to Napoleon's rule in France, however. As emperor, he ensured that law and order were maintained, and that the country kept the benefits of the revolution. He seems to have modelled himself on the 'enlightened despots' of the Ancien Régimes in Europe, where autocratic leaders ruled wisely.

Napoleon's domestic reforms

Napoleon's domestic policies have attracted considerable debate. What were the motives behind them? Did he just want to stay in power? Or was he a genuine heir to the revolution who wished to keep the French people free from the injustices of the Ancien Régime?

In his first years in power, Napoleon brought in a series of major domestic reforms. Making peace in 1801 with France's European enemies enabled Napoleon to focus on the internal affairs of France. The revolutionary years had destroyed much of the Ancien Régime, but in many cases had put little in its place. Partly to secure himself in power, partly to gain popularity and partly to consolidate the gains of the revolution, Napoleon proceeded to reform France.

Legal reform: the Code Napoléon

The civil and criminal legal system in France in 1799 was a complicated mess. Before 1789, there had been about 400 different legal systems in France. Regions and towns often had their own laws. The Church had its own rules, as did other groups of people, such as merchants. Some nobles would be exempt from certain laws.
The revolution had abolished many but not all of these old systems. Over 14 000 new laws had been passed by the various assemblies between 1789 and 1799, but many of them were now unnecessary and discredited. The legal system in France needed radical reform, if the new regime was to convince the French people that it could effectively govern the country.

Although most of the actual work reforming the legal system was done by others, Napoleon realised the importance of the work, ensured it happened, and took credit for it after its obvious success. Under Napoleon's supervision, a new French civil law code was created. Napoleon later claimed this code as one of his greatest achievements. The Code was produced in stages between 1801 and 1806, and formally established as the Code Napoléon in 1807. Its main terms were:

- equality before the law
- freedom of religion
- freedom of conscience
- an end to feudalism
- the rule of law with the right to a proper trial and defence
- freedom to choose one's own profession.

The Code introduced reformed systems of civil law, commercial law and criminal law, and brought in a new penal code. All laws were to be applied uniformly throughout France. The Code covered many areas of life, such as divorce, marriage, adoption, debts, loans and even gambling.

Critics at the time, and since, pointed out that the Code:

- favoured the middle class
- was biased in favour of owners of landed property and neglected the interests of industrial wealth
- promoted the interests of the state over those of the individual
- gave too much authority to the father/husband over women
- offered little to the poor or landless (there was no right to a livelihood)
- favoured the employer over the worker (workers' associations were banned).

Nonetheless, most parts of the Code survived Napoleon's overthrow. The Code was radical for its time, although since then historians have criticised it for not going further in political and social matters.

Figure 1.28: Napoleon handing his Code of Laws to Rome, 1806. The painting is intended to demonstrate that the new legal system was replacing the old one, which was based on Roman Law.

Educational reform

Napoleon brought in major changes in the system of education. Although there had been attempts during the revolutionary period to improve schools, much damage had also taken place. Before the revolution, the Church had been one of the main providers of education in France. Napoleon allowed it to retain control of primary education, up to the age of 10, but made sure that it taught children to respect the emperor and obey the law. The state took control of male education after the age of ten.

In 1801, a report from the prefects on the poor state of education led to important developments, in which Napoleon had a major influence. A state-controlled system of education for boys aged 10 to 16 was set up. The curriculum was controlled by the state and teachers were trained, paid and monitored by the central government. There was little emphasis on religion in this new curriculum. The focus was mainly on subjects such as French and mathematics, designed to produce a middle-class (and non-revolutionary) elite capable of administering France in the future. In addition, 30 lycées were created throughout France to provide advanced and specialist higher education for the future leaders of France. A reformed university system was also created in 1808, led by the 'Imperial University'. This, too, aimed to produce an educated elite in France which would serve the state.

In general, the poor were excluded from these reforms. Like many of the middle class, Napoleon felt that educating the poor was a waste of time and money. The army needed ordinary soldiers and farming needed simple labourers. Neither needed much education. Girls and women did not benefit much from these reforms either. Nonetheless, this system of education was both popular and long-lasting.

Financial and economic reform

Hunger and poverty within the working class had been major factors influencing the course of the revolution before 1799. High taxation and economic and financial instability had done much to influence middle-class attitudes. Napoleon knew that he had to address these issues in order to remain popular and cement his regime. There were some attempts to encourage manufacturing, and protective trade **tariffs** became French policy, to protect French textiles, for example, against the import of cheaper British textiles. Prefects were made to improve the quality of roads, which helped trade and communications (and also the rapid movement of troops). The long, straight, tree-lined boulevards of France today are a Napoleonic legacy. Once stable, the economy was often subordinated to Napoleon's other needs.

KEY TERM

Tariffs: Taxes or duties imposed by a government on goods imported into a country.

Banking

In one financial area there were significant improvements. In 1800, the Bank of France was formed to bring order and stability to the banking system and the French currency, and to end the problem of the assignats. (Napoleon and his family were shareholders.) Banks across the country were tightly regulated by the central bank and only the Bank of France could print the paper currency, which became secure and accepted. Napoleon ended forced loans, where bankers were compelled to lend money to the state, and the cycle of inflation and deflation. He ensured that the state's debts were paid on time and in 1802 there was a balanced state budget in which income matched expenditure. The small financial elite, who had played a part in calling the Estates-General in 1789 and also in ending the Directory and helping Napoleon rise to power, were given a major role in the management of the Bank of France.

Taxation

The sensible and fair system of taxation largely created under the Directory was continued. The system was seen to be just, and that was critical to its success. In the first decade of Napoleon's rule the level of taxation was not a major concern. However, after 1810 the costs of maintaining his armies grew. Taxation, therefore, rose, and this caused increasing resentment which played a part in Napoleon's downfall in 1814.

Bread prices

Aware of the role that hunger had played in the events of 1789 onwards, Napoleon carefully ensured that the price of bread was strictly controlled. Bread was an essential part of working-class diet. Napoleon knew that once it cost more than 40% of a working man's daily income, problems would occur. Prefects were to ensure that this did not happen and were given the powers to enforce strict price controls. Regulations were also imposed on the quality of bread produced and steps were taken to ensure that good quality bread was always available. Napoleon did not want to return to the hunger-driven radicalism of the sans-culottes of the revolutionary period.

Religious reform: the Concordat with the Roman Catholic Church

One issue that had divided France throughout the whole revolutionary period was what should happen to the Roman Catholic Church. France had always been a strongly Catholic country, with some tolerance for both Protestants and Jews. The Church and its members had been fiercely attacked in the early days of the revolution. Revolutionaries had attempted to 'dechristianise' France and many clergymen had been killed or had fled, while most of the Church's wealth and land was confiscated. However, in many parts of France, especially in the Vendée and Brittany, support for the Catholic Church had been an important reason for counter-revolutionary activity. Many deeply conservative people, especially in rural areas, wished to see Catholicism restored to their lives and communities.

Napoleon knew that he had to compromise with the Church and end the bitterness that the revolutionary attacks had caused. Settling this issue would deprive the royalists of Church support and would also ease the fears of those who now owned the former Church property that had been sold during the revolution. Napoleon also had territorial ambitions in Belgium, south Germany and Italy–all strongly Roman Catholic countries. The Church could be a useful ally.

In 1801, Napoleon started secret discussions with the head of the Catholic Church, the Pope. Making a deal was not easy after such violence and the seizure of Church property and wealth. Much bitterness remained. Napoleon believed that religious toleration was necessary but the Roman Catholic Church disagreed, being reluctant to tolerate any rival religions in France. In 1802, however, the Pope and Napoleon reached an agreement, which was published. This agreement was known as the Concordat. Its terms were as follows:

- There was a formal reconciliation between the Roman Catholic Church and the French state.
- The Church formally recognised Napoleon's government as the legitimate government of France.
- Napoleon's government officially recognised Catholicism.
- The Church was free to organise public worship.
- The Church remained subordinate to the state. It retained some influence over primary education, but that was carefully monitored by the government. The state appointed the bishops and paid the clergy.
- The clergy had to take an oath agreeing to be loyal to the state.
- Church lands seized during the revolution remained with their new owners.
- Other religious groups, such as Protestants and Jews, were to be tolerated.
- Clergy were allowed to preach freely.

Although this agreement caused problems later, it was a great achievement at the time. It ended a major source of division in France and was a practical solution to a serious problem. The Concordat played a key part in ensuring the stability of the state and Napoleon's hold on power.

Figure 1.29: Image of the signing of the Concordat. The men signing it, representing Napoleon and the Roman Catholics bishops, are being blessed from above by the Church. Napoleon was anxious to gain the support of the many Roman Catholics in France.

ACTIVITY 1.27

The object of my dearest thoughts has always been the happiness of the French people and their glory the object of my labours. Called by Divine Providence and the Constitutions of the Republic to Imperial power, I see in this new order of things nothing but greater means of assuring national power and prosperity. I take comfort with confidence in the powerful aid of the Almighty God. He will inspire His Ministers to support me by all the means within their power. These Ministers of God will enlighten the

CONTINUED

people by wise instruction, preaching to them love of duty, obedience to the law and the practice of all the Christian and civil virtues. They will call the blessing of Heaven upon the nation and on the Supreme Head of the State.

From Napoleon's proclamation to the French people on becoming Emperor, 1804

a How does the source show that Napoleon was trying to reconcile the Ancien Régime with the ideals of the French Revolution?

b How does the source demonstrate why the Concordat was so useful to Napoleon?

KEY CONCEPT 1.4

Change and continuity

Historians study patterns of development over time, identifying and analysing areas of continuity and areas of change.

Think back over what you have learned about France under the Directory and under Napoleon. Working in pairs, identify the principal changes that Napoleon brought to France in his domestic policies.

- Evaluate how fundamental they were. To what extent was France a very different country as a result of his rule?
- How different was Napoleon's rule to that of the Directory?
- Assess the degree of continuity between his rule and that of the Directory.

ACTIVITY 1.28

In groups, consider the following question: 'The Code Napoléon was Napoleon's greatest domestic achievement.' How far do you agree?

a Each member of the group should take one of Napoleon's achievements. You could choose from the establishment of order and stability, the Code, the Concordat, education, economic stability, a fair system of taxation, the end of privilege among others. You should prepare to argue that your 'achievement' is the most important and lasting.

b Consider factors such as the challenges he faced in achieving it – some reforms may have been easier to achieve than others. Did it last? Did it bring benefits to most people? For a question like this, always pause for a moment and think about your criteria for 'greatest'.

c Organise a whole class debate on the question and try and come to an agreed conclusion. (But bear in mind that historians often disagree!)

Reasons for Napoleon's fall from power

The system of government that Napoleon had built up in France, and the empire that he had created in Europe, came to an end in 1814.There were four main reasons why Napoleon fell from power in France:

- his declining popularity in France
- the destruction of his armies leading to the invasion of France
- losing the support of potential allies such as Germany and Poland
- running out of the resources he needed to maintain his vast empire.

Declining popularity at home

Napoleon had been initially popular after assuming power in France. His successful battles had won him prestige and gained territory for France. Most citizens approved of his early domestic policies and the political, social and economic stability he had brought to France. He was careful not to alienate the elites and ensured the support of his generals by rewarding them with money and lands.

However, by 1815 there was no great popular desire to keep him on the throne. Conscription and the deterioration in the economy caused by Napoleon's constant wars had caused his popularity to decline. When Napoleon's armies began to sustain defeats, he became less popular still. His powerful police chief, Fouché, administering his efficient national police force, began to use increasingly repressive, and much disliked, policies to stamp out dissent. Censorship and propaganda became more important and more obvious, and this caused increasing resentment.

Conscription and the deteriorating economy

A major reason for the gradual decline in Napoleon's popularity was the regular demands he made on all French men to serve in his armies. France had a tradition of conscription. However, during the revolutionary period the government had made it clear that conscription was a temporary requirement to save the revolution from its enemies and the men returned home once the emergency was over. In contrast, Napoleon was at war with most of Europe for most of his rule, and he needed a large army. Significant numbers of men had to go and fight for long periods; this became part of French life and was enforced by law. It was possible for the rich to avoid this duty simply by paying a fine, but the poor had to fight, and significant numbers died. Over two million men were conscripted (from a total population of around 27 million) and over half a million deserted or went into hiding to avoid military service. Conscription became increasingly unpopular.

The shortage in the workforce damaged French agriculture and industry. In addition, by 1813 over 80% of the income from taxation was being spent on war. There were huge losses of men and material. Taxation on essentials was introduced, which hit the poor hardest. A bad harvest in 1812 caused further hardship.

The ongoing war with Britain continued to affect trade and industry. The economy suffered when the British destroyed the French fleet in 1805, meaning that France was unable to trade with its profitable West Indian colonies. The continuing British blockade of French ports prevented exports of French goods from any of the French ports as the British navy patrolled the seas outside them and captured ships entering or leaving. The ports of Marseilles, Bordeaux and Nantes were closed, causing distress. Attempts to create a cotton-based textile industry to replace the British failed, largely through over regulation and the inability to import raw cotton.

Effects of Napoleon's failure to defeat Britain

Napoleon allegedly referred to the British as a 'nation of shopkeepers'. However, fighting a war with Britain, France's old enemy, played a major part in his downfall. The British navy prevented French expansion overseas and did immense harm to the French economy. The British government paid large sums of money to the Russians and the Austrians to fight the French – their payments funded 450 000 soldiers. The small, but well led, British army played a key role in defeating the previously unbeaten French armies. The British had less than half the population of the French, but they had an excellent navy and a great deal of money.

The failure of the Continental System

Determined to try to damage the British and their vast overseas trade, which brought in so much of their income, Napoleon introduced the **Continental System** in 1806.

The Continental System was an attempt to ban all the countries on mainland Europe from trading with Britain. It was designed to damage Britain's trade and wealth and to prevent Britain from providing money to other countries, such as Austria, Prussia and Russia, to fight against France's domination of Europe.

The Continental System caused anger amongst Napoleon's 'subject' nations, as these nations wished to purchase goods, such as textiles, pottery and iron products, which Britain produced at low cost. The system failed, partly because of large-scale smuggling and partly because Britain could sell its goods elsewhere. As a result, the system damaged France and the countries it controlled more than it harmed Britain. In addition, the British navy controlled the seas, and Britain was prepared to blockade and damage the overseas trade of countries who proved too willing to accept the Continental System. The Continental System, therefore, failed to achieve its objective of damaging Britain, and contributed to loss of support for Napoleon in the rest of Europe.

KEY TERM

Continental System: The system introduced by Napoleon which prevented any imports and exports from and to Britain, from France and any of the countries it controlled, and banned any other form of contact with Britain, such as mail.

Outcome of the Peninsular War, 1808–14

Another factor in Napoleon's fall was his invasion of Spain and Portugal. Portugal had a long-standing alliance with Britain. It was strongly opposed to the Continental System as it had an overseas empire in Brazil and Africa and wished to trade both with Britain and with its own empire. Determined to enforce the Continental System, Napoleon invaded Portugal and Spain in 1807. He drove out the Spanish monarch and placed one of his brothers on the throne of Spain.

The Portuguese asked Britain for help. Britain sent a small army to Portugal, which repeatedly defeated the French army and forced it out of both Portugal and Spain by the end of 1813. The British army, led by the Duke of Wellington, then crossed the Pyrenees and successfully invaded the south of France, defeating French armies on French soil. This was a humiliation for Napoleon and meant that France was now being threatened from the south by the British and from the east by the combined armies of Russia, Prussia and Austria.

Napoleon's involvement in Spain and Portugal played an important part in his downfall. The British had showed that the seemingly unbeatable French armies could be defeated, which encouraged the Prussians and Austrians to try again. Trying to control Spain when the Spanish people hated French rule meant that he had to maintain an army of 300 000 men there. Thousands of French soldiers died in Spain and the cost of supporting them there was a huge burden on the French state. There were no gains for France in Portugal and Spain, only losses. As one Spaniard said in 1812 'The first step that Bonaparte made towards his ruin was the enterprise in Spain'. Napoleon later referred to the 'Spanish ulcer' as it drained so much of France's energy.

Growth of nationalism in the empire

By 1812, Napoleon's military conquests meant that he controlled a large part of Europe. However, ideas of **nationalism** were spreading throughout Europe, and this empire was becoming increasing difficult to maintain.

KEY TERM

Nationalism: The belief that people with a common language, culture or history should have the right to govern themselves, and that the boundaries between states should be based on this idea.

The extent of Napoleon's empire by 1812

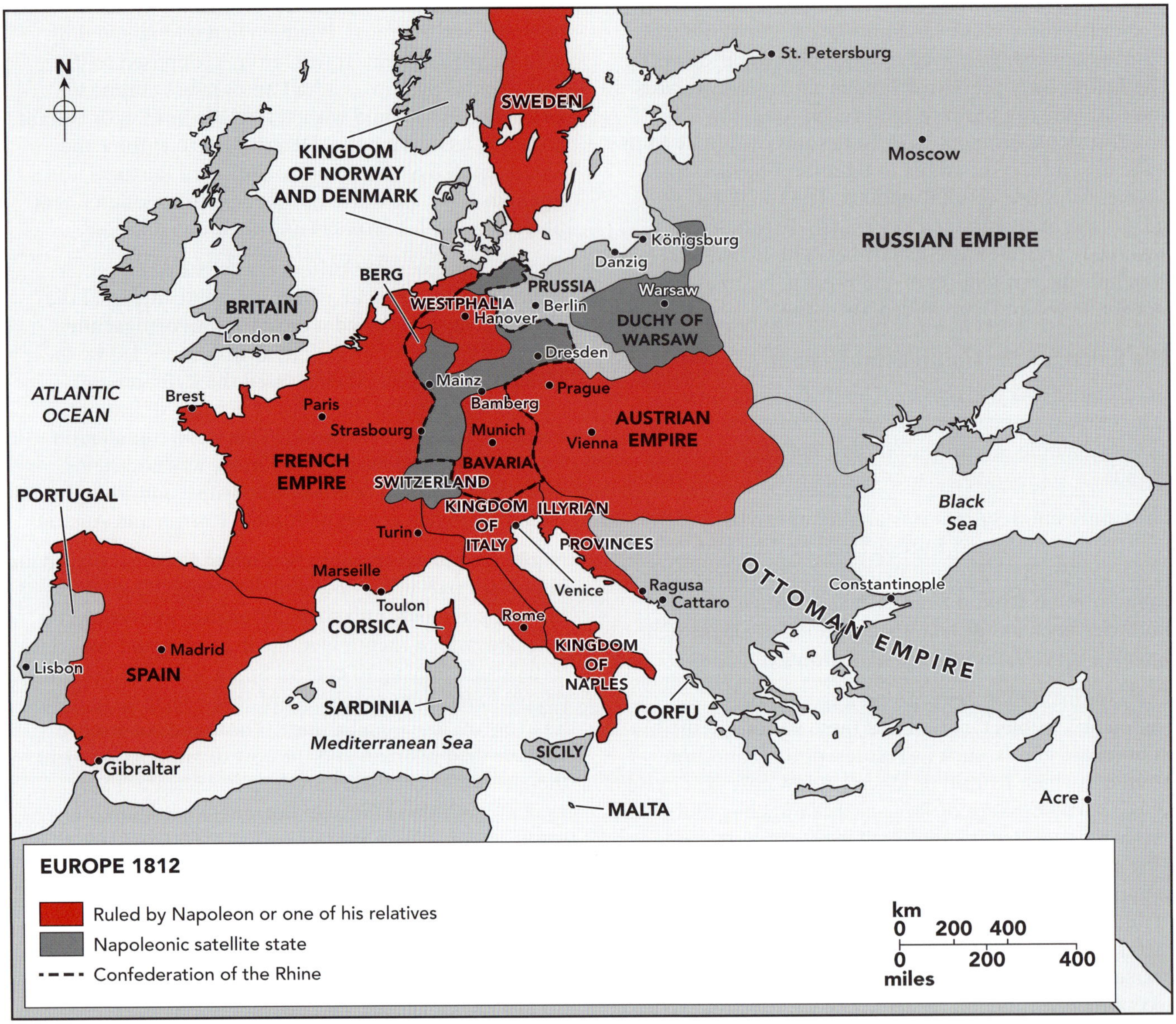

Figure 1.30: The French Empire under Napoleon.

Under Napoleon, France controlled large parts of Europe (see Figure 1.30). His conquests included modern-day Germany (then a large number of small states), and all the states that made up modern Italy, Belgium and Holland, as well as much of modern-day Poland. He invaded Spain and placed his brother on the throne there. He made a second brother king of Naples and Sicily (the kingdom of Naples formed a large part of southern Italy); a third brother became the king of Westphalia (part of what is now Germany); and he made a fourth brother the king of Holland.

In 1810, Napoleon divorced his childless wife, Josephine, and married an Austrian princess, Marie-Louise, who became empress of France and queen of Italy. His new wife gave him a male heir to continue the Bonaparte dynasty and inherit the empire. The Bonaparte family was now as grand a family as the royal family that the revolutionaries had removed.

However, achieving and maintaining Napoleon's many military successes and territorial acquisitions was costly. In the Battle of Friedland against the Russians in 1807 about 10000 of his army died. At the Battle of Wagram, against the Austrians, in 1809, it is estimated that 40000 were killed or wounded. There were limits to the troops and the money that France could provide for Napoleon's wars and also to the areas that the French could police and control effectively. There were also limits to what Napoleon himself could do. He was not good at delegating authority and managing both France and large parts of Europe was proving a major challenge. If Napoleon had stopped expanding his empire in 1810 and had, therefore, avoided conflict with Britain (the one power he could not defeat), he might have established the Bonapartes as the rulers of France for the 19th century and maintained his empire. However, he could not resist embarking on a further campaign in Russia, which played a key role in his downfall.

The spread of nationalist ideas

In many of the territories that Napoleon invaded, particularly in Italy, Germany and Poland, his armies had forced out unpopular monarchs who ruled in 'Ancien Régimes' similar to France before 1789. Behind the invading French armies came the ideas of the French revolution. Such ideas became popular in the conquered territories – for example, the concepts of careers open to talent, equality before the law, and the right of a people to determine their own future, as well as the idea that sovereignty should lie with the people and not with a hereditary monarch. Many people saw that there were benefits to rule by France.

However, by 1810, the benefits of French rule were beginning to be outweighed by increasing disadvantages, while ideas such as the right of a people to determine its own future began to conflict with the reality of being ruled by a foreign country, France. Nationalist feelings were growing across Europe. There was a sense that Poland should not be ruled by France, that Spaniards should not be ruled by the brother of the French emperor, that the economies of Holland and Sweden should not be controlled by France in the interests of the French economy. The idea that each nation should be in control of its own destiny and that sovereignty should lie with its own people was spreading and this idea fuelled a reaction to French domination of Europe.

In Poland, there was initially strong support for French rule. Russia had formerly governed Poland, using brutality to enforce its rule, and Polish traditions were ignored. The ideas of the French revolution were a refreshing change. However, this attitude soon changed. Poland was a strongly Roman Catholic country, and its people disliked France's attitude towards their church. By 1812, 75% of Poland's budget went to supporting France's wars, and 80000 Poles had to fight for France. Many of them died when Napoleon invaded Russia in 1812 and was forced to retreat from Moscow.

Influenced by nationalist ideas from France, the German, Italian, Spanish and Dutch people began to hope that they could throw off their foreign master and form independent nations. When the armies of Russia, Prussia and Austria started to move west in 1813, growing nationalist feelings meant that there was little support for Napoleon within the empire he had created. Some former subject nations fought to defeat the French: Dutch soldiers fought alongside the British to finally defeat Napoleon at the battle of Waterloo in 1815.

Outcome of the failure of the campaign against Russia

Angered by Russia's refusal to obey the rules of his Continental System, Napoleon invaded Russia in June 1812. His intention was to have a short campaign, inflict another defeat on the Russian army (he had done it often before), and force Russia to accept the Continental System and his own domination of Europe. This was his greatest military enterprise. With an army of nearly 650000, many of whom came from his increasingly reluctant German and Polish allies, he aimed at a quick campaign to capture Moscow, force a Russian surrender and impose his terms on them.

The campaign was a failure. The Russians refused to fight, abandoned and burned Moscow, and retreated eastwards into the vast regions of Russia, destroying food stocks and shelter as they fled. By the end of September 1812, Napoleon was short of food and supplies, and was facing the bitter Russian winter with no proper winter clothing for his troops and no shelter. He was forced to retreat back to Poland, chased by the Russian army, which was still intact. Napoleon was driven out of Russia with a total loss of nearly 500000 men, either killed, captured or frozen to death during the bitter Russian winter. About 210000 of those casualties were French. Thousands of horses and guns were lost as well. Napoleon could not afford those losses.

The failure in Russia marked the beginning of the end for Napoleon's empire and played a key role in his downfall. Not only had he lost an irreplaceable number of soldiers but he suffered an immense loss of prestige. His former allies, such as the Poles, were no longer willing to fight for him. The French people were going to be asked to make even more sacrifices in terms of men and money to support his ambitions and help

Figure 1.31: The retreat from Moscow; an engraving based on a painting of 1856.

retain his empire. Countries like Austria and Prussia were inspired to join Russia in an attempt to rid Europe of Napoleon forever. The Russian campaign had been a major error.

Impact of the defeat at Leipzig, 1813

Austria, Russia, Prussia and Sweden were encouraged by the British victories over the French army in Spain and the disastrous defeat of Napoleon in Russia. These countries formed an alliance committed to defeating Napoleon and ending his domination of Europe. The British provided financial support to help pay for their armies. When Napoleon tried, in 1813, to restore his authority in Germany, the allied nations joined forces to drive him out.

This situation reached a crisis in the Battle of Leipzig, in Germany, in October 1813. Although the French suffered fewer casualties than their enemies (38 000 dead to 55 000) France did not have troops to replace them and was forced to retreat. Napoleon's reputation as a military commander suffered yet another blow. He had lost so many of his experienced solders in Russia and his young recruits, often unwilling conscripts, could not stand up to the increasingly experienced and confident soldiers of the alliance against France. The Battle of Leipzig and the retreat that followed led to the end of France's control of Germany. The successful allies together marched on France, determined to end the threat of France forever.

Allies capture Paris

After Napoleon's failure to defeat the allied armies at Leipzig, he retreated back into France. The combined armies of Prussia, Russia and Austria followed him. The British invaded from the south, having crossed the Pyrenees from Spain. To the north, Holland revolted against French rule and a British army landed there as well. Although Napoleon continued to win some minor battles, he was unable to win the war. He no longer had sufficient resources of men and materials, and his military skill was not enough on its own.

Napoleon was offered peace terms which would have enabled him to remain in control of France, but he unwisely rejected them. In March 1814, the allied armies forced their way into Paris and the city surrendered.

Talleyrand persuaded the **Senate** to depose Napoleon formally. Napoleon's own generals then persuaded him to abdicate and leave France. They knew there was no point in continuing to fight.

KEY TERM

Senate: A body created in the Constitution of 1799 designed to give the Consulate legislative support and the appearance of representation. Napoleon ignored it, but it gave the appearance of legality to Napoleon's overthrow.

Abdication, 1814

Napoleon had to surrender and give up his throne. His wife and son had fled to Austria, his generals were no longer prepared to serve him and there was little evidence of popular support for him in France. France was defeated and exhausted. At the allies' demand, Napoleon retired to Elba, a small island in the Mediterranean, agreeing to remain there for the rest of his life. The allies moved to Vienna, the Austrian capital, to agree how Europe should be re-formed. Deposed monarchs wanted to regain their thrones, and many wished to eliminate any traces of the revolutionary ideas that Napoleon's armies had brought and to restore their 'Ancien Régimes'.

Napoleon escaped from Elba in February 1815 and made a desperate attempt to regain his throne. He raised another army in France, but was finally defeated at the battle of Waterloo, in Belgium, by the combined forces of Britain and Prussia in June. This time the allies were determined to ensure that he should never return, and he was sent to a tiny island in the South Atlantic, St Helena. He died there in 1821.

Figure 1.32: How Britain viewed Napoleon's imprisonment in Elba. The text around the figures says things like 'vive Louis' (long live Louis) and 'à bas le Tyran' (down with the Tyrant).

ACTIVITY 1.29

> Bonaparte was a poet in action, an immense genius in war, a tireless spirit, skilful and sensible in administration, a hardworking and reasonable legislator. That is why he had so much hold on the imagination of different peoples and so much authority over the judgement of capable men. However, as a politician he will always be seen as a failure by statesmen. He himself confessed to mistakes over Spain and Russia. The way he killed Enghien only served to anger both France and Europe. The mistakes in Spain aroused the hatred of a nation and provided a school for English soldiers. He angered the Poles, the Germans and the Prussians and let his army die in Russia. His great empire gained by victories of genius lacked a foundation, and it fell when the genius started to fade. Unlike the masterful Alexander the Great centuries before, who founded empires as he advanced, Bonaparte when he advanced knew only how to destroy. His goal seemed to be to master of the world without burdening himself with the means to preserve it.
>
> **Abridged from the memoirs of Chateaubriand, a French nobleman who fought against the revolutionary armies, was wounded and became an émigré. Chateaubriand returned to France after the amnesty and supported Napoleon's regime until the execution of the Duke of Enghien in 1804. Written after Napoleon's death.**

Read the extract and answer the questions using your own knowledge.

a How effectively did the author identify Napoleon's strengths?

b To what extent did the author successfully identify the reasons for Napoleon's fall?

c Given the background of the author and the period in which it was written, how valid a judgement of Napoleon is this source?

Practice questions

Source-based question

Read the sources and then answer **both** parts of the question.

SOURCE A

Sire, the state is in peril. A revolution is being prepared and it is being brought about by the stirring up of minds. Political writings have been published during the Assembly of Notables and the new political demands drawn up by the various provinces and cities. The disastrous growth of this terrible agitation means that opinions which would previously have been seen as treason, today seem reasonable and just to most men. These all prove that there is a new spirit of disobedience and scorn for the laws of the State.

From a memoir written by the royal princes to Louis XVI, December 1788.

SOURCE B

The nobility is a foreigner in our midst because of its civil and political privileges. All departments of the government have fallen into the hands of this noble class that dominates the law, the Church and the army. As a result of their spirit of brotherhood, nobles always prefer each other to the rest of the nation. Their power is total; in every sense of the word, they reign in France. It is not the king who reigns, but the aristocracy of the court, which is the head of the vast aristocracy which overruns every part of France. The aristocracy is fighting against reason, justice, the people and the king.

From a pamphlet written by the Abbé Sieyès, *What is the Third Estate?*, January 1789.

SOURCE C

We beg the king to remove from the clergy the liberty of taxing itself and we wish it to be taxed in the same way as the Third Estate. We likewise wish that all nobles be taxed in the same way,

CONTINUED

and that all tax exemptions be removed. We do not wish to alter the position of the Estates in any way and the other privileges of the First and Second Estates could remain. There is a postmaster who farms many fields for which he is not made to pay any land tax because of his ancient office for which he does no work. He should be included in the taxes which the Third Estate have to pay. The Estates-General should concern itself with the salt tax, which of course falls most heavily on those least able to pay. We would also request that attention be paid to the lack of equality before the law as there is evidence that men of noble rank are escaping justice unnecessarily.

From a list of demands sent in by a district of France before the meeting of the Estates-General, March 1789.

SOURCE D

The most striking of the country's troubles was the chaos in the finances, the result of years of extravagance at Court, as well as the vast expense of the American War of Independence which cost the state over 12 million livres. No one could think of any remedy. The worst of the abuses were the arbitrary system of taxation, the cost of collection and the irresponsible defence of privilege by the richest sections of society. This extended from the great and influential men of the kingdom, to the privileged orders, to the provinces and to the towns, so the burden of taxation fell on the least wealthy part of the nation.

From the memoirs of a French nobleman who became an émigré, written in 1823.

1 a Read Sources **B** and **C**.
Compare the attitudes towards the nobility in Sources B and C. **[15 marks]**

b Read **all** of the sources.
'Anger over privilege was the principal cause of the French Revolution.' How far do the sources support this view? **[25 marks]**

Essay-based questions

Answer **both** parts of each question.

2 **a** Explain why the Bastille was stormed. **[10 marks]**

b To what extent was the French crisis of 1789 caused by economic factors? **[20 marks]**

3 **a** Explain why Napoleon was able to seize power in 1799. **[10 marks]**

b 'The Directory did a good job in difficult circumstances.'
How far do you agree? **[20 marks]**

Improve this answer

1 **b** Read **all** of the sources.
'Anger over privilege was the principal cause of the French Revolution.' How far do the sources support this view? **[25 marks]**

The sources overall make a strong case for arguing that privilege in various forms was a major, if not the principal cause of the revolution. Arguably the principal cause was the refusal of the king to accept the need for reform and the way in which he managed events from the early 1780s until his execution.

> It is a good idea to start with some judgement, an answer to the question set. Doing this demonstrates that the student has grasped all the sources. The paragraph also shows evidence of analytical thinking. However, while it is fine to bring in contextual detail, this detail has to be directly linked to the question asked. It needs to be more relevant than what the student has included here – the point about the king's responsibility is not discussed in any of the sources so is not appropriate to include. Be careful not to waste time!

Source B presents the strongest evidence for supporting the argument. The Abbé strongly attacks both the civil and political privileges of the nobility, referring to the way in which it sees them as 'overrunning every part of France' and that this class 'dominates the law, the Church and the army.' He also feels that this privilege is used to gain absolute power in France and control the king as well. However, it could be argued that Sieyès is writing a political pamphlet designed to persuade public opinion to support his views. Also, it was common for clergymen to be promoted because of their social class, rather than their ability. The author, who did not come from a privileged background, would have witnessed this and clearly feels strongly about this issue.

> A competent paragraph. It is clear which source is being referred to and the paragraph shows a good grasp of the source. There is an analytical focus as well. The quotations are good and well selected and reinforce the points made. The evaluation is very good indeed, but actually seems to weaken the student's initial point that it was the 'strongest' evidence.

Source C also provides evidence to support the hypothesis, but perhaps not so strongly as **Source A**. It shows the wish to end the privilege of exemption from taxation for the nobles and clergy with the wish that 'all tax exemptions be removed'. However, it does not wish to end any of the other privileges of the nobility and the clergy, except, perhaps, in the comment about equality before the law, that 'men of noble rank are escaping justice unnecessarily'. This cahier's demands were very similar to many others from all over France, and clearly show that privilege was an issue, but there were others: the salt tax for example.

> There is good initial focus and again it is clear which source is being used. There is some cross-referencing to back up points made (note: this is not always necessary). However, the focus is very much on the source's content and there is limited evaluation of the source. What are these demands? There is a strong case for showing some contextual knowledge here. The student should look at the date and show some thinking about the provenance of the source. There is some consideration of the nuance of the source here which is a good sign, but it needed more precise evidence to support it as well as greater analysis.

Source D also raises the issue of privilege with the reference to 'the irresponsible defence of privilege by the richest sections of society' and the impact it had. However, the author does not see privilege as the primary cause; he refers to 'the most striking of the country's troubles was the chaos in the finances,' with privilege therefore being just one part of a larger problem. The author, an émigré, is writing long after the events. He had lived through the period and had presumably suffered when he had to flee France. It is worth noting that he is blaming his own class on the issue of the causes of the crisis.

> This paragraph shows a good focus on the question, which is always important. the paragraph continues to demonstrate a good grasp of the sources and an understanding that there are other factors to consider such as France's financial problems. There is good awareness of the provenance of the source and some competent evaluation. The paragraph shows hindsight and some balance. The student could make it clearer to see why the source has limited support for the argument. All evaluation needs to focus clearly and explicitly on the question.

Source A challenges the hypothesis, the author clearly sees the cause of the troubles as the 'stirring up of minds', probably referring not only to the ideas of many of the Enlightenment thinkers which had been seen in the cahiers, like 'equality before the law', but also in the writings of men like Sieyès and the large number of radical newspapers and pamphlets which were being published at the time. How well informed the royal princes might be, probably isolated in Versailles, could be questioned. They might well be unaware of the financial problems mentioned in **Source D** and also the impact that the bad harvests were having on much of the population. Overall, the sources do suggest that privilege played a part – but it was only one factor amongst many.

> This paragraph shows competent focus and good use of the source. The quotations are strong – appropriate and not too long. There is evidence of sound contextual knowledge.

> The point about radical newspapers was well spotted. However, the evaluation is not strong – more on the provenance would help. The answer might have commented on the significance of the date. The final comment is rather a weak – does it match up with the opening statement?

Consider the comments. Now write your own answer to the question.

Improve this answer

2 b To what extent was the French crisis of 1789 caused by economic factors? **[20 marks]**

Economic factors played a very large role in both the longer-term causes of the French Revolution as well as the shorter-term causes. Although there were other factors, such as the summoning of the Estates-General itself in 1788, which led to the actual crisis of 1789, underlying everything was the fact that the French government had run out of money and an important section of the French population was very hungry as a result of bad harvests. There was also a real lack of will on the part of the King and his court to make the necessary changes that might have led to a solution of the many problems which France faced.

> This has a good focus and gives an answer to the 'extent' part of the question by suggesting that it played a 'very large' part. It also shows balance by considering other causes. However does the response really explain clearly how the lack of cash flow and reluctance to lend the government money actually led to the crisis?

The government's shortage of money went back to the 1770s, when the King and his foreign minister, Vergennes, decided to help the American colonies in their bid to become independent from France's old enemy, Britain. Although the government was warned that the French economy was in no position to fight an expensive war, this advice was ignored. Most of the costs of the war were financed by borrowing money at very high rates of interest. When the war finally ended in 1783, France gained little except a very large increase in its national debt and an increasing reluctance by lenders to lend any more money to the French government.

> This paragraph develops the point well. There is good supporting detail here, but there needs to be greater focus on developing the 'very large' point.

Another major problem was that the system of tax collection was inefficient and often corrupt. Much of the money which should have come in to the government simply got lost in the system. What was an even more important factor was that the two richest sections of the community, the nobility and the clergy, were largely exempt from taxation. The heaviest-taxed sections of the population were the middle class and the working class. Many middle-class people disliked paying taxes when they had no involvement in how the money was spent, and they also disliked the fact that many men richer than them paid no taxes simply because they were noblemen. The working class resented the taxes that fell on essentials, such as salt, and also the fact that they often had to do unpaid work on the lands of the nobility. These economic factors meant that when the Estates-General met in 1789, there were a lot of grievances connected to money.

> Again, this has a sound focus and good supporting detail, but needs to be more obviously related to the 'extent' part of the question.

Bad harvests led to there being real hunger in many parts of France, with prices rising and a shortage of the main diet of the working class – bread. No action was taken by the government or the King to deal with this, even though all could see the luxurious lifestyle of the King and his court at his great palace of Versailles. Every attempt at reforming the government's finances by a series of ministers like Necker, Calonne and Brienne after 1781 had failed. The King was reluctant to act and the nobility who surrounded him at court did not want their wealth to be taxed. Necker had attempted to give a true picture of France's finances in 1781, but failed to do so, and painted an over-optimistic picture of the country's finances, hiding the true crisis. It was the knowledge that France was heading for bankruptcy, unable to pay its debts and raise any more money to run the country, that led to the calling of the Estates-General. This was to trigger the revolution.

> This has good focus and depth and demonstrates a good level of understanding. The comment at the end is a good, succinct way to end one paragraph and lead into another.

However, there were other factors which led from the meeting of the Estates-General to the process becoming a revolution, the execution of the King and the end of the monarchy. The King would not compromise and accept that he had to become a constitutional monarch to survive. Many of the nobility and clergy would not give up their privileges and exemption from taxation. Many middle-class men strongly resented paying taxes and having no means of influencing how they were spent. They wanted political representation. Many were influenced by the ideas of the Enlightenment and wanted a much fairer and more just system of government. They wanted things like equality before the law and a much more efficient system of government.

> This introduces other causative factors but does not provide detail on why they were of less importance.

Overall it was economic factors which brought the crisis on and led to the calling of the Estates-General. However, it was other factors which then led to the actual revolution and the death of the King. Much better management of the Estates-General by the King would have prevented further trouble. Many of the nobility and the clergy would not give up their privileges and events like the Storming of the Bastille and the Flight to Varennes made it even more revolutionary.

This is a very competent response. With a greater analytical focus, it could have been excellent. The final paragraph summarises the essay quite well but needs to be more explicitly linked to the initial issues of 'extent'. The degree of knowledge and understanding shown is high, but to improve the essay, there should be more of an analytical focus. More debate on the 'extent' part of the question is needed, and clearer points made as to why economic factors played such a large part in the crisis.

Taking into account all the comments, write your own answer to the question.

SELF-EVALUATION CHECKLIST

After working through this chapter, complete the table.

You should be able to:	Needs more work	Almost there	Ready to move on
explain the principal reasons for the crisis of 1789			
outline the ideological influences of the French Revolution			
analyse the arguments against the political and financial policy of the monarchy			
evaluate if the course and consequences accomplished the goals of the French Revolution			
explain why groups supported or opposed the revolution and how successful they were			
evaluate how the results of the French Revolution changed the nature of French society.			
describe the political instability and conflict caused by the revolution			
assess the steps taken to create the French Republic			
assess the French government's response following Louis XVI's rule			
evaluate the effectiveness of the constitutional revolution of 1792			
explain why the Reign of Terror happened and its implications			
analyse how and why the Directory was created and its successes and failures			
explain the impact of Napoleon's reputation on his rise to power			
assess the impact of the Coup of 1799 on French politics			
analyse the impact of Napoleon's domestic policy as First Consul			
evaluate the causes and consequences of Napoleon's fall from power.			

> Chapter 2

Liberalism and nationalism in Germany, 1815–71

KEY QUESTIONS

This chapter will help you to answer these questions:

- What were the causes of the revolutions of 1848?
- What happened during the 1848–49 revolutions and what were their consequences?
- Why was Bismarck appointed as minister-president and what were his aims in the period up to 1866?
- How and why was German unification achieved by 1871?

Timeline

- **Jul 1806** Napoleon I establishes Confederation of the Rhine
- **Oct 1813** Napoleon defeated at Battle of Leipzig
- **Jun 1815** End of Napoleonic Wars; German Confederation established
- **Jan 1834** Zollverein is founded
- **Jun 1840** Friedrich Wilhelm (Frederick William) IV becomes king of Prussia
- **Mar 1848** Revolution begins in Austria and Germany
- **Jun 1849** Collapse of Frankfurt Parliament
- **Mar 1850** Erfurt Union of German states formed
- **Nov 1850** Humiliation of Olmütz: Prussia abandons Erfurt Union plan
- **Jan 1861** Wilhelm (William) I becomes king of Prussia
- **Sep 1862** Bismarck becomes minister-president (prime minister) of Prussia
- **Jan 1864** War against Denmark begins
- **Jun 1866** Austro-Prussian War begins
- **Aug 1866** Treaty of Prague
- **Jun 1867** North German Confederation set up under Prussian leadership
- **Jul 1870** Franco-Prussian War begins
- **Jan 1871** German Empire established

GETTING STARTED

The map in Figure 2.1 shows central Europe in 1815, at the end of the **Napoleonic Wars**. Look at a map showing the boundaries of modern Germany. How do those of the German Confederation differ?

Figure 2.1: The German Confederation in 1815.

Introduction

Until 1871 a unified German state did not exist. Instead, the area that we now know as Germany consisted of a number of separate states, which varied considerably in size and importance. In the north-east, Prussia was emerging as the strongest economic and military force by the middle of the 19th century. It later became the leading power in the process of German unification. It was not inevitable, however, that Germany would be united into one country. There were many obstacles to the creation of a united Germany.

At the end of the **Napoleonic Wars** in 1815, much of the area that later became Germany belonged to a loosely connected grouping known as the German **Confederation**. The dominant country was Austria, whose monarchy presided over a **multi-ethnic** central European empire. Austria had a strong interest in opposing national unity and in this it was supported by most of the princely rulers of the various German states.

In the three decades after 1815, the main drive towards national unification came from educated, liberal-minded, middle-class people. Their efforts to establish a parliament for the German people ended in failure in 1848, the 'year of revolutions' across Europe. Ultimately it was Prussia, guided by its leading minister from 1862, Otto von Bismarck, which brought about the creation of a united Germany. Unification happened not because Bismarck sympathised with the idea of nationality but because he wanted to make Prussia the dominant power in the German lands. Bismarck achieved Prussian dominance through a series of wars between 1864 and 1871 – against Denmark, Austria and France. The Germany that emerged was made in the image of Prussia's conservative, authoritarian, military nature.

KEY TERMS

Napoleonic Wars: The conflict between France under Napoleon I (Bonaparte) and alliances of various European states, which began in 1803 and ended with Napoleon's defeat in 1815. (See Chapter 1.)

Confederation: A loose association of states which retain some control over their own policies.

Multi-ethnic: Made up of people of different races.

2.1 What were the causes of the revolutions of 1848?

You will have noted that Germany did not exist in 1815 as a single unified country. Instead, it consisted of a series of different states. Much of the territory lay within the boundaries of an organisation known as the German Confederation. This chapter explains how these states came to be united in the mid-19th century.

Before the Napoleonic Wars, most of the area that we know today as Germany had been part of the medieval Holy Roman Empire, a collection of semi-independent states under the Austrian emperor. The Holy Roman Empire had collapsed in 1806, when Napoleon's armies invaded it. Napoleon reorganised the west German states into a single organisation, the Confederation of the Rhine.

The French armies brought with them the ideas of the 18th-century Enlightenment, which stressed the power of reason and aimed to sweep away outdated political and social structures. For example, they replaced the different laws and judicial processes of the various German states with their own legal system. In reaction, many German thinkers began to emphasise the distinctiveness of their own culture. Romantic writers stressed the importance of emotion and imagination, in response to the rational ideas of the French invaders, and they encouraged interest in the historical past of the German people. Particularly influential was the writer J. G. Herder, who popularised the concept of Volksgeist ('spirit of the people'), the idea that each nation had its own individual identity, based on a shared inherited culture and language. These were the first stirrings of a sense of German nationhood.

German people began to understand the importance of uniting against the French occupation. After its defeat by Napoleon, Prussia, one of the most important states, reorganised its government and army. This enabled it to join with Austria and Russia to expel the French forces. The decisive Battle of Leipzig (1813), a major defeat for Napoleon, helped to develop a sense of national pride. The battle was later commemorated as a symbol of emerging German identity, with a 91-metre-high monument constructed on the site to mark its centenary, even though German-speaking troops had fought on both sides.

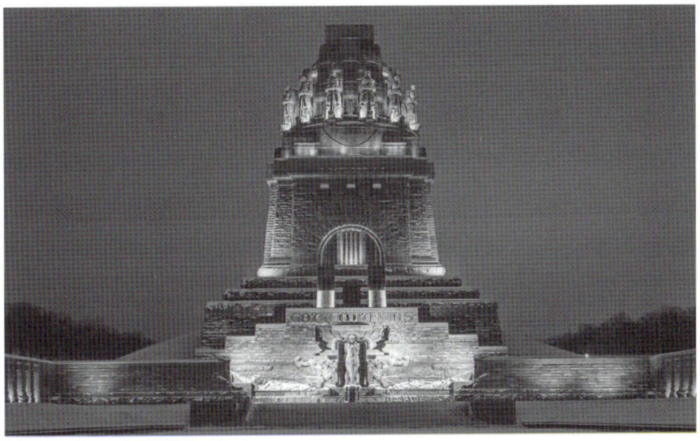

Figure 2.2: The monument to the Battle of the Nations in 1813, erected a century later to commemorate the beginning of German nationalism.

The Congress of Vienna and the formation of the Confederation

In September 1814, a **congress** of European nations met in Vienna to discuss the problems caused by the Napoleonic Wars, and to establish new boundaries on the continent. The most important states represented at this series of meetings were Austria, Prussia, Britain and Russia. France, whose monarchy had been restored after the defeat of Napoleon, attended the congress but had no decision-making powers. The decisions made at this meeting changed the face of Europe.

The European leaders faced a challenge from the related ideas of nationalism and **liberalism**, which were products of the French revolutionary era. The representatives of the countries who met at Vienna regarded these ideas with anxiety. These leaders were political and social conservatives. They were determined to restore stability after the years of upheaval caused by the revolution in France and the movements of French armies across the continent. They wanted to recreate the rule of the old royal families who had lost power during the previous 20 years.

KEY TERMS

Congress: A large, formal meeting of delegates, in this case representatives of different countries.

Liberalism: A belief that government should be reformed to allow as much personal and economic freedom as possible. Nineteenth-century liberals also favoured the concept of representative assemblies, although these would not necessarily be elected by all adults.

Figure 2.3: Delegates at the Congress of Vienna in 1814. How could you evaluate this image as a historical source?

The most significant individual at the congress was the Austrian foreign minister, **Prince Klemens von Metternich**. The Austrian Empire had a population of 25 million and extended over 647 000 square kilometres. It comprised present-day Austria and Hungary, together with a range of other territories in central and eastern Europe. In addition to Austrians (who spoke German) and Hungarians, among the many different ethnic groups under its rule were Czechs, Slovaks, Croats, Poles and even some northern Italians. The majority of the empire's subjects were Roman Catholics, loyal to the Pope.

KEY FIGURE

Prince Klemens von Metternich (1773–1859)

Metternich was Austria's foreign minister from 1809 to 1848 and its chancellor (chief minister) as well from 1821 to 1848. He played a key role in creating the alliance of Austria, Prussia and Russia which defeated Napoleonic France in 1813–14. Metternich was a conservative whose main aim was to uphold international order to protect Austria's interests. He was determined to suppress liberalism and nationalism. Metternich fell from power when the 1848 revolutions broke out and went into exile. He returned to Austria in 1851, after the power of the monarchy had been re-established, but he never again played an important role in politics. Always sure of his own abilities, Metternich famously said of himself that 'error has never approached my spirit'.

The largest German state was Prussia, a mainly agricultural country in the east of the North European Plain, with Berlin as its capital. It was ruled by an authoritarian monarch, King Friedrich Wilhelm III (1797–1840), who governed with the support of a conservative landowning class, the Junkers. The Junkers also provided the majority of the Prussian army's officer class. In the 1815 peace settlement, Prussia gained a great deal of territory, including the Rhineland in the west, an area separated from the main part of Prussia which had undergone **industrialisation**. These territorial gains doubled its population to more than 10 million.

Prussia was the only possible future rival to Austria for the domination of Germany, but at this stage it did not offer a challenge to its more dominant southern neighbour. With their conservative, monarchical forms of government, both Prussia and Austria had an interest in preventing political change in Germany.

KEY TERM

Industrialisation: A process in which an economy that is mainly based on agriculture develops large-scale manufacturing industry.

The German Confederation

Metternich's solution for Germany was to reorganise it into a confederation (Bund) of 39 states under the control of Austria. These varied considerably in size, from kingdoms like Prussia, Bavaria and Saxony to self-governing city states like Hamburg. It was not a united Germany and, in fact, the intention was to avoid such a development.

As shown in Figure 2.1, the Confederation was based on the boundaries of the old Holy Roman Empire. It contained some non-Germans, for example Czechs in Bohemia (a region in the present-day Czech Republic) and French-speaking people in Luxembourg. At the same time, it excluded some areas with German-speaking populations, including parts of Prussia. Presiding over this structure was a conference of ambassadors from the member states, known as the **Diet**, which met in Frankfurt. The Diet controlled the foreign policies of the member states, and federal law took precedence over state law. However, the individual rulers continued to manage their own internal affairs, and the Confederation never developed a strong identity of its own. The rulers used the Diet as a forum – a meeting place in which to exchange ideas and defend their individual states' interests. The Confederation did not have its own **civil service** and there was no attempt to develop it as an economic area. In 1818–19 and again in 1831, Prussia led attempts to create a **federal** defence force. These initiatives caused disagreements over who should command such organisations and how they should be funded. Both Austria and the south German states were cautious about an arrangement that might give more power to Prussia. A federal army was created after 1840, but member states did not give full control of their forces to the Confederation.

The structure of the Confederation was designed to maintain Austria's power over the German states. The Diet was always chaired by the Austrian representative. Austria also had a **veto** over any attempt to change the constitution, and it could usually count on the support of the main southern states–Bavaria, Württemberg, Baden and Hesse-Darmstadt–in a vote. These states were near each other and had mostly Catholic populations. They were culturally more sympathetic to Austria than to northern, Protestant, Prussia. The rulers of these southern states granted their subjects constitutions, with certain civil rights in law, but they retained the real power over the government. Most of the German princes followed Metternich's lead in governing in an authoritarian fashion.

KEY TERMS

Diet: An assembly which meets to debate and make decisions on political matters. Also known as a Bundestag.

Civil service: Professional administrators who provide support to the government of a country.

Federal: Relating to a system of government in which power is shared between a central authority and various regional bodies.

Veto: The right to refuse to accept a proposal or decision.

Strengths and weaknesses of the Confederation

The Confederation had some successes, but it also suffered from several major flaws (see Table 2.1).

The impact of Metternich's system on the states of Germany

Metternich succeeded in maintaining a repressive and authoritarian regime in Germany in the decade and a half after the Congress of Vienna. He established the 'Metternich System', an alliance of conservative European states, which met in congresses after 1815 to uphold their common interests. The aim of the system was to maintain the rule of absolute monarchy in the Austrian Empire and allow similar political systems to continue in the other European states.

Metternich was determined to suppress liberal and nationalist ideas. He was deeply suspicious of change, once describing the words 'liberty' and 'equality' as the source of evil because they were liable to mislead the masses of the people. He knew that the empire was a fragile structure, and that nationalism threatened the rule of the Austrian royal family, the Habsburgs. He feared that if Germans, or members of other nationalities, were allowed their independence, the empire might collapse. He avoided stationing troops in the parts of the empire from which they came, as he believed this would reduce the chances of organised nationalist opposition developing. Metternich's policies were negative and relied on repressive methods such as press censorship. He created a network of secret agents who spied on political radicals and intercepted their correspondence. The Metternich System kept the peace in Europe, but at a cost of building resentment from the states under its rule.

Strengths	Weaknesses
• The Confederation succeeded in its main aim (holding back the growth of liberalism and nationalism) for over 30 years whilst creating a degree of unity between the member states. • Austria's dominance held the Confederation together. With the support of the south German states, Austria was largely unchallenged until the 1860s. • In theory it was illegal to dissolve the Confederation, and no state could leave or join without unanimous agreement from the Federal Diet.	• The Confederation lacked a strong central authority – it had no head of state and no effective federal armed force and could not progress on economic cooperation. • The Diet required unanimous agreement of all members, so few decisions were taken. • The Confederation depended on agreement between its two largest members, Austria and Prussia. It would, therefore, survive only as long as the rivalry between the two remained suppressed.

Table 2.1: Strengths and weaknesses of the Confederation.

Figure 2.4: A cartoon criticising the suppression of free expression by the Carlsbad Decrees. How does the cartoon indicate the viewpoint of the artist?

The Carlsbad Decrees

After Karl Sand, a member of a liberal student association, murdered a conservative writer and Russian spy, August von Kotzebue, Metternich secured the agreement of the main German states in August 1819 for the repressive Carlsbad Decrees. These decrees had three key features:

- Each university would have an 'extraordinary commissioner' assigned to it, to supervise the teaching programme. Liberal professors who undermined the established order would be removed from their posts. Unauthorised student organisations would be dissolved.
- The member states of the Confederation and the Diet would censor the newspaper press.
- A central investigating commission would be set up in Mainz to reveal organisations promoting liberal and nationalist ideas.

The influence of liberal ideas

Despite Metternich's attempts to repress them, liberal and nationalist ideas spread after 1815, and from 1830 there was an upsurge of unrest.

The emergence of the middle class

Liberalism was primarily an ideology of educated middle-class people. The middle class consisted of two main groups: firstly business people and secondly professionals such as lawyers, officials, doctors and university teachers. The growing business class was mainly concentrated in the cities of the Rhineland, and in ports such as Hamburg. Few of its members were owners of large factories. Most were merchants who controlled small workshops or employed large numbers of domestic workers who produced goods in their own homes. In Prussia, these merchants had benefited from the removal of privileges that had been enjoyed up to the early 19th century by the traditional **guilds**, allowing anyone to become an employer without first joining one of these organisations.

KEY TERM

Guilds: Associations of merchants or craftspeople, often dating back to medieval times, set up to protect the interests of their members. By the 19th century, they were widely seen as outdated and restricting free competition.

The most successful merchants often had a well-developed sense of responsibility to their towns or cities that led them to become leaders in their communities. Many middle-class men acquired a university education, which was the gateway to the professions. Germany's university population doubled between 1817 and 1831. The emergence of the middle class also led to the growth of a thriving newspaper press, as levels of literacy and awareness of public affairs increased, and societies were established to promote cultural activities.

The aims of the liberals

Liberals wished to gain greater freedom to improve their position in society, politics and the economy. They hoped to achieve several things.

Increased career opportunities

Liberalism stressed the importance of opening careers to professional people based on their ability rather than inherited power and privilege. Middle-class liberals felt excluded from the upper levels of the social order, which were still dominated by a privileged landowning aristocracy. In Prussia, for example, the aristocratic Junker class, which owned large agricultural estates in the eastern part of the country, controlled most of the higher positions in the army and civil service. Many members of the middle classes wanted to gain access to the opportunities offered by these public service careers and this desire made liberal ideas attractive to them.

A more representative government

Middle-class liberals wanted the people to have some say in government, but they did not want to see the establishment of fully democratic, republican systems of government, which they viewed as dangerous systems involving the seizure of power by masses of poor, uneducated people. Memories were still fresh of the French Revolution, which had been marked by violence against people and property. Liberals wanted countries to have representative assemblies or parliaments, elected by property-owning people like themselves. They preferred constitutional monarchy as their form of government. They also wanted certain guarantees of freedom, such as the right to free speech and fair trials. Liberals saw such a system as a middle way between the authoritarian rule of an old-style monarchy, and the 'mob rule' of democracy.

Greater economic freedom

Many political liberals also believed in the idea of laissez-faire (meaning 'leave it alone') economics, in which trade and business functioned without government interference. They wanted to remove tariffs, which restricted trade between countries. Economic liberals wanted to promote competition between businesses, arguing that competition would reduce prices and improve the quality of goods for consumers.

The concept that linked all these ideas was an optimistic belief in humans' capacity for self-improvement. Liberals believed that if people were given freedom they would work to improve their circumstances, and this would help society as a whole to make progress.

It is difficult to assess the influence of liberal ideas among the wider population of the German states. There was a great deal of intellectual excitement in the period 1815–48; books and pamphlets were published, and public lectures were held. However, it seems unlikely that this activity reached more than a limited circle of like-minded, well-off, educated people. Some liberals took their ideas to working-class areas, for example in Hamburg. There were some workers who were interested in political ideas, but they tended to be radicals who favoured the creation of a democratic republic. Many of them expected to achieve this through a popular uprising rather than rational debate.

The extent of support for liberalism in Prussia

Despite its developing rivalry with Austria, Prussia also used state power to repress liberal movements. After the failed attempt to create a federal armed force in 1831–32, for example, there was unrest in south-west Germany, which Austria and Prussia cooperated to suppress. Prussia also had a close relationship with Russia, the most anti-liberal European power. This relationship was strengthened by the marriage of Friedrich Wilhelm III's daughter Charlotte to Grand Duke Nicholas, the future tsar, in 1817.

Support for liberal reform within the Prussian elite was weak, especially after Friedrich Wilhelm III came under the influence of an ultra-conservative faction in the 1820s. Instead of a national representative body, in 1823 he created provincial diets–assemblies dominated by the nobility–that met infrequently and did not possess law-making powers. Over time, however, the diets did bring about moderate change. The qualification for membership of the noble estate, or section, was property ownership rather than an inherited title. By the 1830s and 1840s, the diets were pushing for greater press freedom and receiving petitions calling for more representative institutions.

The main source of support for liberal ideas was the Rhineland, where a large urban middle class resisted the centralising efforts of the government in Berlin. The Rhineland retained its own legal system, derived from the period of Napoleonic rule. The Prussian education system was also remarkably **progressive**, encouraging children to think for themselves. School attendance and literacy rates were high for Europe in the first half of the 19th century.

KEY TERM

Progressive: Forward-looking, enlightened.

The growth of nationalist ideas

In the first half of the 19th century, liberalism was often associated with nationalism. Nationalists believed that people of the same race, language, culture or history should be united in an independent nation of their own. They should govern themselves without interference from any other country. Support for national unity in Germany at this time was limited mainly to small sections of society – literate, professional people and members of student associations known as the **Burschenschaften**. They were not typical of German society at the time. The majority of people were peasants who worked in agriculture. They faced a daily struggle for existence and probably had little interest in abstract ideas of this kind.

Most ordinary Germans did not have a strong sense of national identity and felt greater loyalty to the region where they lived. Communications were poor and usually people were born, lived, married, worked and died in the same villages or neighbouring towns. Each region had its own traditions and customs. There was little desire to see the creation of a strong central government that might impose additional taxes on the population, interfere with civil liberties and draft people into the armed forces.

In Germany, there was a common language and culture, but there was no religious unity. The southern states, such as Bavaria and Baden, were mainly Catholic. So, too, were Prussia's western provinces, the Rhineland and Westphalia, and West Prussia and Posen in the east. By contrast, Prussia proper, like most of northern Germany, was largely Protestant. In addition, the industrialised Rhineland was economically very different from the agricultural regions to the south and east. Germans enjoyed relatively high levels of literacy, but most early-19th-century newspapers concerned themselves with local rather than all-German issues.

As we have seen, a sense of German cultural nationalism first emerged in the late 18th and early 19th centuries, in reaction to the invasions by France. Between 1815 and 1848, these ideas filtered through to the educated middle classes. In the cities, some workers were influenced by more radical democratic ideas, based on the sovereignty of the people, but they remained a minority of the population.

KEY TERM

Burschenschaften: Student organisations which developed after 1815 to promote ideas of German nationality, freedom and civil rights. (The singular is Burschenschaft.)

The impact of the 1830 revolutions on German states

Liberalism and nationalism took a stronger hold across Germany, especially in the south, after 1830. From 1830 there was an upsurge of unrest across the German states. This sudden growth in unrest was partly in response to a series of European revolutions. In France, Charles X, last ruler of the old royal dynasty, was replaced in July 1830 by King Louis Philippe, a representative of another branch of the French royal family. Charles had never accepted the ending of old-style absolute monarchy and had tried to govern as his predecessors had done

ACTIVITY 2.1

Copy and complete the table to show the differences in mid-19th-century Europe between the terms: liberalism, conservatism, radicalism and nationalism. What types of people in society were most likely to support each idea?

	Liberalism	Conservatism	Radicalism	Nationalism
Definition of the term				
Groups in society who were most likely to support the idea				

before 1789. By contrast, Louis Philippe established a parliamentary monarchy, based on the consent of the educated, property-owning middle class.

There were other liberal revolutions against conservative, monarchical regimes. Belgium declared its independence from the Netherlands and won recognition as a separate state in 1831. Greece won its independence from the Ottoman (Turkish) Empire in 1832. There was an unsuccessful revolt in Poland against the Russian Tsarist Empire. In Modena, Parma and the Papal states, there were uprisings in favour of a united Italy.

These movements encouraged liberals and democrats in Germany to agitate for change. In four small German states–Saxony, Hanover, Hesse-Cassel and Brunswick–rulers were obliged to grant constitutions. Increased press freedom allowed more criticism of governments. A group called 'Young Germany' was established, which called for a united Germany based on liberal principles. It consisted mainly of politically active writers and journalists who were opposed to the German princely regimes. Most of its members did not advocate violent revolution but their radical ideas still drew the hostile attention of Metternich. In May 1832, democratic nationalists organised the Hambach Festival in the Rhineland-Palatinate region of west Germany.

Some 30 000 people came together to demand national unity, freedom of the press and other civil rights, which had been limited since the transfer of Hambach to Bavarian rule after the Napoleonic Wars. The black, red and gold flag that would become the symbol of German nationalism was prominently displayed at the gathering.

ACTIVITY 2.2

For the German, the seed of great events has not yet germinated. What he desires is a festival of hope; a festival not to celebrate what has been achieved, but what is still to be achieved, in constitutional freedom and German national dignity, not a glorious triumph, but a manful struggle to shake off oppression from within and without.

From the invitation to the Hambach Festival, a political demonstration held in Germany, 27 May 1832.

In what ways does the language of this source extract illustrate the ideas of liberalism and nationalism? Note down the phrases which reflect these ideas.

ACTIVITY 2.3

Figure 2.5: *The Procession to Hambach Castle* by Erhard Joseph Brenzinger, 1832.

Look at the painting in Figure 2.5. The artist took part in the Hambach Festival and depicted three of his friends in the foreground of the painting. He has shown the future national flag of Germany being carried upside down.

a What can be inferred from the way that the artist has depicted the scene?

b In the light of this information about the context of the painting, how useful is it as a historical source?

The Six Articles and Ten Articles, 1832

The Bavarian authorities reacted by tightening restrictions on political assemblies and speeches. Although the organisers of the Hambach Festival were acquitted of wrongdoing by an ordinary court, they were then tried and imprisoned by a special police court. As in 1819, Metternich persuaded the princes to accept a new round of repressive measures. The Six Articles of June 1832 limited the rights of elected assemblies in states which had constitutions, and also declared the supremacy of federal law over the laws of the individual states. Rulers were to be supported in dismissing petitions presented by their state assemblies, and in doing what was necessary to fulfil their obligations to the Confederation. The Federal Diet was to appoint a commission, initially for a six-year period, to monitor events within the states. There were also to be limits on freedom of expression, designed to maintain the stability of the Confederation.

The Ten Articles, passed the following month, banned political meetings and festivals. Government permission was required for the publication of any newspaper with political content. Police surveillance was introduced for anyone known to be critical of the authorities. Passport rules were tightened and anyone guilty of a political offence who fled to another member state of the Confederation would be returned to their home state. It was even illegal to wear the colours of the student associations in scarves and ties and to display unauthorised banners. Punishments were to be imposed on anyone who broke these rules. Member states' governments were to provide each other with military assistance as required, and to notify the Federal Diet of the steps they had taken to enforce the articles.

Support for nationalist ideas in the universities

The Burschenschaften remained the main focus for nationalist agitation after the Hambach Festival. One of the speakers at the festival, Karl Heinrich Brüggemann, was arrested for later political activities and actually sentenced to death, although this was later commuted to life imprisonment. He was eventually pardoned, although he was not allowed to follow an academic career in Prussia. In April 1833, members of the Burschenschaften tried to cause an uprising in Frankfurt. The authorities clamped down on them, sentencing some participants to life imprisonment. After this the Burschenschaften were much less open in their activities.

In 1837, the new king of Hanover, Ernest Augustus, abolished the constitution that had been granted by his predecessor, and seven professors who objected lost their posts at the University of Göttingen. The 'Göttingen Seven' included Jacob and Wilhelm Grimm, two famous

Figure 2.6: A bronze sculpture group commemorating the Göttingen Seven in Hannover, Lower Saxony.

brothers whose collection of traditional folk tales helped to promote a sense of German culture. After they were dismissed, however, institutions in Hamburg, Marburg, Weimar and elsewhere offered them posts. The actions of the Seven helped to raise public and media awareness of the nationalist cause, although their influence on its eventual success was indirect.

Although the universities were the main source of demands for national unity, they were powerless to achieve anything substantial. The Burschenschaften lacked a clear plan to achieve their goals and relied too much on the power of education to bring about unification. The princes ensured that they kept the levers of power in their hands when they granted constitutions. They retained the right to veto unwelcome proposals and could usually rely on the support of the upper houses of parliament, dominated by the aristocracy. The princes used various means to limit the power of elected assemblies: restricting the vote to wealthy property owners, using **indirect voting** or having different classes vote in separate estates, with greater weighting attached to those in which the upper classes were represented. These devices restricted the free expression of public opinion.

> **KEY TERM**
>
> **Indirect voting:** A system in which voters choose delegates who then elect representatives to sit in a central assembly or parliament.

Reactions to the growth of nationalist ideas

The authorities reacted harshly to the growth of nationalist ideas, as can be seen from the passing of the Six and Ten Articles after the Hambach Festival in 1832. In fact, there was no real danger of revolution in Germany in this period. The liberals and nationalists were too few, and Austria could always count on its control of the Confederation and the support of Prussia in suppressing opposition. However, the authorities continued to fear the spread of these ideas.

Reasons for the growth of nationalism in the 1840s

The arrival of railways and improved roads indirectly helped the growth of a sense of national identity by bringing people from different German states into contact with each other. This fostered a stronger feeling of unity across the states. High levels of literacy and the growth of a popular German press also helped to spread nationalist ideas. Literature and music drew on traditional German culture. For example, in 1841 the lyrics of the song *Deutschland über alles* ('Germany above the others') were written and this later became the German national anthem. Although later the anthem came to be associated with ideas of superiority over other nations, this was not its original purpose. It was an appeal to place the idea of a united Germany before provincial loyalties. The newspaper *Die Deutsche Zeitung*, launched in 1847, also reflected both nationalist and liberal sentiments. Another important cultural development was the publication of Baedeker's travel guides, designed to be easy for travellers to carry, from the 1830s. These guides, enhanced by a star rating system which encouraged people to visit particular locations, helped Germans to see themselves as a united people.

External tensions with other countries encouraged nationalist feeling. In 1840 there was a border dispute with France over the River Rhine, which at one point seemed likely to result in a French invasion of German territory. This led to the writing of a patriotic poem, *Die Wacht am Rhein* ('The watch on the Rhine') by Max Schneckenburger, which called for all Germans to defend the region. The poem became popular after it was set to music in 1854. Another issue which strengthened national feeling was a dispute with the Danish king, who ruled the province of **Schleswig-Holstein**. This province lay on the Jutland peninsula, linking Prussia and Denmark, and contained a large German population.

> **KEY TERM**
>
> **Schleswig-Holstein:** Two neighbouring territories between the Baltic and North seas. Although not part of Denmark, they were under the personal authority of the Danish king as their duke. Holstein was German-speaking and was also part of the German Confederation. Schleswig had a mixed Danish- and German-speaking population. As a result, their status was disputed, and German nationalists claimed that they should be treated as one and be part of the Confederation.

Liberal and nationalist feeling in Prussia was briefly encouraged and then disappointed by the accession of a new king, **Friedrich Wilhelm IV**, in 1840. He was a complex and unstable character, who believed that God expected him to rule his subjects firmly but kindly. Friedrich Wilhelm spoke in a mystical way which was hard for his subjects to understand.

He had some reforming instincts. For example, he relaxed censorship and gave greater powers to the provincial diets or assemblies. However, at heart the king had no real sympathy with liberal nationalism, and he rejected demands for a single parliament for all Prussian territories.

KEY FIGURE

Friedrich Wilhelm IV (1795–1861)

Friedrich Wilhelm IV became king of Prussia in 1840. He was a romantic and often unpredictable figure, who unintentionally caused liberals to believe that he sympathised with their ideas. He was really a conservative, whose handling of the revolution of 1848–49 left reformers disappointed. He was unable to rule for the last three years of his reign after suffering a stroke, and the country was governed by his younger brother, Wilhelm I, as regent (temporary ruler).

Economic and political developments

The first half of the 19th century saw barriers to trade within Germany broken down. This benefited Prussia, which was becoming the leading German economic power, rather than Austria. Prussia was at the centre of rapid railway development in the 1840s, which also helped to boost economic growth. This did not, however, mean that Prussia would definitely emerge as the leader of a politically united Germany. There were still major differences over the kind of German state that nationalists wished to see.

Impact of the Prussian Customs Union and the Zollverein

One of the most important factors in the long-term development of a united Germany was the economic progress made in the first half of the 19th century. Germany's geographical situation at the heart of Europe was an advantage because it meant Germany could trade easily with both east and west.

However, in the years after the end of the Napoleonic Wars, economic growth was held back by customs barriers between the members of the German Confederation. Customs barriers slowed down trade across Germany because every time a product crossed a border it was likely to be taxed by the territory it was entering. On a long journey across Germany, this could happen numerous times. In addition, larger states, such as Prussia, often had their own internal boundaries and imposed tolls (taxes) on goods as they moved within their own territory. The time-consuming completion of paperwork at borders increased the costs of transport. At the same time, German industries had to compete with foreign products, which did not have to pay duties at the external borders of the Confederation. This meant that German firms within the Confederation had no competitive advantage over non-German ones outside.

Prussia led the way in removing obstacles to trade. In 1818, it established a **customs union**, known as the Prussian Customs Union, abolishing the kingdom's 67 internal customs barriers and encouraging other German states to do the same. Prussia protected its own industries from foreign competition by charging a tariff on imports at its own frontier. The tariff was initially set at a low level, both to discourage smuggling and so that foreign countries were less likely to hit back with high tariffs of their own. The Prussians worked to remove barriers to trade within the German Confederation to create a larger market and reduce the price of goods. In 1828 Prussia and one of its larger neighbours, Hesse-Darmstadt, agreed a customs treaty.

KEY TERM

Customs union: An association of areas or states who agree to abolish tariffs between themselves, and to operate a common set of tariffs on imports from other countries.

Other states tried to set up their own rival customs unions, such as the Middle German Commercial Union, which comprised Hanover, Brunswick, Saxony and others. This attempt to challenge Prussia's dominance of north–south trade collapsed after one of its members, Hesse-Cassel, abandoned the union in 1831. As a result, Prussia was able to expand its customs union, with Bavaria and Wurttemberg joining in 1834.

Prussia now formed the Zollverein, a customs union of 18 German states. The Zollverein was the largest free-trade area in Europe, soon comprising 25 states, with a combined population of 26 million. Income from tariffs was divided among the member states in proportion to their population size. Soon they were linked by a rapidly growing rail network, centred on Berlin, and in time they adopted a common currency and system of weights and measures. The Zollverein promoted economic expansion for all its members. Prussia especially benefited, both from the growth of trade and prosperity and because the Zollverein linked it with its Rhineland territory. The Zollverein also provided a way to isolate Austria economically.

Figure 2.7: The foundation of the Zollverein in 1834.

Austria did not join the Zollverein, because it did not see the importance of economic change and preferred to maintain high import duties to protect its domestic producers from the perceived threat of foreign competitors. Austria preferred to rely on trade within its empire and did not want to lower its tariffs to match those within the Zollverein. In the long term, this was an important reason why Austria lost control of Germany to Prussia. In turn, Prussia decided not to allow Austria to join the Zollverein later, in order to maintain its own advantageous position. Austria's absence from the Zollverein meant that German economic growth was centred on the ports of the North Sea rather than directed southwards to the valley of the River Danube.

The Zollverein helped Prussia assume a leading economic position within Germany, but this did not mean that Prussia would also take on Germany's political leadership. The states that joined the customs union insisted that decisions in its governing body, the Zollverein Congress, had to be unanimous, and the states were determined to keep their independence. Nationalists who hoped that the Zollverein might provide a basis for a political union were disappointed.

ACTIVITY 2.4

Look at the map in Figure 2.8. How does the map help to explain the growing importance of Prussia in the development of a more unified German economic system?

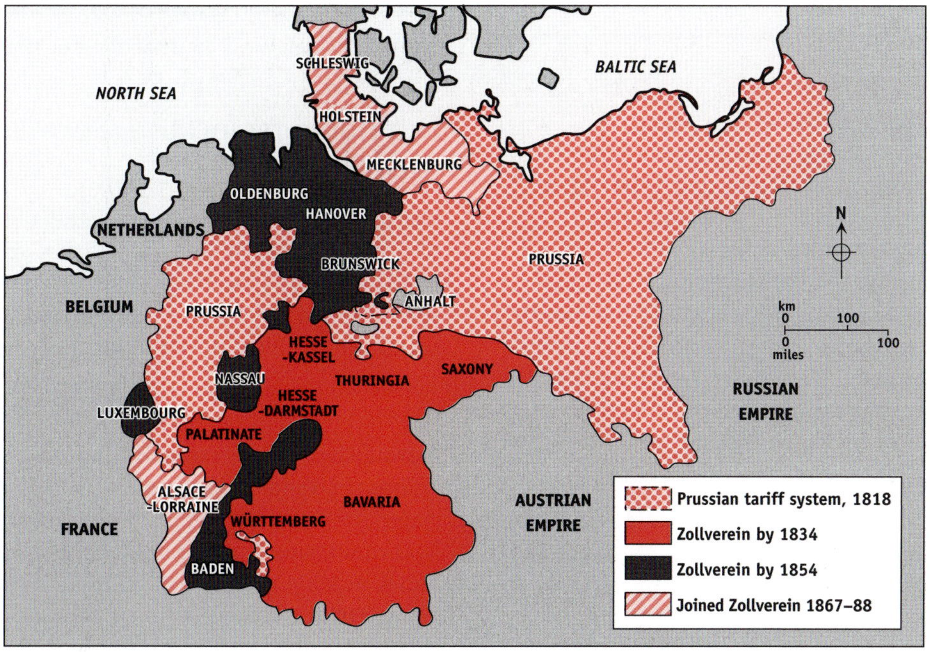

Figure 2.8: A map showing membership of the Zollverein, 1818–88.

One of the nationalists' key weaknesses was that they could not agree on where the frontiers of a German state should be. Some favoured a 'large Germany' (Grossdeutschland) that would include German-speaking regions of Austria, and that would be dominated by Austria. Others preferred a small Germany (Kleindeutschland) without those regions that would, therefore, be dominated by Prussia. To some extent these preferences reflected the continuing cultural differences between Protestant northern Germany and the Catholic southern states. The industrialised Rhineland remained more economically developed than the still largely agricultural east.

ACTIVITY 2.5

The following factors were all obstacles to German unification. From what you have learned so far, which do you think was the most important? Hold a class debate in which you argue the case for the factors. Remember that you must give reasons why you have chosen each factor.

- Austria's opposition to German nationalism
- the smaller German states' hostility to the growth of Prussian power
- divisions within the nationalist movement
- lack of support for nationalism among the poorer classes.

Impact of railway development

Transport was critical to Prussian and wider German economic development. Improved roads and steamboat services on the Rhine and Elbe rivers played an important part. But the real stimulus to heavy manufacturing from the 1840s was the rapid development of railways. At the start of the decade, the Zollverein had fewer than 600 km of rail line but by 1850 it had 5800 km. Railway building attracted capital investment and stimulated the coal and iron industries that provided its two most important raw materials. These developments encouraged the emergence of larger industrial firms and the rise of new urban centres.

The first railway line in Prussia was a privately built one, linking Berlin to the suburb of Potsdam. Constructed in 1838, this was known as the 'Stammbahn' or 'original line'. Prussia was a leader in railway building, expanding its network from 185 km in 1840 to 1106 km five years later. By the late 1840s, alarmed by news of a French construction programme on the borders of the Confederation, and finding that the member states were too slow to respond, the Prussian state was pushing ahead with rail building.

Prussia benefited economically from the ability to move goods more quickly and cheaply over longer distances. Railways also contributed indirectly to Prussia's later role as the driving force behind German nation-building, as Berlin became the most important hub of the network. In the long term, railways would facilitate the movement of troops and military supplies – a key asset in the later wars of unification.

Figure 2.9: A painting of the Berlin–Potsdam railway in 1847.

Problems facing the German states in the 1840s

During the 1840s the German states faced a number of problems, which led to a series of revolutions in 1848–49. The revolutions were not caused just by the spread of liberalism and nationalism. Economic and social factors also played a part.

Economic and social problems in the 1840s

Agriculture was still more important than industry before the 1848 revolutions. Around 70% of the population still made their living from agriculture. Manufacturing was the main economic activity in a few areas, notably the Rhineland and Saxony. The main growth areas were in the production of consumer goods such as textiles. Both rural and urban areas suffered from economic and social problems in the 1840s.

The economic crisis of 1846–47

Deteriorating economic conditions had the potential to create a revolutionary situation in the German states. Poor living standards for the peasants in the countryside were made worse by high rents and two years of bad corn harvests in 1846 and 1847. Living standards fell, with cereal prices increasing by almost 50% in 1847. Potato blight, a disease which ruined the crop, added to the misery as potatoes were the staple diet for most German peasants.

In 1847 problems in the textile industry seriously affected the welfare of urban workers. The economic downturn led employers to cut wages. The wage cuts happened in factories with poor working conditions, where workers worked for long hours in an unhealthy environment.

Increasing population size, due mainly to a declining death rate, made the situation worse. Table 2.2 gives some indication of the rate of growth across the period, with figures for the German states as a whole shown alongside those for Prussia.

	1820	1840	1870
Prussia	10.3	14.9	19.4
Germany	26.1	32.6	40.8

Table 2.2: Population growth (in millions) in Prussia and Germany, 1820–70.

ACTIVITY 2.6

a What does Table 2.2 suggest about the growth of Prussia in comparison with the rest of Germany?

b What other types of data would help you to assess how important it was becoming in this period?

Impact of urbanisation

Rural workers moved to the cities in response to the hardship they faced in the countryside, which increased pressure on the availability of jobs. Urban overcrowding, poor sanitation, disease and unemployment were a dangerous combination. Rising food prices and low wages caused disturbances in cities. The crowds blamed merchants and customs officials for shortages, and they became the main targets of the food riots. One of the most notable cases of looting in Berlin in April 1847, was known as the 'potato revolution'. The riots were an attempt to control the food supply rather than to achieve political goals. However, they helped to politicise those who took part, and caused an intense debate between radicals and conservatives about the response of government to social distress.

Impact of industrialisation on skilled workers

The problems in the textile industry of 1847 led to protests in early 1848. The poorest workers' protests were mainly about their daily lives and were not explicitly political in character. Skilled workers, however, went beyond these basic demands. They were able to make their case more effectively than the unskilled workers, and in cities such as Cologne, they had their own organisations to represent their interests. In spring 1848 they formed workers' committees in Berlin, which called for **trade union** rights, a minimum wage and free education. Others drew up an industrial code, setting out rates of pay and working hours, though this was later turned down when presented to the Frankfurt Parliament, which met in 1848–49 (see Section 2.2).

Karl Marx and Friedrich Engels, authors of the revolutionary *Communist Manifesto* (1848), argued that these developments indicated the growth of a 'working-class consciousness' because industrial workers were driven to revolt by their experience of exploitation under the system of **capitalism**. But the revolutions of 1848 were not primarily about the working classes rising to seize control of the means of production. The disturbances that erupted across Germany in that year would not have occurred without the emergence of a discontented middle class who demanded political and constitutional change.

KEY TERMS

Trade union: An organisation which negotiates with employers on behalf of workers, to improve their pay and conditions of work.

Capitalism: An economic and political system in which individuals, rather than the state, own businesses to make a profit.

KEY CONCEPT 2.1

Similarity and difference

Historians are interested in the ways in which people in the past reacted either in similar or different ways to events.

Austria and Prussia were both opposed to liberal and nationalist movements in Germany between 1815 and 1848. But they had very different approaches to the economic development of the German states, especially after the formation of the Zollverein.

In small groups, discuss why the two states acted as they did in this period.

2.2 What happened during the 1848–49 revolutions and what were their consequences?

The year 1848 is known as the 'year of revolutions' when various European countries were affected by popular uprisings. In 1848–49 there were disturbances across several German states. The disturbances began in February 1848 with the toppling of the monarchy of King Louis Philippe in France. In March, Metternich was forced into exile by disturbances in Vienna. It seemed that the power of the Austrian Empire, and of traditional authorities throughout Europe, was crumbling. Revolutionary hopes proved short-lived, however, and authoritarian regimes soon re-established control.

Figure 2.10: The overthrow of Metternich in the Vienna revolution, March 1848.

The spread of revolution in the German states

As we have noted, educated middle-class people were motivated by a desire to improve their own position as well as being influenced by ideas of liberalism and nationalism. They resented how the privileged nobility held onto power, and dominated the army and civil service, regardless of their qualifications to fill these posts. These middle-class liberals did not want to overthrow the monarchical regimes in power in the German states, but they did want to put pressure on their rulers to introduce political reforms.

Baden in southern Germany was the first state where unrest occurred. This was surprising since Grand Duke Leopold had already granted a free press, trial by jury and other liberal reforms. The immediate trigger for the uprising was news of the February 1848 revolution in France. The disturbances in Baden were partly driven by the grievances of the peasants, who attacked landowners' property. Middle-class liberals met in an assembly at Mannheim at the end of February to demand a **bill of rights**.

KEY TERM

Bill of rights: A declaration of the key freedoms that citizens expect those in authority to recognise.

Demands for liberal political change were made in other German states. The uprisings were uncoordinated but shared certain characteristics. In Württemberg, the ruler, Wilhelm I, was pressured into appointing liberal ministers and granting a new constitution. King Friedrich Augustus II of Saxony agreed to similar changes. The princes of Hesse-Darmstadt, Nassau and other states accepted demands for a bill of rights. The only German ruler who gave up his throne was Ludwig I of Bavaria. The circumstances here differed from the rest of Germany as the first disturbances were caused by conservative opposition to the king's mistress, the exotic Irish-born dancer, Lola Montez. Liberal students then took advantage of the situation to demand constitutional reforms. Ludwig made some concessions, but when these proved inadequate, he abdicated in March 1848 in favour of his son, Maximilian.

Representatives from six states (Prussia, Bavaria, Württemberg, Baden, Nassau and Frankfurt) attended a meeting at Heidelberg in March 1848. The meeting led to the summoning of a 'Vorparlament' or 'pre-parliament'. It met in Frankfurt and resolved to create a national constituent assembly or parliament, whose role would be to draw up a constitution for a united Germany. Each state in the German Confederation would be asked to hold elections to this parliament, using its own voting system.

ACTIVITY 2.7

The calling of a national representative assembly, elected in all German states according to population, must not be postponed; [it is needed] in order to avert internal and external danger, and to develop the power and prosperity of German national life.

In order to assist in bringing about an early and complete representation of the nation, those present have resolved:

To approach urgently their respective governments to provide the whole German fatherland and the thrones [of the German states' rulers] as early and as completely as possible with this powerful bulwark [support].

From the Resolution of 5 March 1848 at the Heidelberg meeting of liberals.

a How does this source show the commitment of the Heidelberg liberals to nationalist ideas?

b What evidence is there in the source to show that they were not seeking the overthrow of the existing political order in the German states?

The fall of Metternich

The 'March Revolution' in Vienna led to the downfall of the long-dominant Metternich. Protestors demanded **universal male suffrage** and a constitution granting civil and political rights to all citizens. Students were killed in clashes with troops near the royal palace. The city's working-class population then supported the revolt. Metternich was forced to resign and flee into exile. Although Metternich returned in 1851, he never held political power again. His downfall was a decisive moment which raised the hopes of those people across the German Confederation who wanted Austrian power reduced.

KEY TERM

Universal male suffrage: Voting rights for all men. The suffrage was also known as the franchise.

Emperor Ferdinand tried to pacify the opposition by proposing a new constitution, but it did not go far enough and further protests occurred, with barricades erected across the city streets.

The emperor offered further concessions, including a directly elected Constituent Assembly, but this still did not appease the protestors. Working-class people demonstrated about unemployment and the threat of wage cuts, leading to further violence. The government was briefly forced to leave Vienna and sent in the army to restore order. In September the Austrian government also faced uprisings in Hungary, Italy and the Slavic nations, which formed part of its empire. At the end of the year, having failed to win over his discontented population, Ferdinand abdicated in favour of his nephew, Franz Joseph.

Revolution in Prussia

A combination of economic distress and desire for political change also caused unrest in Prussia. The Prussian government had decided to build a railway linking the agricultural lands of the east to markets further away (See Section 2.1), but it needed to raise money to do this. The people who stood to gain most from this railway were the Junkers. In April 1847, King Friedrich Wilhelm IV called a national assembly known as the United Diet to win support for the project. The Diet assembled against a background of crop failure and rising food prices. There was unrest among skilled workers, who faced competition from factory production. When the Diet met, its members demanded a constitution before they would consider the king's appeal to support funding of the railway. Friedrich Wilhelm turned them down, declaring, in the old-fashioned language which came naturally to him, that he would never consent 'that a written paper should intrude … between our Lord God in Heaven and this country, to govern us through its paragraphs'. He then dissolved the Diet.

Figure 2.11: A street fighting scene in Berlin during the March 1848 revolution.

The dissolution of the Diet failed, however, to quieten growing demands for political change. Disturbances broke out in Berlin in March 1848, encouraged by news of the fall of Metternich. The first demonstrations involved craftsmen and workers, who were protesting about their pay and conditions. Middle-class citizens then made demands for the protection of their rights. Following a period of street fighting, the army lost control of the situation, leaving the king to attempt to calm the demonstrators. This was the start of the revolution in Prussia.

The role of Friedrich Wilhelm IV of Prussia

Friedrich Wilhelm behaved inconsistently during the revolutionary year. After the rioting in Berlin, he appeared in public cloaked in the black, red and gold colours of the nationalist movement, and declared emotionally that 'henceforward Prussia will be merged in Germany'. There has been debate about his motives for this gesture. He was an erratic figure whose actions are hard to judge. Perhaps he was carried away by the emotion of the moment and genuinely, if briefly, imagined himself at the head of a popular movement. Alternatively, he might have been trying to save his own position by taking charge of the revolution rather than submitting to it. Either could be a possible explanation for his actions.

Immediately after the revolution, Friedrich Wilhelm allowed the election of an assembly, whose purpose was to draw up a constitution for Prussia. He then changed his mind and dissolved the assembly. In December 1848, he announced a more restrictive political settlement of his own. The new constitution, which came into effect in February 1850, established a two-chamber parliament but enabled the king to retain the essentials of power in his own hands. In an emergency, for example, he could collect taxes without parliamentary approval. Ministers would be responsible to him, not to parliament, and he reserved the right to change the constitution.

The voting system for the Prussian lower house of parliament, the Landtag, was intended to favour conservative interests. It would be elected by a 'three-tier suffrage', based on the taxes paid by different classes. Although it allowed all adult males over 25 to vote, it was far from democratic. Voting was indirect and was not secret. The upper house, the Herrenhaus, was appointed by the king. This system guaranteed the continuing political dominance of the Junkers.

Figure 2.12: King Friedrich Wilhelm IV addresses his people in the streets of Berlin during the March 1848 revolution.

The Frankfurt Parliament

The most dramatic consequence of the revolutions was the election of a national parliament, which met in Frankfurt in 1848 to1849. This was a moment of great optimism for people who supported German unification, but their hopes were disappointed.

Formation and actions of the Parliament

The first all-German parliament met in Frankfurt from May 1848 to June 1849. Each state was allowed to choose its own voting system to select its representatives. Most of the poor were not allowed to vote. This meant that the parliament was not truly representative of the German people, though this was similar to national assemblies in other European states. The parliament was all-male and most of the members were wealthy professionals. It was often mockingly described as 'the professors' parliament'. Jacob Grimm and three others of the 'Göttingen Seven' were among those elected. The parliament's first president was typical of the membership. He was Heinrich von Gagern, a lawyer who had been a member of the Burschenschaften at university and had been a member of the legislative assembly in Hesse-Darmstadt. Table 2.3 shows the composition of the parliament.

Occupation	Number of members
Lawyers	200
Nobles	90
University professors	49
Principals and teachers	40
Writers and journalists	35
Merchants and industrialists	30
Clergy	26
Doctors	12
Handicraft workers	4
Peasants	1

Table 2.3: Occupations of members of the Frankfurt Parliament, 1848–49.

ACTIVITY 2.8

Study the data in Table 2.3.

a Convert the numbers for each occupational group in the Frankfurt Parliament into percentages. Tip: add up all the figures to get the total number of members of the parliament, then divide the number in each category (e.g. 200 lawyers) by this total and multiply by 100 to get the percentage. You could create a pie chart to show your findings.

b How far does the Frankfurt Parliament deserve the description 'a parliament of middle-class intellectuals'?

The parliament's members were mostly liberal in politics, although there were also small numbers of radicals who wanted a republic. The parliament wanted a strong central government, with more authority over the German states than the Diet of the old Confederation. However, it was slow to decide what form this government would take or exactly what powers such a government would possess. In June 1848, the parliament set up a 'Provisional Central Power' under a **regent**, the liberal Austrian Archduke Johann, which would govern until a permanent constitution had been agreed. In December, the parliament approved 50 fundamental citizens' rights, including equality before the law, freedom of the press and freedom from arrest without a warrant. It had still not agreed on a constitution to replace the interim government headed by the archduke.

KEY TERM

Regent: An individual who is appointed to govern a country, usually for a limited period, for example if a monarch is too young or unable to rule.

Reasons for the collapse of the Parliament

The Frankfurt Parliament had several key weaknesses.

Internal divisions

The members of the Parliament could not agree on the territorial extent of a new Germany. As we have noted, the old German Confederation included some non-Germans and excluded some German-speaking areas, including parts of Prussia and Austria. There was debate in the parliament about conflicting proposals for a Kleindeutschland, dominated by Prussia, and a Grossdeutschland, which would mean the continued leadership of Austria. After Heinrich von Gagern was appointed to head the Regent Johann's ministry in December 1848, he proposed that Austria should be excluded from the planned federal union but associated with it by treaty. He was a well-intentioned individual who was unable to give a clear lead, and he struggled to determine an agreed position. These long discussions wasted valuable time and allowed the parliament's conservative opponents to regroup.

The parliament's members lacked political experience and took some time to organise themselves and decide how to proceed. They struggled to resolve differences between moderate liberals, radicals and conservatives. The liberals were in the majority, but they faced opposition from the

ACTIVITY 2.9

Figure 2.13: The first session of the Frankfurt Parliament, which was elected during the revolutionary period of May 1848. In this contemporary illustration, the Frankfurt Parliament is shown meeting in a church.

Look at the illustration in Figure 2.13.

a What symbols of German nationality do you observe in this painting?

b Find out what the significance of these symbols was in German tradition and explain their importance. Present your findings to the class in the form of a poster.

radical minority who wanted to move forward with the creation of a republic rather than get the cooperation of the princes. The radicals also wanted social change which brought them into conflict with the economic liberalism of the middle-class delegates. The Parliament rejected an industrial code put forward by the Frankfurt artisans' congress that called for regulation of pay and working hours. At the other extreme was a conservative group who wanted to restrict the parliament's power over the states. The liberal leadership of the parliament was too inexperienced to overcome these divisions.

Friedrich Wilhelm IV's rejection of the imperial crown

The parliament eventually agreed on a constitution in March 1849. An emperor would govern with the support of two houses of parliament. One of these houses of parliament would be elected and the other would consist of the princes of the Confederation. The crown of this empire was offered to Friedrich Wilhelm IV. Supporters of the Kleindeutschland option believed that Friedrich Wilhelm was prepared to place himself at the head of a German national revolution. Prussia was also the only state with the military strength to resist Austria, if it opposed their plans. But Friedrich Wilhelm was a proud man and would not accept a gift from the Frankfurt Parliament because he refused to recognise their legal authority. He rejected the offer in April saying that he would only take an imperial throne offered by his fellow princes. In private correspondence he had already stated the blunt opinion that 'every German nobleman … is a hundred times too good to accept such a crown moulded out of the dirt and dregs of revolution, disloyalty and treason.'

ACTIVITY 2.10

Source A

I undertake today this leadership during the days of peril. My people, which does not shun [avoid] danger, will not forsake me, and Germany will attach herself to me with confidence. I have today accepted the old German colours and ranged myself and my people under the venerable banner of the German empire. From this day onward Prussia is merged in Germany.

From Friedrich Wilhelm IV's proclamation to the people of Prussia and Germany, 21 March 1848.

Source B

The German National Assembly has counted on me in all things which were calculated to establish the unity of Germany and the power of Prussia. I honour its confidence; please express my thanks for it ... But I should not justify that confidence–I should not answer to the expectations of the German people–I should not strengthen the unity of Germany–if I, violating sacred rights and breaking my former explicit and solemn promises, were, without the voluntary assent of the crowned Princes and free States of our Fatherland, to take a resolution which must be of decisive importance to them and to the States which they rule.

From Friedrich Wilhelm IV's message to the Frankfurt Parliament, rejecting the offer of the imperial crown, 3 April 1849.

How do you explain the differences between these two statements by Friedrich Wilhelm IV? Look carefully at the dates of the sources and what had happened in the intervening period.

Lack of executive and military power

The Frankfurt Parliament lacked the means of enforcing any decisions it made. In particular, it had no army of its own. A Prussian general, Eduard von Peucker, acted as war minister, but the Prussian army remained under the authority of the king. The weakness of the army was illustrated by a crisis over the disputed provinces of Schleswig-Holstein. In March 1848, the German-speaking population of these territories rebelled against an attempt to integrate them fully into Denmark. They demanded admission to the German Confederation as a single state. The Frankfurt Parliament authorised the Prussian army to fight Denmark over the issue. Prussian forces advanced, but soon halted and signed a truce at Malmo in August 1848, in response to international pressure. The key point was that Prussia had withdrawn its forces without consulting the parliament. This situation demonstrated the Frankfurt Parliament's dependence on the cooperation of the traditional rulers. The parliament possessed moral authority, but no independent power to impose its will.

The attitude of the German princes

The princes' authority had been weakened by the revolutionary events of spring 1848 and so they did not initially oppose the parliament. By the autumn, however, they were recovering their confidence. The delay in working out a constitution was fatal to the parliament's chances of success. By the time it was ready to present its proposals, its opponents had regained their strength. By March 1849 the new Austrian emperor, Franz Joseph, was once more in control of his territories. None of the princely rulers was prepared to support the creation of a German state to which Austria would be implacably opposed. Austria, Prussia and other states recalled their delegates from Frankfurt. The remaining members moved to Stuttgart, capital of Württemberg, only to be dispersed by troops in June 1849. The collapse of the Frankfurt Parliament marked the failure of middle-class liberalism to establish a united Germany.

ACTIVITY 2.11

Work in groups to produce two different presentations on the reasons for the failure of the Frankfurt Parliament.

a One group should argue that it was doomed from the start because of the weaknesses and internal divisions of its members.

CONTINUED

b The other group should argue that it could have succeeded but for the attitudes of Friedrich Wilhelm IV and the other German princes.

Reflection

Discuss both arguments. Which side do you think is more persuasive?

How did this exercise help you better understand the underlying reason for the failure of the Parliament?

Impact of the 1848 revolutions

As we have seen, most of the German revolutions were not violent. The fighting which erupted briefly in Prussia in March 1848 was not typical of events across the Confederation. In some ways, the restraint of the revolutionaries across Germany was surprising. These events were the culmination of a decade of popular discontent, later known as 'the hungry forties'. Economic depression, combined with food shortages which affected working-class people across northern Europe, were the underlying causes of the uprisings. In the months after March 1848, however, the political demands of the liberals became more prominent. The lack of common ground between working-class and middle-class activists was a fundamental weakness of the movement and it limited the chances of the revolutions having a lasting impact.

By the end of 1848 Prussia was intact as a major state within the German Confederation. Its dominance of the Zollverein had already given it the potential to compete with its only rival, Austria, for the leadership of a united Germany. But at this stage it was not certain that a united Germany would come about. King Friedrich Wilhelm IV was ambivalent about the new forces of liberalism and nationalism and his rejection of the imperial German crown disappointed those who had put their faith in him. Moreover, Austria soon recovered its status as the senior partner within the Confederation in terms of its political and diplomatic standing.

Reasons for the reassertion of Austrian control

The Austrian state and the princes who supported it recovered their authority in Germany. They succeeded in this partly because of their own strengths and partly because the revolutionaries were divided among themselves.

The strength of the conservatives

A key strength of the princely rulers was their ability to wait until the revolutionary movement was beginning to weaken, when they intervened decisively. At first they were alarmed by the strength of popular feeling in the spring of 1848, and made concessions to their opponents. The rulers were worried that if they tried to stand against the revolutionary mood, they would be swept away, so most of them granted constitutions. However, they were careful to retain control of their armed forces. Baden was briefly in the hands of revolutionaries, supported by mutinous troops, but in June 1849, the grand duke asked Prussia to restore order in the country. Prussia also offered military assistance to end the revolts in other states, including Saxony and Württemberg.

The Austrian monarchy had initially been caught off guard in March 1848 and had to deal with popular uprisings in Bohemia, Hungary and its Italian territories. But its leadership was determined to maintain the integrity of the empire. Austrian leaders were, therefore, opposed to a solution that involved Austria's German-speaking lands joining a united Germany. Austria had a weak middle class who were unable to rouse the empire's mainly peasant population in support of liberal and nationalist ideas. Crucially, the army remained loyal to the emperor. By the spring of 1849, the empire had effectively recovered. The Frankfurt Parliament, with its indecisive leadership, lack of an army and failure to win broad support, was too weak to resist.

Divisions between the revolutionaries

The revolutions had been unplanned, and their leaders lacked the necessary organisational skills and resources to achieve their goals. In addition, divisions over aims and methods were fatal to the revolutionary movement's chances of success. Liberals wanted moderate constitutional reform while radicals were hoping for more far-reaching political changes. The working classes wanted improvements to their living and working conditions and most of them were not enthusiastic about the middle-class revolutionaries' political visions. Liberals were unwilling to continue their support for protests that might develop into a radical social revolution. In the Rhineland, for example, wealthier activists abandoned the revolutionary movement when they saw armed working-class crowds taking to the streets, fearing a threat to their property rights.

Overall, the experience of 1848–49 had demonstrated the weakness of liberal nationalism. The reassertion of princely power showed the resilience of long-established institutions, which had been taken by surprise initially, but had proved determined to recover their status. The liberals and nationalists who had such high hopes in the spring of 1848 were left overwhelmingly disappointed.

ACTIVITY 2.12

Consider the question 'How far were economic issues responsible for the German revolutions of 1848–49?' The question asks how far one factor is responsible for a development. First, explain the importance of the factor given in the question. Then look at the arguments for the importance of non-economic factors.

A strong answer will show the connections between the two sets of factors.

Changing relations between Prussia and Austria after 1848

After 1848, Prussia attempted to become dominant within Germany. However, by 1850 Austria had once again re-established its authority.

The 'humiliation of Olmütz', 1850

Friedrich Wilhelm IV might have rejected the Frankfurt Parliament's offer of a German crown, but he was interested in promoting unity in northern and central Germany under Prussian control. In 1849–50 he adopted a complicated plan, proposed by a conservative general, Josef Maria von Radowitz, whose advice he trusted. It involved two unions and, unlike the failed Frankfurt Parliament initiative, would be achieved through agreement between the German princes. There would be a 'Prussian union' or **Reich** of the north German states, excluding Austria, with a strong central government and elected parliament, and with Prussia in control of the army. This union would be in a special relationship with Austria, forming a wider grouping in which Prussia and Austria would be equal but without a central government or parliament.

Saxony and Hanover initially agreed to support the plan, concluding the Three Kings' Alliance with Prussia. Some smaller states agreed to join when the scheme was launched at Erfurt in Saxony in March 1850. Most of the German princes, however, suspected that this 'Erfurt Union' was a vehicle for Prussian domination. Bavaria, the most pro-Austrian of the middle-sized states, refused to join for this reason. Now that Austria was once again able to assert itself, other rulers feared the consequences of its disapproval. The events of 1848–49 had been only a temporary interruption to Austria's status at the head of the Confederation. As Austria recovered from the revolution in Vienna, it reacted to the Erfurt Union project by reviving the Diet of the Confederation. By now, Austria had a new and able chief minister, Prince Felix Schwarzenberg, who was determined to uphold the authority of the Habsburg monarchy. He put forward a rival scheme to the Erfurt Union. It was a Grossdeutschland solution in which Austria, Prussia and the larger states would govern together. In response to this proposal, Hanover, Baden and Saxony abandoned the Erfurt Union, leaving Prussia isolated.

The conflict came to a head when **Elector** Friedrich of Hesse-Cassel (an area between the main part of Prussia and the Rhineland) asked for help in a dispute with his parliament. The Elector appealed to Austria and his parliament asked for Prussian support. Schwarzenberg insisted that only the Confederation could respond to this appeal. Prussia's army was still weak, so, when Austrian troops entered Hesse to restore the ruler's authority, Prussia was not strong enough to resist. In addition, Austria acted with the support of Europe's other leading conservative power, Russia. It was not in Friedrich Wilhelm's nature to try to lead a nationalist movement of German states against Austria.

KEY TERMS

Reich: A German term for a realm or empire. It has been applied to the unified German state of 1871–1918 (the Second Reich) and to Hitler's Germany (the Third Reich, 1933–45).

Elector: A title used by some German princes, derived from the fact that they elected the Holy Roman Emperor until the dissolution of the empire by Napoleon I in 1806.

In the so-called 'humiliation of Olmütz' (modern Olomouc) in November 1850, Prussia agreed to abandon the Erfurt Union. At this meeting, held in the present-day Czech Republic, it effectively gave up its claim to the leadership of the German states. It seemed that Austria had triumphed and that the old, unequal partnership with a 'humiliated' Prussia had been restored. On the other hand, the smaller states rejected the Schwarzenberg plan, as it favoured

Figure 2.14: A meeting of delegates from the German states at Dresden in the kingdom of Saxony, after the humiliation of Prussia at Olmütz in 1850. Why do you think the artist has made the Austrian delegate (in white uniform) so prominent?

their larger neighbours. The result, in May 1851, was an agreement to return to the old framework of the German Confederation.

Yet, Prussia eventually emerged as the state that led German unification. The reality was that, although Austria formally appeared the victor in the dispute over the Erfurt Union, Prussia had some important economic, diplomatic and military advantages over it.

Economic issues

Prussia had several economic advantages over Austria (though these did not mean that Prussia would inevitably become the leading German state).

Economic development and growth in Prussia

Prussia was the most economically advanced of the German states, with its growth overtaking Austria's. Between 1850 and 1860, Prussia's rail network increased by 46%. This impressive growth stimulated other sectors of the economy, such as the iron and steel industry. The output of coal, a vital resource in the age of steam power, grew from 1961000 tonnes in 1850 to 8526000 tonnes by 1865. Railway expansion was achieved through a partnership between the state and the private sector. In return for supplying some of the funding for railway building, the government was able to collect interest payments. Combined with import and export dues from the Zollverein, the sale of timber from the Crown lands and royalties from mining rights, these payments boosted the government's income and reduced the need to raise taxes.

Otto von Manteuffel, minister-president (prime minister) of Prussia from 1850 to 1858, introduced important economic reforms. He was a conservative who wanted to strengthen the bonds between the monarchy and the people. His aim was to promote economic and social development, without making concessions to radicals who wanted a more democratic political system. He also blocked traditionalists who wanted to restrict the foundation of new banks, which they regarded as encouraging risky financial speculation. He helped to foster a culture of private enterprise by reducing state control of the coal and iron industries.

Figure 2.15: A sample of Prussian manufactured goods, on display at an international exhibition in Paris, 1855. Why do you think Prussia would have wanted to take part in such an exhibition?

Manteuffel sought to discourage the poorer members of society from supporting liberal ideas by undertaking social reforms. His government provided low-interest loans to help peasants buy their landholdings from the landowning aristocracy. In areas where there was excessive population pressure on the land, the government provided financial assistance to peasants who were willing to move to less densely populated parts of the country. He also introduced measures to improve the working conditions and pay of factory workers. He achieved these reforms without the involvement of parliament, and without harming the interests of the industrial middle classes.

Prussia was in a strong position to lead German unification by the end of the 1850s. The rapid growth of its population, coupled with its successful banking system and coinage, meant that economically it could dominate its neighbours. Its iron and steel industries provided the materials for its weapons, and its expanding rail network could be used to mobilise its troops. In 1862, a Franco-Prussian trade treaty helped Prussia's development by further integrating it into the economy of western Europe.

Economic and financial problems facing Austria

Prussia's economic lead over Austria made it a believable focus for German nationalist aspirations. Some regions of Austria experienced impressive growth, such as northern Bohemia and Moravia (present-day Czech Republic), which were centres of coal mining, metal and textile production. Overall, however, the 1850s was a time of relative economic stagnation for Austria. For example, Prussia had more than three times the rail track that it possessed. Austria lacked direct access to the most rapidly growing trade routes in Germany – the ones that led northwards to the Baltic and the North Sea.

The empire was hit hard by the onset of an economic downturn at the end of the decade. The costs of maintaining military garrisons throughout its extensive territories added to Austria's problems. In addition, Austria was much less efficient than Prussia in directing the revenues generated by its economy to support its state structure. In the 1860s, this inefficiency had serious consequences for Austria's ability to finance its armed forces.

Austria relied on its prestige and its ability to use diplomatic means to control the other states for its domination of Germany. Increasingly, it lacked the economic and military might to compel other states to obey it. In the era of Metternich, it had succeeded in keeping Prussia on its side by appealing to its fear of revolution. Since the 'humiliation of Olmütz', however, this uneasy partnership had been replaced by outright resentment. As Prussia grew in strength during the 1850s, it became possible for it to challenge Austria's supremacy – if it could find the necessary political leadership to do so.

Disagreements over the Zollverein

One of the most important features of the 1850s was the continued growth of the Zollverein. Hanover became a member in 1851, which enabled Prussia to control the flow of trade to the North Sea ports. By now, the Zollverein was Europe's fourth largest economy, after Britain, France and Belgium. Austria wanted the whole of the Habsburg Empire to join, but this was unacceptable to most of the existing members. It would have involved introducing high tariff barriers to protect Austria's less efficient industries. In 1853, Austria concluded a trade treaty with the Zollverein, leaving the question of it joining the bloc for review by 1860. In the end, Austria never joined the Zollverein. In effect, Prussia had won the battle for economic domination of Germany.

Despite this, we should not exaggerate the importance of the Zollverein to the process of political unification. By joining the Zollverein, German states were getting financial advantages as members of the strongest economic unit in central Europe. This did not mean, however, that they welcomed the possibility of Prussia becoming the dominant political force in Germany. Indeed, some historians have suggested that the Zollverein might have held back unification by helping the finances of smaller states that wanted to retain their independence. The historian Christopher Clark has argued that the main importance of the Zollverein was that it encouraged Prussian leaders to think in a wider 'German' way, while still pursuing the interests of their own state. It also showed liberal thinkers in smaller states that, in spite of its conservative reputation, Prussia could represent a more forward-looking, rational approach in some ways.

Political issues

The 1850s saw several political developments that could affect the balance of power between Prussia and Austria in the longer term.

The growth of liberalism

Prussia's economic growth boosted the prosperity and self-confidence of the middle classes. Growing numbers of middle-class people began to look to the Prussian state to guarantee continued future growth and possibly to bring about unification. They had learned an important lesson from the experience of 1848–49: that liberal idealism without the backing of a powerful state structure was doomed to failure. They, therefore, took a more flexible approach and were more prepared to compromise so that the established authorities would not be driven into opposing all future reform.

ACTIVITY 2.13

	Percentage of labour force in manufacturing		Per capita Gross National Product (in 1960 US $)		Railways (km in operation)	
	1850	1870	1850	1870	1850	1870
Prussia	20	28 (1882)	308	426	5586	18876
Austria	14.8 (1857)	13.1 (1869)	283	305	1579	9589

Table 2.4: Some economic indicators in Prussia and Austria.

a Use the data in Table 2.4 to explain why Prussia was better placed than Austria to become the dominant German state in the mid-19th century.

b How useful is the information presented here?

c Can you think of other indicators that you would need to make a fully informed judgement on the relative strengths of Prussia and Austria?

In 1859, many business and professional people came together to form the National Society, or Nationalverein, an organisation which placed its hopes in Prussia. The society's founding document called for nationwide elections and the creation of a strong national authority, replacing the Confederation. It was prepared to support the transfer of the Confederation's powers to the Prussian government. However, the society was never likely to become the centre of a mass movement. It had only 25 000 members, mostly from the middle classes, so its actual influence was relatively limited.

Nonetheless, liberalism made some advances in Prussia after the 1848–49 revolutions. Prussia's complex three-tier voting system, used for the lower house of its parliament, mainly worked in the interests of the middle classes, who generally supported centre-right liberal or moderate conservative parties.

In October 1857, Friedrich Wilhelm IV became unable to rule after suffering a stroke and in the following year his brother, Wilhelm, became the permanent regent. In elections to the lower house of the Prussian Landtag (legislative assembly), liberal representation increased from 60 to 210 members. Although Wilhelm was fundamentally a conservative, dedicated to preserving the Prussian army, he accepted the principles of constitutional government, and some liberals were admitted to the ministry.

Prussia's international position

Prussia's compact position in north-central Germany gave it an opportunity to dominate its neighbours, but Austria had a large and spread-out southern European empire to govern. Much of its army was tied down by the need to control nationalist movements in Hungary and northern Italy.

Events in Germany were indirectly affected by the outbreak of the Crimean War of 1853–56. Britain and France went to war with Russia, fearing that Russia was planning to extend its influence in south-eastern Europe at the expense of the Ottoman (Turkish) Empire. The Crimean Peninsula bordering the Black Sea was the main area of fighting, and both Britain and France sent troops there. Austria made a major diplomatic mistake by not backing Russia, the other leading power with an interest in maintaining the 1815 European settlement. Russia had supported Austria over the Erfurt Union and was angered by its apparent ingratitude.

Russia's resentment of Austria weakened the alliance between Europe's two most conservative states. If further change occurred in Germany, it was now much less likely that Russia would intervene on Austria's side. On the other hand, the war had no real effect on Prussia, whose interests were not directly involved. Prussia wisely played no part in the conflict, managing instead to remain on good terms with both sides.

Bismarck's role up to 1859

Otto von Bismarck, who later became one of the most important and influential figures in German and European history, was little known in the 1850s. He came from a Junker landowning family which owned estates in rural eastern Prussia. Bismarck first made his name as a conservative member of the Prussian United Diet, where he defended the monarchy against the liberals in the 1848 revolution. He liked to present himself as a typical country squire: unintellectual, with strong prejudices and an ingrained sense of loyalty to Prussian institutions. The truth was more complex, however. Bismarck's mother came from a middle-class professional background, and he inherited his quick intelligence from her. He was cunning, unprincipled and strong-willed but also emotional and short-tempered. His preferred form of government was a monarchy with few constitutional restrictions, and he had little patience with parliament.

KEY FIGURE

Otto von Bismarck (1815–98)

Bismarck was the son of a Junker landowner and a mother who came from a middle-class family of officials and lawyers. He was a boisterous law student at Göttingen and then Berlin University, and was known for fighting duels. Although well-educated, as a young man he could not settle to a career in the civil service because he could not put up with authority. After a period spent managing his estates, he was elected to the Prussian United Diet in 1847.

Bismarck represented Prussia as a diplomat for a decade until his appointment as minister-president in 1862. When the German states were united in 1871, he was the first chancellor of Germany. He helped to expand the German Empire and had great power until he was forced from office after a dispute with Kaiser (Emperor) Wilhelm II in 1890.

Bismarck served as a diplomat, representing Prussia in the Diet of the Confederation in 1851, where he was noted for his rudeness and defiance of the Austrian chairman. He established his position with other delegates by means of a simple gesture at his first appearance at the Diet: he openly smoked – a privilege that had previously been enjoyed only by the Austrian representative. In 1859, he was appointed Prussian ambassador to Russia and later he became ambassador to France, before serving as Prussia's minister-president.

As the 1850s drew to a close, the 'German problem' remained unresolved. Prussia had made great strides in terms of its economic development and possessed a strong state structure. This gave it the potential to challenge Austria for the leadership of Germany. Prussia was an almost exclusively German kingdom, while Austria had an extensive empire to manage and many problems outside of Germany which might distract it.

Yet, Prussia still had significant limitations. Its army needed modernising, and it could not count on the support of many of the smaller German states. In addition, any move to dislodge Austria from its position in Germany would depend on the attitude of the other major European powers. It was by no means a certainty at this stage that Prussia would emerge a decade later as the centre of a united Germany.

KEY CONCEPT 2.2

Change and continuity

Historians are interested in what remains the same in a time period, as well as what changes. Between 1815 and 1860 there were important changes in the following:

- German economic development
- the strength of the German nationalist movement
- the relative power of Prussia and Austria.

Work in pairs. One of you should concentrate on finding out what changed in each of these areas. The other should look for features that changed less or not at all. Compare your findings. Overall, was there more change or continuity in Germany in this period?

2.3 Why was Bismarck appointed as minister-president and what were his aims in the period up to 1866?

The Constitutional Crisis, 1861–62

Otto von Bismarck, the key figure in the process of unification, came to power in 1862 because of a political crisis in which Prussia's new king, Wilhelm I, clashed with parliamentary liberals over the issue of army reform.

The accession of Wilhelm I

After serving for three years as regent of Prussia, **Wilhelm I** ascended the throne in his own right on his brother's death in January 1861. He had gained a negative reputation with the liberals after using troops to crush risings in Berlin and Baden in the revolutions of 1848–49. However, he accepted the constitution and was now seen as politically neutral. The ministry contained both conservatives and liberals.

KEY FIGURE

Wilhelm I (1797–1888)

Wilhelm acted as regent for his older brother, Friedrich Wilhelm IV, before becoming king of Prussia in 1861. He appointed Otto von Bismarck as his chief minister in 1862, and depended heavily on him. In 1871, following victory in the Franco-Prussian War and the achievement of German unification, he became German emperor.

The formation of the German Progressive Party

The German Progressive Party was formed in June 1861 when a group of left-wing liberals in the Landtag broke with the moderate liberals and united with the National Society (Nationalverein). Members included the historian, Theodor Mommsen, and the electrical engineer, Werner von Siemens. The German Progressive Party was the first political party in Germany to adopt a single policy platform. The main Progressive demands were the unification of Germany under Prussian leadership, democratic reform (but not universal suffrage) and respect for the rule of law. The party was the largest group in the Prussian lower house from 1861 to 1865.

The Progressive Party's conflict with royal policy unintentionally brought Otto von Bismarck into mainstream politics. The cause of the dispute was Wilhelm's attempt to strengthen the army.

Proposals for army reforms and the reaction of the liberals

The crisis started with Wilhelm's fears for Prussian security, which had first been aroused in 1859. The occasion was the Franco-Austrian War, part of the process of Italian unification. France supported the kingdom of Piedmont in driving Austrian forces out of northern Italy. The Prussian army was partly mobilised to prevent possible French moves in the Rhineland. Although the army was not eventually called upon to fight, the experience revealed serious organisational weaknesses. Prussia's professional army at the time numbered some 150 000 soldiers. Approximately 40 000 young men had two years of military training followed by two years in the reserve. They then transferred to the Landwehr, a semi-civilian militia force separate from the army. Members of this organisation received limited training, and the officers were not professionals.

Wilhelm wanted to reform the army to make it more effective. This meant increasing the military budget. He and his war minister, Albrecht von Roon, wanted to double the size of the regular army by increasing the annual number called up for military service to 63 000 and extending their term from two to three years, followed by five years in the reserve. Wilhelm also viewed the Landwehr as both militarily ineffective and unreliable in its loyalty to the state. He wanted to reduce its importance by merging it with the army. He first submitted this ambitious plan to the Landtag in 1860. Funding the plan would require a 25% tax increase.

These plans alarmed the liberal majority in the Landtag because they feared that a stronger army could be used to suppress them and raise taxes without their consent. They were also concerned at the proposed downgrading of the Landwehr, which was dominated by middle-class men like themselves. By contrast, the regular army's officers were mostly conservative members of the aristocratic Junker class. The German Progressive Party, therefore, agreed to vote funds for only one year. The king faced a constitutional crisis when the liberals increased their parliamentary representation in the December 1861 elections, winning nearly 40% of the seats.

In September 1862, the Progressives clashed once again with the king over the budget. Wilhelm faced a dilemma: he believed that funds were needed urgently for the army, but the constitution required that taxes be agreed by the *Landtag*. He even considered abdication, rather than give up any of his royal powers. This was where Bismarck became involved.

Bismarck's appointment as minister-president and how he resolved the crisis

Bismarck had served as Prussia's ambassador in Russia since 1859. In the summer of 1862, just as the conflict between the king and the liberals was reaching its climax, he was transferred to Paris. He did not remain there for long. On War Minister Albrecht von Roon's initiative, he was recalled to Berlin to serve as minister-president. Von Roon believed that Bismarck had the strength of personality and intelligence to overcome the budgetary crisis. Although Bismarck's commitment to the Prussian state was not in doubt, it was still a controversial and risky choice. He was regarded in government circles as extreme and even reckless, and Wilhelm had serious reservations about asking for his assistance. 'He smells of blood,' Friedrich Wilhelm IV had once said, 'and can only be employed when the bayonet rules.' In the tense situation which had developed by September 1862, however, it was hoped that Bismarck could find a way of financing the army reforms while preventing the loss of any royal powers.

Bismarck is one of the most controversial figures in German history. It is important to understand the significance of his appointment as minister-president. It started a period in which, after years of frustration, the cause of German unification made rapid strides.

When Bismarck became minister-president, he delivered a speech to parliament that became famous. (It is referred to as his 'Blood and Iron' speech and the key passage is included in Activity 2.14.) Bismarck intended to show the liberals that they shared some common interests with him. The liberals wanted to see German unity achieved at the expense of Austria, and Bismarck wanted to show them that their aims could only be achieved with a strong army. His words reinforced his image as a ruthless politician who was prepared to govern by force if necessary.

ACTIVITY 2.14

> The position of Prussia in Germany will not be determined by its liberalism but by its power ... Prussia must concentrate its strength and hold it for the favourable moment, which has already come and gone several times. Since the treaties of Vienna, our frontiers have been ill-designed for a healthy body politic [state]. Not through speeches and majority decisions will the great questions of the day be decided–that was the great mistake of 1848 and 1849–but by iron and blood.
>
> **From Bismarck's speech to the Prussian parliament, 30 September 1862.**

a What do you think Bismarck meant by his reference to the 'great mistake' of 1848 and 1849, and by 'iron and blood'?

b What does this extract say about the way in which he expected Prussia's position in Germany to change?

Bismarck promptly resolved the army reform crisis by collecting taxes even though parliament had not agreed to a budget. When the liberals suggested that there might be popular resistance to the collection of taxes, he retorted that he had 200 000 troops ready to persuade them. He simply ignored the parliamentary opposition when they declared his actions to be illegal.

Bismarck and the Progressives were not only in conflict over army reform: in fact they had little in common with each other. The Progressives resented Bismarck's willingness to ignore parliamentary convention, his use of the press to manipulate public opinion and his evident contempt for their political values. His repressive measures, including censorship of the press, showed contempt for the liberal belief in the rule of law. In addition, his insistence that he would govern even without parliament's agreement completely rejected what they stood for. In further elections in September 1863, the Progressives won 40% of the seats, but they could not prevent Bismarck from governing without their consent.

There was only one possible basis for a compromise: for very different reasons, both Bismarck and the Progressives supported the idea of German unification. If Bismarck was successful in achieving this, it was likely that they would place their nationalist beliefs before their liberal principles and give him their support.

Bismarck had a reputation for constant loyalty to the monarchy. This had persuaded Wilhelm I to take the risk involved in appointing him as his chief minister. However, relations between king and minister were often stormy. Although he served the monarchy faithfully, Bismarck often tried to push policies through against the king's wishes, using tearful, angry outbursts and threatening to resign when he met opposition. He acted like an ultra-conservative servant of the Crown, but really he was skilled at manipulating Wilhelm. Bismarck was an intensely arrogant, self-confident individual. He once said that he would make his own music or none at all, meaning that he would not take orders from others.

In the end, unification came as the result of a series of short wars in which Bismarck was the key player: against Denmark in 1864, Austria in 1866 and France in 1870–71. Prussia then became the leading state in a new German empire. However, Bismarck did not achieve German unification under Prussian leadership on his own. Prussia had a very effective army and Bismarck was assisted by two outstanding individuals – General **Helmuth von Moltke**, chief of the **general staff**, and Albrecht von Roon, the minister of war, who had been responsible for the expansion of the army and the three-year military service requirement.

KEY TERM

General staff: A group of army officers who assist a senior commander in planning and carrying out military operations.

KEY FIGURE

Helmuth von Moltke (1800–91)

Moltke made his name as a skilful battlefield commander and cemented his reputation with his reorganisation of the Prussian army in the 1860s. He modernised methods of training and understood how important railways could be to transport soldiers and supplies. He was chief of the Prussian general staff from 1857 to 1871, and then of the German general staff until his retirement in 1888.

Figure 2.16: Wilhelm I (second from left) with key members of his staff. On either side of the king are the chief of the Prussian general staff, Moltke (on the left), and Wilhelm's son, Crown Prince Friedrich. Bismarck rides behind the prince on the right of the picture.

The Congress of Princes, August 1863, and relations with Austria

Bismarck's main aim in 1862–66 was to make Prussia the dominant power in northern Germany by excluding Austria from the region. He preferred to achieve this peacefully, but was prepared to use force if necessary. He was determined, however, that any fighting would take place at a time he chose, when he had ensured Austria's isolation and was confident of success.

Bismarck seized an opportunity in January 1863 when the Polish people revolted against Russian control. He used the crisis to improve relations with the Russian government. However, his support for the suppression of the uprising was unpopular with Prussian liberals and France, Austria and Britain also took an anti-Russian position. Because of this hostile reaction, Bismarck did not stick to an agreement to hand over any Polish rebels who crossed the Prussian frontier to the Russians. His change of mind angered Russia's leader, Tsar Alexander II. But Alexander was more offended by Austrian and French criticism, which meant that if a conflict in central Europe arose, Russia was unlikely to join with these two powers against Prussia.

In August 1863, Bismarck thwarted a fresh attempt by Austria to assert its dominance in Germany. At short notice, the Austrian government called a congress of the German princes in Frankfurt. The purpose was to discuss reform of the German Confederation. With great difficulty, Bismarck persuaded Wilhelm I not to attend. There was a stormy encounter between monarch and minister, and Bismarck even threatened to resign. Wilhelm's absence reduced the congress's chances of success because the princes who attended could not agree to any changes without Prussia's consent. Bismarck also insisted that in any reform of the Confederation, Prussia must have equal status with Austria, and its assembly must be elected by universal male suffrage. He knew that these demands would be completely unacceptable to the Austrian government.

War with Denmark, 1864

A complex dispute with Denmark over the territories of Schleswig-Holstein led to the first of three conflicts that were later known as the Wars of German Unification.

Causes of the war

The main cause of the war with Denmark was a dispute over the **duchies** of Schleswig-Holstein. This issue had already inflamed German national opinion during the 1848 revolution, when Prussian troops had intervened in support of Holstein's revolt against Danish rule (see Section 2.1). In 1852, the major European powers had reached an agreement in London, that when the childless King Frederick VII of Denmark died, he would be succeeded as king and as ruler of the duchies by Christian of Glucksburg, a cousin through marriage. It was also agreed that the duchies would not be incorporated into Denmark. When Christian succeeded in November 1863, Schleswig and Holstein refused to recognise his claim. Also, Christian violated the London agreement by proposing the incorporation of Schleswig into Denmark, which angered the German Confederation. Nationalists put forward a German prince, Duke Frederick of Augustenburg, as a rival candidate for the position of Duke of Schleswig-Holstein. The smaller states in the Confederation sent an army into Holstein in support of Augustenburg's claim.

KEY TERM

Duchy: A territory ruled over by a duke. (The plural is duchies.)

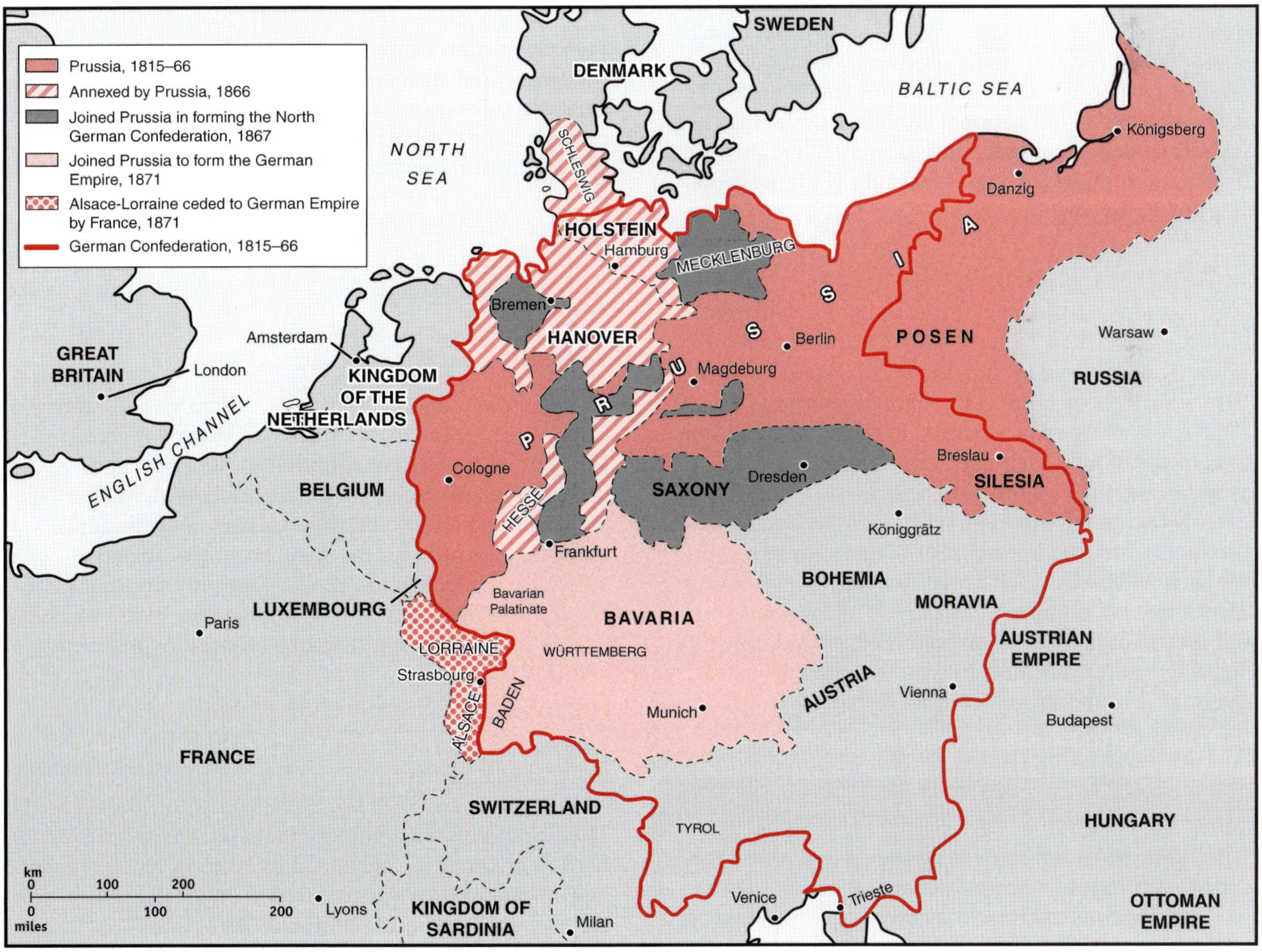

Figure 2.17: A map showing the steps towards the unification of Germany, 1815–71.

Reasons for Bismarck's involvement

Bismarck wanted to secure the two duchies for Prussia. However, he did not want to provoke Austria by acting independently. Nor did he wish to see Schleswig-Holstein occupied by an army of the German Confederation or become an independent state under the Duke of Augustenburg. He was acting in the interests of Prussia, not of a wider German identity. Denmark made the mistake of believing that Austria and Prussia would not cooperate with each other, even against a common enemy. Austria had no direct interest in the region, which was geographically much closer to Prussia, but, when Bismarck proposed joint action against Denmark, it had no option but to take part. For the sake of Austrian prestige, it could not allow such an important issue to be settled without its own involvement. Bismarck was confident that other European powers would not intervene in the crisis. They did not sympathise with the claims of either Danish or German national groups and preferred some kind of compromise settlement. France would almost certainly remain neutral. Britain did not have a large enough army and did not see the outcome of the crisis as a vital national interest. Russia was unlikely to help Denmark, since Bismarck had provided diplomatic support for Tsar Alexander II's repression of the 1863 Polish revolt.

Outcome

Prussia and Austria joined forces to fight a swift war against Denmark in January 1864. Denmark was militarily much weaker than the invaders and, in April, lost the fortress of Düppel (Dybbøl) after a ten-day siege. An **armistice** was arranged in the hope of finding an agreed solution. Denmark's refusal to consider a compromise, such as partitioning Schleswig, meant it lost any remaining international sympathy. Bismarck also made sure that Frederick of Augustenburg would not become Duke of Schleswig-Holstein by presenting terms that would make him a puppet of Prussia, and then blaming him when he turned them down. Fighting resumed in June, leading to a final defeat for Denmark and the surrender of both duchies to Prussia and Austria.

> **KEY TERM**
>
> **Armistice:** An agreement between two sides to stop fighting. It is not necessarily the point at which a war ends but it may allow the negotiation of a peace treaty.

Increased tension between Austria and Prussia: the Convention of Gastein

It was now up to Austria and Prussia to decide the long-term future of the duchies. They ignored German nationalist opinion, which wanted to see both duchies incorporated into the German Confederation under the Duke of Augustenburg. Bismarck knew that Prussia was not yet strong enough for a conflict with Austria, and he could not predict international reaction if he tried to take the duchies by force. He, therefore, concluded the Gastein Convention in August 1865 – a temporary agreement which, in his own words, 'papered over the cracks' between the two victorious powers. It was agreed that Holstein (the duchy nearest to Prussia) would be administered by Austria, and Schleswig by Prussia. This was a provisional arrangement which gave Bismarck time to decide how to proceed. Bismarck could now build up Prussia's armed forces knowing that he could argue with Austria over the status of Holstein when it suited him.

Some historians claim that the war against Denmark was proof that Bismarck planned and carried out his aims carefully, using Austria as an ally when needed, but turning against it later. In fact, Christian instigated the crisis, and Bismarck came under great pressure within Prussia to take decisive action. He began the war without a clear idea of the settlement that would follow, and the terms of the treaty were largely a result of Denmark's refusal to compromise.

War with Austria, 1866

Unlike the war against Denmark, Bismarck was largely responsible for the Austro-Prussian War of 1866. While more states were admitted to the Zollverein, Austria was still excluded. Disagreements also arose over the government of Schleswig-Holstein, and Bismarck made no effort to conceal these, hoping to stir up anti-Austrian feeling in Prussia. Knowing that war with Austria was likely to occur at some point, Bismarck began to seek foreign allies in the hope of isolating his enemy.

Meeting with Napoleon III at Biarritz

Bismarck was so concerned about which side France might take in an Austro-Prussian conflict that he travelled to France to meet with the French emperor, **Napoleon III**. The emperor was a complex character whose motives are hard to understand. He aimed to extend French influence in Europe, but also sympathised in an idealistic way with the aspirations of other nationalities.

Figure 2.18: Prussian soldiers after the storming of the fortress of Düppel during the war with Denmark, April 1864. Photography had not advanced enough by this time to allow pictures to be taken of fighting as it happened. Why do you think this photograph was taken?

KEY FIGURE

Napoleon III (1808–73)

Louis Napoleon (Napoleon III) was the nephew of Napoleon (I) Bonaparte, whose achievements he tried to imitate. As a young man, he was involved in plots to restore his dynasty to power and in 1848 he was elected president of the Second French Republic. In 1851, he carried out a *coup d'état* to make himself dictator and the following year he proclaimed himself Emperor of the French. He governed until 1870, when he was removed from power in a revolution triggered by his defeat in the Franco-Prussian War. He died in exile in Britain just over two years later.

At Biarritz in October 1865, Napoleon III decided to remain neutral, but, as a supporter of the newly united Italy, made it a condition that Prussia would hand the area of Venetia (at the time governed by Austria) to Italy after the war. (Italy, like Germany, was in the process of being unified in the 1860s, and its king wanted to enlarge his new state by acquiring this region.) The French emperor expected that a war between Austria and Prussia would be prolonged, and he believed that France would benefit by acting as a peacemaker. He wanted an outcome which left neither state as the dominant power in northern Germany. Bismarck's anxiety that Napoleon should not ally with Austria led him to make vague promises about territorial concessions in the Rhineland, the area of Germany on the Franco-German border. It is not clear whether he deliberately intended to mislead Napoleon, but certainly Bismarck did not concede any land after the war was won.

Secret alliance with Italy

Although Russia decided to remain neutral in any conflict, Bismarck succeeded in making an alliance with Italy. The Italian army was small, but Bismarck felt that it might provide a useful distraction during a war and prevent Austria from focusing its entire force on Prussia. In April 1866, he concluded a secret treaty which committed Italy to follow Prussia in going to war with Austria within a three-month period. Italy was prepared to help Prussia in return for gaining Venetia.

Bismarck now had to act quickly to benefit from this time-limited commitment.

Most of Europe, including the German states, shared Napoleon III's opinion that the war would be a long one, and public opinion in Prussia was against the conflict. Some people believed that Prussia could not win against the strength of Austria while others did not want to fight against the German states that would support Austria. Field-Marshal Moltke was uncertain about the chances of victory and even Bismarck had doubts about Prussian success.

Reasons why war broke out

Bismarck planned a rapid war with Austria in the early summer of 1866 that would enable Prussia to win control of northern Germany.

Bismarck's proposal to the Federal Diet for a new constitution

To provoke Austria, in April 1866 Bismarck proposed a new constitution to the Federal Diet. This constitution involved a representative assembly which would be elected by universal male suffrage. Bismarck knew that this would be unacceptable to the Austrian government. The prospect of a more democratic Germany, unified under Prussia, also worried middle-sized states such as Hanover and Bavaria.

Austria knew that its army was slow to mobilise, so it made the first move to avoid being caught unawares. Austria's move enabled its opponents to portray Austria as the aggressor. It began calling up troops in April in response to news of Italian military movements and had to continue mobilising them while talks with Prussia carried on. Austria greatly feared having to fight a war on two fronts and committed 100 000 troops to its southern border (though in fact the Italians did not perform well on the battlefield when war broke out).

Austria's violation of the Convention of Gastein

In early June, the Austrian government asked the Diet of the German Confederation to review the Schleswig-Holstein question, which Bismarck condemned as a violation of the Gastein Convention. Prussia at once sent forces into Holstein but Austria did not strike back militarily. Instead, the Federal Diet voted to back Austria against Prussian aggression. Bismarck now withdrew from the German Confederation and called on the other members to join with Prussia. He invaded Hanover, Hesse-Cassel and Saxony, which had sided with Austria, rapidly overrunning their territory.

The outcome of the Seven Weeks' War

Austria was a tougher opponent than Denmark, and it was likely that it might defeat Prussia. After all, it was generally felt that the Austrians had performed better than the Prussians in the Danish War. Table 2.5 shows that the two sides were fairly evenly matched in terms of numbers of men and weapons. However, the Austrians had some fundamental weaknesses that these figures do not reveal. In fact, it took Prussia just seven weeks to win a decisive victory.

There was only one major decisive battle in the Seven Weeks' War, at Königgrätz, a fortress on the River Elbe in Bohemia. The battle is sometimes named after the town of Sadová because it was fought between there and Königgrätz. The Prussian army, commanded by Moltke, headed southwards in three sections into Bohemia. Moltke's plan was to use the rail network to move his forces rapidly in the direction of the main Austrian army, and for them to meet up on the battlefield. He could use five railway lines to move his troops, while Austria had only one line, from Vienna to Bohemia. The Prussian strategy was daring and depended on good coordination, and the result of Königgrätz hung in the balance until the Prussian Second Army, under Wilhelm's son, Crown Prince Friedrich, arrived at the very last moment.

	Austrian forces	Prussian forces
Troop numbers	245 000	254 000
Artillery	650	702

Table 2.5: Relative strengths of the Austrian and Prussian armies in Bohemia (in the present-day Czech Republic), 1866.

Figure 2.19: The arrival of the troops of Crown Prince Friedrich on the battlefield of Königgrätz, July 1866. The image is taken from a British newspaper, the *Illustrated London News*. How good an idea does it give you of the nature of the fighting?

Weaponry was an important factor in the outcome of the battle. The Austrian artillery included many guns with rifled barrels that were of better quality than those used by the Prussians. The Prussians fought in small units, however, which reduced the damage caused by the heavy guns and their infantrymen were also better equipped than Austrian infantry soldiers. Prussian soldiers used an early form of bolt-action rifle known as the Dreyse rifle or needle gun–so called because of the shape of the firing pin–which could fire seven shots a minute. The Dreyse gun gave them an advantage over the old-fashioned rifle muskets used by the Austrians, which had to be laboriously reloaded by pushing the ammunition down the muzzle and could manage only two shots per minute. Rifle muskets also had to be reloaded in a standing position, which exposed the user to enemy fire. The needle gun could be reloaded by a soldier kneeling or even lying down. It outranged the rifle musket, and, in trained hands, it had a devastating effect on the closely packed Austrian ranks.

ACTIVITY 2.15

> The Prussian infantry rifle is still capable of combining its great accuracy at up to 600 paces [480 metres] with the possibility of extraordinarily rapid fire, an indisputable advantage if its application is saved for the really decisive moments of battle. Within this extended sphere of activity for infantry, even enemy swarms in loose formation are incapable of holding out when unprotected and at a standstill.
>
> **From Helmuth von Moltke's memorandum on the effects of improvements in firearms on battlefield tactics, April 1861.**

a How useful is this source in helping you to explain the Prussian army's success against Austria?

b What else might you want to know about the two sides' armies?

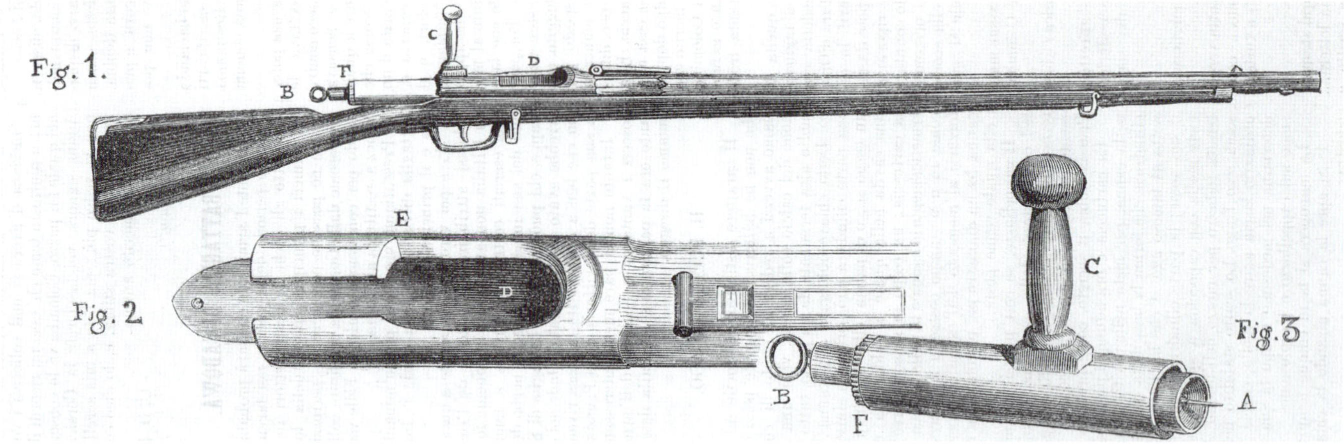

Figure 2.20: A drawing of the Dreyse needle gun used by the Prussian army in the war of 1866, showing its revolutionary loading mechanism.

The electric telegraph was another key technological development of the mid-19th century that helped Moltke to direct the advance. Training and transport helped the Prussians to victory. The Prussian troops were well prepared, had better officers and were able to move quickly to take decisive positions on the battlefield. An Austrian general later observed that 'wars now happen so quickly that what is not ready at the outset will not be made ready in time ... and a ready army is twice as powerful as a half-ready one.'

Figure 2.21: Prussian soldiers listening to French telegraph messages in the Franco-Prussian War, 1870. The telegraph was an important means of communication in both the Austro-Prussian and Franco-Prussian wars.

Finally, Austria's forces were led by an indecisive commander, Ludwig Benedek. Benedek positioned his forces with their backs to the River Elbe, but a more mobile strategy might have been more successful. Benedek's best hope was to defeat the Prussian First Army before the other two armies arrived. By not acting first, Benedek allowed the Prussians to encircle his forces. He was no match for Moltke, who had the ability to adapt to changing circumstances and to delegate (pass down) decision-making to officers lower down the chain of command. The Austrians' command structure was not effective, and they could not combine the forces of the smaller states (except Saxony) with their own. For example, Bavaria had 65 000 troops, but it refused to act quickly against Prussia.

The Treaty of Prague, August 1866

The Austrians were quick to seek peace, fearing that prolonged conflict might cause further problems in their multi-ethnic empire. The peace terms were laid down in the Treaty of Prague, but they were not harsh. Others in the Prussian leadership, including the king, favoured a triumphal entrance into Vienna. Bismarck, however, had no desire to humiliate Austria by seeking territorial concessions, other than granting Venetia to Italy. Although defeated, Austria was still a powerful state and Bismarck did not want to make it a permanent enemy of Prussia. He was looking to the future when Prussia might need Austria as an ally. He was also cautious about weakening Austria so much that France or Russia might decide to intervene. This was unlikely, but these powers would not want the Habsburg Empire destroyed while it could act as a useful balance to Prussia's growing strength. In any case, weakening Austria might create a dangerous power vacuum in southern Europe,

ACTIVITY 2.16

a Copy and complete the table to organise your thoughts on the reasons for the Prussian victory in the Seven Weeks' War of 1866. This encourages you to think about the different characteristics of the two sides.

b Which of these factors do you think was most important in bringing about the outcome of the war?

	Prussian strengths	Austrian weaknesses
Planning and preparation for war		
Ability to mobilise troops		
Types of weaponry		
Command and control of armies		

Reflection

How did you decide which factor was the most important? Explain your thinking to another student. How would you defend your choice? Have you changed your mind after listening to your partner's choice?

where it performed a useful function holding together a collection of different national groups. As long as Austria's power in northern Germany was permanently broken, Bismarck was content. He was willing to leave Austria to focus its priorities on eastern Europe and the Balkans. The treaty did not, therefore, include the surrender of any Austrian territory to Prussia. The most far-reaching provisions were the ones that affected the north German states.

The formation of the North German Confederation

The treaty allowed Bismarck to replace the Austrian-dominated German Confederation with the North German Confederation. The North German Confederation was not an association of free states, but a political union in which Prussia simply took over the states north of the River Main: Hesse-Cassel, Nassau, Hanover, the city of Frankfurt and Schleswig-Holstein. Several rulers, including the king of Hanover, were effectively deposed, as Bismarck did not want to risk these royal families recovering and seeking revenge.

The establishment of the North German Confederation meant that, from the west bank of the Rhine across to eastern Prussia, there was a continuous stretch of Prussian territory. Saxony retained its king, Johann I, and some limited independence within the Confederation. These concessions were won for Saxony by Austria, as Saxony was Austria's leading north German ally.

The new Confederation established Prussian power over an additional 4 million people in northern Germany. The king of Prussia controlled the Confederation's foreign policy and decisions about war and peace. The Confederation was governed by a Federal Council (Bundesrat), representing the states, and a parliament (Reichstag), elected by universal male suffrage. Although the parliament was supposed to be democratic and was given some powers, the reality was that Prussia dominated the Confederation, under Bismarck's direction. He was appointed federal chancellor, a post that was theoretically responsible to the Reichstag but in practice answered to the king of Prussia as president of the Confederation. Crucially, the Reichstag did not control military spending, which was 90% of the annual budget. It was a model of government that was deliberately very different from the kind of western parliamentary democracy supported by traditional German liberals.

Figure 2.22: King Wilhelm I opens the first Reichstag of the North German Confederation, February 1867.

Liberals change their attitude to Bismarck

Bismarck did not enter the Austro-Prussian War with the goodwill of the liberals. They did not believe that a minister with his authoritarian views should propose a democratically elected parliament for the German Confederation just before the war. They still mistrusted him because of his decision to rule without parliamentary approval in 1862. However, the victory over the hereditary enemy, autocratic Habsburg Austria, now made Bismarck popular with the liberals. One group broke with their irreconcilable liberal colleagues to show their support for Bismarck's foreign policy. They recognised that 'blood and iron' had achieved partial German unification where their methods had failed. This group went on to form the National Liberal Party in February 1867.

Not all conservative Junkers supported the new Confederation, fearing that Prussia's identity would be watered down. However, moderate members of their grouping established the Free Conservatives, who supported Bismarck's plans. They and the National Liberals became the main parliamentary supporters of Bismarck in the coming years. Bismarck had succeeded in dividing his opponents at home as well as defeating Austria.

The Indemnity Bill, September 1866

Bismarck introduced an **Indemnity Bill** to legalise the raising of taxes of without parliamentary approval over the previous four years, and only seven members of the Prussian Diet voted against it. This tactic showed Bismarck at his most politically imaginative: he created an alliance between moderate liberals and flexible conservatives in support of his bold moves and isolated the hard-liners at both extremes. Bismarck had succeeded in placing Prussia at the head of the nationalist movement, and, from now on, many liberals and conservatives saw him as a heroic figure. He had achieved these successes partly through good fortune. As a royal courtier reminded him after the Battle of Königgrätz, 'You are now a great man. But if the crown prince had arrived too late, you would be the greatest scoundrel in the world.'

Bismarck had justified the trust that had been placed in him by King Wilhelm I–even if reluctantly at first–less than four years earlier. He had done something which old-fashioned Prussian conservatives would never have dared to do, and which the liberals had clearly failed to do in 1848–49. He had shown that the forces of German nationalism could be allied to the interests of the

Prussian state. Most importantly, the historic struggle for power in northern Germany between Prussia and Austria had been finally settled. The status of the southern German states, however, remained to be decided. The next section examines their fate.

KEY TERM

Indemnity bill: A law passed to protect people who might otherwise face penalties for illegal conduct.

ACTIVITY 2.17

> [Article] 6. The Federal Council consists of the representatives of the members of the Confederation, amongst whom the votes are divided according to the rules for the full assembly of the late Germanic Confederation, so that Prussia, with the late votes of Hanover, Hesse-Cassel, Holstein, Nassau and Frankfurt, has 17 votes, Saxony 4 … Mecklenburg-Schwerin 2, … Brunswick 2, [all other states one each], Total 43 …
>
> [Article] 11. The Presidency of the Confederation appertains to the Crown of Prussia, which … has the right of representing the Confederation internationally, of declaring war and concluding peace, of entering into alliances and other treaties with foreign states …
>
> [Article] 63. All the land forces of the Confederation form one single army, which in war and peace is under the command of His Majesty the King of Prussia, as federal Commander-in-Chief …
>
> **From the Constitution of the North German Confederation, 14 June 1867.**

How does this source reveal Bismarck's aims in setting up the North German Confederation?

a Note carefully the features of the constitution that favoured Prussian interests.

b Present the structure of the Confederation in the form of a diagram.

KEY CONCEPT 2.3

Cause and consequence

Cause: Look at these possible reasons why northern Germany was unified under Prussia by 1867. In small groups, discuss which, in your opinion, was the most important:

- Prussia's economic strength by the mid-19th century
- Bismarck's diplomatic skill
- Prussia's military effectiveness
- the support of the German nationalist movement.

Consequence: In small groups, discuss the consequences of the formation of the North German Confederation for:

- Prussia
- the other German states
- the other European powers, especially Austria and France.

2.4 How and why was German unification achieved by 1871?

Bismarck fought a third and final war with France in 1870–71. As a result of this war, the south German states were united with the North German Confederation to create a united German state.

Pressure from nationalists to complete the unification process

For many nationalists in the north, the process of unification was still not complete. They hoped that passing modernising legislation in the North German Confederation might attract the support of progressive opinion in the south and encourage the southern states to join the new Reich. National Liberals and Free Conservatives wrote these laws that extended citizenship rights and commercial freedom. National Liberals also wanted to invite Baden, the southern state that was most positive in its attitude to Prussia, to join the Confederation. However, Bismarck discouraged this as he feared the effect on opinion in the other southern states, as well as the international reaction. Nationalists did not expect that their goals would soon be achieved.

Problems with the southern states

When the North German Confederation was formed, Bismarck guaranteed the independence of the southern German states of Bavaria, Wurttemberg, Baden and Hesse-Darmstadt. He openly stated that he had no plans to incorporate the southern states and unify all of Germany. At this stage, he did not want to provoke a hostile reaction from France by going too far. He may also have felt that the new Confederation needed time to establish itself before Catholic south German states were admitted. Bismarck did not want to risk a dilution of Prussia's traditional culture. Moreover, he was aware that there was strong resistance to Prussia's values, which many southern Germans summarised as 'pay taxes, be a soldier, and keep your mouth shut'. The states did not want to see the creation of a Prussian-dominated Germany in which they were likely to lose their independence.

However, Bismarck did try to strengthen the links between the two parts of Germany. The southern states concluded defensive military alliances with Prussia. These alliances meant that, if they faced a common threat, their armies and railways would come under Prussian control. The alliances were important when Bismarck went to war with France in 1870.

The Zollparlament

Bismarck hoped at this stage that political unity might come about through closer economic integration. Prussia remained president of the Zollverein and in 1867 he set up an elected body to consider the Zollverein's future. This body was known as the Zollparlament or customs parliament. Members of the North German Reichstag were joined by representatives from southern Germany elected by universal male suffrage. However, elections to the Zollparlament in March 1868 showed that the new members did not favour political union. In Bavaria the largest party was an anti-Prussian Catholic party, while in Württemberg, a Grossdeutsch-democratic party won most of the seats.

Lack of political unity

It is arguable that the southern states could not have indefinitely maintained an independent existence. The larger and more prosperous part of Germany was now united and in the long term its economic strength would have exercised a powerful pull on its neighbours on the other side of the River Main. Their all-important lines of communication ran through the North German Confederation to the Baltic ports. In any case, the southern states did not form a united bloc of their own. The key factor that would lead to their incorporation into united Germany was the attitude of Emperor Napoleon III, who was keen to gain some territorial compensation for his neutrality during the Austro-Prussian War. Fear of French expansion would ultimately prove stronger than anti-Prussian feeling in the south.

Figure 2.23: A Prussian military parade, watched by admiring civilians. Prussia's culture was strongly militaristic.

Napoleon III's ambitions

It is not clear that Bismarck actively sought war with France as a long-term objective, but he was prepared to accept it if necessary. He considered that it might even work in Prussia's interests. A conflict with an external enemy, which could be portrayed as threatening both southern Germany and the North German Confederation, might be a way of bringing about complete unification.

Relations between Prussia and France deteriorated after the Austro-Prussian War. Napoleon III was under pressure from French public opinion to gain some compensation for tolerating this powerful neighbour on his eastern border. He wanted to revive the glory of his uncle Napoleon Bonaparte's empire, with the important difference that he wanted to acquire territory peacefully. In particular he wanted to take over an area on the west bank of the Rhine that had been under French control before the fall of Napoleon Bonaparte in 1814.

The Luxemburg Crisis

Bismarck exploited tensions with France in order to arouse German national feeling against Napoleon III's empire. These tensions eventually led to war between France and the German states.

Causes

In July 1866, Napoleon III submitted a proposal for France to acquire part of the Rhineland, which belonged to Bavaria and Hesse. Bismarck did not intend to help him gain possession of any German land but did not want to alienate France at this stage. So instead, he encouraged Napoleon to turn his attention to the Duchy of Luxemburg (spelt Luxembourg in French), a mainly French-speaking independent state to the north, whose ruler was the king of the Netherlands. Some of the inhabitants were German-speaking, and a Prussian garrison had been stationed there since 1815 as part of the German Confederation. Bismarck initially supported Napoleon's claim. However, he changed his position when news broke that the king was willing to give up Luxemburg, which sparked a storm of protest in Germany.

Why Bismarck encouraged the crisis

Once he had secured his peace settlement with Austria, Bismarck did not need to reward France with any territory. He deliberately whipped up German public opinion to prevent the deal between France and the Netherlands from going through. In March 1867, he increased the tension with France by revealing details of the secret military alliances with the south German states. The king of the Netherlands agreed to sell the duchy to France, subject to Prussian approval–something which was extremely unlikely to be given.

It is unlikely that Bismarck was trying to start a war with France at this stage. However, he must have been aware that by obstructing Napoleon's plans to gain territory, he was provoking him into possible future aggression. The crisis showed that Bismarck was willing to use nationalist feeling as a political weapon to put pressure on France.

PUNCH, OR THE LONDON CHARIVARI.—August 25, 1866.

PEACE—AND NO PIECES!

BISMARCK. "PARDON, MON AMI; BUT WE REALLY CAN'T ALLOW YOU TO PICK UP ANYTHING HERE."
NAP (*the Chiffonnier*). "PRAY, DON'T MENTION IT, M'SIEU! IT'S NOT OF THE SLIGHTEST CONSEQUENCE."

Figure 2.24: 'Peace – and no pieces' – a cartoon from the British magazine *Punch*, August 1866, showing Bismarck (right) politely refusing to grant Napoleon III any land following the end of the Austro-Prussian War. Napoleon is dressed as a rag-picker, someone who picks up waste material from the streets for a living. Bismarck says, "Pardon mon ami. But we really can't allow you to pick up anything here." Napoleon says, "Pray, don't mention it, monsieur. It's not of the slightest consequence." What does this cartoon suggest about the changing balance of power between Prussia and France in this period?

Outcome and effects on relations with France

The crisis was defused by a conference held in London in May 1867, which resulted in Luxemburg being declared a neutral state. The Prussian garrison was withdrawn. The agreement was a face-saving compromise for France, but the fact remained that Napoleon had failed in his attempt to gain territory.

The south German states were horrified to discover that Napoleon wanted to take control of Luxemburg and turned against France. But they were not willing to commit their armed forces to fight alongside Prussia. It needed a greater crisis to make this happen.

The Hohenzollern candidature

It was a dispute over the succession to the Spanish throne that finally triggered the war of 1870–71.

Spanish crown accepted by Prince Leopold

In 1868, the Spanish queen, Isabella, was forced to abdicate by politicians who wanted to end the rule of the Bourbon royal family in Spain. They selected Prince Leopold of Hohenzollern-Sigmaringen as their new monarch. Leopold was from a south German state and a Catholic, like the Spanish, but he was also related to the Prussian royal family. Encouraged by Bismarck, Leopold accepted the offer – a move that was certain to increase French anger as a further example of Prussian expansionism. As king of Prussia, Wilhelm I was head of the Hohenzollern family. He was unsure of the wisdom of Bismarck's policy.

Reaction of Napoleon III

A major international incident occurred in early July 1870, when a document announcing Leopold's acceptance arrived in Madrid at a time when the Spanish parliament was not in session. This was not supposed to happen. Napoleon should not have heard the news until the Spanish had publicly chosen Leopold. The French government concluded that there was a Prussian plot to encircle France, and so put Wilhelm under pressure to persuade Leopold to withdraw.

The Ems Telegram

The king sent Bismarck a telegram describing a meeting about the matter he had just had with Benedetti, the French ambassador, at the spa town of Ems. When he received the Ems Telegram (as it is now known), Bismarck saw an opportunity to portray France as the unreasonable party in the negotiations. He changed the original wording of the telegram to make it appear that the French were demanding a humiliating pledge from Prussia never to support any future renewal of Leopold's candidature (claim to the Spanish throne). He also gave the impression that Wilhelm had abruptly broken off the discussion with the ambassador. Moltke, who was present when Bismarck edited the telegram, instantly grasped the important difference between the two versions. 'Now it has a different ring,' he declared. 'It sounded before like a parley [a negotiation]; now it is like a flourish in answer to a challenge.'

Bismarck then released the telegram in both Germany and France, anticipating that each side would believe that it had been insulted in the conversation between the king and the ambassador. Its contents were also released to foreign governments. The editing of the telegram provided the final push into war. It would be almost impossible now for France to retreat without losing face.

ACTIVITY 2.18

After the news of the renunciation of the hereditary Prince von Hohenzollern had been officially communicated to the Imperial Government of France by the Royal Government of Spain, the French Ambassador further demanded of His Majesty the King, at Ems, that he would authorise him to telegraph to Paris that His Majesty the King bound himself for all time never again to give his consent, should the Hohenzollerns renew their candidature. His Majesty the King thereupon decided not to receive the French Ambassador again and sent the aide-de-camp [an officer who acts as an assistant to a person of high rank] on duty to tell him that His Majesty had nothing further to communicate to the ambassador.

Bismarck's version of the Ems Telegram, 13 July 1870.

a Explain why the Ems Telegram would cause anger and alarm when published in this form.

b Is the telegram proof that Bismarck intended to go to war with France, and had been planning for this?

Reflection

Discuss your response to the Ems Telegram with another student. Did you reach similar conclusions about Bismarck's conduct? Would you change your mind about him in the light of your discussion?

Declaration of war by France

Urged on by public opinion, Napoleon decided on war. After originally governing France in an authoritarian fashion, he had begun a cautious process of liberalisation in the 1860s. Napoleon's increased tolerance made it much harder to restrain the expression of French public opinion. He went to war partly to improve his weakened domestic position. The failure in 1867 of a poorly thought-out scheme to establish a French client state in Mexico, headed by the Austrian Archduke Maximilian damaged his prestige.

The French declaration of war referred to the Ems Telegram and emphasised the threat to national security posed by the Hohenzollern candidature, and 'the consequent need to take immediate steps for the defence of French honour and injured interests'. Napoleon hoped to restore France's international standing and reunite the country behind him by winning a military victory in Europe. He was overconfident of the strength of his armed forces.

It is not clear how long Bismarck had been thinking about war with France, but war was the outcome of his manipulation of the Ems Telegram. War would almost certainly unite the south German states with the North German Confederation against the common enemy. In the event, the French played into his hands, enabling him to present the war as a defensive action by Prussia and the other German states.

The Franco-Prussian War, 1870–71

The Franco-Prussian War began in July 1870 and lasted until January 1871.

Why Bismarck was in a strong position

Despite Napoleon's confidence in his armed forces, Bismarck was in a strong position.

Lack of international support for France

France's decision to initiate war in July 1870 was risky. Although it had attempted to establish alliances, France was relatively isolated. It was seen as the aggressor while Prussia claimed only to be defending itself. Britain believed that France was not justified in going to war over the Spanish throne and refused to offer support. Italy also refused to help France while French soldiers were still present in its country, defending Rome on behalf of the Pope. Rome was the last area in the peninsula to remain independent of the new Italian state, and its leaders wanted the French to withdraw so that they could take it over.

The old conservative alliance of Russia and Austria, which had maintained the 1815 settlement for a generation, was now dead, and Russia decided to remain neutral after Bismarck said he would help secure a revision of the treaty which had ended the Crimean War. Austria had been weakened by its defeat in 1866 and was now focusing on its empire in south-eastern Europe. It would require all of Austria's remaining energies to keep its empire together.

By contrast, the German national movement supported Prussia. The south German states committed their troops to the war, viewing France as a threat to the whole of Germany, and they fought as well as their Prussian allies. Prussia was able to move half a million troops to the French border while France had only 250000 men concentrated in the Rhineland. The Prussian rail network proved its worth, just as it had four years earlier against the Austrians. Prussia had six rail lines that ran to the French frontier but France had only two.

The relative strengths of the Prussian and French armies

The Prussian army under General Moltke was a vital asset for Bismarck. The military was well-respected and was considered an honourable occupation for men of noble families. The training of army officers was well organised and they spent three years at a military academy. Elsewhere in Europe, wealthy young men could buy their positions as officers and had little further training as they were promoted. Officer training was rigorous and the best candidates were promoted to the general staff after an intensive course in the theory and practice of war. Most importantly, they were expected to think for themselves when carrying out the commander's overall strategy.

Prussia was also capable of mobilising for war more quickly and efficiently than France. As in 1866, the Prussian general staff system was valuable. By contrast, the French leaders' command and control over their forces was not effective. Their army reservists had to go to depots to collect equipment before moving to the points where they were meant to assemble. They did not have maps of their own country and had only been given maps of Germany because they expected soon to cross the border to win a swift victory.

The Prussian military combined short-term, universal conscription with intensive training. In contrast, France relied on long-serving professionals, recruited by annual lottery. France's reserve force, the Garde Mobile, had

Figure 2.25: An engraving showing the Battle of Gravelotte (just west of Metz), August 1870.

only 14 days of training each year. One of the French generals claimed that their army was 'ready to the last gaiter button', but this was an empty boast. The French allowed the Prussians to take the initiative, so that most of the war was fought on French territory.

France had some advantages in weaponry. The recently issued Chassepot rifle was superior to the Prussian needle gun, and they also possessed an early kind of machine gun, the Mitrailleuse. However, their troops had not learned how to use these weapons effectively to support their infantry. The French battlefield tactics were faulty. They concentrated their troops in prepared defensive positions and controlled their rate of fire as the enemy approached. The Prussians were more mobile and had improved their artillery. Moltke had learned from his army's experience against the Austrians, and had adopted rifled, steel breech-loading field guns. These guns outclassed the French in terms of range, accuracy and rate of fire.

Impact of the German victory at Sedan, September 1870

These improvements helped the Prussians and their allies to win the decisive battle of Sedan, near the Belgian border, in September 1870. Here a French army of 100 000 men was surrounded and shelled by the Prussian artillery until it surrendered. The French lost 17 000 troops while Prussian casualties were closer to 8000. Napoleon III surrendered to Bismarck. The French emperor was in poor health but felt that he should be present at the battle, even though he had a weak grasp of military matters. News of the defeat triggered a revolution in Paris. Napoleon was forced to abdicate, and a republican government was established.

Meanwhile, Marshal Bazaine allowed himself to be confined with 180 000 troops in the border fortress of Metz, instead of proactively using his resources. In short, France's leaders could not make up their minds whether to fight an offensive or a defensive war. Their lack of a clear strategy critically influenced their chances.

ACTIVITY 2.19

Create a table showing the similarities between the reasons for Prussia's defeat of Austria in 1866 and its defeat of France in 1870. Did Prussia's opponents make similar mistakes? Compare your key points with those chosen by other members of your class and discuss the reasons for your choice.

Armistice agreed, January 1871

The war took a different turn when the new republican government in Paris decided to hold out against the invaders in the capital city through the winter. In the countryside, the French used guerrilla warfare to harass Prussian forces. The siege of Paris demonstrated the ruthlessness of the Prussians. A combination of starvation, exhaustion and prolonged artillery bombardment finally led to the signing of an armistice on 28 January 1871. The French republican leaders knew that they could not resist any longer and wanted to bring the siege to an end. The armistice included a provision for the election of a French national assembly, with the authority to negotiate a final peace treaty.

Treaty of Frankfurt, May 1871

Bismarck took advantage of France's weakness to impose harsh peace terms. By the Treaty of Frankfurt, the defeated country had to pay a sum of 5 billion francs as **reparations**, and a German army was posted in northern France until the sum was paid. The border province of Alsace and the northern part of its neighbour, Lorraine, were granted to Germany, mainly to protect the newly unified state from the possibility of a French war of revenge. Although the annexed areas were largely German-speaking, they had belonged to France since the 18th century.

The harshness of the settlement contrasted starkly with Bismarck's relatively generous handling of Austria four years earlier. However, it was a way of binding the south German states to the new Reich. The annexed territory was a **buffer zone** between France and the states of Bavaria, Württemberg and Baden. Acquiring it was part of a strategy of viewing France as an aggressor, who must be punished as part of the peace settlement.

Bismarck had decided that, unlike Austria, France could never develop into an ally in the future, and so the relationship between Germany and France must be based purely on superior strength.

The settlement created lasting resentment in France. A statue in the centre of Paris, representing the Alsatian city of Strasbourg, was permanently shrouded in black cloth as a reminder to the population of the loss they had suffered. The French desire to avenge the loss of the two provinces was a long-term cause of the tensions that led to the First World War of 1914–18.

The defeat of France proved Bismarck's skill as a diplomatic 'chess player'. As in 1866, before beginning military action, he made sure that his opponent was isolated among the European powers. He also showed skill in manipulating the growing sense of German nationality, using the French threat as a way of binding the south German states to the war effort. He could not have achieved anything, however, without the successes of the Prussian army. The army's readiness to fight was a result of Moltke's effectiveness as a commander and improvements since the defeat of Austria four years earlier. Finally, Prussia was fortunate that the French army was badly prepared even though it had advantages in weaponry. Prussia won the war largely because of superior Prussian planning, combined with Bismarck's willingness to take a calculated risk when pursuing his objectives.

KEY TERMS

Reparations: Money that one country has to pay another as compensation for war damage.

Buffer zone: A protective area separating two potentially hostile countries.

The creation of the German Empire, 1871

The new German state was officially established during the Franco-Prussian War, in a manner which confirmed the domination of Prussia over the other members.

Concessions to the southern states

Germany was fully united as a result of the war with France. However, this was not entirely a triumph for German nationalism. Prussia remained the dominant state in the new Germany. It was a Kleindeutsch solution to the German problem, with Austria excluded from the new Reich.

ACTIVITY 2.20

Figure 2.26: Siege of Paris: Emperor Wilhelm I on the rampart of a Prussian artillery position the day after the surrender of the city, January 1871 (contemporary wood engraving).

Look at the engraving in Figure 2.26.

a Does this drawing give any clues to the reasons for the Prussian victory over France in the war of 1870–71?

b What else would you need to know in order to evaluate its usefulness as a source?

Some southern states were still reluctant to be part of a 'Greater Germany' under Prussian control. Bismarck had to compromise to persuade them to join the union. Bavaria, the largest southern state, wanted special powers to keep some independence, including control over its own armed forces. Bismarck also gave money to its king, Ludwig II, who was heavily in debt and open to bribery. This money came from the confiscated fortune of the king of Hanover, who had unwisely backed Austria in the war of 1866 and was then forced to abandon his throne and flee to Austria.

Wilhelm proclaimed Kaiser

It was not only the southern states that were concerned about the unification of their country. The Junkers also feared that Prussia would have less power and influence in a larger Germany. There was an argument about the exact title that Wilhelm would take. He wanted to be known as 'Emperor of Germany' but was eventually proclaimed 'German Emperor' or Kaiser on 18 January 1871, at a ceremony held in the Hall of Mirrors in the royal palace of Versailles. Bismarck preferred this title because it did not sound as though Prussia was making an unreasonable claim to authority over the south German states, whose cooperation he needed. The choice of venue was symbolic, since the palace had been created by one of the greatest French monarchs, Louis XIV. Proclaiming Wilhelm Kaiser at Versailles was a visible sign of France's humiliation.

ACTIVITY 2.21

Figure 2.27: King Wilhelm I of Prussia being proclaimed German Emperor in the Hall of Mirrors in the Palace of Versailles. Bismarck is the central figure in white uniform. Moltke is to the right of Bismarck, raising his hat. Behind them are the leaders of the German states.

Look at the painting in Figure 2.27.

a This painting by Anton von Werner, produced in 1877, is not accurate in all details. Bismarck did not actually wear white, for example, so why has the artist portrayed him like this?

b What can you learn from the painting about the way in which Germans wanted to regard the achievement of unification?

The constitution of the new Reich

The new Reich was very different from the national state that German liberals had struggled for in the revolutionary years of 1848–49. This time, the imperial crown was offered to a Prussian king by his peer group, the princes, rather than by a popular assembly. Unity had been imposed by means of force from above, not achieved from below by the people.

The constitution was modelled on the North German Confederation. Prussia had a deciding voice in the Bundesrat since it was allocated 17 out of a total of 58 votes, and 14 votes were sufficient to block any new proposals. It also had a majority of the seats in the Reichstag.

The king of Prussia was the Kaiser and commander-in-chief of the armed forces. Bismarck was appointed as imperial chancellor and remained the effective decision-maker in Germany until his downfall in 1890. The heads of the government departments, such as the treasury, justice and the interior, were designated as state secretaries who answered to the chancellor, rather than acting as a team of equal ministers. As Prussian foreign minister, Bismarck was also in control of Germany's external policy.

However, the individual states retained a number of powers, for example over direct taxation, education and welfare policies, and their local parliaments had different relationships with the government in each of the states. It was a Fürstenbund or grouping of states with individual royal rulers. The imperial government was granted certain specific, but important powers: over foreign policy, peace and war and the customs system.

Most importantly, the Prussian army was far greater than the military establishments of the other German states. The military exercised a special role in the new Reich. The army budget was not subject to parliamentary control. Under the North German Confederation, it had been set in 1867 at a fixed level for five years. During the Franco-Prussian War, the time period was extended until 1874 and, in practice, the Reichstag never gained control of military spending. This meant that the power of the Reichstag to evolve as a genuine parliamentary government, and to hold the Kaiser's ministers effectively to account, was always limited. The new Germany reflected the authoritarian, monarchical, military culture of Prussia.

KEY CONCEPT 2.4

Interpretations

How far was German unification the result of Bismarck's actions?

When Bismarck wrote his memoirs, in retirement in the 1890s, he presented himself as the architect of German unification, who had acted in accordance with a pre-determined plan. Historians have contested Bismarck's evaluation of his own role. Many scholars see him as a clever politician, who reacted to events as they occurred. He may have had broad long-term goals, but he was an opportunist in his pursuit of those objectives. Was he ever sincere in his support for German nationalism or did he see it as a movement that he must harness in the interests of the Prussian state, which remained the primary focus of his loyalty?

The first view sees Bismarck as both a visionary and a ruthless planner. Support for this interpretation comes from his remarks in 1862 to Benjamin Disraeli, the British politician and future prime minister. Bismarck said that his first task was to reorganise the army and after that he would 'take the first opportunity to declare war with Austria, break the German Confederation, bring the middle and smaller German states under control, and give Germany a national union under Prussia's leadership.' These comments suggest that Bismarck did indeed plan events over the long term. In a later conversation with Disraeli, he claimed that he had always planned the stages by which Germany was unified.

These conversations should nonetheless be treated with caution as evidence of Bismarck's political vision. There is some debate around the credibility of the 1862 conversation. Bismarck referred to it in a letter to his wife at the time, but one of his biographers, A. J. P. Taylor, argues that the story may have been manufactured later. It seems unlikely that Bismarck would reveal accurately his long-term plans to a British politician he knew only slightly. He might simply have been trying to impress Disraeli in the course of a casual conversation.

The alternative interpretation is that Bismarck was primarily concerned with the interests of Prussia. As a Junker landowner, he aimed to maintain Prussia's monarchy and its conservative social structure. He did not believe in German nationalism for its own sake but only as a way of advancing Prussia's power. On one occasion he said of nationalism that 'this kind of emotional sentimental policy is totally alien to me; I have no time at all for German nationality; I would as soon make war against the kings of Bavaria and Hanover [as] against France.' Bismarck was determined that if German unification took take place, then it should work to Prussia's advantage. This meant a Kleindeutschland solution: one in which Austria was excluded from any new German state. He knew it was unlikely that Austria and Prussia would ever agree to divide Germany between them, and that a conflict between the two was almost unavoidable.

CONTINUED

Figure 2.28: Bismarck (left) pictured with Benjamin Disraeli, then British prime minister, at a later meeting in 1878.

Although sometimes Bismarck liked to suggest that he had a carefully worked-out master plan, at other times he emphasised his pragmatism (practicality). For example, he said that a person should not play chess assuming that their opponent was bound to make a certain move: 'for it may be that this won't happen and then the game is lost … one must always have two irons in the fire.' This comment suggests that he was good at making use of opportunities as they arose.

Look back on the information in this chapter on the role of Bismarck. How significant do you think his actions were in the move towards German unification? By contrast, how much did that process owe to other factors, such as the economic strength of Prussia, its military power, or the mistakes and miscalculations of its opponents in the wars of 1864, 1866 and 1870–71? Overall, how important do you consider Bismarck was as an individual, relative to the other forces at work?

Practice questions

Source-based question

Read the sources and then answer **both** parts of the question.

SOURCE A

It remains to be remarked that the feeling of uneasiness in Germany is augmented [increased] by the impression that … when France shall have completed Her military preparations, She will seek a war with Germany so as to obtain those compensations for the aggrandisement [increased power] of Prussia, which She has sketched out, but which She has already learnt will only be yielded to superior force. Whether the fears thus entertained in regard to the eventual course of France and to the alliances to which it may give rise will be realized or not, some seventeen or eighteen months hence, their existence produces a feeling of uncertainty as to the future and furnishes a motive for military preparation on the part of Germany.

From a report by the British envoy to Bavaria, Sir Henry F. Howard, to the British foreign secretary, Lord Stanley, 3 December 1866 (abridged).

SOURCE B

In regard to the South German situation I think the line for Prussian policy is set by two diverse aims … the one distant, the other immediate … The distant and by far the greater aim is the national unification of Germany. We can wait for this in security because the lapse of time and the natural development of the nation which makes further progress every year will have their effect. We cannot accelerate it unless out of the way [unexpected] events in Europe, such as some upheaval in France or a war of other great powers among themselves offer us an unsought opportunity to do so … Every recognisable effort of Prussia to determine the decision of the South

CONTINUED

German Princes will endanger our immediate aim. I consider this to be … to keep Bavaria and Württemberg in such political direction that neither will cooperate with Paris or Vienna … nor find a pretext to break alliances which we have concluded [with them].

From a letter from Bismarck to Wilhelm I, 20 November 1869 (abridged).

SOURCE C

The [governments of the North German Confederation] have felt that they have done all which honour and dignity permit to maintain for Europe the blessings of peace; and the clearer it appears to all eyes that the sword has been forced into our hand, with greater confidence we turn, supported by the unanimous will of the German governments of the South, as well as of the North, to the love of the Fatherland and willingness for sacrifice of the German people to the summons to protect her honour and independence.

From the speech of the king of Prussia at the opening of the North German Reichstag, 19 July 1870.

SOURCE D

After I had read out the concentrated edition to my two guests, Moltke remarked: 'Now it has a different ring; it sounded before like a parley [a negotiation]; now it is like a flourish in answer to a challenge.' I went on to explain: 'If in execution of his Majesty's order I at once communicate this text, which contains no alteration in or addition to the telegram, not only to the newspapers, but also by telegraph to all our embassies, it will be known in Paris before midnight, and … will have the effect of a red rag upon the Gallic [French] bull.

> **CONTINUED**
>
> Fight we must if we do not want to act the part of the vanquished without a battle. Success, however, essentially depends upon the impression which the origination of the war makes upon us and others; it is important that we should be the party attacked …'
>
> **From Bismarck's memoirs, published in 1898, recalling the evening when he edited the Ems Telegram, 13 July 1870.**

1 a Read Sources **C** and **D**.

Compare Sources C and D as evidence of Prussia's responsibility for the outbreak of war with France in 1870. **[15 marks]**

b Read **all** of the sources.

'Bismarck planned in advance to complete the process of German unification by means of a war with France.' How far do the sources support this view? **[25 marks]**

Essay-based questions

Answer **both** parts of each question.

2 a Explain why the rulers of the German states survived the revolutions of 1848–49. **[10 marks]**

b To what extent was Prussia's military strength the most important reason for the unification of Germany? **[20 marks]**

3 a Explain why the king of Prussia refused the imperial throne in 1849. **[10 marks]**

b 'Growing German nationalism between 1815 and 1850 was mainly influenced by economic factors.' How far do you agree? **[20 marks]**

Improve this answer

1 a Read Sources **C** and **D**.

Compare Sources C and D as evidence of Prussia's responsibility for the outbreak of war with France in 1870. **[15 marks]**

Source C is taken from an address by the Prussian King, Wilhelm I, to the North German Reichstag, the parliament of the North German Confederation. This body had been created as a result of the Austro-Prussian War of 1866, in which Prussia defeated Austria to become the dominant power in northern Germany. The King is speaking to the Reichstag at the point when the war between France and Prussia broke out. Source D is Bismarck's own account of the outbreak of the Franco-Prussian War in his memoirs, published at the end of his life in 1898.

One similarity between Source C and D is that both portray Prussia as acting defensively, suggesting that France was responsible for the outbreak of war, not Prussia. In Source C it says that the North German Confederation felt that they had done everything they could to 'maintain … the blessing of peace' and that 'the sword has been forced in our hand', both of which suggest that Prussia wanted peace but had to go to war because of France's actions. Source D agrees that the outbreak of war was not Prussia's responsibility as it says that Bismarck realised that 'it is important that we should be the party attacked' which shows that he was determined not to been seen as the aggressor, he wanted France to attack first so that it was not Prussia's fault that war broke out. The reason they both show that Prussia was not responsible for the outbreak of war with France is because they are both by Prussians. Source C is by the King of Prussia and Source D is by Bismarck, so these men are bound to be biased and want to show their enemy, France, as the aggressor.

> This paragraph explains a point of similarity between the two sources, using references to the text to support the points made. This should be developed further by adding a point of difference. In the closing sentences of the paragraph, there is an attempt at evaluation but the comments are simplistic. To access the higher levels of the mark scheme, the student should explain why the similarity (or difference) occurs, linking the points clearly to the historical context of the sources.

The different dates of the two sources are important in explaining the differences between them. Both are primary sources because they are written by participants in the events of 1870, but Source C comes directly from the time whereas Source D is written almost 30 years later. In July 1870, it was important for Prussia to persuade the other German states to join the war, and this was Wilhelm's main purpose. The other German states would not have supported Prussia if they felt it had acted as the aggressor. We cannot be sure, but it may be that the speech was written for him by Bismarck, as his chief minister and the mastermind behind the conflict with France. By the 1890s, however, the war was in the past and it would not affect the course of events for Bismarck to be honest about how he had manipulated the situation. In fact it may be that he wanted to show his cleverness. He quotes Helmuth von Moltke, chief of the Prussian general staff at the time, as recognising the likely effect of his editing of the telegram, which underlines his own brilliance to the reader.

This paragraph begins to analyse why, as well as how, the two sources differ. However, the points need to be supported with clear evidence from the sources.

The intended audiences of the sources are also important in understanding why they differ. The immediate audience for Source C would have been the leading politicians of North Germany, but it would also have been published abroad and can be interpreted as justifying military action against France, so that other countries felt less inclined to take the French side. Source D's audience is the general public, particularly those interested in recent political history. Politicians write memoirs when they retire partly to make money but also to justify their earlier actions. Neither source will give a completely reliable account of the events of 1870 because they are both written for particular purposes and will distort reality in order to make their point. However, Source D, as an insider's account written later, is probably more useful as evidence than a public statement made at the time – although we need to make allowances for a retired politician's desire to exaggerate his own role.

This is an insightful paragraph which considers the issue of provenance and uses outside knowledge to evaluate the sources for usefulness and reliability. However, the student could have commented further on the content of the sources. The way that Source C enlists the cause of German nationalism ('love of the Fatherland' and the 'sacrifice of the German people') in support of Prussian interests is worth noting. It is also relevant to highlight the dubious argument here, that the North German Confederation has done its best to maintain 'the blessings of peace'. This claim could have been examined. In D, Bismarck is careful to state that he was acting in obedience to the king, whereas in fact he was acting with considerable independence. His caricature of France as the 'Gallic bull' is a striking use of language. In conclusion, this is a good response which explains and evaluates the sources and makes some effective use of contextual knowledge – but it could have gone a little further in making greater use of the evidence presented in the sources.

When you have studied these comments, write your own answer to the question.

Improve this answer

2 a Explain why the rulers of the German states survived the revolutions of 1848–49. **[10 marks]**

The German princes were taken by surprise by the revolutions which swept across their territories in 1848–49, but within a year they had recovered their power. This was partly because of their own instinct for survival and the support they received from the two most powerful states, Austria and Prussia. However, it was mainly because of the internal weaknesses and divisions of the revolutionaries. In this essay I will explore these different factors, in order to explain why the princes survived the revolutionary upheavals of this period.

> This introduces the key aspects of the explanation quite concisely, so that the reader knows what to expect in the main body of the answer. It also shows awareness of the need to assess the relative importance of different factors. But does the final sentence really add anything? Remember that time is limited. It would have been better to add a sentence to explain what is meant by an 'instinct for survival'.

The princes initially granted the revolutionaries some of their demands, setting up constitutions which limited their own power. This showed their ability to react to circumstances; they knew that they could be swept from power if they tried to use military force at a time when support for the revolutions was strong, in the spring of 1848. But they were waiting for the right time, when the revolutions started to run out of steam, to fight back. Most of the princes had made sure that they kept their armed forces under their control. This meant that when the revolutionaries started to fall victim to internal divisions, the princes were able to step in and recover control.

> This is a valid explanation, and the last sentence links neatly to the next paragraph, which deals with the weaknesses of the revolutionary movement. But it lacks examples to support the points it makes. It could include, for example, the support provided by Prussia to the rulers of Baden, Württemberg and elsewhere in suppressing the uprisings in 1849. On a point of style, the phrase, 'started to run out of steam' is not wrong, but a more formal expression, such as 'began to lose momentum', might create a more 'professional' impression.

It is doubtful that the princes would have recovered their power so easily, if they had been confronted by more united and better organised revolutionary forces.

The revolutions of 1848–49 in the German states were undermined by divisions between liberal, middle-class groups and more radical, working-class elements. They were struggling for different objectives and did not see eye-to-eye with each other. For example, in the Rhineland, better-off middle-class revolutionaries abandoned the revolution because they feared that armed working-class crowds were presenting a threat to their property. This weakened the movement and helped the princes to regain control.

> This is a stronger paragraph because it uses a specific example, events in the Rhineland, to illustrate the point it is making. But a sentence or two to explain the different aims of the two types of revolutionaries would have helped to develop the argument. What were the liberals and radicals seeking?

The weakness of the revolutionary movement was illustrated by the failure of the Frankfurt Parliament, which the liberal nationalists hoped would create a new constitution for Germany as a whole. It was too slow to agree on a form of government and was also divided between those who wanted a smaller Germany, led by Prussia (Kleindeutschland) and those who wanted a larger Grossdeutschland which would include Austria. The Parliament did not have armed forces of its own and when a crisis occurred in Schleswig-Holstein, which German nationalists wanted to see join the other German-speaking provinces, they had to rely on Prussia for help. In August 1848 the Prussians made their own peace with Denmark, whose King was the ruler of Schleswig-Holstein, when it suited their interests.

This paragraph concisely highlights the key weaknesses of the Frankfurt Parliament, whose failure was a key reason why the liberal revolutions of 1848 ended in disappointment. It uses appropriate terminology (Kleindeutschland/Grossdeutschland). It would have been better with a concluding sentence linking to the theme of the essay – the power of the princes. It could have ended, for example: 'This showed that the goals of liberal nationalism could not be realised without the cooperation of the princes, who had shown that they still possessed the vital resource of armed strength, which they would use to serve their own interests.'

Finally, the recovery of the two largest states, Austria and Prussia, from the shocks of March 1848 helped the princes to recover. Austria was soon in a position to use its leadership of the German Confederation to its advantage, under a new prime minister, Prince Schwarzenberg. In Prussia the key role was played by King Friedrich Wilhelm IV, who had first seemed to show sympathy for the revolution but, when he felt strong enough, crushed its hopes. This occurred when he turned down the offer of the German imperial crown in April 1849. This showed that he refused to accept the authority of the parliament, and he would only receive such a crown if it was offered by his own peer group, the German princes. The fact that the revolutionaries had such high hopes of the King, rather than pushing for the more radical solution of a German republic, shows how unlikely they were to succeed.

This is another strong paragraph. It would have benefited from more material on the recovery of Austria, but the analysis of Friedrich Wilhelm IV's role is particularly good. The final sentence nicely links the part played by the king with the weaknesses of the revolutionaries.

The princes recovered so rapidly from the upheavals of 1848–49, partly because they were resourceful, and they knew when to retaliate. They had never given up their most important powers, even when they had been forced to grant their subjects more freedoms and had introduced constitutions. But the main reason for their survival was the weakness of liberal nationalism, which from the start was not well enough organised or united to succeed.

This conclusion highlights the most important points of the argument, which have been developed in the main body of the essay. But it does not fully show the connections between the different causes. The essay demonstrates good knowledge of the topic, although, as noted, more examples would have helped – few princes and their states are actually mentioned and, perhaps understandably, the focus is mainly on Prussia. It explains the main factors with relevant supporting information, and there are no factual inaccuracies. It would benefit from a little more detail and a more fully supported conclusion.

Consider the feedback. Now write your own answer to this question.

SELF-EVALUATION CHECKLIST

After working through this chapter, complete the table.

You should be able to:	Needs more work	Almost there	Ready to move on
explain how the Congress of Vienna and the Confederation worked			
outline the successes and failures of Metternich's system			
analyse how liberalism and nationalism created pressure for reform			
evaluate how economic and political changes across the 1840s encouraged radical calls for change			
explain how the German revolution of 1848–49 spread			
explain the failure of the Frankfurt Parliament			
analyse the revolutions of 1848 and the Austrian counter-revolution			
evaluate the changing relationship between Prussia and Austria after 1848			
explain the main features of the 1861–62 constitutional crisis			
outline the importance of the Congress of Princes (1863)			
analyse the impact of the war over Schleswig-Holstein with Denmark			
evaluate how Prussia's war with Austria changed the course of German history			
explain how supporters of nationalism impacted German unification			
outline the impact of the Luxembourg Crisis and the Hohenzollern Candidature			
analyse how the Franco-Prussian War influenced German politics			
evaluate the causes and consequences of the creation of the German Empire in 1871.			

› Chapter 3

Russia from autocracy to revolution, 1881–1924

KEY QUESTIONS

This chapter will help you to answer these questions:

- What challenges faced the tsarist regime between 1881 and 1894?
- What were the causes and outcomes of the 1905 Revolution up to 1914?
- How and why did the Bolsheviks seize power in October 1917?
- How were the Bolsheviks able to consolidate their power up to 1924?

Timeline

Mar 1881 Alexander II assassinated; Alexander III becomes tsar

Nov 1894 Nicholas II becomes tsar

1903–06 Wave of anti-Jewish pogroms results in 2000 deaths

Jan 1905 Start of the 1905 Revolution

Oct 1905 October Manifesto issued

Apr 1906 New constitution – the Fundamental Laws; First Duma

Jul 1914 First World War begins

Feb 1917 Nicholas II replaced by Provisional Government

Apr 1917 Lenin returns to Russia from exile

Oct 1917 Bolsheviks seize power

1918–21 Civil War: terror and War Communism

Jan 1918 Constituent Assembly dissolved

Mar 1918 Treaty of Brest-Litovsk; Bolshevik Russia withdraws from the war

Jul 1918 Royal family murdered

Mar 1921 Crushing of sailors' uprising; one-party state established

Note: Dates up to February 1918 are given in the traditional Julian Calendar, which was used in Russia until then. By the end of the 19th century, the calendar needed to be adjusted because it was running 13 days behind the newer Gregorian Calendar that was being used in western Europe. Russia adopted the Gregorian Calendar in February 1918. In this book we refer to the 'February Revolution' since it began on 23 February 1917 in the old calendar (8 March on the new calendar). The 'October Revolution' occurred on 25 October 1917 on the old calendar (6 November on the new one).

GETTING STARTED

Why might Russia's rulers have found it difficult to govern an empire as large and diverse as this? Use the map in Figure 3.1 to help you answer.

Figure 3.1: A map showing the expansion of the Russian Empire between 1795 and 1914.

Introduction

In the period from 1881 to 1924, Russia experienced a process of profound political and social change. At the start of the period, the country was governed by an all-powerful hereditary ruler – the tsar. Russia was in the early stages of industrialisation. Most of the population were peasants who worked in agriculture. Up to 1861 the peasants had been owned by aristocratic landlords or the state. Although this was not the case after 1861, they remained poor and had limited personal freedom. In the late 19th century, several political opposition groups emerged but they had no legal way of showing their grievances against the tsarist system. In 1905 social and economic pressures, along with demands for political change, led to the outbreak of revolution. The government made some concessions, such as allowing the election of a duma or parliament, but it soon recovered its authority.

Just before the First World War, Russia was in the process of limited internal reform. Some historians consider that the regime might have survived if it had not had to cope with the economic and social strains of war. But by 1917, growing hopelessness among the military, as the soldiers faced increasing battlefield losses, along with rising discontent on the home front, led to the fall of the tsarist system. In the February Revolution, the tsarist government was replaced by a Provisional Government that tried to continue fighting the war against Germany. In October this administration was swept away in a second uprising, led by a disciplined revolutionary party, the **Bolsheviks**. By 1924, under the capable and ruthless leadership of Lenin and Trotsky (see Section 3.2), the Bolsheviks had established a one-party government. They had defeated their internal enemies and aimed to transform Russia into a society organised according to a system of **communism**.

KEY TERMS

Bolshevik: A member of the more radical faction of the Russian Social Democrat Party, which seized power in the revolution of October 1917. The party was renamed the Russian Communist Party in 1918, but the term Bolshevik is used throughout this coursebook for simplicity.

Communism: A system of government based on a classless society in which property and wealth are owned by the community rather than by private individuals.

3.1 What challenges faced the tsarist regime between 1881 and 1894?

In the last two decades of the 19th century, Russia still had an old-fashioned, highly authoritarian system of government. This period saw the beginning of some major changes to the Russian economy and society, but Russia remained underdeveloped compared to western European countries.

How Russia was ruled in the period 1881–94

In the middle of the 19th century, Russia was the largest state in Europe, covering over 20 million square km. It had a population of around 70 million, which grew to more than 125 million by the time of the Russian Empire's first and only census in 1897. This empire covered large parts of both Europe and Asia, stretching from the Baltic to the Pacific. It consisted of many different ethnic and religious groups, all with their own very different cultures and traditions. Russia was governed by an all-powerful emperor, the tsar, supported by a landowning noble class, the army and the **Orthodox Church**.

Over 80% of the population were peasants, employed by their landlords or the state. Until 1861, those in the former category were **serfs** who were legally bound to work on the land. They had to pay rent (obrok) or to give labour service (barschina) to their landlords, who owned them like any other form of property. The serfs were under the authority of village councils known as the mir. These were headed by village elders and were responsible for collecting taxes, organising agriculture and selecting men for the army. Peasants had to endure severe restrictions on their personal liberty, with physical punishment allowed, and harsh working and living conditions. State peasants, who worked on the crown lands, had more freedom in their villages, if they paid their taxes.

KEY TERMS

Orthodox Church: The branch of the Christian Church to which most believers in Russia and eastern Europe belong. The Orthodox Church separated from the Roman Catholic Church in the 11th century.

Serfs: A class of unfree agricultural workers who worked on the land and had to obey their landlords.

In 1861, Tsar Alexander II legally gave the serfs their freedom (a process known as **emancipation**). Serfdom was no longer delivering economic growth, and the nobility were falling into debt. The system hindered innovations in agriculture and industry and there was not enough food for the growing population. Poverty and food shortages among the peasantry resulted in growing unrest, causing the tsar to fear for long-term social stability. In addition, the Crimean War of 1853–56 against Britain, France and Turkey (see Chapter 2, Section 2.2) had shown that the army's dependence on recruitment from the peasantry had led to military weakness.

In February 1861, Alexander emancipated all privately owned serfs, and state peasants were freed five years later. Peasants could now own land and enjoy other freedoms, such as the right to marry without permission from their landlords. The nobles had to transfer some of their land to the peasants in return for generous financial compensation from the state. To pay for this, peasants were expected to make '**redemption payments**' over a 49-year period. They could not become legal owners of their land until these payments had been made in full.

In practice, the peasants were not completely free. They still had to obey the mirs that managed the redemption payments and made decisions about the cultivation of the land. The mirs administered justice through their own law courts, separate from the legal system used in the rest of Russia.

KEY TERMS

Emancipation: Freeing someone from being legally controlled by another person.

Redemption payments: In 19th-century Russia, annual fees paid by peasants to the government. These payments were to cover the debt that the government incurred when it compensated the landowners for the abolition of serfdom.

There were fewer urban workers than rural peasants. In the mid-19th century, only 7.8% of Russians lived in cities (the equivalent figure in Britain was 50%). Conditions were as poor for factory workers as for the peasants. Compared with the other great powers–Britain, France and Germany–Russia was economically underdeveloped. This was a consequence of an underdeveloped banking system that was unable to raise enough capital to invest in industry. Communications were also poor, with just 23 600 km of railway track in 1880. As a result, Russia's commercial and professional middle class was much smaller than that of most other European countries.

Autocracy: The role of the tsar, the State Council and key ministries, the army and the Church

Russia was ruled by the tsar, a member of the Romanov family which had governed Russia since the early 17th century.

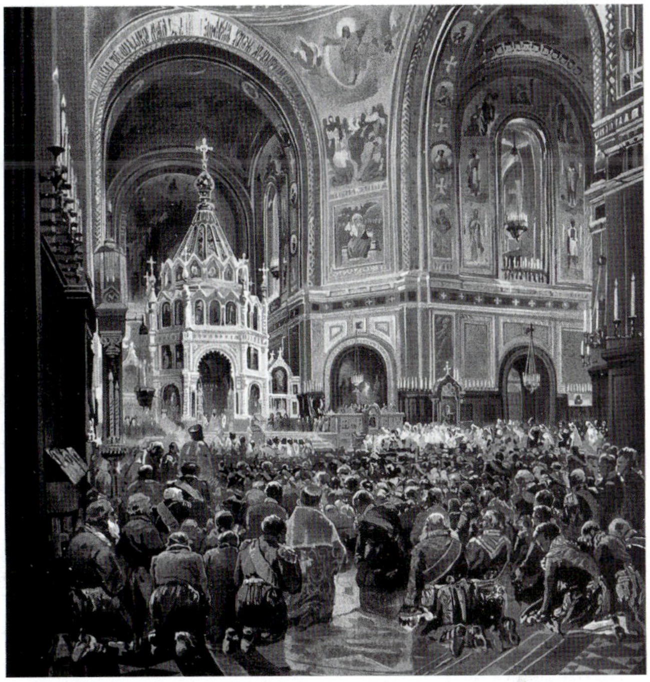

Figure 3.2: The coronation of Tsar Alexander III. What impression of the tsarist system of rule does this painting give?

The tsar, the State Council and the key ministries

The tsar was an autocrat with unlimited power. He governed with the support of the landowning aristocracy. Unlike in western European countries, the nobility did not act as a check on the power of the monarchy. The social position of members of the nobility depended largely on military and civil service to the state. There were no truly independent institutions in Russian society.

Government was centred in the capital, St Petersburg. All the institutions of government were responsible to the tsar, who had ultimate decision-making power. The Imperial Council of State, which consisted of senior government servants, gave advice to the tsar. Most of its members were old men appointed because of their long service to the state, rather than for their strength and skill in managing affairs. The tsar usually appointed them for life, but he could dismiss them when he chose, and he did not have to follow their advice. Members, therefore, usually gave the tsar advice that they knew he would welcome, rather than what they truly believed to be in Russia's best interests.

The Senate was Russia's supreme court up to 1917. The tsar also appointed the Senate's members. The Senate was the final court of appeal and oversaw the operation of the law, but its powers were unclear. Neither the Senate, nor the Council of State, restricted the tsar's personal power.

A Council of Ministers reviewed draft laws and passed them to a further body, the Committee of Ministers, for further examination. The ministers were administrators rather than people who devised policies. A major weakness was that they did not work together in a collective way.

A large and unmanageable bureaucracy linked the central government with the localities. The country was divided into 97 regions. This was too many, even for a state as extensive as Russia. Officials were often unpaid and some resorted to corrupt practices to make money.

The secret police, known as the **Okhrana**, possessed wide powers to enforce the tsar's will.

KEY TERM

Okhrana: The name for the secret police between 1880 and 1917. It had wide powers to carry out surveillance and arrest of political opponents, and to censor publications.

The army

In the 20 years before the accession of Alexander III, the Russian army had undergone many major reforms. In the 1850s, heavy defeat in the Crimean War against France, Britain and Turkey had humiliated Russia and highlighted the need for major improvements.

By 1880, the army numbered around 900 000 men. Officer training had been improved by the creation of army schools that were open to all and modelled on the efficient Prussian system. This marked the beginning of a slow movement away from promotion based on social background and connection, rather than on merit. Military service was made less harsh by reducing the period of compulsory service from 25 years to 15. From 1874 conscription was extended to all classes, with wealthy men banned from paying substitutes to take their place. However, there were reductions in service for the educated, a ruling which obviously discriminated against the peasants. This discrimination caused resentment that led to problems for the government later.

It was remarkable that these reforms were introduced, considering the desire of the nobility to preserve their privileges. The performance of the army improved, although there was still some way to go. By the time of the Russo-Japanese War (1904–05) the empire still lacked an effective general staff. The outbreak of the First World War in 1914 showed that in terms of quality, the Russian army was not equal to that of its German opponents.

The Church

The Orthodox Church was the official religion of the Russian state. It originated in the eastern part of the Roman Empire, was independent of foreign influence and acted as a vital support of the tsarist political system. The tsar appointed the Church's leaders. The Orthodox Church had great influence over society, especially in rural areas, and used its influence to promote a conservative, backward-looking ideology that mistrusted liberalism and change. The chief procurator of the Holy Synod was its leading administrator, and he was a government minister who advised the tsar on Church policy. From 1880 until 1905 this position was held by Konstantin Pobedonestsev, who had earlier served the regime as a legal expert and tutor to Tsar Alexander II's sons. Pobedonestsev's main goal was to preserve political and religious unity. He constantly resisted reform. He was hostile to Jewish people, seeing them as an alien presence within Russia, and to all varieties of Christianity other than the Orthodox faith.

Figure 3.3: The Winter Palace, St Petersburg; the official home of the tsars up to the 1917 revolution.

Reform and repression

Alexander III became tsar in 1881 at the end of a period of great change in Russia. From 1855 to 1881, Tsar Alexander II had introduced some far-reaching reforms while still trying to retain control over Russia as its absolute ruler. Following on from his emancipation of the serfs in 1861, these reforms included:

- **Local government reform:** After emancipation, the nobility no longer controlled the peasants, so their political role was reduced. From 1864, Alexander II filled the gap with the creation of elected councils called **zemstvos**. Their powers and composition reflected the tsar's desire to balance a degree of reform with continued autocratic control. The zemstvos took control of local services such as public health, education and roads, but could not make decisions on the use of imperial taxes.

  From 1870, the towns were given councils known as dumas. These dumas were elected by male property holders and had similar powers to the zemstvos. They did not control the police, which showed that the regime regarded law and order as a key responsibility. Elections and representation were introduced into local government, replacing the old autocratic rule. It gave many people the opportunity to point out local complaints and demand further reform. These changes to local government were very important later. Alexander II started a process that his successors were unable to stop.
- **Reform of the judicial system:** At the beginning of Alexander's reign, the law courts were inefficient and full of poor practice. Officials were badly trained and corrupt, and it was hard for individuals to get justice. Alexander II recognised the need for reform and, from 1864, introduced trial by jury, with public rather than closed trials. The courts became more efficient, and the public respected them more. The courts were also surprisingly independent of the authorities. Judges were better paid, which made them less likely to be tempted by bribes. Alexander also allowed the training of a new generation of lawyers. Although this was not his intention, these lawyers became a focus for the development of liberal ideas.
- **Education reform:** The traditionally strict control of education was relaxed from 1861. Primary schooling had been limited, so it was expanded, and controlled by school boards run by the zemstvos. This was a major step forward as literacy rates were historically low among the peasants, and schools had been provided either by the Church, or the generosity of wealthy individuals. From the 1860s, the state and the Church shared educational provision.

  Universities had greater freedom in how they taught subjects, although the government still set the curriculum. They were also allowed to use books from abroad without censorship, and to give financial assistance to students from low-income backgrounds. With the ending of censorship, students could get hold of and read books that had been banned in the past.

The reign of Alexander II brought many profound changes to Russia. The abolition of serfdom had a great impact on Russian society and the economy. The reforms to local government gave the middle-class greater involvement in the administration of their towns and rural areas. The huge changes in education led to a growth of literacy among the poor (making them more open to radical ideas) and the increased freedom from censorship in universities opened the way to new liberal ideas. The men who led the revolution in 1917 were largely educated in Russian universities in the 1870s and 1880s and their radical messages to the urban and rural working class could be read by the newly literate. Alexander II started a process which ultimately led to the collapse of the tsarist system because his successors could not adapt to deal with that process.

> **KEY TERM**
>
> **Zemstvo:** An elected local assembly set up in rural areas as a consequence of the ending of serfdom.

Alexander III's policies

Alexander III came to power after his father was assassinated by political radicals. This shocking event shaped his 13-year reign. He was completely opposed to reform, believing that it was responsible for undermining autocratic power.

KEY FIGURE

Alexander III (1845–94)

Alexander came to the throne aged 36. His personality was uncomplicated and hard. He had an uncompromising belief in the principles of Orthodoxy, autocracy and Russian nationality. During his relatively short reign he showed no sympathy for ideas of reform.

Alexander III was determined to reverse his father's liberalisation of Russia, as he believed that this liberalisation had led to his father's murder. He was committed to suppressing any opposition to his rule, and to rigidly imposing his three fundamental beliefs on the Russian people. These beliefs were:

- **Autocracy:** The tsar was the supreme authority in all Russia – there was no place for democratic ideas in Russia.
- **Orthodoxy:** The Greek Orthodox Church was the official religion in Russia – there would be little tolerance of religious minorities, such as Jewish people.
- **Nationality:** The desire for independence in countries that had been conquered and taken over by Russia, such as Poland and Kazakhstan, would be stamped out. Citizens of these countries had to become 'Russian' in language, religion, culture and values, and to obey all the rules and laws that came from their Russian masters.

Repression

Advised by the ultra-conservative procurator of the Holy Synod, Konstantin Pobedonestsev, the new tsar introduced a series of repressive policies, starting in 1881 with the Statute of State Security. This law gave the authorities wide-ranging powers to ban meetings and arrest suspects. Alexander set up government-controlled special courts and removed officials who were sympathetic to liberal ideas. The judicial reforms of his predecessor were slowly being undone.

Alexander reduced the power of the zemstvos because he felt that they were becoming too independent and straying from the original intention of improving the efficiency of local administration into trying to influence policy in the locality. From 1889, the administration of peasants would be supervised by government-appointed 'land captains'. The land captains were wealthy individuals, typically drawn from the nobility, with wide powers to overrule local law courts and order punishments. They had to stamp out any sign of local initiative or autonomy (self-government). Universities also came under strict government control. Unrest was dealt with firmly. When a plot against Alexander was uncovered in 1887, the ringleaders were executed. Among them was the elder brother of the future revolutionary leader **Vladimir Ilyich Lenin**.

KEY FIGURE

Vladimir Ilyich Lenin (1870–1924)

Lenin came from a middle-class family. He was regarded as politically dangerous from the age of 17, when his older brother was executed for involvement in an assassination plot against Alexander III. Lenin was first sentenced to exile in Siberia and then lived in western Europe. He returned to Russia two months after the 1917 February Revolution. He opposed the Provisional Government, which replaced Tsar Nicholas II, and played a decisive role in the October Revolution of 1917, which brought the Bolsheviks (communists) to power. He governed Russia until his death in 1924.

Russification

In partnership with his repressive policies, Alexander worked hard to impose the Russian language and culture, and the Orthodox religion, on the empire's diverse peoples. Russian became the country's official first language and was imposed in schools attended by Baltic Germans, Poles, Finns and other national minorities.

Alexander's policy of 'Russification' alienated the different ethnic groups by treating them as second-class citizens and showing hostility to their national traditions. This was later very damaging to the tsarist system.

When the revolution happened in 1917, many of the minorities either supported the revolutionaries or failed to support a tsar whose predecessors had done so much to destroy their language and culture.

Russia's five million Jewish people endured particularly harsh persecution. They were blamed for Russia's troubles and subjected to periodic **pogroms**. Many Jews fled to western Europe or the United States. Those who stayed were often drawn into revolutionary activity.

> **KEY TERM**
>
> **Pogroms:** Outbreaks of mob violence against Jewish people, often approved by the authorities.

The development of the Russian economy in the period 1881–94

In the latter part of the 19th century Russia's economy slowly began to modernise. However, Russia remained primarily an agricultural country that was more backward than other great European powers. There was limited industrial development.

Economic developments

In general, the reign of Alexander III was one of reaction and repression, dominated by conservative ministers and a tsar determined to stamp out any sign of liberalism and undo all the reforming work of Alexander II. However, there was one important exception. This was the work of Nikolai von Bunge (1823–95), who was appointed finance minister in 1881 and remained in office until 1886. He was a professor of economics and had been heavily involved in many of the reforms of the previous reign, especially the emancipation of the serfs. He had gained a reputation as an effective managerial moderniser.

Bunge's policies

Bunge introduced significant reforms between 1881 and 1886, including:

- He developed a safe, secure banking system at both the local and national level. Such a system was essential for economic development.
- He created widely available and secure savings banks, available to all classes and incomes. Those savings could provide investment for agricultural improvement and new industries.
- He created an effective system of credit. He ensured that people who wanted to borrow money at a realistic level of interest could easily find capital to invest in industry or agricultural improvement.
- He created the Peasants' Land Bank. This was designed to enable any enterprising newly emancipated peasants to buy their own land, increase agricultural productivity and eliminate the many weaknesses in the outdated agricultural system existing in Russia.
- He altered the income tax system to make it more progressive and introducing import duties to help develop Russia's growing metal industries. He also reduced the direct tax on the peasantry.

Bunge originated genuinely liberal reforms which paved the way for Witte's reforms of the 1890s (see Section 3.2), and also helped to lay a firm basis for Russia's growing industrialisation. He encouraged railway building and introduced laws to improve factory working conditions and reduce child labour. However, being the only liberal in a very conservative administration, he was increasingly marginalised by the forces of repression and had to resign in 1886. He left an important legacy, giving the Russian economy secure foundations on which his successors could build.

Industrialisation

It was expected that emancipation would lead to a more productive agricultural sector to generate surplus capital (wealth) that could be used to finance industrialisation. In practice, however, although some growth occurred, Russia remained backward in relation to rival countries. This was partly because Russian agriculture continued to perform badly.

Development of the Russian rail network helped industrial growth. By 1890 Russia had 31 000 km of rail track. This was impressive and made possible because the government supported railway builders who ran into financial difficulties, and compensated investors who lost money investing in new railways. Railway growth enabled the movement of bulky goods, such as coal and iron ore, in large quantities. But Russia's vast size meant that the railways were still thinly spread throughout the country.

Bunge's work had laid a good foundation for rapid Russian industrial expansion towards the end of Alexander III's reign. Production of steel and iron increased by 500% between 1887 and 1900, as did oil output, and the coal mined increased by 300%. This, together with the improved banking and credit system, meant increased foreign investment in Russian heavy industry, particularly from France. This led to even more rapid industrial expansion after 1900.

Economic problems including taxation and famines

The condition of the peasantry was perhaps Russia's most serious problem towards the end of the 19th century. Famines were frequent and poor transport infrastructure prevented the government from moving food from places where it was plentiful to places where it was lacking. The worst famine was in 1891–92, when up to 400 000 people died. It was caused by prolonged dry weather, leading to a bad harvest, and worsened by the government's slowness to ban grain exports.

There were some attempts at reform. In 1883, the Peasants' Land Bank was founded to provide money for local communities and individual peasants to buy land. In response to the famine of 1891–92, Alexander III established a ministry of agriculture to encourage better farming methods, but this did not have much effect. Officials often blamed problems on the laziness and alcoholism of the peasants and saw everything from a law-and-order perspective. The fundamental problems of rural poverty and low production levels were not tackled.

ACTIVITY 3.1

Figure 3.4: *The Return Journey* by Illarion Pryanishnikov (1883).

Look at the painting in Figure 3.4, depicting peasants returning home from market. The artist belonged to a group of painters known as the Peredvishniks. These painters were active in the 1870s and 1880s. They aimed to represent the lives of ordinary Russian people in a realistic manner.

Do paintings like this have value for someone studying Russia in this period? How could you judge the accuracy of the painting?

Peasants were encouraged to move from the west of Russia to Siberia, where land was plentiful, but natural conditions in Siberia were too harsh for successful agriculture. Redemption payments were not cancelled until 1905 and even then the cancellation made little difference to the peasants. The main problem was that, despite its size and potential, Russia could not generate enough agriculturally to feed its population adequately. Neither the peasantry nor the landowners were interested in modernising to improve output.

Profits from grain exports did not benefit the peasantry. The expanded railway system, along with increased industry, did help Russia to export more wheat, which helped foreign trade – but the money was not equally shared.

The central government was dominated by landowners, who did not impose a fair level of taxation on the Russian ruling class. The government put less tax on income and land than on commodities and food (which were taxed through indirect taxes), and this system disadvantaged the peasants and the poor who lived in towns. The system for collecting taxes was inefficient and corruptible, with most taxes disappearing into the pockets of tax collectors and other middlemen before they could reach the central government.

The regime also spent its money unwisely. Funds were given generously to the army and to the police, but little was spent on improving the economy. The result was that the general Russian populace became increasingly alienated from the government and their landlords, although it seems that most peasants continued to believe in the tsar (the 'little father') as an individual. Their dislike of government officials, who demanded taxes and forced service from them, deepened over time.

Figure 3.5: Peasants seeking help from their priest during a famine – an illustration from a British newspaper, 1891. What does this picture suggest about the nature of Russian society and the influence of the Orthodox Church in this period?

Social change in the period 1881–94

Although Russia remained a mainly peasant society, towards the end of the 19th century there was some urban growth and the beginning of a small but politically significant middle class.

Social development

Russia's social structure remained relatively unchanged throughout this period. The only national census to take place under the tsars was held in 1897. Look at Table 3.1 to see the data the census gave for different classes as a percentage of the population.

Social class	Percentage of the Russian population
Ruling class (tsar, court and government)	0.5
Upper class (nobility, higher clergy, military officers)	12.0
Middle classes (merchants, factory owners, bankers)	1.5
Working classes (factory workers, small traders)	4.0
Peasants (agricultural workers)	82.0

Table 3.1: Census figures showing different groups in Russia, 1897.

Urban growth

As Table 3.1 shows, Russia remained a mainly agricultural society. Urban growth was uneven across the country. The main centres were St Petersburg, Moscow and other parts of western Russia, Warsaw in Russian Poland, Kiev (Kyiv) in Ukraine, and the Baltic regions. But a significant minority of peasants were moving to the cities to find jobs in the manufacturing industry. There were about 1.4 million factory workers by the early 1890s. The main industries were textiles, steel and coal mining.

Living and working conditions for the urban workforce were poor, although there was some regulation of working hours, child labour and factory safety from 1882. Working-class housing was poor quality, and overcrowding and lack of sanitation led to the spread of diseases such as cholera. Even St Petersburg, with 1.25 million citizens by the turn of the century, did not have a sewerage system until 1911. Poor transport links meant that many factory workers lived in barrack blocks close to their workplace. Accommodation was usually basic and unhygienic. Low wages and insecure employment added to the misery of daily life for the urban workers. The lack of strong trade unions to protect workers helped to keep living standards low. These conditions led to the growth of revolutionary feeling.

Development of the middle class

The middle class consisted of business owners, merchants and professional people such as doctors, lawyers, managers, bureaucrats and rural landowners with small estates. This class remained very small by European standards. It grew in importance as the power and influence of the nobility declined, in the decades after the emancipation of the serfs. However, some historians argue that it is not possible to speak of a unified middle class with an identity of its own. There was not much agreement between the officials, who remained loyal to the tsarist system, and the educated, liberal-minded intellectuals. It was the liberal-minded intellectuals who later challenged the autocratic tsarist political system in the early 20th century.

The role of opposition

Opposition to tsarist autocracy took many forms. However, opposition was not united. Some thinkers wished for an economic and social revolution to bring about a more equal society. Other thinkers were influenced by liberal ideas of reform and wanted greater freedom and regional autonomy in legal ways. There was a split between Slavophiles, who wanted reform to be influenced by the values of traditional Russian peasant society, and westernisers, who argued that Russia was culturally isolated and backward, and that Russians should adopt western liberal ideas. The different views about how to respond to the political system, and what should replace it, weakened the opposition.

The development of opposition from the peasants and urban workers

Opposition grew slowly among the peasants. It took many different forms and had many different causes. Some peasants were bitter about the terms imposed on them by emancipation. Many hated the compulsory conscription for the army. Deeply conservative peasants disliked attempts to reform agricultural processes and improve productivity. There was resentment of the few who managed to increase their farms and start to make large profits. Low levels of literacy weakened the ability of opposition thinkers to communicate their ideas and build a mass following. The conservative Church was an

ACTIVITY 3.2

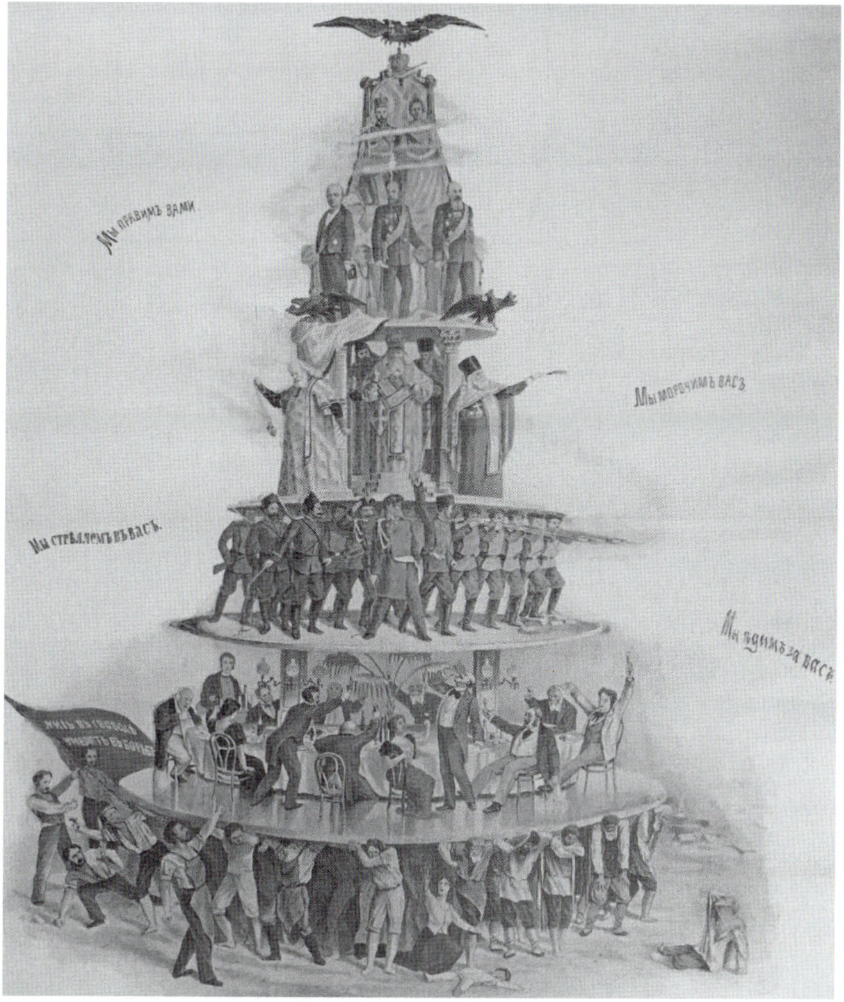

Look at the cartoon in Figure 3.6. The cartoon was drawn in 1901 by a Russian artist who opposed the tsarist system. It shows how Russian society was dependent on the labour of the workers. The workers are at the base of the pyramid. The tsar and tsarina are on the top level.

a Can you identify the different social groups depicted?

b How does the artist convey his message in the way he has drawn the cartoon?

Figure 3.6: Cartoon *Social Pyramid* (1901) by Nicolas Lokhoff.

important influence in peasants' lives and it preached loyalty to the tsar and opposition to any reformers or radicals. Most peasants were not influenced by ideology but expressed discontent with their physical conditions through occasional rioting and setting fire to landowners' property.

The beginning of industrialisation led to the formation of illegal trade unions among factory workers. In January 1885, 8 000 workers at the Morozov textile factory in Moscow went on strike in protest at wage cuts and fines imposed by the employers. Troops were called in to suppress the workers and the ringleaders were tried and exiled. The government did, however, pass a law to stop the fining of workers in 1886. Lenin later used the strike as an example of what organised labour could achieve. Further strikes occurred ten years later but a large-scale organised urban working-class movement did not emerge in this period. Bunge's suggestions about good working conditions were largely ignored so the bad working conditions, poor wages and often dreadful living conditions proved damaging to tsarism in the long run. Later, the revolutionary leaders of 1917 gained their most enthusiastic supporters from an angry urban working class, who went on to bring down the tsarist regime.

Political opposition

Inevitably, Alexander's brutal approach to the Russian people, liberals, religious minorities and the conquered subject nations led to strong opposition, which was difficult to control, and he had to use many resources to impose his principles on Russia.

The temporary ending of censorship at universities under Alexander II had allowed many students to study formerly banned books about liberalism and **socialism**. The ideas of liberal democracy appealed to many of the middle and upper classes, while the writings of socialist, communist and anarchist thinkers appealed to people who wanted much more radical change. All the opponents of tsarism who emerged after 1900 were influenced by these new (to Russia) ideas. Just as many French Revolutionary leaders were strongly influenced by the ideas of the Enlightenment thinkers of the 18th century, the leaders of the Russian Revolution gained many of their ideas while reading and arguing as students in the 1870s and early 1880s.

In addition, the zemstvos had introduced elections and representation in Russia, and many people who demanded change after 1900 had learned about organising elections and working together to achieve solutions to their grievances in zemstvo meetings during Alexander II's reign. Alexander II had never intended to undermine tsarism, but his attempts to reform proved important to its downfall.

KEY TERM

Socialism: A system in which society is equal, based on cooperation, rather than on the capitalist concept of competition.

The growth of Marxism

The ideas of the German socialist thinker, Karl Marx (1818–83), circulated among Russian intellectuals in this period. Marx argued that:

- The course of history was determined by economic forces.
- In primitive societies people did not own property. Primitive ways of living had been replaced by private property ownership.

Figure 3.7: The assassination of Alexander II by terrorists from an opposition group known as 'People's Will', March 1881. How accurate do you think this engraving is? How can we tell?

- The economy of the Middle Ages was based on the ownership of land by the aristocracy (feudalism). This system had been replaced by capitalism.
- Establishment of the capitalist system had given power to the moneyed middle class, or **bourgeoisie**.
- Under capitalism, workers were treated like machines and exploited for the profit of the bourgeoisie.

Marx called for a revolution by the lower classes–the **proletariat**–to overthrow the capitalist system. He claimed that a dictatorship of the proletariat would lead to a classless society, national boundaries would disappear and state governments that suppressed workers would no longer exist.

KEY TERMS

Bourgeoisie: The middle class, mainly business people who owned the means of production in capitalist society, such as factories.

Proletariat: The urban, industrial working class. They generally had no savings or property, and their only source of income was their own labour.

In the period between 1881 and 1894 there was a rapid spread of increasingly radical and revolutionary ideas in Russia, including Marxist ideas. These ideas spread partly as a reaction to the conservative repression of Alexander III and partly as a result of the relaxation of censorship and expansion of higher education under Alexander II. As with the French revolutionaries, there were great differences of opinion about the revolutionaries' objectives and the methods they should use to achieve them.

People influenced by the ideas of Marx held sharp divisions of opinion. Marx was a German academic living in London who knew little about Russia, so when people tried to apply his ideas to conditions in Russia they interpreted these ideas differently. Some Marxist thinkers believed that a revolution would emerge from the industrial workers and overthrow the tsarist regime, even though the industrial workers were a tiny minority at the time. Others believed that the educated middle class would lead the revolution and bring communism to Russia. There were arguments about the role the large rural peasantry might play in a future revolution. There were debates about the need for violence – would another Terror like that of the French Revolution be required? There were also ideas put forward by anarchists who strongly disliked the Marxists, thinking that they were too authoritarian.

The only ideas that all these thinkers had in common were a hatred of the tsarist system and hostility towards cooperating with middle-class liberals who wanted a liberal democracy. These divisions continued in the following reign and played a significant part in events after 1900.

KEY CONCEPT 3.1

Change and continuity

Review the topic up to this point. How much change was there between 1881 and 1894 in these four key areas?

- the nature of the Russian political system
- opposition to the tsarist system
- economic development
- the structure of society.

Overall, was there more continuity or change across the period? Present your findings as a table.

Continuity across the period	Change across the period

3.2 What were the causes and outcomes of the 1905 Revolution up to 1914?

The 1905 Revolution was a series of protests, strikes, mutinies and other events, involving a range of social groups across the Russian Empire. It was a spontaneous outbreak of popular discontent, which was not coordinated by a single revolutionary party or group. Tsar Nicholas II was forced to introduce political changes in response, although he later recovered control of the country. The revolution was a warning of what could happen. It has been regarded by some historians as a dress-rehearsal for the more serious uprisings of 1917.

The causes of the 1905 Revolution

The 1905 Revolution was caused by a combination of pressure for political change and the growing discontent of the urban and rural poor with their conditions of life.

Discontent with the regime of Nicholas II

Nicholas II became tsar on the death of Alexander III in November 1894, announcing, 'I shall maintain the principle of autocracy just as firmly as did my unforgettable father'. Nicholas kept his promise throughout his reign, resisting change however much circumstances within Russia altered. He kept the structures of government passed on to him by his father.

KEY FIGURE

Tsar Nicholas II (1894–1917)

Nicholas II was the last tsar, reigning from 1894 to 1917, when he was forced to resign in the wake of the February Revolution. He was no less committed to autocracy than his father but less intelligent and a far less commanding figure. After his abdication from the throne, he and his family were held prisoner by the Bolsheviks and murdered in July 1918.

The new tsar was disastrously out of touch with the feelings of his subjects. This impression was unfortunately established early in his reign, with his reaction to the 'Khodynka tragedy', which occurred during the festivities of his coronation in May 1896. When rumours spread that there was not enough food and drink for everyone in the crowd, the crowd stampeded. The authorities were unable to control the situation – more than 1300 people were crushed to death and a similar number injured. Although Nicholas shared the sense of shock which followed this event, he was insensitive enough to attend a celebratory ball the same evening.

Nicholas' only son, Alexei, suffered from the blood disorder haemophilia (meaning that even a slight injury could cause him to bleed severely), and it was doubtful that he would survive into adulthood. This situation left uncertainties over the succession to the throne and played a significant part in the instability of Nicholas' regime.

Nicholas was a kind man on a personal level, devoted to his wife and children. He possessed some characteristics which might have made him a respected nobleman but he lacked many of the qualities required in an effective ruler. He was also a committed **anti-Semite**. He could be swayed easily by advice, usually from courtiers who opposed reforms. He typically chose his ministers because of their social position rather than for their abilities. These men competed for the attention of the tsar rather than cooperating with each other or offering objective advice. Nicholas focused on the detail of day-to-day administration, and found it hard to delegate even unimportant tasks, which meant that he failed to grasp larger issues. In short, he claimed the power of an autocrat without possessing the personality needed for the role.

KEY TERM

Anti-Semite: Someone who exhibits hostility towards Jewish people (known as anti-Semitism).

Resentment caused by the lack of political reform

By 1905 there was growing nationalist unrest among racial groups such as the Finns, Baltic peoples, Armenians and Georgians, who resented the policy of Russification. Other groups within the empire wanted a more democratic form of government. Members of the educated middle classes wanted political change, although, as we have seen, they were divided, supporting various forms of liberalism and socialism. Their fundamental objection was to the autocratic nature of Nicholas II's rule. It distanced him from the population and made the situation worse. Supporters of political reform faced the brutal workings of the tsarist police state. The lack of political reform under Nicholas II was a key cause of the 1905 Revolution.

Political opposition

By the end of the 19th century, liberals in Russia were pressing for constitutional political change, and increased civil liberties, similar to those enjoyed in western European states. The liberals had a power base in the zemstvos and by 1904 had formed an organisation known as the Union of Liberation. They were not very powerful, however, because they drew their support mainly from the relatively small middle class and did not appeal to the peasants. There were no official liberal parties until the outbreak of the 1905 Revolution, when the political climate became slightly more favourable to their activities. The main liberal party in 1905 was known as the Kadets (or the Constitutional Democrats). This party campaigned for a reformed monarchy, with limitations on its power.

The oppressive nature of the tsarist political system meant that opposition tended to be driven underground. Critics of the government could not find legal opportunities to express their views. Consequently, they often turned to political violence. It was a common saying among educated foreign observers of Russia in the 19th century that its political system consisted of 'autocracy tempered [moderated] by assassination'.

The Socialist Revolutionaries

One radical political group was the Socialist Revolutionaries (SRs), founded in 1901. The group emerged from a populist movement which had first appeared in the reign of Alexander II after the emancipation of the serfs. The main aim of its members was the confiscation of land and its redistribution to the peasants and this won them mass support in the countryside. The Socialist Revolutionaries differed over tactics. One wing of the group supported violence and carried out many political assassinations in the years leading up to the 1905 Revolution, including the assassination of the unpopular minister of the interior, Vyacheslav von Plehve. An opposing faction was also committed to revolution but was prepared to work with other parties. From 1906 the Socialist Revolutionaries were a divided party.

The Social Democrats

In the long run, the most important opposition group was the All-Russian Social Democratic Labour Party, founded in 1898. The Social Democrats (SDs) were a Marxist party.

The industrial growth of the 1890s made Marxist ideas appealing to many revolutionaries who wanted to transform Russian society. The key figure in the early years was Georgi Plekhanov, who aimed to build a broad alliance of pro-reform, anti-tsarist activists although he was in exile until the February 1917 Revolution. He was challenged by Vladimir Ilyich Lenin (see Section 3.1), who argued that only a highly centralised, disciplined revolutionary party could successfully lead a revolution in an autocratic state like Russia.

The second congress of the Social Democrats met in London in 1903. Lenin wanted to restrict membership of the party to those people who were active in the cause of revolution and socialism. These people would necessarily be a minority. Lenin wanted a revolution in Russia to defeat tsarism. **Leon Trotsky** and Julius Martov (a Russian politician who was exiled for his views on reform) disagreed with these steps. Trotsky and Martov believed that revolutionary success depended on a wider, rather than a more restricted membership. They took the longer-term view of Marxism: that capitalism had to collapse from within before communism could triumph. The deciding vote at the congress was very close, but Lenin's group won by two votes. This group took the name Bolshevik (a word meaning 'the majority'). Martov's group, the minority, became the Mensheviks. The Mensheviks maintained a separate organisation of their own after this split in the Social Democrat Party. At this stage, Trotsky belonged to the Mensheviks.

The various revolutionary groups were not the main cause of the 1905 Revolution. The disturbances which led to revolution were largely unplanned, and mishandling of the crisis by the authorities made it more serious. The Bolsheviks and the Mensheviks were, therefore, not expecting this revolution to happen. Nevertheless, when unrest broke out, Trotsky and other Mensheviks and radicals tried to promote strikes and other workers' actions. In fact, in 1905, Lenin was the right man in the wrong place. He was in exile and returned to Russia 11 months after the revolution broke out – too late to play an effective part.

KEY FIGURE

Leon Trotsky (1879–1940)

Trotsky came from a prosperous Jewish Ukrainian family. As a young man, he sided with the Menshevik faction of the Social Democrat Party. In the 1905 Revolution, he organised workers in St Petersburg. He was sentenced to internal exile but escaped abroad. In 1917, he joined the Bolsheviks and played a key role in their seizure of power, later organising the Red Army. After Lenin died in 1924, Trotsky lost a power struggle with Stalin. He was expelled from the party and exiled from Russia. He was assassinated in Mexico in 1940 by an agent sent by Stalin.

Economic problems

The 1905 Revolution was the culmination of years of discontent caused by several factors. These factors were primarily economic.

Bad harvests

A major cause of the revolution was the poor economic condition of the peasantry, who had seen little improvement in their lives following emancipation. Between 1891 and 1901 there were several bad harvests. Inequality in the distribution of land made the situation worse for poorer peasants. Lack of land meant that they had no way of improving their conditions. Rapid population growth further reduced the amount of land available, and so did the practice of dividing land among the next generation after a person died. Peasants who lacked sufficient food for themselves were also expected to produce food to export, and to do this with outdated farming methods.

Taxation

The peasants continued to bear the burden of taxation. They were still expected to make redemption payments in return for the land granted to them after emancipation. Another grievance was the government's decision in 1894 to create a state monopoly (total control) of vodka production and sales. The monopoly became a major source of government revenue, leading to widespread peasant unrest. Also, despite Alexander II's reduction of the length of time that peasants had to serve in the army, compulsory military service continued to be a major grievance. In 1903–04, the so-called 'Years of the Red Cockerel', peasants responded to their financial hardship by seizing land and attacking warehouses.

Unemployment

There was an economic recession in the early years of the 20th century that resulted in high rates of unemployment among the industrial working class. The St Petersburg metal-working industry, for example, experienced a fall in orders, leading to job losses. Strikes also contributed to the rise of unemployment. Baku, the centre of the oil industry in the Caucasus, was hit by a strike in 1903, when workers were sacked and a period of growth came to an end.

Meanwhile, real wages declined in this period by an estimated 20%. Workers had virtually no employment rights. Trade unions were banned, and the police cracked down on protests. Urban overcrowding, bad housing and poor working conditions were a dangerous combination.

Witte's policies

Sergei Witte was minister of finance from 1892 to 1903. Witte believed that the answer to Russia's problems lay in foreign loans and foreign exports. He realised that the country was rich in raw materials, but it needed industrial growth to be able to compete with the more economically advanced nations of the West. Modernisation was also required to increase the country's military strength.

Russia, therefore, needed large-scale investment to promote industrialisation, and Witte was convinced that the power of the state must be used to drive the growth of capitalism. He brought in engineers and managers from western countries to advise the government on how to go about this.

KEY FIGURE

Sergei Witte (1849–1915)

Witte was one of the few officials in Nicholas II's government who supported reform. As minister of finance from 1892 to 1903, Witte believed that rapid industrialisation was the solution to the country's economic problems. Nicholas II never fully supported Witte's ideas and dismissed him, though he recalled him briefly as prime minister after the 1905 Revolution.

Witte increased taxes and raised money abroad by giving investors high rates of interest. He imposed tariffs on imports to protect Russian industries, and increased the value of the Russian currency, the rouble, by linking it to the **gold standard** in 1897. The aim of this step was to increase the confidence of foreign investors in the currency – though it also raised the cost of imports.

KEY TERM

Gold standard: An international monetary system in which the value of a country's currency was linked directly to a fixed quantity of gold. The system aimed to give long-term price stability.

Witte was particularly interested in railways, having been director of the state rail network before becoming finance minister. The length of railway lines almost doubled during his term of office, opening up previously inaccessible parts of the country to economic development. The most high-profile development was the Trans-Siberian Railway, which eventually linked Moscow with Vladivostok on Russia's eastern coast, although sections of it remained incomplete between 1900 and 1910. These policies led to impressive increases in industrial growth, with coal production in southern Russia more than trebling. Russia became the world's fourth-largest producer of steel and the second-largest producer of petroleum. One historian called this the 'great spurt'.

However, Witte's policies also caused problems. Twice as much was spent on repaying the foreign loans as was spent on education. Taxes were increased to repay the loans, and this affected the peasants most severely. Economic growth was distorted because Witte focused on heavy industry and neglected agriculture and industries such as light engineering and textiles. Railway expansion was impressive, but it still lagged behind Russia's most important European rival, Germany. By the early 1900s, Germany had almost 64 000 km of rail line, compared to less than 50 000 km constructed across Russia's much larger land area. Reliance on imported technological expertise discouraged the development of Russian talent.

Members of the court and other nobility despised Witte and considered his ideas dangerous. They were suspicious of his support for rapid industrialisation, which they feared would destabilise rural society. Many members of the upper class also disliked him for having married a divorced Jewish woman. After Witte was dismissed, Nicholas recalled him briefly as prime minister at a time of crisis after the 1905 Revolution, mostly to negotiate a loan from France. His support for reforms was still unpopular with influential courtiers and Nicholas dismissed him again as soon as the loan was secured.

During Witte's period as finance minister, the country's national debt increased and the standard of living of most the population declined. At the turn of the century, these problems were certainly serious, but there was no indication that they would be fatal for Nicholas II. The national situation was no worse than it had been for many years, and most people believed that the tsarist government could survive if it did not have to face a major crisis such as a foreign war.

Defeat in the Russo-Japanese War

Defeat in the Russo-Japanese War of 1904–05 contributed to the outbreak of revolution because it gave the impression that the tsarist government was

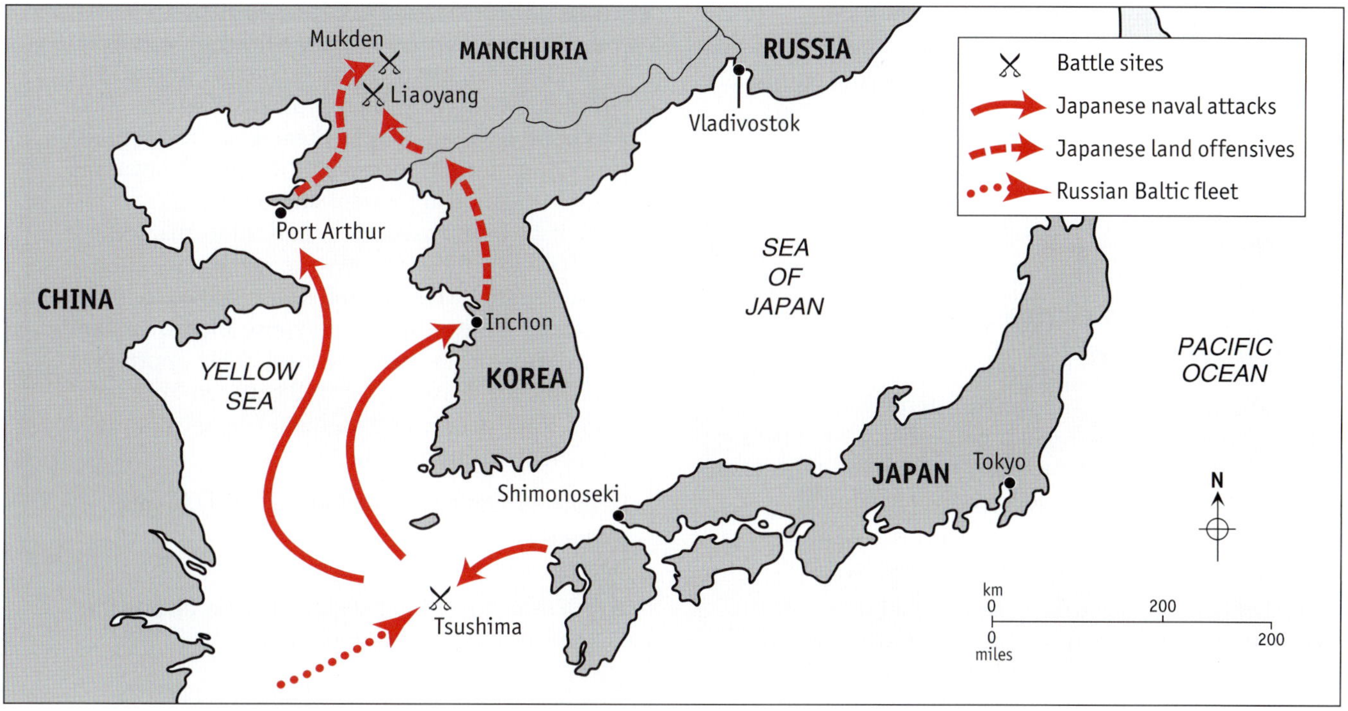

Figure 3.8: A map showing the progress of the Russo-Japanese War, 1904–05.

incompetent and vulnerable to challenges by hostile foreign powers. It was a serious blow to the prestige of the regime and fuelled criticism by liberals who wanted a reformed, more efficient monarchy.

The war arose from the weakness of China at the start of the 20th century. China was suffering from internal conflict and poor government. Both Japan and Russia saw the possibility of expanding their influence in Manchuria, eastern China, and Korea. Port Arthur in Manchuria offered Russia an ice-free harbour, which would be useful because its other ports were either in the Arctic north or on the Black Sea, with difficult access to other oceans. Japan suggested that Russia could take control of Manchuria if Japan itself could have Korea. However, these negotiations broke down, and war broke out in 1904, after Japan attacked Port Arthur. During the Russo-Japanese War, the poor quality of the Russian navy became clear when ships had to be sent from the Baltic to confront the Japanese navy. The fleet took eight months to arrive, and then suffered a devastating defeat at the Battle of Tsushima in May 1905. In a stunning victory for the Japanese, two-thirds of the Russian fleet was destroyed, demoralising the surviving Russian sailors.

The Russian army was larger than the Japanese army but inferior in quality. It failed to prevent the capture of Mukden, the capital of Manchuria. With the Trans-Siberian railway not yet complete, the Russian government struggled to transport troops and equipment from western Russia to the battle zone. Ultimately, Russia had to agree a humiliating peace in the Treaty of Portsmouth, arranged by the United States, in 1905. Japan was left as the dominant power in Korea and Manchuria.

The events and consequences of the 1905 Revolution

The 1905 Revolution saw a wave of unrest across the Russian countryside and major cities. The government was initially taken by surprise and made some concessions to the revolutionaries, but soon recovered control.

'Bloody Sunday', strikes and unrest in 1905

In December 1904, a strike began at the Putilov steel works in St Petersburg in protest at the dismissal of four workers. This soon spread to other workplaces. In January 1905, a priest named Father Gapon led a non-violent march to the tsar's Winter Palace in St Petersburg, to petition him for an assembly elected by universal suffrage. The crowd also called for basic civil liberties, land reform, fairer taxes and a voice for workers in the running of factories. The crowd was dispersed violently by Cossack soldiers. The Cossacks came from the Volga region of Russia and were known for their extreme loyalty to the tsar. An estimated 130 people were killed and hundreds more injured. The incident became known as 'Bloody Sunday'. Up to this point, many workers had described the tsar as their 'little father', and seen him as different from the unfeeling, unpopular state bureaucracy. They believed that the tsar did not know of their terrible conditions. Many of the marchers had carried images of Nicholas. Now he was widely blamed for the repression, even though he was not present at the time. The marchers were unarmed, and they had not intended to behave in a revolutionary manner, but their harsh treatment stimulated other popular outbreaks. Strikes began in Moscow and rapidly spread to other cities as industrial workers organised themselves into trade unions. In March the government closed higher education institutions, which had the unintended effect of encouraging students to join the striking workers. A railway strike in October turned into a general strike in Moscow and St Petersburg. In total an estimated 800 000 workers went on strike.

ACTIVITY 3.3

Sire, here are many thousands of us, and all are human beings only in appearance. In reality in us, as in all Russian people, there is not recognised any human right, not even the right of speaking, thinking, meeting, discussing our needs …
We have been enslaved … under the auspices of YOUR officials … We are seeking here the last salvation. Do not refuse assistance to Your people … Give their destiny into their own hands. Cast away from them the intolerable oppression of officials. Destroy the wall between Yourself and Your people and let them rule the country together with Yourself.

From the petition of the crowd on Bloody Sunday, January 1905.

a What does this extract suggest about the intentions of the marchers?

b Does its language indicate a desire to overthrow the tsarist system of government, or just to make it work more fairly?

ACTIVITY 3.4

Figure 3.9: A painting by Ivan Vladimirov showing the 'Bloody Sunday' shooting of workers in front of the Winter Palace, St Petersburg, 9 January 1905.

Look at the painting in Figure 3.9. How reliable do you think this painting is? What would you need to know about the artist and the circumstances in which the painting was made to assess its value to historians?

In an important development, workers' committees known as **soviets** were set up in factories in St Petersburg and Moscow. They demanded improved conditions for workers and became a focus for wider political agitation. Sailors on the battleship *Potemkin* mutinied, and the government feared more unrest among sailors and soldiers. Middle-class liberals, organised as the Kadets (or Constitutional Democrats), wanted the tsar's powers to be limited by an elected assembly. They attempted to form a 'Union of Unions', linking up with workers and peasants to demand further political change. Peasants refused to pay rent and attacked the property of the aristocracy, burning 3000 manor houses in the summer of 1905.

However, the revolutionaries were largely disorganised, with no central coordination, and protests were geographically scattered across the empire. Few determined revolutionaries were involved in the protests. Fortunately for the tsar, the army remained loyal to him.

KEY TERM

Soviets: Workers' councils, which first appeared in industrial cities in 1905. They played an important part in the October 1917 Revolution.

The reactions of Nicholas II to the 1905 Revolution

As unrest continued, Nicholas II was reluctantly persuaded to make concessions to the masses. He did this on the advice of Witte, who had been recalled as prime minister. The document in which Nicholas promised reform was called the October Manifesto.

The October Manifesto and the formation of the Duma

The October Manifesto promised free speech, voting rights for those who had previously been denied an opportunity to participate in politics, and an elected assembly called the Duma (from the Russian word 'dumat', which means 'to think'). The Duma would be the lower chamber of a parliament consisting of around 500 members (the tsar's State Council would be the upper chamber). The Duma's agreement would be needed before any laws could be passed. Nicholas II initially promised greater liberties and said that the Duma would have the power to act to uphold these liberties. However, he did not allow the Duma to elect government ministers or hold them to account, and he claimed the right to dissolve it.

Reaction to the October Manifesto was divided. Many of the rebels felt that their voices had been heard, and that the landowners would have to accept their demands. Moderate liberals, who became known as 'Octobrists', were pacified by the introduction of the Duma. They were drawn mainly from the landowning and business classes and had been alarmed by the violence of working-class protests. They were relieved to have order restored. In November, peasant unrest was calmed by an announcement that redemption payments would be phased out.

However, a minority of extreme revolutionaries (including the Bolsheviks) felt that the manifesto did not go far enough in addressing the grievances of the Russian people. There was some armed resistance, but the tsar's soldiers suppressed this. It seemed, for a time, that stability would return to Russia.

Reasons for the survival of the tsarist regime

The tsarist regime survived through a combination of its own willingness to fight back against the revolution, after initially making concessions, and the weaknesses of the opposition.

The Fundamental Laws and the Dumas

Nicholas II's insincerity in presenting the October Manifesto soon became apparent. He proved unwilling to enforce the reforms that he had promised, and in April 1906 he issued the Fundamental Laws, which asserted his full autocratic powers. The first statement of the Fundamental Laws was that 'supreme autocratic power belongs to the tsar'. This denied the hopes of those who saw the Duma as a means of bringing more representative government to Russia. The tsar could introduce laws and veto those passed by the Duma. Furthermore, the elected Duma would be balanced by the State Council, most of whose members would be appointed by the tsar. Ministers were still appointed by the tsar, who also controlled military and foreign affairs. The Duma had no way of enforcing its decisions.

ACTIVITY 3.5

8 The initiative in all branches of legislation belongs to the Tsar. Solely on his initiative may the Fundamental Laws of the Empire be subjected to a revision in the Council of the Empire and the Imperial Duma.

9 The Tsar approves of the laws, and without his approval no law can come into existence.

10 All governmental powers in their widest extent throughout the whole Russian Empire are vested in the Tsar.

From the Fundamental Laws of the Russian Empire, 23 April 1906.

a How does this extract conflict with the October Manifesto?

b How would you expect the reformers in Russia to react to this document?

Some historians have argued that Nicholas II missed an opportunity in 1906 to carry through the reforms that would have made Russia a more modern and stable country. However, autocratic rulers rarely prove willing to surrender any of their power, and Nicholas II was particularly reactionary. It soon became apparent that the reforms lacked substance. The factors that had caused the 1905 Revolution remained largely unresolved even after Nicholas had put down the revolt and tried to carry out reforms. His treatment of the Dumas in 1906–14 showed his contempt for representative government, and his refusal to provide effective leadership laid the foundations for future troubles.

The first Duma, May to July 1906

Although the Duma was an elected body, like many other constituent national assemblies in the world at that time, it represented only a section of the adult population. The right to vote was not universal: it applied only to male citizens over the age of 25. They did not vote directly for their own representatives, but for committees known as electoral colleges, which selected members of the Duma. Crucially for its political influence, its powers were limited to control of a small part of the budget. The limitations to the Duma's powers meant that Nicholas II was increasingly able to ignore its debates and resolutions.

The Duma's members were first elected in 1906. They were drawn from a range of political parties, except for the socialists, as the Social Democrats and Socialist Revolutionaries boycotted the elections. The Kadets won 153 of the 448 seats and demanded more powers for the Duma. The tsar rejected the demand and dissolved the Duma barely two months later. The Kadets assembled at Vyborg in Finland in protest and appealed to the Russian people not to pay taxes or submit to military service. Their appeal led to scattered outbreaks of resistance, which the government was easily able to crush.

The second Duma, February to June 1907

The second Duma met for a few months. The Kadets had been damaged by their earlier failure and the more radical Social Democrats and Socialist Revolutionaries were successful in the elections, winning more than a hundred seats between them. Their successes led to deep divisions within the Duma over land reform and the government's law and order policies. Nicholas was not prepared to see the Duma become a forum for opposition, and once again it was dissolved. He continued to call elections, however, believing that an appearance of parliamentary government made his regime more acceptable to Britain and France as he was building closer relationships with them to counter the rise of Germany.

Figure 3.10: A group of representatives of the Second Duma. The dress of some of these deputies suggests that they came from peasant or working-class backgrounds.

The third Duma, November 1907 to June 1912

Before the next Duma was elected, the voting arrangements were changed to give greater representation to landowners and urban property owners. The new arrangements enabled the third Duma to last longer than its predecessors. With right-wing parties now controlling 287 of the 443 seats, the third Duma's relationship with the government was more harmonious than before and there was progress on land reform, military reorganisation and the introduction of national insurance for workers. However, the third Duma was denounced by radicals as a 'Duma of lords and lackeys [servants]', and seen as too subordinate to the government. Even the liberals were uneasy with the way in which the Fundamental Laws had been manipulated to bring about the change in the electoral law.

The fourth Duma, November 1912 to August 1914

Divisions between socialists and Octobrists hindered the fourth Duma's chances of success. It voluntarily dissolved itself when war broke out in 1914, so that party politics would not be a distraction at a time of national emergency. Many Soviet-era historians saw the third and fourth Dumas, in particular, as part of a worthless experiment in fake democracy, viewing them as docile puppets of the tsarist regime. They held this view because Marxist writers were committed to dismissing all reforms undertaken before the Bolshevik seizure of power. Since the end of communist rule, and the decline in the influence of Marxist historical thinking, more historians have been willing to appreciate the Dumas' attempts to criticise the government and their successes in passing legislation. It is impossible to judge whether, given more time, the Dumas might have developed more power and influence in the state. What is certain is that, for as long as the tsar and his ministers controlled the electoral system, the Dumas could not gain sustained popular support, nor give representative voice to the Russian people's wishes.

Repression

Nicholas felt strong enough by late 1905 to use force against continued opposition. Troops returning from the Russo-Japanese War were used to suppress the St Petersburg and Moscow Soviets with violence. Ringleaders, including Trotsky, were arrested. The police and the army continued to harass real or imagined critics of the regime: it is estimated that 15 000 people were killed and 70 000 arrested within a year. Nicholas' prime minister in 1906–11, Pyotr Stolypin, believed strongly in strict law and order. He ruthlessly repressed peasant uprisings. 'Stolypin's necktie' (death by hanging) was used widely to punish rebels. The regime used divisive methods to promote a sense of Russian nationality. The tsar approved an extreme right-wing grouping called the Union of the Russian People, which organised the paramilitary 'Black Hundreds' – violent gangs who terrorised supporters of democracy. Their most prominent victims were Jews. At this time, anti-Semitism was widespread in Russia. Conservatives highlighted the presence of Jews in left-wing and revolutionary political parties, regarding them as a threat to social stability and order. They used popular prejudice against the Jews to rally 'patriotic' Russians behind the tsar and his government, with the cooperation of the police.

These tactics were a worrying development in a country that was supposed to be moving towards parliamentary government. The experience of 1905–06 had shown that the tsar's government was not serious about reform. Fear of the state preserved Russia's fragile stability much more than loyalty and affection for the tsar.

The nature and extent of opposition

The opposition's lack of unity was an important reason for the failure of the 1905 Revolution. Although workers, peasants and liberals had been united at the start of the revolution, they had different interests and did not work together for a common goal. The regime had effectively persuaded the moderate liberals by offering mild political reforms. However, these reforms would never be enough for the socialist opposition, who wanted a fundamental transformation of Russian society.

In the years 1906–14 the police and the army kept the radical opponents of tsarism under control, but they could not eliminate them altogether. The exile of Lenin and other revolutionaries kept them safe and allowed them to continue their work abroad, where they gained increasing support. Radicals in internal exile in remote parts of Siberia still managed to spread their ideas and keep in contact with others. They evaded censorship and illegal newspapers, pamphlets and books were distributed widely.

However, the Bolsheviks had been weakened following extensive infiltration by the Okhrana. Even the leader of the Bolshevik group in the fourth Duma, Roman Malinovsky, turned out to be a police spy, although Lenin refused to believe this at first. Only the outbreak of the First World War gave the opposition a real chance of success.

The extent of changes in Russia between 1905 and the start of the First World War

Under a new prime minister, **Pyotr Stolypin**, reforms of the rural economy and society were made. The aim was to create greater political stability. There was some industrial development, although workers' conditions remained poor.

KEY FIGURE

Pyotr Stolypin (1862–1911)

Stolypin came from a noble family and was politically conservative. However, unlike many of his class, he demonstrated an awareness of the hardships that most Russians faced. He made his reputation by his tough handling of disturbances as a provincial governor in 1905. As prime minister, Stolypin aimed to counter unrest by agreeing to reforms that could vastly improve life for the peasants in Russia.

Stolypin's agrarian reforms and their impact

In May 1906, Nicholas appointed Pyotr Stolypin as minister of the interior. Two months later, Nicholas made Stolypin prime minister. Stolypin saw agrarian reform (changes to the system of land holding and cultivation) as his main priority and wanted to improve the peasants' situation. In many ways, his work complemented that of Witte, whose focus had been on industrial growth, although the two men did not work together in government. Some historians consider that if Nicholas had fully backed these men, who were his two most talented ministers, they could possibly have prevented revolution.

Although Stolypin wanted reform, he was not a democrat. His first objective was to restore order, and he embarked on a policy of social and economic reform only after he had achieved this. Stolypin believed that the most beneficial change would be to encourage the growth of a wealthy peasant class, whose members were known as kulaks. He said that Russia should 'bet on the strong', meaning that, if peasants became property owners, it would be better for them to maintain the current system, so they would be less likely to support revolutionary change.

Stolypin intended to make the peasants independent of the mirs, which still exerted a restrictive influence on agriculture. The mirs directed what land a peasant could work on, and which crops could be grown. This limited the ability of an ambitious peasant to make improvements. The high price of land, combined with rural overpopulation and a series of poor harvests, had worsened conditions in the countryside. Stolypin carried out the following reforms:

- He allowed the peasants to combine their individual strips of land (which might be spread over several fields) into smallholdings, which could be farmed more efficiently. To create a class of landholders, peasants were not allowed to sell land to non-peasants.
- He made underused land available to the Peasant Land Bank (established by Alexander III) so that peasants could buy it on favourable terms.
- He cancelled outstanding redemption payments. In doing so, he aimed to remove one of the reasons why the peasants had taken part in the 1905 Revolution.

It could be argued that Stolypin sacrificed the interests of the poorer peasants by prioritising the creation of a strong kulak class of better-off peasants. Peasants who had little or poor land were encouraged to move to unfarmed areas in the east. In places such as Ukraine and Crimea in the south, where the land was fertile, peasants had an incentive to secure their own land. In the harsh north and east, there was no such incentive.

Agricultural production increased in the most favourable regions, making the kulaks more prosperous and benefiting the government and those who exported wheat. Exact figures are difficult to calculate, but output may have increased by 14% between 1900 and 1914, and the income of some landowners and kulaks rose by as much as 80%. Some historians believe, however, that most of the increase was the result of a series of naturally good harvests rather than Stolypin's reforms. They point out that many Russians did not benefit from these policies. Agriculture was improving by the outbreak of war in 1914, but the attempt to create a new, independent class of peasant proprietors had not developed very far. Stolypin said that his policy would need 20 years to see results. In 1906–14 only 15% of peasant households were consolidated into farms. Peasants were suspicious of change and did not want to risk leaving the security of the mirs. They even questioned the authorities' attempts to measure the land in readiness to enclose it into smallholdings, fearing that they would not get a fair share. They were especially resistant in central Russia, where peasant support for revolution would be strongest in 1917.

Rural landlords and other property owners became more conservative in their attitudes after seeing the violence of 1905. Stolypin planned to carry out reforms of local government which would increase peasant representation on the zemstvos and challenge traditional aristocratic domination of the countryside, but the nobles successfully opposed these reforms. Stolypin was assassinated in September 1911 at the Kiev (Kyiv) Opera. He was already losing the favour of the tsar, and it is possible that agents of the state were behind his murder. In the Duma, he had built a good working relationship with the Octobrists, who supported his policies, but his successors as prime minister, Vladimir Kokovtsov (1911–14) and Ivan Goremykin (1914–16), lacked his drive and commitment to reform.

Developments in industry and their impact

There was significant industrial growth in the five years before the First World War. Russia's overall growth rate was 8.5%. However, some key industries, such as coal, continued to stay behind competitor countries. The key issue was that productivity did not increase. The growing size of the labour pool, a result of Russia's increasing population, could not compensate for the lack of investment in modern technology. The proportion of the population that worked in agriculture had hardly changed since the 1850s. Industry and the transport network would struggle to meet the needs of the country after the outbreak of war in 1914. The situation did not indicate an economy that was going through effective modernisation.

The growth of industry did not bring an improvement in workers' conditions. Between 1909 and 1914, strikes became more common, as workers demanded increased wages and improved housing and working conditions. Shop workers and railway employees, among others, went on strike. Violent repression by the authorities only encouraged further protests. One significant example of violence against strikers during this period was the massacre in the Lena gold mine in Siberia in April 1912. During the strike, 270 miners were killed and almost as many were wounded by tsarist soldiers. The violence caused an adverse public reaction and encouraged an upsurge in industrial militancy. Poor working and living conditions allowed radical opposition ideas to spread.

Growing unrest did not mean that another revolution was inevitable. In the years immediately before the First World War there were increases in strikes in Britain and the United States, for example, where revolution was avoided. However, the strikes contributed to an atmosphere of growing confrontation in Russia.

Figure 3.11: The tsar and his family at the 300th anniversary celebrations of the Romanov dynasty in Moscow, 1913. They were making their first public appearance since the 1905 Revolution, celebrating tsarist rule with a tour of Russia. At the same time, political unrest in Russia was growing. Do you think that this photograph is evidence of genuine public support for the regime, or was it part of a propaganda exercise?

KEY CONCEPT 3.2

Similarity and difference

Compare the aims and achievements of Witte and Stolypin. In what ways were their aims and achievements similar? How were they different? Consider:

- their political objectives
- the nature of their policies
- their relationships with the tsar
- their individual levels of success.

KEY CONCEPT 3.3

Interpretations

How secure was the tsarist regime in 1914?

There is a debate about whether Russia was on the brink of revolution at the outbreak of the First World War. Outwardly the regime appeared secure in 1914, having survived the 1905 Revolution, and some scholars claim that it was, in fact, mostly stable, with an improving economy and a government that controlled dissent. They believe the monarchy could have survived if it had been allowed a longer period of international peace.

In contrast, Marxist historians have argued that the fall of tsarism and the triumph of the Bolsheviks were the inevitable consequence of economic forces which generated a rapidly increasing class struggle. Most modern historians, however, do not support this view. They believe that in 1914 the tsar ruled over a fragile society; internal tensions destabilised the state and the strains of war caused an already worn-out structure to collapse.

You may like to keep these views in mind as you complete Activity 3.6. Look back at the information you have gathered so far and add material from other sources. A useful resource is the website of historian Orlando Figes, whose book, *A People's Tragedy: The Russian Revolution 1891–1924* (Jonathan Cape, 1996), is a classic study.

ACTIVITY 3.6

In your opinion, how strong was the likelihood of revolution in Russia in 1914? Make sure you justify your opinion by setting out arguments based on evidence.

a Review what you have read so far and copy and complete the table. This will help you to organise the evidence for and against the claim that Russia stood on the brink of revolution by the time war broke out.

	Evidence that the tsarist regime faced challenges by 1914	Evidence that the regime was still secure in 1914
Strength of Russia's traditional institutions		
Success of the Dumas		
State of the Russian economy		
Success of Stolypin's reforms of agriculture		
Levels of public support for the regime		
Strength of opposition to tsarism		

b On balance, which side of the argument do you agree with?

Reflection

In making your judgement, how far do you think you have been influenced by hindsight – in other words, by the knowledge that revolution did occur just three years later? Would you change your answer if you did not know this?

3.3 How and why did the Bolsheviks seize power in October 1917?

Lenin and the Bolsheviks came to power in 1917 following two separate upheavals: the February and October revolutions. These revolutions were caused by Russia's inability to cope with the pressures of fighting the First World War.

The impact of the First World War on tsarist rule

Russia claimed that it did not go to war in 1914 to win territory, but rather to protect Serbia–a small state with a population of fellow Slavs–after it became involved in a dispute with Austria-Hungary. The July 1914 crisis, which led to the outbreak of war, was triggered by the assassination of the heir to the Austrian throne, Archduke Franz Ferdinand, on a state visit to Bosnia. Austria-Hungary blamed Serbia for the killing and presented the Serbian government with an **ultimatum** setting out a series of demands, including a requirement to allow Austrian officials to investigate the assassination.

KEY TERM

Ultimatum: A final demand that, if rejected, will lead to serious consequences such as war.

There was a long history of tension between Austria-Hungary and Russia. Austria-Hungary was allied to Germany, whose leader was Kaiser Wilhelm II, the tsar's cousin. Despite these family ties, Russia feared Germany as the main threat to its security. In turn Austria-Hungary believed that Russia was using Serbia to extend its influence in the Balkans, so that Russia would benefit if the Austro-Hungarian Empire broke up in future. At the end of July, Russia announced that it was mobilising troops, ready to support Serbia. On 1 August, Germany declared war on Russia. Russia was now at war with both Austria-Hungary and Germany – a difficult position for a country with such major weaknesses.

At first, the Russian population rallied around the tsar as a symbol of national unity. Germany was unpopular and there was an upsurge of patriotic feeling. In the Duma, all except the five Bolsheviks declared their support for the war. Lenin, who had fled to neutral Switzerland, was unhappy that the working class failed to start a revolution. He was an isolated figure at the start of the war. However, events soon began to turn against the tsarist regime. Its inability to manage the pressures of war led to its downfall.

The impact of defeats in the First World War on the tsar's position

The Russian military had made some improvements by the start of the conflict. Defeat by Japan in 1904–05 had encouraged the government to tackle the failings in the Russian army and navy, and considerable sums of money had been spent in enlarging and improving the armed forces. In 1914, the Russian army was larger than Germany's and it mobilised more swiftly than expected, invading eastern Germany. The Kaiser's army had invaded Belgium and France and was, therefore, fighting a war on two fronts.

However, it was clear that the increased spending on the military had not made the Russian army capable of fighting a modern war. It still relied on its cavalry, which caused problems because horses required large quantities of food and transport. The cavalry was ineffective against modern weapons like machine guns and brave cavalry charges resulted in terrible slaughter. Most commanders relied on bayonets (the sharp blades attached to the soldiers' rifles), so many soldiers were shot before they reached the enemy. Russian military planning was weak in important respects, for example, large numbers of soldiers and weapons were kept in strongpoints behind the front lines. The Russian army was inexperienced in methods of modern warfare. Its unity was based on harsh discipline and an insistence on regulation and display.

The conflict began badly for Russia, and despite some early victories against the Austro-Hungarian army, and a success against Turkey, it soon became clear that Russia would not be able to defeat Germany in an offensive war. Defeat at the Battle of Tannenberg in August 1914 showed that the German forces were superior in

Figure 3.12: Russian soldiers taken prisoner after the Battle of Tannenberg, August 1914. What does this photograph suggest about the state of the Russian army at the start of the First World War?

ACTIVITY 3.7

Study the data in Table 3.2 which shows casualties for the major combatant countries in the First World War.

a What does it tell you about Russia's capacity to cope with the stresses of war?

b What other data would be helpful to you in your analysis?

Country	Number mobilised	Dead	Wounded	Missing / prisoners of war
Russia	12000000	1700000	4950000	2500000
France	8410000	1357800	4266000	537000
Britain and empire	8904467	908371	2090212	191652
Germany	11000000	1773700	4216058	1152800
Austria-Hungary	7800000	1200000	3620000	2200000
USA (1917–18)	4355000	116516	204002	4500

Table 3.2: Troop losses to the major combatant countries in the First World War.

terms of weaponry, tactics and speed. The Germans also had better military intelligence, intercepting radio messages which told them where the Russian forces were. Around 70000 Russian soldiers were killed or injured at Tannenberg, and a further 92000 captured. The Russian commanders found that they needed to use defensive tactics, for which the troops were not well trained.

The human cost of the war steadily increased for Russia, and the cost in resources also grew. The ordinary soldiers were mostly peasants forced into military service. These soldiers were short of clothes, food, weapons and ammunition. Guns and shells were piled up, unable to reach the front lines due to the inefficient transport system and the vast distances to be travelled. Weak generals did not alter their tactic of throwing masses of badly equipped soldiers against steady gunfire.

Military losses had a drastic impact on the civilian population. They directly caused an enormous displacement of population – half a million peasant households were forced to abandon their farms in 1914–16 and move eastwards, away from the German armies, leading to further disruption to society. Attempts by the authorities to maintain popular support often had the reverse effect, by drawing attention to the hardships that people faced. The propaganda put out by the state completely failed to match the public mood.

Unrest was not confined to the lower classes. Courtiers and generals expressed dissatisfaction with the conduct of the war. Liberals such as the Kadet leaders had supported the regime because they saw it as offering protection against working-class violence. Their leader, Pavel Milyukov, had encouraged patriotic support for the government on the outbreak of war. Yet the Duma had been suspended when war began.

As pressure mounted on the regime for a change of direction, the Duma was recalled in July 1915. Its members were not revolutionaries, but they wanted a more efficient tsarist government.

However, the tsar rejected calls for a new government of national unity. He continued to reshuffle his government, appointing few–if any–competent ministers. The liberals and moderate conservatives in the Duma formed a '**progressive bloc**', which increasingly became a focus for criticism of the regime. The Duma was suspended after less than two months and not recalled until February 1916.

KEY TERM

Progressive bloc: A group in Russia consisting of 236 of the Duma's 442 members, made up of Octobrists, Kadets, moderate nationalists and others. It called for a 'ministry of confidence' and extension of civil liberties.

In response to the continuing military failures, in August 1915, Nicholas II decided to go to the front to take personal charge of his armies. His decision was a fatal mistake. The tsar had no military skill or training, and his presence did not inspire either the army generals or the common soldiers. Nicholas' absence from court left a power vacuum in Russia. His new position as leader of the military also meant that he was seen as personally responsible for defeats. (Such criticism was unfair, since Nicholas took few important decisions and his role was largely a ceremonial one, consisting of attending parades and visiting field hospitals.)

Perhaps the most serious problem of all was that Nicholas' headquarters were in Mogilev, 600 km south of Petrograd. (The name of the capital city had been changed from the German-sounding St Petersburg to Petrograd at the start of the war.) Nicholas was, therefore, far away from developments in Petrograd, and he did not appreciate what was happening there. As a result, he became increasingly out of touch with public opinion. As tsar he was blamed for the growing unrest, but he was both unable and unwilling to do anything about the worsening conditions experienced by both soldiers and civilians.

Weaknesses in the government during the war

Despite some successes, the overall military situation continued to worsen. In June 1916, General Brusilov made some progress against the Austro-Hungarian army in western Ukraine, but when the Germans sent support, Russian forces were pushed back, suffering almost a million casualties. After this, Russia was never able to make an effective attack on its enemies.

This inability to recover from continuing defeats led to growing criticism of the regime from the Duma, after it met again in November 1916. The liberal leader, Pavel Milyukov, delivered a speech in which he repeatedly asked of the government's actions, 'Is this stupidity or treason?' The speech signalled that progressive politicians were becoming increasingly willing to oppose the regime openly.

The tsarina, **Alexandra Feodorovna**, was left in charge of the government while her husband was at the front, but she was not able to use this power effectively. Born a German princess, she was viewed with suspicion, and some people even accused her of being a German spy. As a woman, she found she had little power or influence over traditionally minded ministers.

KEY FIGURE

Tsarina Alexandra Feodorovna (1872–1918)

Alexandra (Alix) was the German-born granddaughter of Queen Victoria. In 1894 she married Nicholas II, becoming the last tsarina (empress) of Russia. A foreigner and a strong believer in autocracy, she was never popular in Russia. Nicholas, Alexandra and their five children were held prisoner and executed by firing squad after the Bolsheviks seized power.

One significant factor in the decline of the tsar's reputation was the royal family's association with **Grigori Rasputin**. A self-professed healer, Rasputin seemed able to calm the heir to the throne, Alexei, during his frequent periods of illness, and this made him a great favourite of the tsarina, in particular. However, many royal courtiers despised Rasputin because of his low birth and lack of education, and many people grew concerned over the influence he seemed to have on the tsar and tsarina. Alexandra defended Rasputin fiercely. Courtiers who were appalled at his crude manners fell out of favour, and she dismissed critical ministers. In letters to the tsar, Alexandra referred to Rasputin as 'Our Friend' and they show the significance she gave to his advice. For instance, in a letter written in September 1916, she wrote: 'Our Friend says about the new orders you gave to Brusilov etc.: "Very satisfied with Father's orders, all will be well." He won't mention it to a soul, but I had to ask His blessing for your decision."

Before the First World War, Rasputin's unpopularity was confined to the court and higher circles of government. However, once Alexandra was in control of the country, she sought Rasputin's advice on many matters. This brought him to the attention of the wider public, but he was equally unpopular with them. Rasputin was murdered in December 1916 – not by political radicals striking a blow against the monarchy, but by a group of conservative courtiers who wanted to save the tsar's reputation.

KEY FIGURE

Grigori Rasputin (1869–1916)

Rasputin came from Siberia. He was illiterate and had a reputation as a drunkard, a womaniser and a petty criminal. He spent a few months in a monastery but was too badly educated to become a monk. He described himself as a holy man and healer. Rasputin arrived in St Petersburg in 1903, and came to the attention of the royal family, who hoped he could heal their son. He was murdered by a courtier in 1916.

ACTIVITY 3.8

Figure 3.13: An undated cartoon showing Rasputin (centre) with the tsar and tsarina.

Look at the cartoon in Figure 3.13. What features of this cartoon make it clear that it was produced by opponents of the tsarist system?

The causes and effects of the February Revolution

The downfall of Tsar Nicholas II was caused by his failure to manage the war successfully, which led to a loss of public support for the monarchy.

Economic and social problems on the home front

Traditional Russian Marxists argued that the fall of the Romanov regime and the triumph of the Bolsheviks were inevitable because of the backward state of Russia and the efficiency of Lenin and his followers. However, most historians now argue against this view. They emphasise the importance of the war as an immediate cause of the fall of Nicholas II in February 1917.

Food shortages and inflation

Russia had industries, the railway system had been enlarged and, in peacetime, the harvests were sufficient to feed the population. Its major problem during the First World War was a lack of organisation. The needs of the military were given priority on the railways, at the expense of the civilian population. The system could not transport food and supplies from areas of plenty to where they were needed. As the network failed to cope with the pressures placed upon it, food rotted in depots instead of being moved to the towns and cities. The movement of raw materials to manufacturing centres was also disrupted. Labour supply was another problem, as workers and peasants were conscripted into the army, placing additional burdens on the people who remained in the factories and on farms.

Local government tried to support the war effort with two new organisations: the Union of Towns in the towns and the Union of Zemstvos in rural areas. The purpose of these organisations was to offer help to refugees and orphans, and to assist with providing medical aid and provisions for the army. They were united in a single organisation known as Zemgor from the spring of 1915. The unions had some success in organising hospitals and relieving suffering. They never enjoyed consistent support from central government, however, and they were not equipped to deal with the scale of the economic and social crisis facing the country.

The fundamental problem was that Russia was not prepared for a long war. The conflict cost 15 times more than the Russo-Japanese War, and the government had to borrow heavily and print money to finance it. These policies led to terrible inflation.

Average incomes doubled in 1914–16, but the price of fuel and foodstuffs quadrupled. Rising prices affected the lower classes in towns and the countryside. As peasants ceased to get a good price for their produce, they hoarded it, making the food shortages in urban centres worse. Strikes spread in major cities such as Moscow and Petrograd.

Land seizures

Meanwhile, many front-line soldiers began to abandon the war effort. Conditions at the front were unbearable and stories spread of hardships at home. Soldiers drifted back to their homes in large numbers, afraid that their families would die if they did not return to help them. In the countryside, they joined other peasants in carrying out land seizures and random 'adjustments' of the rents they were prepared to pay. Landlords were often driven off their property. This process continued on a larger scale after the February Revolution.

Events of February 1917 and the abdication of the tsar

Food shortages and a desire for an end to the war were the two main grievances of the urban population. On 18 February, workers went on strike at the Putilov steel works, the most important and most politically active factory in Petrograd. Other workers followed. On 23 February, thousands of women demonstrated in the streets on International Women's Day. Sergei Khabalov, the governor of Petrograd, proclaimed **martial law** and ordered his soldiers to restore order. Many soldiers had too much sympathy with the protestors to do this. They refused and fired on their officers instead. Even the Cossacks–once the most loyal of the Romanovs' soldiers–turned against Nicholas.

KEY TERM

Martial law: The replacement of civilian rule and legal processes by military power.

The tsar was over 600 km away from Petrograd, at his military headquarters, and was out of touch with the developing crisis. Radical Duma members formed a provisional committee. At the same time, the Petrograd Soviet of soldiers, sailors and workers was established. Two quite different steps had thus been taken towards an alternative government. This situation immediately raised the question of whether the two bodies would merge, cooperate or come into conflict.

Nicholas decided to return to Petrograd as he mistakenly believed that his presence would calm the situation. On the way, troops forced his train to divert to Pskov, 160 km from the capital. Here he was met by army leaders and members of the Duma who persuaded him to give up the throne for his own safety. They included Mikhail Rodzianko, president of the Duma and previously a loyalist, who had tried in vain a few days earlier to warn the tsar that he needed to appoint a government which had popular support. On 2 March 1917, Nicholas decided that his only remaining option was to abdicate. Feeling that his son was too young and unwell to assume such responsibility, Nicholas nominated his brother, Grand Duke Michael, as his successor in the hope of preserving the monarchy, but Michael was not willing to accept the throne in these circumstances. The monarchy was instead replaced by the Duma committee, which declared itself the Provisional Government.

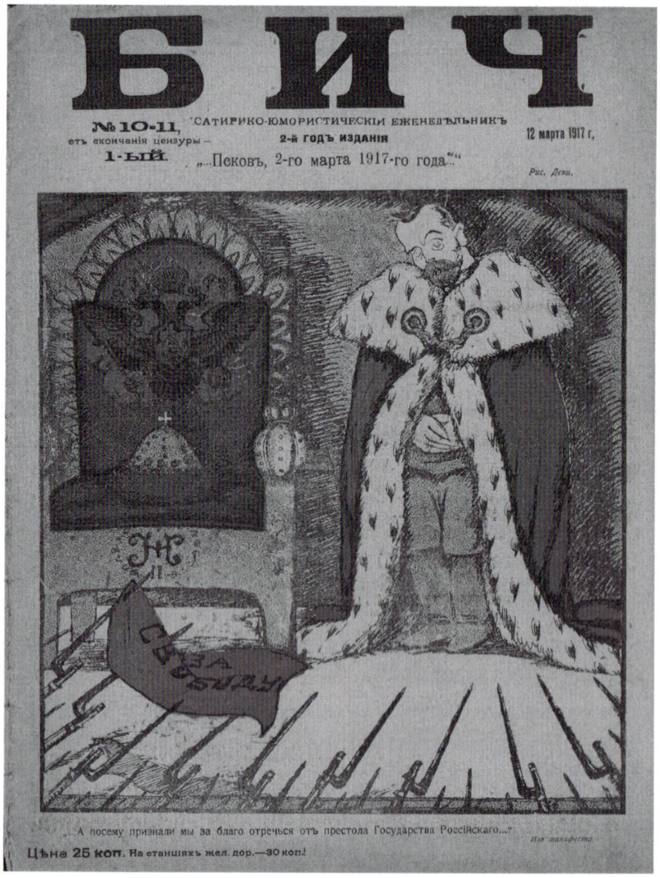

Figure 3.14: A cartoon from a satirical Russian journal, showing Nicholas II abdicating the throne when faced with the bayonets of the Petrograd revolutionaries. Does this image give a complete explanation of why the tsar abdicated in March 1917?

The Bolsheviks played no real part in the downfall of the tsar. Most of the key figures were out of the country and were taken by surprise by events in Petrograd. In December 1916, Lenin had told fellow Bolsheviks, in exile with him in Switzerland, that he did not expect to live to see the revolution.

The regime collapsed partly because those who might have been expected to defend it, in particular the senior military figures, failed to do so. Their assessment of the disturbances in Petrograd was that by late February the situation was hopeless and Nicholas must step down. By this stage, the tsar himself had lost the will to resist the unfolding events. His own personality played a large part in his downfall. He was unable to empathise with his people's suffering during the war and was too distant from their daily struggle for survival. He lacked the drive and imagination to provide effective leadership at a time of supreme crisis.

The deeper reason for the end of the tsarist system was the way in which prolonging the war tested Russia's economy, transport system, political institutions and armed forces nearly to destruction. Growing casualties and food shortages weakened the morale of the population and undermined support for the war. By taking personal command of his forces, the tsar had identified himself with military failures. This made his own political survival virtually impossible.

ACTIVITY 3.9

The situation is serious. The capital is in a state of anarchy. The Government is paralysed; the transport service is broken down; the food and fuel supplies are completely disorganised. Discontent is general and on the increase. There is wild shooting on the streets; troops are firing at each other. It is urgent that someone enjoying the confidence of the country be entrusted with the formation of a new Government. There must be no delay.

From a telegram sent to Tsar Nicholas II by Mikhail Rodzianko, president of the Duma, 26 February 1917.

a Find out more about the background and views of Mikhail Rodzianko.

b What was his purpose in writing like this to Nicholas? Was he trying to save the monarchy or bring it down?

The formation and aims of the Provisional Government

After the abdication of the tsar, the Provisional Government tried to restore stability and to continue the war. It could not achieve these objectives and in the October Revolution it was swept away, after Lenin's Bolshevik Party seized power.

The Provisional Government consisted mainly of liberals with a small number of socialists, but no members of the Bolshevik Party. In its eight months of existence it had two prime ministers. The first was a liberal aristocrat, Prince Georgy Lvov. He was a moderate reformer who had acted as a spokesman for rural interests for many years, and he headed the Union of Zemstvos. As prime minister, he was not a strong figure. He believed in the ability of the people to govern themselves, optimistically assuming that peaceful democratic change could be achieved in the middle of a great war. Lvov was increasingly overshadowed by **Alexander Kerensky**, a leading member of the Social Revolutionary Party, who served as minister of justice and minister of war before succeeding Lvov as prime minister in July 1917.

KEY FIGURE

Alexander Kerensky (1881–1970)

Kerensky is shown in the image (left) reviewing his troops as minister of war. He trained as a lawyer and was a democratic socialist in the wartime Duma. He became the second prime minister in the Provisional Government in July 1917. He was a popular leader and tried to hold together the different factions. However, he made the fatal error of deciding to continue the war, which the country could no longer sustain. In addition, he postponed land reforms, a long-standing goal for which the peasantry would wait no longer. Meanwhile, the economy worsened. After the October Revolution, Kerensky moved to western Europe and then to the United States, where he taught at university, dying there in 1970.

The Provisional Government had two serious weaknesses from the start. First, it had developed from a committee of the Duma, and government domination and manipulation of the electoral system had seriously undermined the people's trust in the Duma. Second, it had to share power with the Petrograd Soviet that claimed to speak for workers and soldiers. Following the creation of the Petrograd Soviet, soviets were formed in other towns and cities too.

The Petrograd Soviet was not actually hostile to the Provisional Government and was not initially dominated by the Bolsheviks. The two bodies cooperated on a number of reforms, including an amnesty for political prisoners, the introduction of universal voting rights, the abolition of capital punishment (the death penalty) and recognition of trade unions. However, the existence of the Petrograd Soviet potentially presented a challenge to the government's authority. In 'Order Number 1', issued at the beginning of March, the Petrograd Soviet

ACTIVITY 3.10

Figure 3.15: A women's demonstration in Petrograd in February 1917. The banners, though patriotic in tone, express demands forcefully. One reads: 'Feed the children of the defenders of the motherland', and another: 'Supplement the ration of soldiers' families, defenders of freedom and the people's peace'.

Look at the photograph in Figure 3.15.

a What information does this source provide about the involvement of ordinary Russians in the events of February 1917?

b How does it help to explain the downfall of the tsarist system of government and what are its limitations as evidence?

stated that it would obey the orders of the Military Commission of the State Duma (an organisation created by the Duma during the February Revolution to manage the army) only if these orders did not clash with its own decrees. This order meant that the government did not possess unqualified control over the army, which proved a significant issue. In effect, the government had to accept the existence of a 'dual authority'. Together with its failure to redistribute land to the peasants (the rural population's most important demand) and its attempt to continue an unpopular war, the government's acceptance of dual authority condemned it to eventual disaster.

Reasons for the failure of the Provisional Government

The Provisional Government fell from power in the October Revolution because it failed to satisfy the demands of the peasants for land reform and because it tried to continue fighting an unpopular war.

Challenges facing the Provisional Government

The Provisional Government faced a number of challenges, which ultimately caused it to fail.

The need for land reform

Russia was internally unstable, and the Provisional Government lacked the strength to restore order. Popular uprisings and army unrest were common in Europe at this time, but the emergence of the soviets in the cities, countryside and the army was a particularly big challenge. The soviets were not highly organised, but they were sufficiently coordinated to represent a major threat.

Food distribution was still a problem, and peasants demanded that land should be redistributed. After the fall of the tsar, the peasants had expected that they would acquire the estates of the nobles and the Church, and when this did not happen they seized land anyway. The government lost support in the countryside by its failure to deal with the problem of land seizures. Its leading members were property owners who were not keen to legalise this behaviour. It was also extremely difficult to distribute food during a wartime emergency. Lenin's return to Russia in April 1917 was a further problem. The Bolsheviks did not have a worked-out policy of their own towards the peasants, so they adopted the ideas of the Socialist Revolutionaries on land redistribution. This meant that they recognised the land seizures on the basis of 'revolutionary legality'. This was an opportunistic, tactical move by the Bolsheviks. It improved their previously weak support in the countryside, where historically the Socialist Revolutionaries had been dominant.

Failure to end the war

Continuing the war was the most important reason why the Provisional Government eventually failed. The Provisional Government believed that continuing to fight was a matter of both honour and national survival – and indeed Russia was pressed to remain in the war by its allies, who provided vital financial aid. The government hoped that war might appeal to Russian nationalism and unite the country, but instead the loyalty of the soldiers continued to decline. Heavy casualties reinforced a growing sense of war weariness, and troops were open to the agitation of Bolsheviks, who encouraged them to disobey their officers and abandon the war effort. The Petrograd Soviet was openly opposed to a continuation of the war. It demanded 'peace without annexations or indemnities' (meaning an end to the war without losing territory or paying compensation to the other side). It also demanded that the government should concentrate on defending the gains of the February Revolution.

In April, the foreign minister, Pavel Milyukov, leader of the Kadets, triggered street demonstrations by declaring that the government intended to fight on to achieve victory. He was forced out at the beginning of May and Prince Lvov attempted to broaden the base of the government by including moderate socialists. The war minister, Alexander Guchkov, was replaced by Kerensky. These events weakened the government by separating it further from the soviets. The soviets became more critical of the government, as it failed either to bring about major democratic reforms or to end the war. After a disastrous offensive against Germany in June 1917, in which up to 60 000 troops were lost, it became clear that the army was in no condition to fight and demands to make peace increased. The failure of the offensive damaged Kerensky's own reputation since he had personally ordered it to go ahead. The continuation of the fighting worsened the problems of food shortages and inflation, increasing popular unrest.

The July Days

Sailors at Kronstadt, the naval base close to Petrograd, established their own government in defiance of the Provisional Government. There were then numerous demonstrations by workers and soldiers in Petrograd between 3 and 6 July. It is not clear who started these disturbances. The Bolsheviks later claimed that they were started by the Socialist Revolutionaries and Mensheviks. The Socialist Revolutionaries and Mensheviks argued that the Bolsheviks were responsible but had tried to distance themselves from a failed attempt at revolution.

The rising was poorly organised, and the participants were divided. The Provisional Government gathered enough soldiers to put down disorder, and Lenin had to leave the centre of action and flee to Finland. Kerensky succeeded Lvov as prime minister. The episode showed that the Provisional Government still possessed some authority. The government accused Lenin of being a German agent, closed the Bolsheviks' newspaper, *Pravda*, and dispersed the party's members.

The Kornilov Revolt

The Kornilov Affair restored Lenin's fortunes. Lavr Kornilov, the commander-in-chief of the army, was a conservative army officer who supported strong action against the Bolsheviks. The Germans were now approaching Petrograd. Kornilov was concerned by the worsening war situation, and he believed that he must take action to restore internal stability. In August, he attempted to march on Petrograd at the head of a troop of soldiers known as the 'Savage Division' because of its warlike reputation. It is uncertain how far Kerensky approved of the plan and how far Kornilov acted independently, but the scheme failed. Kerensky quickly accused Kornilov of attempting a takeover to establish a military dictatorship and dismissed him from his post. He also called for support from the workers to resist the army. The Bolsheviks now reappeared and gained credit by leading resistance among the workers and soviets. In fact, the attempted takeover collapsed because rail workers refused to transport Kornilov and his men to Petrograd, and he was then arrested.

The affair demonstrated the weakness of the Provisional Government. Kerensky had lost the favour of the conservatives by turning against Kornilov, but he had also alienated the radical opposition, who suspected him initially of being involved in counter-revolutionary plotting. The episode also further undermined military discipline, and soldiers deserted and turned to the soviets. By the end of August, the Bolsheviks had a majority on the Petrograd Soviet. Soon afterwards, they gained control of the Moscow Soviet. These events convinced Lenin, who returned to Russia on 7 October, that the time was right for a second revolution.

Figure 3.16: General Lavr Kornilov reviewing troops in 1917.

How and why the Bolsheviks were able to seize power in October 1917

Under Lenin's leadership, the Bolsheviks were ruthless in exploiting the unpopularity of the Provisional Government and offering the people the three things they wanted: peace, land and bread.

Lenin's leadership

One of Lenin's greatest strengths was his ability to be both idealistic and practical, and his government of Russia after 1917 showed his willingness to compromise when necessary. He was a skilled orator (which contributed to his success in 1917), but more importantly for developing the Bolshevik movement, he was also a talented writer and a profound political thinker. His adaptation of Marxism began a new political philosophy that became known as 'Marxism-Leninism'. For decades Lenin had aimed to incite a revolution that would bring down the tsarist autocracy, but, ironically, he did not tolerate any challenges to his own leadership.

Lenin reached two decisions that shaped the future of Russia. First, he appreciated the importance of organisation and discipline within a revolutionary party. The disorganised and fragmented radical groups had achieved very little and spent a great deal of time quarrelling among themselves. Second, he recognised the value of the industrial working classes for the success of any revolution. He believed that the peasantry could not mount a united challenge to the tsarist regime. The proletariat worked in factories and lived in towns. Lenin believed that it was more likely that the proletariat could be shaped into an effective revolutionary weapon.

At the start of 1917, Lenin was in exile in Switzerland and could not influence events in Russia. To return to Petrograd he would have to travel through Germany. This would not normally be possible in wartime conditions. However, Lenin had a stroke of luck that he could not have calculated. His isolation ended when the Germans, intending to weaken Russia by stirring up disorder, transported him in a train to the Russian frontier. It consisted of one carriage and was known as the 'sealed train' because the Germans did not inspect the passengers' passports and belongings, and it made as few stops as possible.

Lenin was afterwards accused by his enemies of being a German agent, and it was true that the Bolsheviks had received financial support from the Germans. However, the reason for their cooperation was simply that Lenin's aims coincided with theirs. Lenin wanted Russia to withdraw from the war so that he could start to transform the country into a socialist society. The Germans wanted him to progress their military objectives by undermining the Russian war effort.

Lenin arrived at Petrograd's Finland Station on 3 April, the most important among several opposition politicians who were now returning to Russia from exile. As he had spent so much of his life abroad, he did not know Russia and its people well, and he could not automatically become the leader of the Bolshevik Party without challenge. Nevertheless, he quickly set out his strategy for revolution. He condemned the 'dual authority' approach on the grounds that the Provisional Government was a 'parliamentary–bourgeois republic' which was nothing more than a front for capitalism. True socialists should not cooperate with it but should seek its overthrow.

Figure 3.17: Lenin at the Finland Station in Petrograd: a painting produced after the Bolshevik seizure of power. How can you tell that this is a propaganda painting?

In calling for a second revolution, Lenin was departing from traditional Marxist teaching, which argued that society had to pass through a bourgeois capitalist phase before the proletariat could come to power. He justified his strategy on the grounds that the Russian middle classes were incapable of carrying out a revolution, and that the war had transformed the situation, making widespread socialist revolution likely across Europe. Lenin quickly realised the potential power of the soviets. He saw them as an alternative to the Provisional Government and adopted the slogan 'All power to the soviets'. His aim was for the Bolshevik Party to take control of the soviets and to use them as a springboard to power. (In practice, the Bolsheviks did gain control of the soviets during the following few months and Russia later became a one-party state under the Bolsheviks.)

Lenin did not have a fully worked-out plan for the seizure of power. He set out his call for a second revolution and withdrawal from the war in a speech, and the main points were later written down in a document known as his 'April Theses', but, at the time, his demands did not seem realistic to most socialists. However, his absolute self-belief and single-minded dedication to revolution enabled him to dominate those around him. No one else had Lenin's ruthlessness or his clarity of vision. He knew when to retreat, as well as when to take decisive action. He could be brutally harsh towards his opponents, but also immensely persuasive. He understood the importance of propaganda in undermining support for the government and also in keeping the workers in a state of readiness for when the time was right to seize control.

Bolshevik promises

Lenin memorably offered the Russian working people 'Peace, Land and Bread'. This simple slogan helped Lenin to win control of the Bolshevik Party's agenda. It appealed powerfully to the Russian masses, meeting the wishes of the industrial workers, soldiers and poorer peasants, and showing them why they should support the party.

- **Peace:** Lenin offered an end to the universally unpopular war which, as we have seen, was going badly for Russia.
- **Land:** Lenin promised to seize all landed estates and to transfer agricultural land from the nobility to the peasants.
- **Bread:** Lenin offered food for Russia's hungry population. There was an urgent need for food since the war had disrupted the transport of food and created shortages in the cities.

ACTIVITY 3.11

It must be explained to the people that the Soviets of Workers' Deputies are the *only possible* form of revolutionary government, and that therefore our task is, as long as *this* government yields to the influence of the bourgeoisie, to present a patient, systematic and persistent *explanation* of the errors of their tactics ...

Not a parliamentary republic–to return to a parliamentary republic from the Soviets of Workers' Deputies would be a retrograde [backwards] step–but a republic of Soviets of Workers', Agricultural Labourers' and Peasants' Deputies throughout the country, from top to bottom.

From Lenin's April Theses, 4 April 1917.

What kind of future is Lenin calling for in this document? Explain carefully the difference between a 'parliamentary republic' and a 'republic of Soviets'.

The role of the Petrograd Soviet and Trotsky

The Petrograd Soviet of Workers' and Soldiers' Deputies, formed in March 1917, had played an important part in weakening the authority of the Provisional Government, forcing it to govern alongside the Petrograd Soviet in a 'dual authority'. In September, the Bolsheviks gained a majority on the Soviet and Leon Trotsky became its chairman.

Trotsky played a key role in bringing about the October 1917 Revolution. Later, after Joseph Stalin became leader of the **Soviet Union**, Trotsky was exiled and eventually murdered. Trotsky was removed from official Soviet histories and his image was systematically deleted from photographs. He became in effect a 'non-person'. However, most historians regard him as the chief organiser of the Bolshevik seizure of power. He was also a brilliant public speaker who knew how to energise audiences and was widely recognised as having more charisma than Lenin.

In some ways it was surprising that Trotsky was so central to the Bolshevik takeover. Like Lenin, he was abroad when the February Revolution took place, and he did not arrive in Russia until May. At that point, he was not a Bolshevik; instead he still belonged to the Menshevik Party. He changed his loyalties during the summer of 1917 because, following the July Days, he realised that only the Bolsheviks could supply the leadership needed to bring about a socialist revolution. He recognised that their increasingly dominant position in the trade unions and factory committees was the key to winning power. Apart from his involvement in the Petrograd Soviet, Trotsky's main contribution to the revolution was his role in organising the **Red Guards**, an armed workers' group.

Trotsky joined the Bolshevik Party's Central Committee, where he soon became Lenin's most trusted supporter in planning and carrying out the October Revolution. As commissar (minister) for foreign affairs, he was responsible for peace negotiations with Germany in 1917–18, and as war commissar, he played a key role in defeating the Bolsheviks' opponents in the Russian Civil War of 1918–20.

KEY TERMS

Soviet Union: Shortened form of the Union of Soviet Socialist Republics (USSR), the communist state officially established in 1922 and dissolved in 1991, comprising Russia and other republics.

Red Guards: Armed volunteer groups, consisting mainly of urban workers, led by the Bolsheviks. From 1918 they formed the basis of the Soviet Union's military force, the Red Army.

The Military Revolutionary Committee

Trotsky also introduced a Military Revolutionary Committee (MRC) of the Petrograd Soviet in October 1917. It was one of several similar committees founded across Russia in response to German army advances in the Baltic region.

The Petrograd Military Revolutionary Committee was supposedly designed only to defend the city in the event of a German attack but its real purpose was to carry out an armed insurrection against the Provisional Government. It rapidly won the support of the Petrograd garrison.

The events of the October Revolution

The short-term causes of the October Revolution in 1917 can be summarised as follows:

- The Provisional Government had no control over events. Disobedience from the soviets and the Kornilov Revolt had undermined its authority.
- The Russian army was suffering huge losses in the ongoing war, and this made the Provisional Government even more unpopular.
- Kerensky could not deliver other reforms, such as the redistribution of land or a new constitution.

As the German army advanced, Kerensky could not provide enough soldiers to defend key points in the major cities. Rumours spread that he was preparing to abandon Petrograd to the Germans. Lenin overruled doubters among the Bolsheviks who believed that Russia was not ready for a revolution. He claimed that he was acting for the soviets and demanded that his supporters should rise up at this critical point. Some members of the Bolshevik Party's Central Committee wanted to wait until the meeting of the All-Russian Congress of Soviets, composed of delegates from soviets across Russia. This body was scheduled to meet on 20 October, but the meeting was postponed until 25 October. Lenin did not want to wait for the meeting because it would mean a transfer of power to a coalition, including the Socialist Revolutionaries and Mensheviks, rather than to the Bolshevik Party on its own.

The announcement of elections to a 'constituent assembly' in November was another concern for Lenin. This body was meant to be the first fully democratic all-Russian parliament. It would have the legitimacy which the Provisional Government, as a self-appointed authority, did not have. Lenin did not know how well the Bolsheviks would perform in the elections to the constituent assembly, so he was determined to seize power before it met. Lenin did not automatically sway the Central Committee to support his viewpoint, and he had to struggle to win the argument with his colleagues.

The uprising itself was triggered by Kerensky's government. The government decided to act before the Bolsheviks could make a move. Kerensky announced that the majority of the Petrograd garrison would be transferred to meet the German advance on the northern front. The transfer of troops would enable him to remove the most rebellious troops from the capital, thus provoking a poorly planned Bolshevik uprising, which he then expected to easily crush. The Military Revolutionary

Committee took over the Petrograd garrison on the grounds that a counter-revolution was imminent. Acting swiftly, the Bolsheviks gained control of Petrograd and seized the Winter Palace, the former residence of the tsar, where members of the Provisional Government were gathering. It was Lenin who gave the critical direction to carry out the takeover and decided its timing. But it was Trotsky, as leader of the Red Guards, who carried it out.

The revolution lasted from 25 to 27 October. The Bolsheviks claimed that it was a popular action, a revolution of the people. In fact, it was a tightly organised takeover by a minority, made possible by the weakness of the Provisional Government. The Winter Palace was easily taken and only five people were killed. Unlike in the February Revolution, there were no mass strikes and demonstrations. Trotsky himself admitted that no more than 30 000 people were actively involved, which was only 5% of all the workers and soldiers in Petrograd. Large numbers were not needed because there was very little resistance from the Provisional Government. There were few troops loyal to Kerensky in the capital by this stage. Kerensky had already left Petrograd in an unsuccessful attempt to organise forces still loyal to the ideas of the Provisional Government. His ministers either fled or were taken prisoner by the Bolsheviks. Although Soviet mythmaking later presented the events of October as a heroic struggle, the truth was that the Bolsheviks had moved into a vacuum created by the weakness of the Provisional Government. The worst violence in the capital actually occurred after the occupation of the Winter Palace, when Bolsheviks looted the wine cellars then went on a drunken rampage. Outside Petrograd, the Bolsheviks' hold on power was less secure, with fighting in Moscow between their supporters and those who remained loyal to the Provisional Government.

Nevertheless, the October Revolution certainly took place against a background of growing chaos. Many parts of the country saw the election of workers' factory committees, peasants forcibly redistributing land, and soldiers rebelling against their officers. The Petrograd and Moscow Soviets were increasingly important bodies. National movements in Ukraine and Finland were starting to put their own demands for independence. All of these developments helped to weaken the authority of the Provisional Government.

ACTIVITY 3.12

Figure 3.18: *The storming of the Winter Palace in Petrograd in October 1917* by Valerian Shcheglov.

Look at the drawing in Figure 3.18. It was made in the 1930s, after the establishment of the Soviet government. What do you think its purpose was?

Lenin announced the seizure of the Winter Palace to the delegates at the Congress of Soviets on 27 October. Internal tensions within the Socialist Revolutionary Party now came to a climax. The mainstream group (labelled the Right SRs) walked out, together with the Mensheviks. The members of both groups were angry at what they regarded as a takeover by the Bolshevik Party rather than an assumption of power by the Soviet. The walk-out was a mistake – in doing so, the Right SRs and Mensheviks lost any influence over future events. Trotsky savagely denounced them as having passed into the 'dustbin of history' and organised a vote of the remaining delegates to give some legitimacy to the Bolshevik government. The vote left a breakaway Socialist Revolutionary faction, known as the Left SRs, in alliance with the Bolsheviks for the time being.

KEY CONCEPT 3.4

Interpretations

There are different views on whether the events of October were a popular revolution or a simple takeover. The Menshevik analysis was that the February Revolution marked the overthrow of the feudal aristocracy by the bourgeoisie.

Following Marx's teaching, the Mensheviks did not believe that Russia had yet reached a stage of economic development where it possessed a sufficiently strong and numerous industrial proletariat. For that reason, they were willing to ally temporarily with bourgeois parties until the time was right for the proletarian revolution. Lenin and the Bolsheviks, however, were not prepared to wait. They were focused on seizing power at all costs, and they did not intend to share it with other parties, as events after the capture of the Winter Palace quickly showed.

The alternative view is that there was a genuine popular element in the events of 1917. This interpretation starts with the breakdown of central government after the February Revolution. Its supporters argue that power was widely spread, and the Provisional Government was already fatally weakened by popular uprisings across Russia. However, this argument does not contradict the essential fact that, once in power, the Bolsheviks started to work towards a one-party state and to prevent the moves towards democracy which had begun between the spring

CONTINUED

and autumn of 1917. Their call for 'all power to the soviets' was a cover for their own desire for power.

Consider these points as you complete Activity 3.13.

ACTIVITY 3.13

To the Citizens of Russia!

The Provisional Government has been deposed. State power has passed into the hands of the organ of the Petrograd Soviet of Workers' and Soldiers' Deputies – the Revolutionary Military Committee, which heads the Petrograd proletariat and garrison.

The cause for which the people have fought, namely, the immediate offer of a democratic peace, the abolition of landlord ownership, workers' control over production, and the establishment of Soviet Power – this cause has been secured.

Long live the revolution of workers, soldiers, and peasants!

From the Proclamation of the Military Revolutionary Committee of the Petrograd Soviet on the success of the Revolution, 25 October 1917.

Does this source support the view that October 1917 in Russia was a popular revolution or the view that it was a coup d'état?

Use the source and information from this section to create a poster showing the two competing arguments in bullet point form. Include a box setting out your own judgement on which you consider is the stronger argument.

3.4 How were the Bolsheviks able to consolidate their power up to 1924?

The most urgent task for Lenin and his followers after the fall of the Provisional Government was to ensure the survival of their only just established regime. They desperately needed a period of stability that would allow them to begin creating a socialist state. Yet the country was still at war with Germany, and at the same time the Bolsheviks faced a range of internal opponents.

In Petrograd, civil servants and bank clerks went on strike, paralysing the institutions of government until the Bolsheviks forced them to obey. Fighting continued in Moscow, and the Bolsheviks' hold on rural areas was even less secure. The railway workers' union, Vikzhel, threatened to cut off vital supplies to Petrograd unless the Bolsheviks agreed to form a government with the Mensheviks and Socialist Revolutionaries. This threat forced Lenin to authorise talks with the other parties, but he broke these off in early November when he felt strong enough to do so. He remained true to the concept of 'democratic centralism': the view that only the Bolshevik Party represented the workers, and that multi-party electoral politics was a deception that would merely preserve the power of the bourgeoisie.

Bolshevik policies

The Bolsheviks asserted their authority through a series of emergency actions in the critical early months of their rule, when they might have been overthrown by their many opponents.

№ 209.
Суббота,
28 октября 1917 г.

ИЗВѢСТІЯ

ЦѢНА:
въ Петроградѣ 15 коп.
на ст. жел. д. 13 коп.

ЦЕНТРАЛЬНАГО ИСПОЛНИТЕЛЬНАГО КОМИТЕТА
И ПЕТРОГРАДСКАГО СОВѢТА
РАБОЧИХЪ И СОЛДАТСКИХЪ ДЕПУТАТОВЪ.

Адресъ конторы: Лиговка, Сайкинъ пер., д. № 6. Телефонъ № 218-41.
Адресъ редакціи: Смольный Институтъ, 2-й этажъ комната № 144. Телефонъ № 38-89.

Въ виду созыва въ теченіи ближайшихъ дней Второго Всероссійскаго Съѣзда Совѣтовъ Крестьянскихъ Депутатовъ, **крестьянъ-делегатовъ** пріѣхавшихъ на Второй Всероссійскій Съѣздъ Совѣтовъ Рабочихъ и Солдатскихъ Депутатовъ **просятъ остаться** для участія въ работахъ этого съѣзда.

ДЕКРЕТЪ О ЗЕМЛѢ

СЪѢЗДА СОВѢТОВЪ РАБОЧИХЪ и С. Д. (ПРИНЯТЪ НА ЗАС. 26 ОКТ. ВЪ 2 Ч. Н.).

Figure 3.19: Announcement of the Decree on Land, passed in November 1917. This decree abolished private property and gave the lands of the nobles to the peasants.

The establishment of Sovnarkom

The main governmental body was the **Council of People's Commissars (Sovnarkom)**, founded in October 1917, which declared that it had the right to pass laws independently of the Petrograd Soviet. It was effectively a cabinet of ministers, although the Bolsheviks avoided this label since it had been used by both the 'bourgeois' Provisional Government and the tsarist government. Sovnarkom consisted of 17 commissars, who each took responsibility for an area of government activity. It was chaired by Lenin, while Trotsky was the commissar for foreign affairs. Sovnarkom was the main decision-making body. It issued the decrees that shaped the new state.

Alongside it was the Central Committee of the Bolshevik Party, the body that had directed the October Revolution under Lenin's leadership. The Central Committee was the highest authority within the party between its annual congresses. From 1919, it appointed a five-member body, the Politburo, which became the real centre of power in the Soviet Union.

KEY TERM

Council of People's Commissars (Sovnarkom): The supreme government body in Russia, created in October 1917. Commissars acted as ministers, in charge of the various government departments.

Decrees on land, peace, workers' control and rights

The new government's first acts, which took place in October and November 1917, were attempts to pass into law elements of the Bolshevik slogan, 'Peace, Land and Bread'. The 'Decree on Land' urged the break-up of large estates and the transfer of land to the peasants, something which was already happening unofficially in the countryside. The decree had the effect of speeding up the breakdown of military discipline, as soldiers abandoned their posts to return home to secure land. The 'Decree on Peace' stated that Russia aimed to withdraw from the war without 'payment of indemnities or annexations' – the demand of the Petrograd Soviet before the October Revolution. This decree was an appeal to the war-weary soldiers still fighting at the front. The 'Decree on Workers' Control' recognised the takeover of factories by workers' committees. The 'Declaration of the Rights of the Peoples of Russia' stated the right of all the peoples of the Russian territory to determine their own future. The government passed this decree in a bid to win the support of non-ethnic Russians, such as the people of Latvia, Estonia and Lithuania.

The establishment of a dictatorship

The Bolsheviks used ruthless tactics to suppress opposition, including establishing a new secret police force and suppressing Russia's only democratically elected assembly. They also ended the war against Germany – this was a controversial decision, intended to give them a breathing space to ensure their control over Russia.

The Cheka

Various measures indicated that the Bolsheviks intended to construct a police state. The opposition press was banned, and members of other parties were arrested. The Left SRs were admitted to Sovnarkom because it suited the Bolsheviks to have their cooperation at this stage. They had broken away from the mainstream Socialist Revolutionaries to accept the October Revolution, and their links to the peasants made them useful.

The functions of the Military Revolutionary Council were transferred early in December 1917 to a new body, the Cheka, a secret police force modelled on the tsarist Okhrana. Its leader, the Polish-born Felix Dzerzhinsky, was a ruthless individual who instructed the organisation's members to fight a 'battle to the death' against supporters of counter-revolution.

Figure 3.20: Felix Dzerzhinsky (left), head of the Soviet secret police from 1917 to his death in 1926.

The establishment of the Cheka marked the beginning of the 'Terror' – the use of force to crush any form of opposition to the Bolshevik state. At least 8500 died in the first year of the terror (1918–19). Countless others were arrested, imprisoned and tortured. Anyone could be a target of the Terror: not just supporters of the tsarist regime and other political opponents but also priests, better-off peasants, people who hoarded grain or sold other goods for profit, and, indeed, anyone who came under suspicion on account of their bourgeois background or appearance. The confiscation of property, under the slogan 'Loot the looters', happened alongside physical abuse and murder.

One of the most violent episodes was the killing of the former tsar and his family in July 1918. The family had been kept under house arrest since the revolution and in their final months were moved to Ekaterinburg in Siberia. On the orders of local Bolsheviks, and with the approval of the government, they were shot in a cellar of the house where they were being detained.

The closure of the Constituent Assembly

Elections to the Constituent Assembly were held in November 1917. All Russian citizens over the age of 20 were allowed to vote, using a secret ballot. The Bolsheviks did well in Petrograd and Moscow, and they were popular with the military, but they did poorly in rural areas, and overall their share of the vote was only 24%. They won only 175 of the 715 seats. The Socialist Revolutionaries emerged as the largest party with 40% of the vote and a total of 370 seats. The breakaway Left SRs, who were still allied to the Bolsheviks, gained just 40 seats.

The Constituent Assembly met for only one day, 5 January 1918. The Socialist Revolutionaries refused to approve a Bolshevik decree declaring Russia a 'soviet republic' and tried to substitute their own policies. Lenin's solution to this challenge to the Bolsheviks was simple. He had the Assembly dissolved by Red Guards. This action met with almost no resistance and the workers seemed content to allow government to remain in the hands of the soviets.

This action marked the end of the most democratically elected body in Russian history to be assembled up to that point. Nothing like it would be possible again for 75 years, until after the collapse of the Soviet Union. The dispersal of the Assembly showed unquestionably that the Bolsheviks refused to give up power. It was justified by Lenin as 'a complete and open liquidation of democratic forms for the sake of revolutionary dictatorship'.

The Treaty of Brest-Litovsk, March 1918

The traditional Bolshevik view of the First World War was that it was an imperialist conflict which could be ended only by socialist revolution in the participating countries. If this revolution did not occur spontaneously, the Bolsheviks were prepared to start it by carrying 'revolutionary war' into the rest of Europe. With the Russian armed forces disintegrating, however, Lenin became convinced that Russia must seek a separate peace with Germany. It was important to end the fighting to give space to establish a socialist state in Russia. The Bolsheviks could not expect moderate terms from the victorious Germans – but by prolonging the conflict they might have to accept even worse conditions. As a Marxist, Lenin believed that any concessions would turn out to be ultimately meaningless, as revolution would eventually occur across Europe.

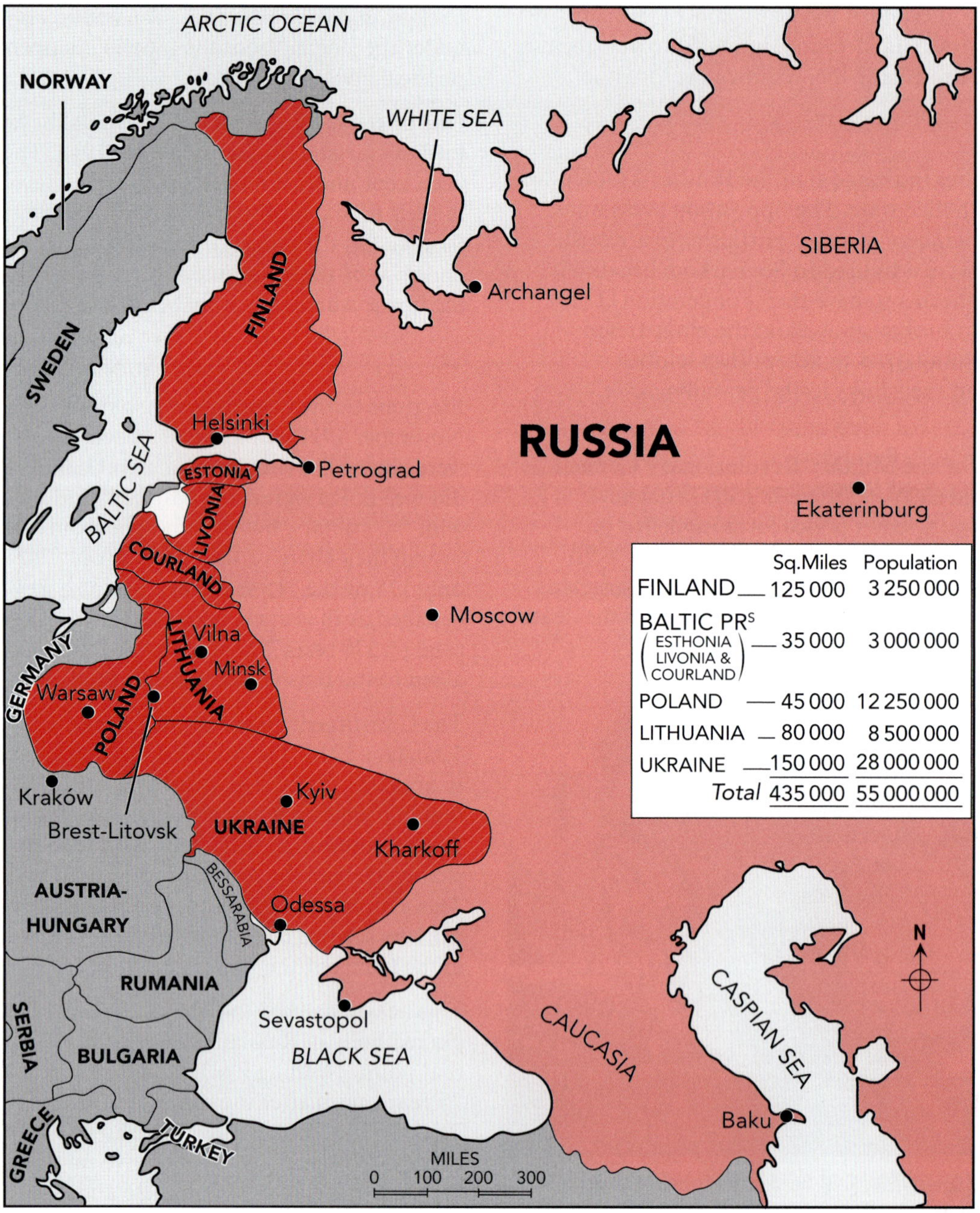

Figure 3.21: A map showing western Russia after the Treaty of Brest-Litovsk. Areas in red are those lost by Russia.

Lenin's proposal was controversial within the Bolshevik Party. The idea of conceding land to Germany contradicted the 'Decree on Peace'. Trotsky, the commissar for external affairs, argued for a policy of 'neither war nor peace'. By this he meant dragging out negotiations as long as possible, hoping that the enemy's war effort in the west would collapse and be followed by a revolution inside Germany.

Lenin was convinced that this approach would result in more German victories and might cause the revolution to collapse. He was not abandoning the long-term prospect of European-wide revolution, but the current priority was to defend socialism in Russia. By mid-February 1918, the German armies were only 600 km from Petrograd, threatening the survival of the revolutionary state. In March 1918, Russia signed the treaty of Brest-Litovsk, now located in Belarus, close to the Polish border. The peace treaty was overwhelmingly in Germany's favour. Russia lost control of Ukraine, its Polish and Baltic territories and Finland – an area which was one million square kilometres in size. It contained half of the old Russian Empire's industry and farmland, and a third of its population. Still fearing the German threat, the Bolsheviks reluctantly decided to transfer the Russian capital from Petrograd to a more secure location in Moscow, 700 km to the south-east and further from the border.

The treaty was extremely unpopular within the Russian leadership. The Left SRs, who had envisaged a people's war against the invaders, left the government in protest. Lenin's critics within the Bolshevik Party only reluctantly accepted the treaty. However, the course of events justified Lenin's approach. The Bolsheviks gained a little time to strengthen their control before the civil war broke out in Russia later that year. In August 1918, the German position on the Western Front began to collapse, leading to the withdrawal of German troops from the areas they had occupied since Brest-Litovsk. In November Germany surrendered to the allies, which meant that the terms of the treaty were now void. At last, events were now starting to move in Lenin's favour, enabling him to consolidate his hold over the government.

ACTIVITY 3.14

'The Treaty of Brest-Litovsk was an apparent failure, but in reality was a major success for Lenin's leadership of Russia.'

Consider this statement about the Treaty of Brest-Litovsk. Copy and complete the table to help organise your thoughts.

In defence of the treaty	Criticisms of the treaty

Reasons for the Bolshevik victory in the Civil War

From 1918 to 1920 various different groups opposed the Bolsheviks. The conservative counter-revolutionaries were known as the 'Whites', a colour traditionally associated with the monarchy, while the Bolsheviks were the 'Reds'. However, the opposition to the Bolshevik regime was much broader than just supporters of the monarchy. It consisted not only of ex-tsarists but of a variety of other groups. Initially, Bolshevik control of the country was insecure except in the party's urban heartlands. By the end of 1920, however, the Bolsheviks had defeated all their opponents.

Weaknesses of the Whites

The Bolsheviks defeated the Whites for several reasons.

Leadership and lack of unity

The first reason was the Whites' weak and divided leadership. There were several White armies, scattered across the Russian territory, and they failed to cooperate effectively with each other. One army, led initially by General Kornilov, was based in the Caucasus region of southern Russia. It was led by General Anton Denikin after Kornilov was killed in April 1918. Denikin attempted an attack on Moscow in 1919, but was driven back to the Crimea. General Pyotr Wrangel led another White army in the south. Unlike Denikin, he did not favour a frontal assault on Moscow, but attempted to link up with White forces in Siberia. The army in Siberia was led by Admiral Alexander Kolchak. Known as the 'Supreme Ruler', he organised an expedition into western

Russia in March 1919 but failed to link up with Denikin. If these two White armies had combined at this stage, they might have won. Losing support, Kolchak was betrayed to the Bolsheviks and executed in January 1920. A further army was assembled on the Baltic coast, with British support, under another former tsarist general, Nikolai Yudenich. He nearly captured Petrograd in the autumn of 1919 while Bolshevik forces were occupied elsewhere, but failed to gain control of the railways and was defeated.

A critical weakness was that various White groups had different objectives. Armed peasant resistance groups, known as Greens, had little in common with conservatives who were fighting for the restoration of tsarism. Their main motivation was anger at Bolshevik seizure of supplies from their communities. Opposition also came from the Socialist Revolutionaries, who tried to stage a takeover of the Moscow Soviet. Fanny Kaplan, a Socialist Revolutionary activist, made an unsuccessful attempt on Lenin's life in August 1918.

Another source of opposition was found in Ukraine, Georgia and other territories, where, as the German war effort collapsed, nationalist groups arose which wanted to maintain their independence from Russian rule. The White generals did not try to appeal to the national minorities' desire for greater self-governance. Their failure to appeal to these minorities was particularly damaging because their armies were based mainly in areas such as the Caucasus and the Baltic, where there were large non-Russian populations.

Finally, we should note the so-called Czech Legion, an armed force of 35 000 subjects of the Austro-Hungarian Empire. They had joined the Russian side in the war, attempting to win their independence, and were then stranded in central Russia after the Treaty of Brest-Litovsk. Clashes between the Czech Legion and the Bolsheviks along the Trans-Siberian Railway in May 1918 helped to spark the Civil War. The Czechs eventually reached Vladivostok on the Pacific coast and they were evacuated from there.

Issues of supply

Issues of supply were a related problem for the Whites. The size of Russia made it difficult for them to move their supplies over long distances. The Whites depended heavily on aid shipped from Britain, the United States and France, who intervened in the Civil War in an attempt to crush the Bolshevik Revolution.

Foreign intervention

Foreign intervention was another source of weakness for the Whites. British and US forces occupied Archangel in the White Sea and the British also intervened in Murmansk in the Arctic. The Germans intervened in the Baltic, while French-led forces appeared in the Black Sea region and southern Russia. Meanwhile, Japan, which was allied to the western powers, occupied Vladivostok. By identifying themselves with foreign intruders, the Whites lost the chance of depicting themselves as champions of the Russian motherland.

In addition, the allies wanted to punish Russia for withdrawing from the war, and to prevent supplies loaned to its government since 1914 from falling into German hands. They continued the intervention for a time after the end of the First World War because they opposed the ideas of the Reds, and because the Bolsheviks had refused to repay the debts incurred by previous Russian governments. The foreign powers began to lose interest, however, and they sent only enough aid to keep the White armies in the field, not enough to give them a real chance of victory. After four years of European war, Britain, France and the United States were not keen on further conflict. Lacking determined commitment to the cause, they withdrew their troops from Russia in 1919–20.

Use of conscription and failure to win popular support

The Whites did not just rely on recruiting volunteers. In many cases they conscripted peasants into their ranks. The Reds did this too, but the difference was that the Whites gave the impression that they were fighting to restore tsarism and the power of landlords over the peasants. Conscription and the requisitioning of food from villages made the Whites very unpopular.

As former prime minister Prince Lvov acknowledged: 'We were mistaken to think that the Bolsheviks could be defeated by military force. They can only be defeated by the Russian people. And for that the Whites would need a democratic programme.'

Strengths of the Bolsheviks

Leadership, unity and organisation

United, strong leadership was a key advantage for the Bolsheviks. As commissar for war, Trotsky was in charge of the Red Army. Trotsky and Lenin worked together effectively. Trotsky realised the importance of making the Red Army more professional. He recruited former tsarist officers because they possessed the necessary military skills and experience, even though this was unpopular with the Bolsheviks. Their loyalty was guaranteed by threatening to take the families of deserting officers hostage. Party workers known as political commissars

Figure 3.22: A Bolshevik cartoon showing the western powers in control of the White leaders, Denikin, Kolchak and Yudenich. How can this cartoon help to explain the eventual defeat of the White forces?

were attached to each army unit to supervise the officers. There were severe punishments for desertion and disloyalty. Distinctions of rank had been abolished after the revolution, but these were restored. Despite these measures, Red Army soldiers were never as disciplined as their opponents. Mass conscription, however, increased the size of the Red Army until, at its peak, five million soldiers were under arms – more than double the number of White troops.

Popular support

The Bolsheviks were just as brutal as the Whites, but much more successful in their dealings with local people. Propaganda posters, films, and speeches by Trotsky and other leaders helped to win support across the country. Above all, they drove home the message that if the Whites won, they would take back the land that the peasants had gained since 1917.

There was an underlying sense of purpose, arising from a combination of Bolshevik ideology and the force of the Red Terror. By contrast with their divided opponents, the Bolsheviks had a shared ideology and a clear commitment to achieving victory.

Geographical factors

Geographical factors also played a part in the Bolshevik victory. They controlled the country's central area, between Petrograd and Moscow, where most of its railways were concentrated. Controlling this area enabled them to move men and supplies rapidly to where they were needed. Trotsky conducted his campaigns from an armoured train, giving him the advantage of mobility across the vast distances of Russia. The central area was also the most industrialised part of Russia, giving the Bolsheviks access to munitions and other vital equipment. Access to the necessary equipment gave them an important advantage over the less well-resourced Whites, whose armies operated mainly on the margins of Russian territory.

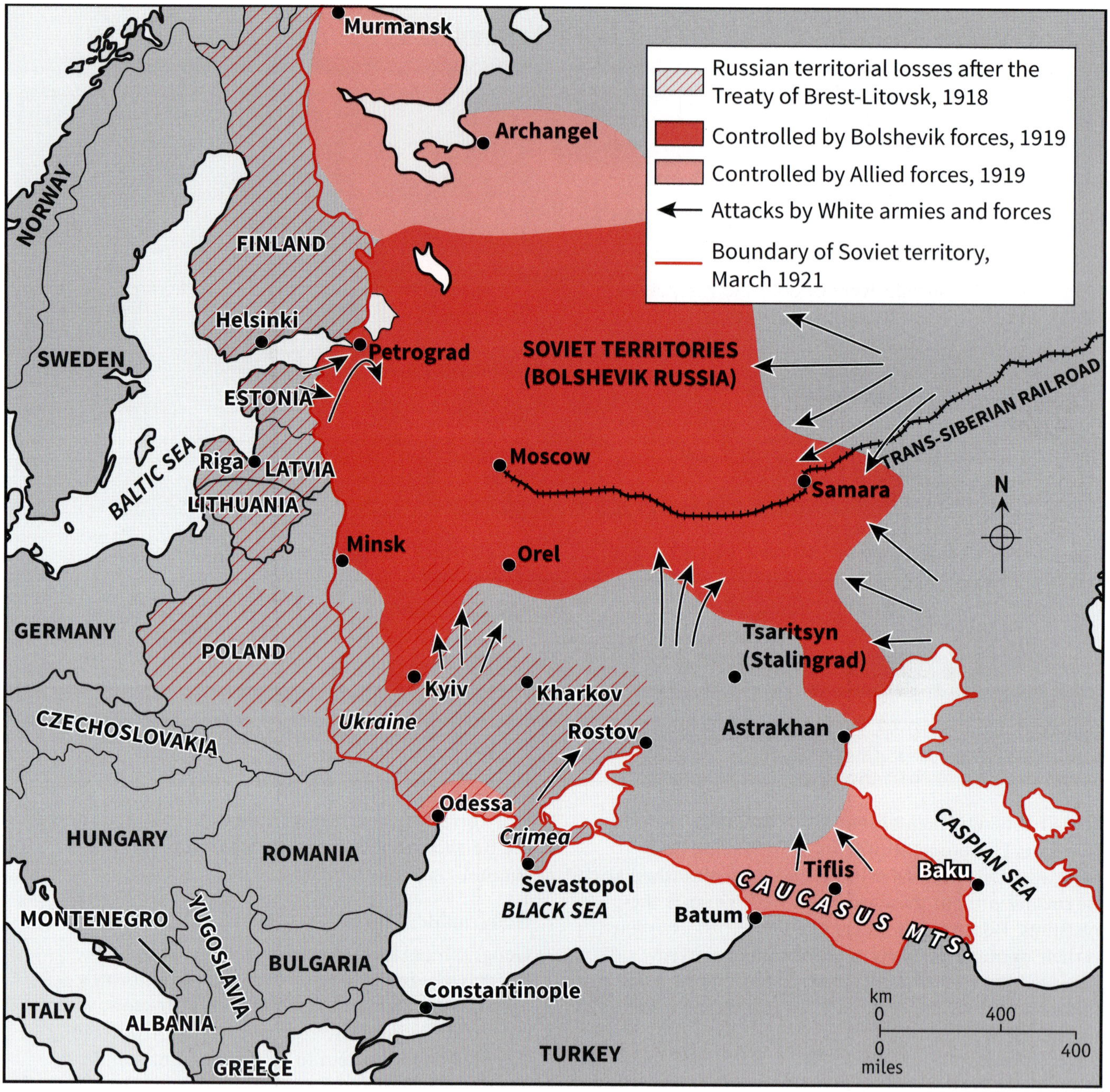

Figure 3.23: A map showing the positions of the Whites' armies during the Russian Civil War.

The introduction and impact of War Communism

Finally, the Bolshevik policy of 'War Communism', introduced in June 1918, helped to bring about the defeat of the Whites. War Communism involved nationalising large-scale industry, abolishing private markets and forcibly requisitioning surplus grain from the peasants. In 1920, the policy expanded when the Bolsheviks attempted to replace money with a system of state rationing. War Communism increased central government control over the economy. The tightening of discipline over the workforce enabled the Bolsheviks to produce more weapons than their opponents.

As we will see, War Communism was unpopular with the people and it generated problems of its own, but in the short term it introduced some order into a chaotic economic situation.

There are different explanations for the introduction of War Communism. Some historians see it as a sensible response to the economic problems of the civil war period – the shortage of food and the decline of industrial production. They argue that it was an attempt to cope with an emergency and was only a temporary diversion from a more moderate policy of state-managed capitalism. Other historians regard War Communism as the true expression of Marxist ideology, part of a long-term drive towards a fully planned economy.

Although the Bolsheviks were opposed to market economics, they were divided over the policy of War Communism. Its details were improvised and often changed. One important factor was the Bolsheviks' suspicious view of the peasants as fundamentally selfish and hostile. Marxist teaching had always stressed the importance of industrial workers and had generally dismissed those who lived in the countryside as uninterested in a socialist revolution. The Bolsheviks were also worried by the movement of large numbers of urban workers to the country in search of food, depriving industry of vital manpower. The non-agricultural labour force fell from 3.6 million to 1.5 million in 1917–20.

ACTIVITY 3.15

How far do you agree that the Whites lost the Civil War because of their own weaknesses and divisions, rather than the strengths of the Reds?

Hold a class debate in which students make the case for each side of the argument. You must support your viewpoint with facts.

The importance of the Kronstadt mutiny

In February 1921 the sailors at the naval base on Kronstadt, an island outside Petrograd, rebelled against the Bolshevik government. The mutiny was the most serious opposition movement that the newly established Bolshevik government faced.

The Kronstadt Mutiny: Causes, events and impact

The main causes of the rebellion were the authorities' introduction of War Communism, which inflicted severe hardship on the population, and anger at the tightening of the Soviet dictatorship.

Although War Communism played a part in winning the Civil War, its economic consequences were disastrous for the Russian population. Nationalisation of industry did not lead to an improvement in economic growth. By 1920–21, large-scale industrial production had fallen by 82% compared with 1913, the last full year of peace before the First World War. Food shortages worsened as peasants produced only what they needed to survive, knowing that the authorities would seize any surplus. By 1920, Russia was facing famine. The government maintained that the problems were due to the peasants' concealment of grain, and its officials introduced increasingly harsh measures to make them give up what they were hiding.

There were hundreds of peasant revolts. The most serious one began in Tambov, 350 km south-east of Moscow, in the autumn of 1920. It was suppressed by Red Army troops, who used brutal tactics, including using poison gas. Officially, the government described such uprisings as the work of 'bandits', but it became impossible to make people believe this as opposition to government policies spread beyond the peasantry. Starving industrial workers went on strike. There was also growing anger about the increasingly centralised power of the party. A 'Workers' Opposition' movement arose in 1920 to protest at the subordination of trade unions to the authority of the party. Workers' meetings called for a restoration of freedom to trade and of civil liberties.

The situation became critical in February 1921 with an uprising of sailors at the Kronstadt naval base. Joined by urban workers, they formed a revolutionary committee which put a series of demands to the government. The sailors had once been described by Trotsky as the 'pride and glory of the revolution'. They had taken part in the July Days and the crushing of the Kornilov coup in 1917. A shot fired by the cruiser *Aurora* in October 1917 had signalled the start of the Bolshevik takeover. Now the sailors were arguing that the Bolsheviks had betrayed the socialist ideals for which they had fought. The party had accumulated too much power and denied ordinary workers essential freedoms.

Under Trotsky's direction, 60 000 Red Army troops, backed by Cheka units, assaulted Kronstadt in March, advancing across the frozen sea that surrounded the base to do battle with the 15 000 defenders. After a siege of two weeks, the base fell, and the survivors were executed or imprisoned.

The rebellion had a major impact on the development of Soviet Russia. To defuse popular anger, the government introduced economic reforms which answered some of the demands of the rebels. But political control was not relaxed. The crushing of the uprising showed that Lenin and the Bolsheviks were determined to create a single-party dictatorship.

Figure 3.24: This photograph shows Red Army troops loyal to the Bolsheviks in the frozen Gulf of Finland to suppress the 1921 Kronstadt uprising.

ACTIVITY 3.16

1 In view of the fact that the present Soviets do not represent the will of the workers and peasants, immediately to re-elect the Soviets by secret voting …

3 Freedom of meetings, trade unions and peasant associations …

5 To liberate all political prisoners of Socialist Parties, and also all workers, peasants, soldiers and sailors who have been imprisoned in connection with working class and peasant movements …

11 To grant the peasant full right to do what he sees fit with his land and to possess cattle, which he must maintain and manage with his own strength, but without employing hired labour …

From the demands of the Kronstadt sailors, 1 March 1921.

The government tried to depict the Kronstadt rebels as agents of the White counter-revolution. Using this extract from the sailors' demands, what do you think were the real reasons for the uprising? Refer closely to the extract in your answer.

Reflection

Compare your list of reasons and supporting evidence from the extract with a partner. Have you used different parts of the extract to support similar reasons? Discuss your approach to how you decided which parts of the extract to use. Would you change how you choose supporting evidence from sources following your discussion?

The introduction and impact of the New Economic Policy

Despite the brutal nature of the repression, it was clear that the regime would have to moderate its policy of War Communism. In March 1921, at the tenth Party Congress, which opened while the uprising was being put down, Lenin declared that the events at Kronstadt had 'lit up reality like a flash of lightning'. Food requisitioning was replaced by a **tax in kind** and, once they had paid this, peasants were now allowed to sell their surplus grain on the market. This concession was the foundation of the New Economic Policy (NEP) – Lenin's recognition that the party needed to reach a settlement with the peasantry. The change in direction did not mean that the government had abandoned its long-term plans to take the peasants' landholdings into state ownership, but the plans were certainly to be delayed.

KEY TERM

Tax in kind: A tax paid in goods or services rather than in money.

Lenin depicted the NEP as a compromise between socialism and capitalism. The 'commanding heights' of the economy, including large-scale industry and banking, remained in the hands of the state. A central planning agency, known as Gosplan, had to give advice on the long-term development of industry. Small-scale businesses, however, were returned to private ownership to encourage the production of consumer goods. Restrictions on private sales of goods and services were lifted, and the State Bank was empowered to make credit available to enterprises.

Figure 3.25: An open-air market in Smolensk, allowed by the Soviet authorities under the New Economic Policy.

The NEP was a controversial move back towards the market economy. A new class of merchants and profiteers known as the 'Nepmen' emerged to make money from the new opportunities. Such capitalist activity had been illegal since the Bolsheviks took power. Lenin insisted that it was necessary to take this step, since the uprisings faced by the government were 'far more dangerous than all the Denikins, Yudeniches and Kolchaks put together'. It was the only way to deal with the desperate food situation and to avert the collapse of the Russian economy. He described it as 'a peasant Brest-Litovsk' – comparing it with the unpopular treaty with the Germans, which he had defended as taking one step backwards to take two steps forward.

The NEP was broadly successful in leading to increased agricultural and industrial output. But there was a downside, known as the 'scissors crisis' because the widening gap between agricultural and industrial product prices resembled the open blades of a pair of scissors. Good harvests in 1922–23 led to falling food prices, while the slow recovery of industries from the Civil War meant that factory production struggled to keep pace, keeping products relatively expensive. This situation meant that peasants were expected to sell their produce cheaply, leaving them unable to afford to buy manufactured goods. Fortunately, by 1924 the gap between the two was closing as industry began to recover. But at the time of Lenin's death in January 1924, Soviet Russia seemed to lack a coherent overall economic policy.

The Soviet state survived largely because of Lenin's insistence that the political control of the party would not be relaxed. At the 1921 Congress, he secured a vote banning **factionalism** within the party. The Central Committee would be the supreme body in the party and the country. This was the logical outcome of the policies followed by the Bolsheviks towards all forms of opposition since the October Revolution. Russia was now officially a one-party state.

KEY TERM

Factionalism: Arguments between small groups within a larger organisation such as a political party.

KEY CONCEPT 3.5

Significance

Historians assess the significance of key events and individuals in terms of their impact on later developments. The Kronstadt uprising demonstrated the ruthlessness of the Bolshevik government in suppressing opposition. It also showed that the regime could be flexible in how it reacted to events, since it contributed to the adoption of the New Economic Policy. In small groups, discuss the importance of the uprising for the development of the Soviet state and economy.

Practice questions

Source-based question

Read the sources and then answer **both** parts of the question.

SOURCE A

In commanding the responsible authorities to take measures to stop disorders, lawlessness, and violence, and to protect peaceful citizens in the quiet performance of their duties, We [i.e. the tsar] have found it necessary to unite the activities of the Supreme Government, so as to ensure the successful carrying out of the general measures laid down by Us for the peaceful life of the State.

We lay upon the Government the execution of Our unchangeable will:

1 To grant to the population the inviolable right of free citizenship, based on the principles of freedom of person, conscience, speech, assembly and union.

2 … to include in the participation of the work of the Duma those classes of the population that have been until now entirely deprived of the right to vote …

3 To establish as an unbreakable rule that no law shall go into force without its confirmation by the State Duma …

From the October Manifesto, issued by Tsar Nicholas II, 17 October 1905.

SOURCE B

A satirical cartoon by the Russian artist Boris Kustodiev. The title is 'Introduction to the revolution' or 'Bugaboo of revolution', 1905. The cartoon shows the revolution as a skeleton rampaging through the city. A 'bugaboo' is an imaginary monster used to create fear.

SOURCE C

The supreme autocratic power is vested in the Tsar of All the Russias. It is God's command that his authority should be obeyed not only through fear but for conscience' sake …

7 The Tsar exercises the legislative power in conjunction with the Council of the Empire [the State Council] and the Imperial Duma.

9 The Tsar approves of the laws, and without his approval no law can come into existence.

10 All governmental powers in their widest extent throughout the whole Russian Empire are vested in the Tsar.

72 No one can be prosecuted for an offence except according to the process established by law.

CONTINUED

78 Russian subjects are entitled to meet peaceably and without arms for such purposes as are not contrary to law.

From the Fundamental Laws of the Russian Empire, 23 April 1906.

SOURCE D

A cruel disappointment has befallen Our expectations. The representatives of the nation, instead of applying themselves to the work of productive legislation, have strayed into spheres beyond their competence … and have been making comments upon the imperfections of the Fundamental Laws, which can only be modified by Our imperial will. In short, the representatives of the nation have undertaken really illegal acts, such as the appeal by the Duma to the nation.

The peasants, disturbed by such behaviour, and seeing no hope of the improvement of their lot, have resorted in a number of districts to open looting and the destruction of other people's property, and to disobedience of the law … We shall not permit arbitrary or illegal acts, and We shall impose Our imperial will on the disobedient by all the power of the State.

From the announcement of the dissolution of the First Duma, 21 July 1906.

1 a Read Sources **A** and **C**.
Compare Sources A and C as evidence of the tsarist government's response to the revolution of 1905. **[15 marks]**

b Read **all** the sources.
'The tsarist regime in Russia's main aim in 1905–06 was to suppress opposition.' How far do the sources support this view? **[25 marks]**

Essay-based questions

Answer **both** parts of each question.

2 a Explain why the New Economic Policy was introduced in 1921. **[10 marks]**

b To what extent was Tsar Nicholas II's weak leadership in the First World War the most important reason for his downfall? **[20 marks]**

3 a Explain why Lenin agreed to the Treaty of Brest-Litovsk. **[10 marks]**

b 'Russian military defeats in the First World War caused the February 1917 Revolution.' How far do you agree? **[20 marks]**

Improve this answer

2 b To what extent was Tsar Nicholas II's weak leadership in the First World War the most important reason for his downfall? **[20 marks]**

Nicholas II was not trained as a general and he was not really suited to the role of wartime leader. He did not fully understand what was needed to bring about victory in war. A major error was his decision to take command of the Russian armies in person in August 1915, replacing his cousin who had been commander-in-chief up to this point. He hoped that this would reverse Russia's poor military performance during the first year of the war, but it turned out to be a serious mistake. However, there were other reasons for his downfall in the February 1917 Revolution. The Russian economy was failing under the strain of the war. The population was suffering from food shortages and the morale of the army collapsed in 1916–17.

This opening paragraph has two main strengths. It focuses immediately on the factor highlighted in the question. It also indicates that the answer will provide some balance, as other factors are referred to. However it is a little descriptive and could do with a sharper analytical focus.

The war had been going badly for the Russians since the start of the fighting in August 1914. The army had been defeated by the more effective German commanders when they invaded Germany, at the Battle of Tannenberg, and they had won few battles since then. The Russians were not properly equipped for a war of this kind. Soldiers lacked training and good weapons, and they were short of food and basic supplies. One of the main problems was that the rail network was not adequate when it came to moving troops and supplies, as well as taking vitally needed food to the cities. Soldiers started to desert the army in 1916, as they became concerned about the problems facing them. They were demoralised by the defeats and heavy casualties, and they wanted to go home to help their starving families. The tsar was unable to cope with these problems because he lacked the ability to be an effective leader.

> This is an accurate summary of the deteriorating situation in Russia, but it does not fulfil the expectations raised in the introduction because it does not link the tsar to the problems described. The paragraph needed a sharper focus from the outset which directly links it back to the question and the answer suggested in the opening paragraph.

The tsar's decision to lead his armies in 1915 was one of his worst mistakes because the government in Petrograd was left in the hands of his wife, Alexandra. She was unpopular with the Russian people because of her German background and because she relied on Rasputin, a strange holy man who had great influence at court. The monarchy lost the respect of the people as rumours spread about Rasputin's relationship with the tsarina and other ladies in the royal circle. Another way in which this was damaging was that Rasputin influenced the appointment and dismissal of ministers, something he was not qualified to do. The level of leadership in Petrograd was poor. Rasputin was murdered in late 1916 by supporters of the monarchy, who were disturbed by the damage he was doing to it, but by then it was too late to reverse it.

> This is a stronger paragraph because it makes a direct link between an important aspect of the tsar's faulty leadership–his personal command of the armies–and the problems of government. This offers some focused explanation of what went wrong for the Russian war effort. The material on Rasputin does, however, need to be linked more explicitly to the fall of the tsar.

There were deeper reasons why the tsar fell from power. The root cause of the crisis was the fact that the Russian economy was not equal to the task of supporting a long war. Although average incomes actually rose during the first two years of the war, prices rose by a much larger factor. This was because the government used borrowing to finance the war, causing the value of money to fall. The food crisis became worse as peasants hoarded grain rather than selling it, because they could not get a fair price for it. Combined with the breakdown of the transport system, this led to food shortages in the cities, leading to protests and strikes by early 1917. A strike in the Putilov steel works, the most important factory in Petrograd, was a major blow. This in turn further weakened the war effort. The economic crisis was critical to the downfall of the tsar because it had a direct impact on people's living conditions, thus reinforcing the feeling that Nicholas was not truly concerned with their welfare.

The poor suffered most from the collapsing home front, and it was their anger which led to the breakdown of order in Petrograd. However, the country's elites were also becoming critical of the government. When the Duma was recalled in 1916, liberals and moderate conservatives joined together in the 'Progressive Front' to demand a change of direction. It was the military and civilian leaders, for example Mikhail Rodzianko, who in the end advised Nicholas to abdicate in March 1917 to protect his personal safety, and in the hope that this would allow the monarchy to continue under a new tsar. The police and army, on whose support the regime relied, could not by this stage be depended upon to put down hostile crowds in Petrograd. They had sympathy for those who were protesting and failed to exert themselves to defend the tsarist system.

Here the essay introduces some balance: these two paragraphs help to meet the requirement to show 'how far' one factor was the most important. It is a little brief, however: we are not told much about the reasons why the Progressive Front was critical of the government, and the jump to the abdication is sudden. The essay states that the elites played an important role in the final crisis of the monarchy but does not fully explain this point. While the first of the two paragraphs above starts well – with a valid point being made – it becomes a little descriptive. The level of detailed support is good here, but the information needed to be more sharply focussed on the question.

The tsar was partly responsible for his own failure. He had always been distant from his people's everyday living conditions, and his decision to attempt to run the war from his military headquarters, 600 km from Petrograd, made this problem worse. He did not understand the situation which had developed in his capital city and believed that he could calm the situation there by returning. Nicholas was on his way there when some of his generals and leading politicians intercepted his train and advised him to abdicate. He gave way with little persuasion required, suggesting that he had never really measured up to the role of tsar. His personality was poorly suited to governing his empire and this was especially so in the middle of war. However, there were long-term reasons for the fall of the monarchy. The state of the Russian economy and army, and the fact that the country could not meet the demands of war on this scale, were the underlying causes of the tsar's fall.

The conclusion has some important strengths. The revolution is linked to the quality of the tsar's leadership, and there are some insights into his personality and poor qualifications for government. The relative significance of different factors is considered, and the judgement is consistent with the line taken earlier in the essay, pointing towards deeper reasons for the tsar's fall. However, the conclusion would be improved still further if the judgement were fully supported. The key prompt in the question, about the tsar's war leadership, is not developed sufficiently in the body of the essay. For example, the fact that by taking command in person, the tsar was unintentionally associating himself with military failure, is not covered. The point about his isolation from political affairs at his headquarters is not addressed until near the end of the essay.

Consider the suggestions for improvement. Now write your own answer to the question.

SELF-EVALUATION CHECKLIST

After working through this chapter, complete the table.

You should be able to:	Needs more work	Almost there	Ready to move on
evaluate the causes and effects of Russian autocracy from 1881 to 1894			
outline the growth of the Russian economy between 1881 and 1894			
assess the effects of societal changes across Russia from 1881 to 1894			
analyse the formation and effectiveness of opposition to tsarist rule			
explain the reasons for the revolution against tsarist rule			
analyse the events of the 1905 Revolution			
outline the immediate changes brought by the revolution			
examine how the revolution changed Russian life from 1905 to the start of the First World War			
analyse how the First World War changed tsarist rule			
assess the causes and consequences of the February Revolution			
explain the creation and rule of the Provisional Government			
examine how the Provisional Government failed and how this helped lead to the October Revolution			
analyse how the Bolsheviks created a dictatorship			
assess the results of the treaty of Brest-Litovsk in March 1918			
explain why the Bolsheviks succeeded			
examine the significance of the Kronstadt mutiny.			

> Chapter 4

Preparing for assessment

The information in this section is based on the Cambridge International Education syllabus. You should always refer to the appropriate syllabus document for the year of examination to confirm the details and for more information. The syllabus document is available on the website: www.cambridgeinternational.org.

Introduction

As we saw in the Getting started with Cambridge International AS Level History section of this book, to achieve success in Cambridge International AS Level History you need to develop skills that enable you to analyse and interpret your historical knowledge in depth. The methods of assessment reflect this requirement. This chapter focuses on those skills and helps you prepare for assessment.

4.1 Overview of assessment and assessment objectives

For the Cambridge International AS Level History (9489/9981) assessment, you will take two papers:

- Paper 1: Historical Sources (1 hour 15 minutes) This paper is worth 40% of the AS Level. You will be asked to answer one two-part question based on historical sources.
- Paper 2: Outline Study (1 hour 45 minutes) This paper is worth 60% of the AS Level. You will be asked to answer two two-part questions.

There are three assessment objectives (AOs) which are used in AS Level History. These objectives describe the skills that are assessed in the course. Table 4.1 lists the AOs and the proportion of marks which are allocated to each one.

Marks are allocated between the two papers as follows:

- Paper 1: AO1 – 25% of the marks. AO3 – 75% of the marks.
- Paper 2: AO1 – 50% of the marks. AO2 – 50% of the marks.

These allocations show us that while learning knowledge and using it appropriately (AO1) is important, you cannot be successful in your course without being able to show the higher-level analysis and evaluation skills of AO2 and AO3.

4.2 Understanding what a question is asking you to do

Broadly, there are two main types of question: source-based questions and essay-based questions.

There are certain key words that appear in many AS Level History questions. These 'command words' are the instructions that specify what you need to do. They make it clear what is expected from a response in terms of skills, knowledge and understanding.

We will discuss the two main types of question separately, considering the command words that they might contain.

Assessment objective	Description	Percentage of total marks
AO1 Historical knowledge	Recall, select and use appropriate historical knowledge.	40%
AO2 Historical explanation, analysis and judgement	Identify, explain and analyse the past using historical concepts: • cause and consequence • change and continuity • significance. Explain and analyse connections between different aspects of the past. Reach a judgement.	30%
AO3 Historical sources	Understand, analyse, evaluate and interpret a range of historical sources in context.	30%

Table 4.1: Assessment objectives from the Cambridge International AS Level History syllabuses (9489/9981) for examination from 2027.

Source-based questions

You were introduced to the concept of source analysis in the Getting started with Cambridge International AS Level History section. We can now look at historical sources in more detail as you have the necessary topic knowledge from studying Chapters 1–3.

Dealing with sources

How you understand, analyse, evaluate and manage different types of sources is vital to success in assessments at AS Level. You must take time to reflect critically when you look at sources, and not just accept them at face value. This means that you must:

- Show that you have fully grasped what the source is saying. Try highlighting the key points. Remember that the key point can often be in the last sentence.
- Evaluate the sources clearly and weigh up their value individually and as a set of evidence. You can do this by demonstrating that you have thought about each source's provenance (background) and reliability. You must not just accept what the source is saying. Think about what the author might have left out. You need to test a source's reliability by:
  - comparing what it says with what other sources say and with your own subject knowledge
  - looking carefully at who created it, when, why and for what purpose or audience
  - establishing if there are any reasons to doubt the reliability of the source.

  Always include as much contextual knowledge as you can to develop a point – particularly when commenting on the accuracy/validity of a source by linking it to its historical context.
- Interpret. What can be learned from the source, taking into account your judgement on how reliable the source is?
- Remain objective. Always look at a source objectively and with an open mind.
- Never make assumptions. For example, do not assume that a source must be biased because it was written by a certain person from a certain place at a certain time. These points might establish a motive for bias, but do not necessarily prove that a text is biased.
- Never make sweeping or unsupported assertions. A statement such as '*Source A is biased …*' must be accompanied by evidence that you know exactly what bias is, as well as evidence and examples to demonstrate in what way it is biased, together with reasons to explain why it is biased.
- Compare sources. If you are asked to compare two sources, make sure you analyse both sources carefully before you start to write your answer. Draw up a simple plan.
- Draw conclusions. What can you learn from your analysis of the sources? How does it enhance your knowledge and understanding of a topic or event?

To analyse a source effectively, you need to consider certain questions:

- Who wrote/spoke/produced the source?
- When was it written/produced/published?
- What is the context?
- What does the source say/what is its message?
- Who was the intended audience?
- Why was it written/produced? What was the author's motive?
- How does it compare with other sources?
- How reliable is it likely to be?

It may be that one or two of those questions are more important when considering a specific source or answering a specific question, but the general principles are the same for all sources. After you practise thinking about these questions for a number of different types of sources, you will find yourself naturally asking the right questions when you look at a source.

Understanding, analysing and evaluating a text source

As you will have seen in Chapters 1–3 there many different types of text sources from private diaries, to journalists' articles in newspapers, to memoirs written by actual participants some years after the events. All these sources need careful evaluation.

Let's look at an example and see how it works in practice. The following source is an extract from a letter sent by the Austrian ambassador to Prussia to the foreign minister in Vienna in February 1866, just after Austria and Prussia had waged a successful war against Denmark.

> So far, the differences between Austria and Prussia have been limited to the Governments of the two countries. Now they have been translated to the field of public opinion. I am clear that Bismarck feels that the time has come to mount a great Prussian action abroad, and if it can be done in no other way, to go to war if he thinks the time is right for it. Such an action has been his ambition from the beginning of his political career. It would deal with his ungoverned and unscrupulous [unprincipled], but daring, wish for great achievement.
>
> If he is successful, especially if it was attained [achieved] by means of a victorious war, the government in Prussia would more easily master its internal problems. It would be difficult to deal with Prussia's internal problems without the diversion of war. It has been suggested that the king of Prussia might end his domestic problems by a coup d'état, simply assuming total power, which Bismarck may have recommended, but the king refused absolutely. The only means by which Prussia's many domestic problems can be overcome must be sought in an active and successful foreign policy. It is this that guides Bismarck's policy. How far Bismarck has succeeded, or will succeed, in winning over the king of Prussia to his extreme warlike policy is the question on which the whole future depends. A solution using force goes against the grain with the king, but he is very open to persuasion.
>
> **From a letter sent by the Austrian ambassador to Prussia to the foreign minister in Vienna in February 1866.**

- **Who wrote this letter?** The Austrian ambassador to Prussia. His job was to represent Austria's interests in Prussia and to report back to Vienna all events in Prussia which might affect Austria.
- **When was it written?** In February 1866. This was after the war against Denmark that had been fought by Prussia with Austria as an ally, and before the war between Austria and Prussia later in 1866.
- **What is the context?** The conflict with Denmark had ended successfully. Both Austria and Prussia had gained from it, though Prussia had done a great deal better than Austria. There was internal conflict in Prussia, however, which was threatening Bismarck's position. This internal conflict would also affect his ambitions for Prussian expansion and German unification under Prussia. (Bismarck was known to dislike Austria and wanted to reduce its influence in Germany.)
- **What does the letter say?** The main point is the internal unrest in Prussia and the ambassador's opinion that one way of dealing with it is for Bismarck to mount a successful foreign war. It is a warning about Prussia's future intentions.
- **Who was the intended audience?** The foreign minister of Austria and other members of the Austrian government. It is unlikely that it would have been published, or given to a wider audience, or appeared in the press.
- **Why was it written? What was the author's motive?** Ambassadors were expected to give accurate reports based on carefully gained evidence. Austria's policy towards Germany would be strongly influenced by this report. It would be important for the ambassador to make the report as accurate and reliable as possible.
- **How does it compare with other sources?** We know from other sources that Bismarck wished to limit or destroy Austria's domination of Germany.
- **How reliable is it likely to be?** Ambassadors were usually educated and experienced men who were paid to report accurately. There might, however, be some pro-Austrian bias as well as personal dislike of Bismarck.

So, overall, do you think that this is a very important source which tells us a great deal – or do you think the ambassador could be giving a wrong impression of what was happening in Prussia?

Understanding, analysing and evaluating a visual source

Many of the sources you will encounter are texts, but you will also be required to use visual sources. Visual sources may be cartoons, posters or photographs. You will analyse and evaluate visual sources in much the same way as text sources, so do not worry. However, it is a good idea to practise working with visual sources, so that you are comfortable with using them.

Let's look at some examples and see how they work in practice.

Cartoons

Cartoons can be difficult to analyse. In most cases they are drawn and published for one or more of three reasons:

- to amuse and entertain
- to celebrate
- to criticise and send a message.

To achieve these aims, cartoons might use symbolism and a subtle form of humour that people at the time might have understood, but which is less obvious to us.

Look at the cartoon in Figure 4.1. The clergyman on the left, looking thin and hungry, represented the clergy in France after the confiscation of the Church's wealth, while the one on the right, representing the clergy before the confiscation, looks very well fed and prosperous.

Figure 4.1: This cartoon was published in a radical anti-clerical pamphlet circulating in France in the early 1790s. The caption at the bottom of the cartoon reads 'The Abbot today and the Abbot formerly'.

- **Who produced the source?** It was one of many radical pamphlets circulating in France in the revolutionary period.
- **When was it produced?** In the 1790s, after the early stages of the revolution.
- **What is the context?** The clergy and the Roman Catholic Church in France, the First Estate, were not only very wealthy, but also generally did not pay any taxes. The majority of taxation was paid by the Third Estate. Most of the clergy strongly opposed the demands of the Third Estate for reform after the meeting of the Estates-General.
- **What does the source say / what is its message?** That the reforms put forward by the National Convention were having an impact, and that the wealth and privilege of the clergy had been destroyed. The abbot 'today' looks poorly fed and dressed, quite a contrast to the well-fed and prosperous looking abbot of the past.
- **Who was the intended audience?** As wide as possible within France. This type of pamphlet was getting a wide readership all over France and was playing a significant role in driving forward the revolutionary process.
- **What were the motives of the cartoonist and the editors of the newspaper?** To maintain the attack on counter-revolutionary forces and emphasise the gains of the revolution.
- **How does it compare with other sources?** The message is very clear and the images of the two clergymen are good evidence of the opinion that the cartoonist holds of the two men and what they have done. (You would have to study other sources to be able to make comparisons.)
- **How reliable is it likely to be?** It is a cartoon and therefore intending to make a point and not convey acccurate information – so potentially unreliable. However contextual knowledge would show that 1789 led to a considerable reduction in the wealth of the church.

When you study a cartoon like this, you need to reflect carefully on how far your own subject knowledge supports or challenges the views represented.

Posters

Posters are created with a specific intention. They aim to convey a message, for example, to encourage people to join the army, or to vote for a candidate in an election. They do not give us a balanced view of a situation, but they can give a clear idea of what might have inspired and motivated people at the time.

Look at the poster in Figure 4.2, which depicts a small ship being destroyed by a much larger vessel. What can this source tell us?

Figure 4.2: A Bolshevik poster, published probably around 1920. The caption beneath the image translates as 'The forces of the counter-revolution smashing themselves to pieces against the strength of the USSR'.

- **Who produced the source?** The Bolshevik government, which controlled all the media in Russia at the time.
- **When was it produced?** The civil war period in Russia, probably 1920.
- **What is the context?** The newly established regime was involved in a life-and-death struggle against its many opponents, both inside Russia, and externally with its former allies such as France and Britain.
- **What is its message?** That Russia is secure against the forces of counter-revolution.
- **Who was the intended audience?** As wide a readership as possible, making a clear visual message which might appeal to the many illiterate people in Russia at the time.
- **What were the motives for producing the poster?** To convince the Russian people that the new regime was secure, and that supporting it, and not the counter-revolutionary Whites, was the most sensible course of action.
- **Additional contextual knowledge?** It demonstrates Bolshevik propaganda techniques well. The Bolsheviks were anxious to secure support from the mass of the Russian people.
- **How does it compare with other sources?** It is likely to be less balanced than other sources, but gives a clear idea of the sense of strength that the Bolsheviks wanted to demonstrate.
- **How reliable is it likely to be?** Posters are designed to influence and inspire. They can give a good picture of one side of an issue.

Posters can be very useful in gaining understanding of issues and what motivated people at the time.

Photographs

Posters and cartoons are drawn or painted. Photographs are different from posters and cartoons because they can generally only visualise a scene that existed at a specific place and at a specific time – a scene that a camera captured. Photos can add to the understanding of issues and the grasp of specific events.

What does the photograph in Figure 4.3 tell us?

- **Who produced the source?** In the case of photographs, the photographer is often anonymous, as is the case here. Was the photographer employed by the Bolsheviks, who might be anxious to demonstrate the heroism of the Red Guards? It might have been by someone neutral and, therefore, present a realistic picture of what happened.
- **When was the photograph taken?** The Bolshevik government claimed that it was taken during the attack. It was later discovered that the photograph in fact shows a re-enactment staged well after the event.
- **What is the context?** Part of a propaganda exercise designed to emphasise the heroism of the Red Guards. The Red Guards played a key role in the Bolshevik seizure of power in November 1917 and in the overthrow of the Provisional Government.
- **What does the source show?** It shows a group of armed men charging towards the Winter Palace, apparently being fired on by opposition within it.
- **Who was the intended audience?** This depends on whether it was published, and where. In this case, it was published as widely as possible, both within Russia and outside as part of a sustained Bolshevik propaganda campaign.
- **What were the motives of the photographer?** It is impossible to say. The photograph could be used to keep a record of what actually happened or for propaganda purposes. The latter is the most likely.
- **How does it compare with other sources?** In this case the source shows the violence which had to be used by the Bolsheviks to gain power in Russia. Other sources focus on different aspects of the revolution.
- **How reliable is it likely to be?** Photographs always need to be treated with caution before accepting them as evidence. This photograph was staged long after the event that it supposedly shows.

Like all sources, photographs can be of tremendous value to a historian, but they need to be used with care. Photographs can easily be stage-managed. Captions can be misleading, and the action captured might actually be a re-enactment production. We should also remember that photographs can easily be altered to give a totally different impression to that originally intended. Airbrushing (manually altering) to remove individuals from photographs was common practice in Russia in the 1920s.

Figure 4.3: The storming of the Winter Palace by the Red Guards, October 1917.

Comparing two sources

Very often, two sources will offer contradictory views. Whenever you compare two or more sources, you should draw attention to the similarities and what they have in common. You should also draw attention to the differences and points where they disagree.

At AS Level, you are expected to do much more than just give a summary of the two sources. You must show that you have reviewed the content of the sources and that you fully understand them and can use your knowledge and understanding of them to answer the question. Make sure you demonstrate your full grasp of the points made in each source and establish very clearly what the main similarities and differences are. Quote briefly from each source to evidence your points – no more than five or six words is usually fine. Take care to explain clearly **why** there are similarities and differences as well. That explanation is important. Do demonstrate contextual knowledge and show that you are fully aware of the sources' provenance. When evaluating each source do not just make a vague comment, comment quite specifically on each source.

Let's look at an example and see how it works in practice. Study Source A and Source B on the causes of the French Revolution.

SOURCE A

The democratic ideal which was stifled under all European governments while the feudal system remained powerful, has gathered strength and continues to grow. As the arts, trade and the pursuit of luxury make industrious people richer, making the rich landowners poorer and bringing the different classes closer together through money, so science and education bring them closer in their daily lives, and recall men to the basic idea of equality. To these natural causes can be added the influence of royal power: long undermined by the aristocracy, it had called the people to its aid. Conditions in France were ripe for a democratic revolution when the unfortunate Louis XVI ascended the throne; the governments' actions favoured its explosion.

The two privileged orders which still retained control of the government were ruined through their taste for luxury and had degraded themselves by their way of life.

Continued

The Third Estate, by contrast, had produced enlightened thinkers and acquired enormous wealth. The people were restrained only by their habit of obedience and limited hope they had of breaking their chains. Government had succeeded in containing this hope, but it still flourished in the heart of the nation. It was already apparent that, amongst the growing generation influenced by the Enlightenment, for royal power to remain it would have required a great tyrant or a great statesman on the throne. Louis XVI was neither; he was too well intentioned not to try and remedy abuses which had shocked him, but he had neither the character, or the talents to control an imperious nation in a situation which cried out for reform. His reign was a succession of feeble attempts at doing good, showing weakness and clear evidence of his failings as a ruler.

From the memoir of Antoine Barnave, a revolutionary, in prison awaiting execution, 1793.

SOURCE B

The turning point was 1789. It was that year that the Revolution, already apparent in the minds, customs and way of life of the French nation, began to take effect in government. I will describe the principal reasons for this and some of the events to which it led. The most striking of the country's troubles was the chaos of its finances, the result of years of extravagance intensified by the great expense of the American War, which had cost the state over twelve hundred million livres. No one could think of any remedy but a search for fresh funds as the old ones were exhausted.

M de Calonne, minister of finance, had produced a bold and wide-ranging plan. This plan changed the whole system of financial administration and attacked all its vices at their root. The worst of these were: the arbitrary [random] system of allocating taxes, the high cost of collection and the abuse of privilege by the richest of taxpayers. The whole weight of public expenditure was borne by the most numerous, but the least wealthy part of the nation which was being crushed by the burden. This plan was submitted to the Assembly of Notables. All the Assembly did was to destroy M de Calonne and he was abandoned by the king. Shortly afterwards the king was unwise enough to make Brienne principal minister.

Continued

> Brienne tried to put through some parts of Calonne's plans, but the parlements resisted strongly. Then the troubles began. They broke out first in Brittany, where the government was compelled to bring in armed forces but did not dare use them owing to the reluctance shown by the troops to be used against such people. In Paris, where the people's discontent had already been raised to the point of rebellion by angry members of the parlement, there were serious riots which had to be put down by force. The upheavals became even more violent in 1788, and then the government made a great mistake: it promised to call the Estates-General. They had not met for almost two hundred years and in the long period of time there had been such great changes in the minds, the way of life, in the character, customs and government of the French nation that their meeting could now only produce upheaval
>
> **From *Memoires* by Marquis de Bouillé, a French aristocrat in exile, 1797.**

In order to look at the similarities and differences between the two sources, you first need to analyse them. You might want to think about these questions:

- **Who wrote these sources?** Source A is by a revolutionary directly involved in the revolution. Source B is by an aristocrat who had fled France.
- **When were they published?** 1793 and 1797. Both are, therefore, primary sources.
- **What is the context?** Source A was published in 1793, after the author's death during the early stages of the Terror. Source B was published in 1797, after the death of the king and the end of the Terror, and during the rule of the Directory.
- **What do the sources say?** Both sources are trying to explain why a revolution occurred in France starting in 1789.
- **Who was the intended audience?** In both cases, as many people as possible.
- **What were the authors' motives?** In both cases, the writers are trying to explain what had happened and why. There might be an element of trying to justify their positions.
- **How do the sources compare?** For help with comparing the sources, see the guidance in the following bullet point.
- **How reliable are the sources likely to be?** In both cases, the information they provide is accurate, if selective. Both writers were involved in the events in France at the time, although on different sides of the revolutionary divide. While they might have been trying to justify their actions, they both tried to reach similar conclusions. Although the author of Source B is an aristocrat, notice that he is critical of both the king and his own class, which adds to the validity of his comments.

So how do you organise these ideas and use them to answer the question?

A good way of comparing the views contained in these two sources is to make some brief notes on the key points, focusing strictly on the issue of what were the causes of the French Revolution.

For example, Source A:

- stresses the growth of democracy – conditions were right for it
- points out that social and economic changes are bringing classes together
- notes that royal powers being undermined by the aristocracy was 'unfortunate'
- emphasises the failings of the First and Second Estates
- raises the point about Enlightenment ideas
- mentions the failings of the king.

And Source B talks of:

- France in 'chaos'
- the failure to back Calonne
- the privileges of the nobility
- taxation
- the failings of the Notables
- wider unrest in Brittany, spreading to Paris
- the summoning of the Estates-General and the lack of awareness of what had changed since it had last met.

From this plan it is easy to see where the authors agree and disagree. They both mention the financial chaos and social changes in France, the failings of the king and are critical of the nobility. However, they disagree about the effects of the Enlightenment and the causes of the violent upheavals.

Source-based questions in assessment

Now that we have looked at different types of sources and the key source analysis skill of comparing sources, let's look at types of question that you might meet in assessment.

Source-based questions test your ability to:

- understand a question and its requirements
- understand the content of a source in its historical setting
- consider how we need to understand a source's meaning in relation to who produced it, and what the writer of the source was trying to achieve
- analyse and evaluate source content and the sources themselves
- reach a focused and balanced judgement based on evidence
- communicate your argument in a clear and effective manner.

TIP

When answering, remember:

- You do not need to provide a summary of the sources, or copy out large parts of them. However, you might need to quote just a phrase or two to back up your points.
- Evaluate the sources. You must show clearly that you have really thought about their provenance and validity.
- Include relevant contextual knowledge.

Consider the source-based question provided in Chapter 2. It contains four sources on the outbreak of war between Prussia and France in 1870. Then, it asks two questions:

1 a Read Sources **C** and **D**.

Compare Sources C and D as evidence of Prussia's responsibility for the outbreak of war with France in 1870. **[15 marks]**

b Read **all** of the sources.

'Bismarck planned in advance to complete the process of German unification by means of a war with France.' How far do the sources support this view? **[25 marks]**

First of all, you must study the sources carefully.

SOURCE A

It remains to be remarked that the feeling of uneasiness in Germany is augmented [increased] by the impression that … when France shall have completed her military preparations, She will seek a war with Germany so as to obtain those compensations for the aggrandisement [increased power] of Prussia, which She has sketched out, but which She has already learnt will only be yielded to superior force. Whether the fears thus entertained in regard to the eventual course of France and to the alliances to which it may give rise will be realized or not, some seventeen or eighteen months hence, their existence produces a feeling of uncertainty as to the future and furnishes a motive for military preparation on the part of Germany.

From a report by the British envoy to Bavaria, Sir Henry F. Howard, to the British foreign secretary, Lord Stanley, 3 December 1866.

SOURCE B

In regard to the South German situation I think the line for Prussian policy is set by two diverse aims … the one distant, the other immediate … The distant and by far the greater aim is the national unification of Germany. We can wait for this in security because the lapse of time and the natural development of the nation which makes further progress every year will have their effect. We cannot accelerate it unless out of the way [unexpected] events in Europe, such as some upheaval in France or a war of other great powers among themselves offer us an unsought opportunity to do so … Every recognisable effort of Prussia to determine the decision of the South German Princes will endanger our immediate aim. I consider this to be … to keep Bavaria and Württemberg in such political direction that neither will cooperate with Paris or Vienna … nor find a pretext to break alliances which we have concluded [with them].

From a letter from Bismarck to Wilhelm I, 20 November 1869.

SOURCE C

The governments of the North German Confederation have felt that they have done all which honour and dignity permit to maintain for Europe the blessings of peace; and the clearer it appears to all eyes that the sword has been forced into our hand,

Continued

with greater confidence we turn, supported by the unanimous will of the German governments of the South, as well as of the North, to the love of the Fatherland and willingness for sacrifice of the German people to the summons to protect her honour and independence.

From the speech of the king of Prussia at the opening of the North German Reichstag, 19 July 1870.

SOURCE D

After I had read out the concentrated edition to my two guests, Moltke remarked: 'Now it has a different ring; it sounded before like a parley [a negotiation]; now it is like a flourish in answer to a challenge.' I went on to explain: 'If in execution of his Majesty's order I at once communicate this text, which contains no alteration in or addition to the telegram, not only to the newspapers, but also by telegraph to all our embassies, it will be known in Paris before midnight, and … will have the effect of a red rag upon the Gallic [French] bull. Fight we must if we do not want to act the part of the vanquished without a battle. Success, however, essentially depends upon the impression which the origination of the war makes upon us and others; it is important that we should be the party attacked …'

From Bismarck's memoirs, published in 1898, recalling the evening when he edited the Ems Telegram, 13 July 1870.

Look at how you might answer these questions.

You will see that the part **a** question requires you to compare two sources.

Here is some advice on answering part **a**.

1 **a** Read Sources **C** and **D**.

Compare Sources C and D as evidence of Prussia's responsibility for the outbreak of war with France in 1870. **[15 marks]**

A response to this question should include:

- Evidence that you have really understood the points made in both sources and grasped their overall argument.

  For example, *Source C suggests that it was the other governments in both north and south Germany that put pressure on Prussia and that they 'forced' Prussia to go to war. Source D however makes it very clear that it was Bismarck, the Prussian chancellor, who was actively provoking France to declare war.*

- evidence that you have identified areas of both difference and similarity between the two sources. A good response will comment on whether there are more similarities than differences, and why. The answer should provide a clearly developed explanation of both similarities and differences, making careful use of both sources.

  For example, *Both sources make it clear that France was the main instigator of the war, with C saying that France was the 'peace and honour' of Germany while Source D also refers to the fact that France was ready to attack Germany. The principal differences are that Source C sees France as the nation keen to provoke war, while Source D makes it clear that it was Bismarck who took care to provoke France into declaring war against Germany.*

- Contextual awareness, showing that you have background knowledge on the topic.

  For example, *The summer of 1870 was when Bismarck was taking the opportunity provided by the Hohenzollern candidature issue to complete his final stage in German unification. He needed to defeat France, the last barrier to his objective. Bismarck was particularly anxious not to upset the other major European powers by being seen as the aggressor. The Prussian king at this point in time would say what Bismarck told him to say and Source D is an accurate representation of what actually happened. Bismarck knew that Napoleon III would be easily provoked into declaring war.*

- Evaluation of both sources and consideration of their validity and provenance. Which would you trust more and why?

  For example, *Source C–the speech of the Prussian king–was actually written by Bismarck and was part of his plan to make it clear that France was the cause of the coming war. It was not true: several German states did not want to see Prussia dominating Germany. It is a good example of Bismarck's cunning. Source D, written in hindsight, shows Bismarck's methods. Although possibly boasting, it was largely accurate.*

- Look at the dates of the sources and reflect on what had been happening of relevance when the sources were written. Think about the authors of the sources.

For example, *1870–with the Hohenzollern candidature issue–provided a superb opportunity for Bismarck to attain his final goal: the unification of Germany under Prussian domination, with the Prussian king becoming the ruler of all Germany. The Prussian king, reading a speech written by Bismarck, was going to be the principal beneficiary of this result. Bismarck, the author of Source D, was naturally bound to take the opportunity of his memoirs to praise his own role in the affair.*

Have a look at the other part **a** source questions at the end of Chapters 1 and 3. You will see that although the wording may differ, the questions are looking for similar skills.

> **TIP**
>
> When a question asks you to compare two sources, make sure you use only the two sources mentioned.

The part **b** question asks you to consider four sources together. Here is some advice on answering this type of question where information from a number of sources needs to be evaluated.

b Read **all** of the sources.

'Bismarck planned in advance to complete the process of German unification by means of a war with France.' How far do the sources support this view? **[25 marks]**

A response to this question should include:

- A clear answer to the question. Set out your judgement at the beginning of your response and be firm and specific. You need to make it clear how far the sources do, or do not, support the view – do not just give a vague 'to some extent'.

  For example, *There is ample evidence in the sources that Bismarck had a long-term plan to complete the unification of Germany with a successful war against France. He was just waiting for the right opportunity to fight it having ensured that France would be seen as the country provoking the war.*

- A balanced argument to support your judgement, demonstrating source analysis skills. A balanced argument is one that considers several different points of view. The supporting paragraphs after your judgement are a good place to do this. Always carefully study the sources while considering what the question is actually asking. Make it clear that you have understood all four sources (not just the two specified in the first question!) and grasped their overall arguments. You must use all four sources in your answer.
- A good way of structuring a response to this type of question is to start by discussing the sources which **support** the view, and then follow with the sources which **oppose** it. You must identify the key points showing agreement and disagreement. Some sources will fully support or oppose the view, others may be divided on the issue. You need to include evidence that shows the extent to which each source supports it. Do not just copy out parts of the sources in your answer but do quote short phrases to back up points that you make.

  For example, *Sources B and D both strongly support the view as both refer to his 'long term plan'… while Source A suggests that it is France who is anxious to fight Prussia and Prussia is not prepared for war. Source C is ambivalent on the issue.*

> **TIP**
>
> You do not need to spend time on 'background' or 'setting the scene'. Keep to the point and show clearly that you fully understand all the sources as well as the question.

- Often there is one source which can both support and challenge the hypothesis. The best way of dealing with this is to mention the source in both the support and challenge sections of the response.

  For example, *while Source C largely supports the hypothesis when it mentions … there is some suggestion of challenge when it refers to …*

- Make sure that you evaluate all the sources in context and consider their validity and provenance. Have you considered the nature, origin and purpose of each source? Is the date of the source important? Use your own ideas on the provenance of the sources, and your own contextual awareness, to support your argument. You need to show that you have background historical knowledge and understanding and that you are not just relying on the sources for information.

  For example, *Source A, written by the British envoy in Bavaria, a German state hostile to*

Prussia, may well be unaware of what the situation was in France at the time. The fact that he is unsure about Prussia's military ability is odd, given that Prussia had just defeated Austria and crushed what was seen at the greatest military power in Europe at the time. Also for Source B: It was well known that the then King of Prussia very much did as Bismarck told him to do when it came to public speeches, and his incorrect assertion that all German states were supportive of unification under the direction of Prussia was completely wrong.

- A good way to end your response is to suggest whether you think the weight of the evidence supports the view or not – and why. You also need to show that you have thought about the 'extent' to which the sources agree or disagree with the view and made up your own mind about it. You do not need to cross-reference the sources, but if you feel that using cross-references can back up your judgement, then do so.

  For example, *The sources overall strongly support the assertion in the question. Sources B and D make this clear and they are the most reliable and contextual knowledge backs them up. Source A's author is obviously not well informed and Source C is just another part of Bismarck's elaborate deception plan.*

As with part **a**, have a look at the other part **b** source questions in the Practice question sections at the end of Chapter 1 and Chapter 3. Although the wording of each question is slightly different, all these questions ask you to consider how far the four sources support a view, so what you are being asked to do is the same.

Essay-based questions

You were introduced to essay-writing skills in the Getting started with Cambridge International AS Level History section of this book. Now you will see how to apply the earlier information to some specific examples.

In this book, you have met the following examples:

Chapter 1:

1 a Explain why the Bastille was stormed. **[10 marks]**

b To what extent was the French crisis of 1789 caused by economic factors? **[20 marks]**

2 a Explain why Napoleon was able to seize power in 1799. **[10 marks]**

b 'The Directory did a good job in difficult circumstances.' How far do you agree? **[20 marks]**

Chapter 2:

1 a Explain why the rulers of the German states survived the revolutions of 1848–49. **[10 marks]**

b To what extent was Prussia's military strength the most important reason for the unification of Germany? **[20 marks]**

2 a Explain why the king of Prussia refused the imperial throne in 1849. **[10 marks]**

b 'Growing German nationalism between 1815 and 1850 was mainly influenced by economic factors.' How far do you agree? **[20 marks]**

Chapter 3:

1 a Explain why the New Economic Policy was introduced in 1921. **[10 marks]**

b To what extent was Tsar Nicholas II's weak leadership in the First World War the most important reason for his downfall? **[20 marks]**

2 a Explain why Lenin agreed to the Treaty of Brest-Litovsk. **[10 marks]**

b 'Russian military defeats in the First World War caused the February 1917 Revolution.' How far do you agree? **[20 marks]**

You will see that in fact each numbered question contains two separate question types. Each question type needs to be approached slightly differently, so we will discuss each question type in turn.

Questions that highlight knowledge and understanding

These questions may ask you to show your knowledge and understanding by explaining why something happened.

Let's look at an example:

a Explain why the Provisional Government in Russia failed. **[10 marks]**

A good-quality answer to this type of question will:

- Be entirely focused on this question. It should only discuss the reasons why the Provisional Government failed in its objectives and was overthrown – not why the Bolsheviks were successful (which is a different question!). No reference to other important factors is expected.
- Identify three or four relevant points and develop them with supporting detail. It is a good idea to add them in order of importance.

For example, *The task facing the Provisional Government in governing Russia was enormous. There was both a complete military and economic collapse in 1916–1917.*

They had no experience in governing Russia – they were not trained administrators.

They were faced by great hostility by the Left and by the tsarist supporters. They made the decision to continue the war against Germany and Austria.

- Indicate which of those points you feel are the most important, and why. This is vital in an 'explain why' type of question to demonstrate that you have thought about the relative importance of the points you are writing about. There is no 'right' answer to this question, and one is not expected. Great historians often disagree!

    For example, *The only chance the Provisional Government had of surviving was if they ended the war, which had been the root cause of all the major problems facing Russia at the time. Their failure to do so led directly to their losing the support of the army and the working class of Russia and their overthrow by the Bolsheviks in 1917.*

- Be written in as clear English as possible.

This type of question is testing understanding as well as knowledge. It is not enough just to remember one relevant point. It is also very important to show that you understand its significance in context.

In addition, the question is assessing your ability to select and apply your in-depth knowledge effectively and your ability to explain something clearly.

TIP

When answering, remember:

- Explain why.
- Answer the question that was asked. Do not spend much time on other factors.
- Do not just list facts which might or might not be linked to the question.
- Make specific points and back them up with relevant and accurate detail.

Questions that highlight analysis and evaluation

There are many forms of question that ask you to show analysis and evaluation. These include questions that ask you to what extent/how far something was the case, or how important/significant something was. You might also be asked (for example) how effective or successful something was, or how far you agree with a view. All these questions are assessing your skills of analysis and evaluation.

Let's look at an example and see how it works in practice:

b 'The revolutions of 1848 in Germany were caused primarily by economic factors.' How far do you agree? **[20 marks]**

- Your answer should contain a clear judgement or argument.
- Your answer should be entirely focused on this question. The question is not asking how successful the invasion was. It is not asking about why the revolutions failed. It is asking whether you think economic factors were the primary cause of the revolutions, or whether they were among many causes, or if there was another primary cause. Be careful not to write a narrative of the revolutions themselves or spend much time on the background history of Germany, unless you can show how such an account is directly linked to the question set.
- Demonstrate that you have thought about causative factors in general. What do you really think led people to take the risks they did in 1848? Did participation in the various revolutionary acts vary between classes? Were people driven by the simple fact that they were hungry, or was idealism more influential?
- Be balanced: show that you have considered both the case for economic factors being the major cause, and the case for other factors.
- Demonstrate that you have thought about a wide range of issues, weighed them all up and reached your own conclusion.
- Offer knowledge and understanding by backing up the various points you make with accurate and relevant detail.

TIP

Tips for answering questions that ask 'How far do you agree?'

'The revolutions of 1848 in Germany were caused primarily by economic factors.'

How far do you agree?

Try thinking about this in terms of a scale, with 'I completely agree because …' at one end and 'I completely disagree because …' at the other, with 'I somewhat agree' and 'I somewhat disagree' in between:

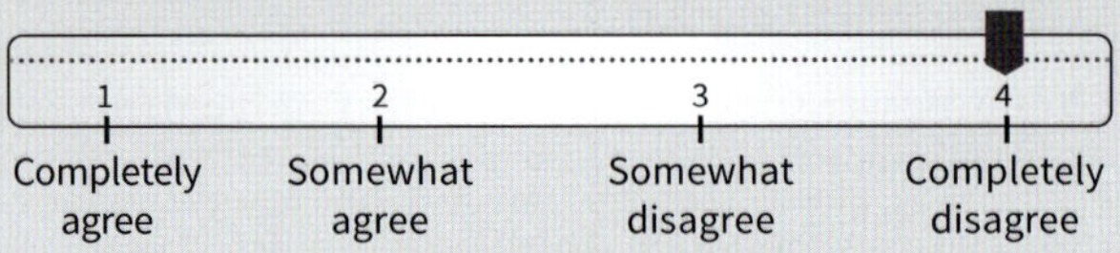

Depending on where you are on the scale, your responses could begin with an opening section similar to one of these:

1. Economic factors, such as poverty, unemployment and hunger, were the principal causes of the revolutions because without them the vital working-class support would not have been forthcoming. While there were other causative factors, such as … and …, they did not play nearly such an important part as the economic factors.
2. Although economic factors did play an important role in causing the revolutions of 1848, the most important cause was the desire by many middle-class people for greater freedom and an end to the rule of autocratic monarchs. This was more important because …
3. Economic factors only played a minor role in causing the revolutions of 1848. The major causes were the desire by many middle-class people for greater political freedom and the wish to unite Germany and end the domination of Austria. In one or two states, there was hunger, and unemployment, which did lead to some working-class unrest, but the revolts were always led by middle-class men aiming at political reform or unification.
4. Economic factors rarely played any role in causing the revolutions of 1848. Much more important were … and … as it was these two factors which …

CONTINUED

Opening sections like these demonstrate thinking about the relative importance of causes and not just trying to remember what all the causes were. Such opening sections show analytical skills and understanding, not just knowledge. Remember that all three are being assessed at AS Level.

Let's look at some other examples of questions that highlight analysis and evaluation.

A question might ask you to consider how effective someone or something was. If you were analysing the effectiveness of Lenin's economic policies, a good response would:

- Be entirely focused on the effectiveness of those policies. The question does not ask about the reasons for the revolution of 1917, or whether the Provisional Government's policies were unsuccessful. The response needs to be only about how *effective* Lenin's policies were.
- Demonstrate evidence of thinking about what effective policies might be in the very challenging circumstances of Russia between 1918 and 1924. Would such policies reduce unemployment, end inflation or restore the people's confidence in their leaders? Would they rebuild the Russian economy, feed the people, prevent a return to tsarism, establish socialism? It is important to show that you are thinking analytically.
- Demonstrate knowledge and understanding by identifying the various policies adopted by Lenin and the Bolsheviks.
- Use analytical ability by weighing up the identified policies and commenting on the extent to which you consider them to be effective or otherwise. The focus should be on the effectiveness of each policy, but you should also comment on the overall effectiveness.

Similarly, a question might ask how successful something was at achieving its aim. For such a question, you would use a similar approach as when analysing how effective something was. For example, if assessing the success of the tsar's reforms after the 1905 Revolution, you should show some reflection on what the criteria for success might be in the context of 1905. Would the reforms be considered a success if they helped the regime to survive longer? Or only if they brought benefit to the Russian people? You need to show that you know and understand what the tsar did and the impact of those actions. After examining the nature and extent of the success achieved you should conclude with a firm judgement on the degree of success attained. Avoid vague responses such as 'It had some effect'. Argue your case strongly.

Another question might ask 'how far' or 'to what extent' something was the case. This type of question is also assessing your analytical skills. You would have to give a firm judgement on the issue of extent. So if you are analysing the extent to which Russia's entry into the First World War was the reason for the downfall of tsarism, your response should show evidence that you have analysed the implications of entering the war on the tsar's position and considered the degree to which joining the war led to his downfall, compared with other factors which might have played an important part. (Remember to keep the focus firmly on his downfall and do not get sidetracked by a narrative of the war.) Then you should come to a conclusion based on the evidence.

Whatever the wording of the question, remember that you need to show strong evidence of analysis and evaluation as well as knowledge and understanding.

TIP

Plan your answer before you start to write. You could set out plans for the longer essay-based questions, such as 'To what extent …', in columns headed 'case for' and 'case against' – or as a mind map, which has a focus on thinking out an answer. A plain list of facts will not be much help as a plan. Use the plan to clarify your ideas on what the question is asking.

Structuring an answer

Consider the following practice question:

b 'Louis XVI must take full responsibility for causing the French Revolution.' How far do you agree? **[20 marks]**

Different students will take different approaches to this type of question, and you will find your own preferred approach. While you are developing your techniques, you might find the structure in Table 4.2 helpful. Even if you choose to organise your essay differently, it is important to note the strengths of this one and apply the same principles in your own writing.

Paragraph	Content
1	This needs to contain a clear answer to the question. Should Louis take full responsibility for causing the revolution, or not? An answer might be, for example: *Louis must take most, but not all, responsibility. There were many other causes which were beyond his control. The reasons why he should take most responsibility are:* *(a) …* *(b) …* *(c) …* *But there were other factors which played an important part, such as:* *(d) …* *(e) …* This paragraph does not need to contain much detail, just broad reasons, and should demonstrate that you are focusing on the question and thinking analytically. Mention briefly possible points 'against'–(d) and (e)–to develop later and show the required analysis and balance. Avoid vague introductions or trying to 'set the scene'.

Continued

Paragraph	Content
2	In this paragraph you could take point (a) and develop it in detail. Make sure that the objective of the paragraph is made clear from the start, for example: *The principal reason for suggesting that Louis must take much of the responsibility was ...* Then include three or four accurate and relevant facts (the evidence) to back up your point. This section might also explain why you feel this particular issue was the most important point, highlighting an analytical approach.
3	You could develop point (b) here in a similar way. Again, take care to ensure that the objective of the paragraph is made clear, so that you are relating what you write very obviously to your answer that Louis must take most responsibility. There is often a tendency to forget the purpose of the paragraph and simply list the facts. A list of facts often leaves the reader asking, 'So ...?'
4	Make the objective clear and add as much commentary as you can to explain why this point is less important than (a).
5	This is a good place to develop the case 'against' the view in points (d) and (e), to demonstrate the balance required in this type of response. There is nothing wrong with strong arguments, however, and if you feel there is no case 'against', say so and why. It might still be a good idea to start this paragraph with, for example: *Defenders of Louis might argue that ...* and bring out a possible defence of this view, however weak you might think it is.
6	If you have developed your response, your final paragraph can be quite brief. Avoid repetition and do not just summarise previous points but make it clear why you have reached your conclusion. The best final paragraphs contain either a definitive judgement (avoid a vague 'to some extent ...' and make sure your judgement doesn't conflict with the initial one – don't change your mind!) or a final clinching argument (the main reason why you have come to that conclusion) which reinforces your opening views.

Table 4.2: An example answer structure for a question that highlights analysis and evaluation.

TIP

- Make sure you that you answer the question in your introduction. Writing an introduction means that if you run out of time, you will still have answered the question. Otherwise you may find that you have to stop writing when you have only presented the case 'for' and 'against' the view, without demonstrating analysis or judgement.
- Avoid getting into a situation where you present a long and detailed 'for' the view in the question and a briefer and undeveloped case 'against' the view – and then briefly conclude that the case 'against' is stronger, even though all the facts presented point the other way. This would mean that you cannot provide enough analysis to fully answer the question.

4.3 Revision techniques

Too often, students think that the purpose of revision is to get information into their brain in preparation for an assessment. It is seen as a process where facts are learned. However, if you have followed the course appropriately and made sensibly laid-out notes as you have gone along, all the information you need is already there. The key purpose of revision is not to gain new information, but to ensure that you can retrieve the knowledge you have learned when it is required.

Revision needs to be an ongoing process throughout the course, not just in the days or weeks before an exam. The focus of your revision should be identifying the key points, on, for example, why Napoleon was able to seize power in 1799. Making good notes as you study the course content will help you do this (see the Getting started with Cambridge International AS Level History section).

Quality revision and plenty of practice in attempting questions under timed conditions are essential. If you feel you have not practised enough at school, you could ask your teacher to provide some questions so you can practise on your own under timed conditions.

4.4 Assessment preparation

This section offers a few general points about how you could approach an assessment. Some might seem obvious, but it is worth remembering that, under pressure, we are all capable of making mistakes. It is useful to be aware of potential pitfalls.

The syllabus includes details of what you need to know during your course and for assessment. You should be aware of:

- What topics the questions can be about. This will be covered during your course.
- What form the questions can take. Your teacher can help you understand the types of tasks you are likely to face, and the syllabus will give details of wording.
- How long you will have to answer a question paper.
- Which parts of a question paper you can ignore. Some papers might have separate sections for those who have studied International History and for those who have studied US History.
- The equipment you will need for writing and what you may or may not bring into an exam room. There are very strict rules on mobile phones, for example, and smart watches. Check if you are allowed to bring water in.

Rubric

All question papers contain rubric. This provides you with essential information about how long a timed assessment will last, how many questions you must answer and from what sections, and so on. Students can make rubric errors by attempting too many questions, for example, or questions from inappropriate sections of a paper. These basic errors can really damage your chances of success.

Timing

It is a good idea to work out in advance how long you have to complete each question or part of a question. Make a note of it and make every effort to keep to that timing.

Practising answering questions under timed conditions is something you can do on your own as part of your revision. Take care not to make the mistake of spending too much time on a question which you know a great deal about and leave yourself insufficient time for a question which might carry twice as many marks.

If you run out of time, you will not be able to answer all the questions fully. If you have spent too long on your first question with its two parts, it might be a good idea to attempt the second part of the next question if it carries more marks.

Planning

There is nearly always the temptation in an exam to just get started rather than spending time on planning. Without planning, however, there is a risk that you will include irrelevant information, or not fully explain the relevance of information. So, make a plan before you start to write!

How much should I write?

There is no requirement to write a specific number of words in a response, nor to fill a certain number of pages. Aim to keep your focus on writing a relevant response to the question set and making sure that you are aware of the assessment criteria for the type of question you are dealing with. Do not worry if another student seems to be writing more than you are.

What can I use to help me prepare for assessment?

Exam boards provide materials to help students and their teachers prepare for assessment. It is important to make full use of these materials. They include:

- the syllabus
- past papers
- mark schemes for those papers
- examiner reports on students' performance in examinations
- the assessment objectives for papers.

The syllabus

The syllabus provides:

- details of the options to be studied at AS Level
- how many options have to be taken
- how long each examination is
- what proportion of the overall marks are allocated to each paper
- the assessment objectives and the relationship between them and the different papers you take
- details of each of the papers
- the Key Questions (these indicate broad areas of history for study; all questions will be based on the Key Questions)
- key content.

It really helps to have the syllabus available so that you know what to expect during your course and for assessment.

Past papers

Past papers are helpful in two ways. First, past papers show you the types of question that have been set in the past. You can see how marks were allocated and calculate how much time you should spend on similar questions or sub-questions. Be careful, however – syllabuses are updated regularly so you may see past paper questions on subject content which is no longer included in the syllabus, or there may have been other changes. Always refer carefully to the syllabus for your year of examination.

Second, past papers help you to revise and practise. The same questions will not be asked again, but you can see the type of question that could be asked, and check whether you have the knowledge and understanding to answer a similar question. Planning an answer to a past question will encourage you to think about that topic and consider the points that you might make when answering such a question.

Mark schemes

Mark schemes accompany the question papers and make it clear how your work will be assessed. They are usually in two parts, a generic one and one for each question set:

- A **generic mark scheme** will help you to understand how answers are marked and what needs to be included in a good answer. It specifies the elements that make up high-quality work, such as developed analysis, balance or source analysis/evaluation.
- An **indicative content mark scheme** will give you a good idea of the sort of answer that is expected. Remember that there is never a 'right' answer to a question in History at this level.

For example, for a question asking you to compare two sources, you can see the sort of similarities and differences in the two sources that you should discuss, the sort of contextual knowledge that you might include in your answer, as well as comments on the provenance of the sources. You can also see how you can develop points from the sources to support your answer.

For an essay-based question you can see the level of explanation needed and the sort of points you might make. The mark scheme will give you a clear idea of the depth you will need to write a good answer and the sort of arguments that you might develop. You do not have to mention every point or fact in the mark scheme.

In summary, mark schemes help you to see what a good-quality answer looks like. You can use this knowledge to reflect on your own work and consider how it might be improved.

Examiner reports

After every examination, a detailed report is written on how students performed. These can be helpful as they highlight both the stronger answers (so, note those answers' strengths!) and the weaker answers (so, do not repeat these answers' weaknesses!). It is worth looking at several examiners' reports for both source-based and essay-based papers. You will see what types of answer have performed well.

Common errors (and how to avoid them!)

When preparing for assessment, try to avoid the following errors – they are more common than you might think!

- **Poor time management.** Do not spend too long on the first part of a question, leaving yourself too little time to answer the second part. So, practise writing answers under timed conditions.
- **Lack of planning.** Clear planning will help to you to make sure that your answer is focused on the question being asked.

> **TIP**
>
> You might like to write a little mind-map or similar, to help you pause and think about your topic before starting to write. Have a think about what style of plan works best for you.

- **Long introductions to essay-based questions asking you how far you agree with a view (or similar).** Such introductions are not necessary and waste a lot of time. So, avoid these – get on and answer the question.
- **Supporting paragraphs which contain a lot of detail but no clear point.** If you provide facts that are relevant and accurate, but it is not clear what point you are making, you are likely to demonstrate your historical knowledge well, but not your skills in historical explanation, analysis and judgement. So, make sure the purpose of a paragraph is clear. Link it carefully back to the argument being made.
- **An implicit answer.** This means that the answer to the question is hinted at but not clearly stated. This weakness is especially common in essay-based questions which ask students how far they agree with a view. Students sometimes provide a list of factors 'for' the view and a list of factors 'against' the view – but they do not actually answer the question. The facts might point to a conclusion, but the response never actually provides one. So, answer the question.
- **Lack of awareness of what the command words require.** So, explain or compare when you are asked to – do not just describe.
- **Writing the answer to a question you wished you had got, not the one you did get.** You may have done a brilliant essay on Bismarck's foreign policy some months ago – but the question set now was on Bismarck's domestic policy. So, do not write about foreign policy!
- **Too little time spent reading the sources.** Often key points which just happened to be towards the end of the last source just never get mentioned. So, spend enough time reading all the sources very carefully (highlighting key points etc.) – and make sure you double-check the last source!

Careful preparation is the key to success in assessment. We hope this guidance will help you to achieve to the best of your abilities.

Glossary

Abdicate: To give up a public office (for example, for a king to give up his throne).

Absolute monarch: A king or queen who has complete power in a state. They can make laws and there are no limits to their power.

Advocate: To support something in public; someone who publicly supports something.

Anarchism: Belief in the abolition of all forms of authority and opposition to having any state or government or any form of capitalism. Several anarchist writers influential in Russia in the late 19th century had been involved in the revolutions of 1848 in Europe.

Ancien Régime: This means 'the old system of government' and describes how France was governed before 1789. It covers not only the government and administration, but also the structure of society and the role of the Church.

Anti-Semite: Someone who exhibits hostility towards Jewish people (known as anti-Semitism).

Armistice: An agreement between two sides to stop fighting. It is not necessarily the point at which a war ends but it may allow the negotiation of a peace treaty.

Assembly of Notables: A group of noblemen and senior members of the Church. The Assembly had no authority – it could only consult, but not actually do anything.

Authoritarian: Preferring to enforce obedience to authority and to limit personal freedom.

Autocratic: Where all power in a state belongs to a single monarch (the autocrat), whose authority is unlimited.

Bill of rights: A declaration of the key freedoms that citizens expect those in authority to recognise.

Bolshevik: A member of the more radical faction of the Russian Social Democrat Party, which seized power in the revolution of October 1917. The party was renamed the Russian Communist Party in 1918, but the term Bolshevik will be used throughout this coursebook for simplicity.

Bourgeoisie: The middle class, mainly business people who owned the means of production in capitalist society, such as factories.

Buffer zone: A protective area separating two potentially hostile countries.

Burschenschaften: Student organisations which developed after 1815 to promote ideas of German nationality, freedom and civil rights. (The singular is Burschenschaft.)

Capitalism: An economic and political system in which individuals, rather than the state, own businesses to make a profit.

Censorship: The suppression of ideas which challenge authority, whether expressed in speech, writing or other media.

Civil Constitution of the Clergy: The law of 1790 in France by which the state took control of the Church and its wealth and lands.

Civil service: Professional administrators who provide support to the government of a country.

Communism: A system of government based on a classless society in which property and wealth are owned by the community, rather than by private individuals.

Concession: A concession is when one person agrees to the demands of another person or other people.

Confederation: A loose association of states which retain some control over their own policies.

Congress: A large, formal meeting of delegates.

Conscription: Compulsory entry into the army as a service to the state.

Conservative: Generally opposed to change; a conservative (or a conservative person) is someone who wants to uphold traditional ideas and institutions in government and society.

Constitution: A written document which sets out the rules by which a country is governed: for example, how much power the government should have and what limits there should be on that power.

Constitutional monarchy: A system of government in which a monarch's powers are limited by laws and rules. These are set out in a constitution which is usually written down.

Constitutional revolution: A constitutional revolution takes place when the rules that state how a country is governed–for example how leaders are chosen–are completely changed.

Continental System: The system in France introduced by Napoleon which prevented any imports and exports from and to Britain, from France and any of the countries it controlled, and banned any other form of contact with Britain, such as mail.

Council of People's Commissars (Sovnarkom): The supreme government body in Russia, created in October 1917. Commissars acted as ministers, in charge of the various government departments.

Coup d'état: The sudden, and often violent, overthrow of government power by a group of citizens or military personnel.

Customs union: An association of areas or states who agree to abolish tariffs between themselves, and to operate a common set of tariffs on imports from other countries.

Democratic: When citizens have equal rights and take part in political decision-making. This system is known as a democracy.

Depose: To remove someone from power or from their position (for example, to remove a king from his throne).

Dictatorship: Rule by one individual without any limits to their power.

Diet: An assembly which meets to debate and make decisions on political matters. Also known as a Bundestag.

Duchy: A territory ruled over by a duke. (The plural is duchies.)

Elector: A title used by some German princes, derived from the fact that they elected the Holy Roman Emperor until the dissolution of the empire by Napoleon I in 1806.

Emancipation: Freeing someone from being legally controlled by another person.

Émigrés: Members of the French population who left France during the first years of the revolution, and later the Terror, in many cases fearing for their lives. Most were nobles, but some were middle-class people who disagreed with the extremism of the Jacobins.

Estates-General: An assembly which represented the three social classes (Estates) of France under the Ancien Régime: the nobility, the clergy and the Third Estate, who represented the majority of the French people. The Estates-General of 1789 was the first to be called since 1614.

Faction: A group within a larger group, where members of the larger group share a common objective, but different smaller groups (factions) within it disagree on how best to achieve that objective.

Factionalism: Arguments between small groups within a larger organisation such as a political party.

Federal: Relating to a system of government in which power is shared between a central authority and various regional bodies.

Feudalism: A social system in medieval Europe, in which the nobility held lands from the Crown in exchange for military service, and the lower classes were tenants of the nobles. These tenants were obliged to live on their lord's land and serve him with their labour and a share of their crops (or other taxes).

Franchise: The right to vote. The franchise was also known as suffrage.

General staff: A group of army officers who assist a senior commander in planning and carrying out military operations.

Gold standard: An international monetary system in which the value of a country's currency was linked directly to a fixed quantity of gold. The system aimed to give long-term price stability.

Grievances: Causes for complaint, usually over unfair treatment. For example, the complaint that the poor had to pay taxes, while the nobility did not.

Guilds: Associations of merchants or craftspeople, often dating back to medieval times, set up to protect the interests of their members. By the 19th century, they were widely seen as outdated and restricting free competition.

Guillotine: A method of execution invented by a French doctor, Guillotin, in 1789 to replace other, often cruel and inefficient, methods of execution. It was designed to behead quickly and cause no suffering in the process. The weighted blade dropped and killed instantly. Thousands died this way during the French Revolution.

Ideological: Based on a set of political ideas and beliefs (an ideology).

Indemnity bill: A law passed to protect people who might otherwise face penalties for illegal conduct.

Indirect voting: A system in which voters choose delegates, who then elect representatives to sit in a central assembly or parliament.

Industrialisation: A process in which an economy that is mainly based on agriculture develops large-scale manufacturing industry.

Inflation: Inflation happens when prices rise rapidly. This means that a worker on a fixed income has to pay more for food or other items, while not earning any more money.

Judiciary: The justice system, including the judges who enforce a country's laws.

Legitimate: Legally entitled. A legitimate ruler is someone who is legally entitled to govern.

Liberal: Believing that government should allow as much personal and economic freedom as possible. A liberal (or a liberal person) is someone who believes that government should allow personal and economic freedom.

Liberalism: A belief that government should be reformed to allow as much personal and economic freedom as possible. Nineteenth-century liberals also favoured the concept of representative assemblies, although these would not necessarily be elected by all adults.

Martial law: The replacement of civilian rule and legal processes by military power.

Middle class: The social class between the nobility/aristocracy at the top of the social structure and the labouring working class and rural peasants at the bottom. Its members were usually educated: either small rural landowners or professionals such as lawyers, doctors, local government officials and successful business owners in the towns and cities. They usually owned property and had to pay taxes.

Moderate: In a political context, a moderate person is one who does not hold extreme or radical views.

Multi-ethnic: Made up of people of different races.

Napoleonic Wars: The conflict between France under Napoleon I (Bonaparte) and alliances of various European states, which began in 1803 and ended with Napoleon's defeat in 1815.

National debt: The amount of money borrowed by a state or country, often at very high rates of interest.

National Guard: A largely middle-class militia, created in 1789 to act as a national police force. It played a vital role in trying to maintain law and order in France during the revolutionary period.

Nationalism: The belief that people with a common language, culture or history should have the right to govern themselves, and that the boundaries between states should be based on this idea.

Nobility: The highest class in society, also known as the aristocracy. A nobleman/aristocrat usually had a title (for example, duke or count), and when he died his eldest son inherited the title. Other members of the noble family, such as wives and younger sons, also had noble rank. (The terms nobility and aristocracy can be singular – when referring to the class as a whole; or plural – when referring to the members of the class.)

Okhrana: The name for the secret police between 1880 and 1917. It had wide powers to carry out surveillance and arrest of political opponents, and to censor publications.

Orthodox Church: The branch of the Christian Church to which most believers in Russia and eastern Europe belong. The Orthodox Church separated from the Roman Catholic Church in the 11th century.

Pamphlet: A small booklet or leaflet.

Parlements: Courts of appeal in the justice system. There were 13 local parlements in France at this time, of which the one in Paris was the most powerful. They were not elected bodies and did not represent all French people.

Parliament: A group of (usually) elected politicians or other people who make laws for their country.

Petition: To request something from someone. A petition is a document, usually signed by many people, making a request to those in authority.

Plebiscite: Like an election, a plebiscite is a popular vote. Instead of being called to choose a national assembly and a government, however, a plebiscite puts a question to voters about a specific issue and is almost always organised around a 'yes/no' decision. Essentially, it is another word for a referendum.

Pogroms: Outbreaks of mob violence against Jewish people, often approved by the authorities.

Principles: Basic or fundamental rules or beliefs which act as a guide for action. For example, a principle that emerged during the American War of Independence was that 'all men are equal'.

Progressive: Forward-looking, enlightened.

Progressive bloc: A group in Russia consisting of 236 of the Duma's 442 members, made up of Octobrists, Kadets, moderate nationalists and others. It called for a 'ministry of confidence' and an extension of civil liberties.

Proletariat: The urban, industrial working class. They generally had no savings or property, and their only source of income was their own labour.

Propaganda: Communication designed to influence an audience to support a specific action or political agenda. It does so by spreading ideas, information or rumours in ways that appeal to people's beliefs and feelings.

Radical: Far-reaching or extreme. A radical (or a radical person or organisation) is someone who supports extreme social or political change.

Red Guards: Armed volunteer groups, consisting mainly of urban workers, led by the Bolsheviks. From 1918 they formed the basis of the Soviet Union's military force, the Red Army.

Redemption payments: In 19th-century Russia, annual fees paid by peasants to the government. These payments were to cover the debt that the government incurred when it compensated the landowners for the abolition of serfdom.

Reform: Change for the better; in this context, improvement in the system of government.

Regent: An individual who is appointed to govern a country, usually for a limited period, for example if a monarch is too young or unable to rule.

Reich: A German term for a realm or empire. It has been applied to the unified German state of 1871–1918 (the Second Reich) and to Hitler's Germany (the Third Reich, 1933–45).

Reparations: Money that one country has to pay another as compensation for war damage.

Representative: Typical of a class or group of people, or speaking and acting on behalf of other people. A representative body is an organisation whose members are elected or appointed to speak and act on behalf of different groups of people.

Repression: Repression by a government is when individuals or groups are prevented from expressing their views or acting in a way the government dislikes.

Republic: A form of government in which the head of state is not a hereditary ruler (someone who rules because they are related to the previous ruler), such as a king; instead they are a leader chosen by those people in the state who have the right to vote.

Sans-culottes: Working-class radicals of Paris and other French cities. They were named after the type of clothes usually worn by the urban working class, trousers, rather than the expensive culottes (knee breeches) usually worn by the rich. 'Sans' in French means 'without'.

Schleswig-Holstein: Two neighbouring territories between the Baltic and North seas. Although not part of Denmark, they were under the personal authority of the Danish king as their duke. Holstein was German-speaking and was also part of the German Confederation. Schleswig had a mixed Danish- and German-speaking population. As a result, their status was disputed, and German nationalists claimed that they should be treated as one and be part of the Confederation.

Senate: A body created in the Constitution of 1799 in France designed to give the Consulate legislative support and the appearance of representation. Napoleon ignored it, but it gave the appearance of legality to Napoleon's overthrow.

Serfs: A class of unfree agricultural workers in Russia who worked on the land and had to obey their landlords.

Socialism: A system in which society is equal, based on cooperation rather than on the capitalist concept of competition.

Sovereignty: Ultimate political authority within a state.

Soviet Union: Shortened form of the Union of Soviet Socialist Republics (USSR), the communist state officially established in 1922 and dissolved in 1991, comprising Russia and other republics.

Soviets: Workers' councils, which first appeared in industrial cities in Russia in 1905. They played an important part in the October 1917 Revolution.

Tariffs: Taxes or duties imposed by a government on goods imported into a country.

Tax in kind: A tax paid in goods or services rather than in money.

'The Terror': Also known as the 'Reign of Terror', this was the name given to the period of extreme violence in France in 1793 and 1794 when thousands of French people were either executed after a brief trial by a revolutionary tribunal or murdered by mobs. Those who died were mainly royalists, nobles, clergy or just political opponents of the Jacobins.

Trade union: An organisation which negotiates with employers on behalf of workers, to improve their pay and conditions of work.

Ultimatum: A final demand that, if rejected, will lead to serious consequences such as war.

Universal male suffrage: Voting rights for all men. The suffrage was also known as the franchise.

Veto: The right to refuse to accept a proposal or decision.

Zemstvo: An elected local assembly set up in rural areas as a consequence of the ending of serfdom.

Acknowledgements

The authors and publishers acknowledge the following sources of copyright material and are grateful for the permissions granted. While every effort has been made, it has not always been possible to identify the sources of all the material used, or to trace all copyright holders. If any omissions are brought to our notice, we will be happy to include the appropriate acknowledgements on reprinting.

Thanks to the following for permission to reproduce images:

Cover Leemage/Corbis via Getty Images;

Inside Chapter 1 Clu/GI; Photos.com/GI; Duncan1890/GI; Ivy Close Images/Alamy Stock Photo; The Picture Art Collection/Alamy Stock Photo; Bildagentur-online/GI; Nastasic/GI; Mikroman6/GI; Culture Club/GI; Print Collector/GI; Photos.com/GI; UniversalImagesGroup/GI; CBW/Alamy Stock Photo; Christophel Fine Art; Nastasic/GI; Clu/GI; G. Dagli Orti/GI; Clu/GI (x3); Svintage Archive/Alamy Stock Photo; PHAS/GI; Mikroman6/GI; Heritage Images/GI; Mikroman6/GI; Heritage Images/GI; Clu/GI; Vernon Lewis Gallery/GI; Print Collector/GI; Wikimedia Commons; Heritage Images/GI; Marka/GI; Pictore/GI; M. Seemuller/GI; Hulton Archive/GI; The Picture Art Collection/Alamy Stock Photo; GraphicaArtis/GI; E. Lessing/GI; A. Dagli Orti/Bridgeman Images; G. Dagli Orti/GI; Zu_09/GI; Clu/GI; Achim Thomae/GI; **Chapter 2** Universal History Archive/GI; Frank Waßewitz/GI; Print Collector/GI; Ullstein Bild Dtl./GI; Hulton Archive/GI; Ullstein Bild Dtl/GI; Bildagentur-online/Universal Images Group via Getty Images; Hulton Archive/GI; Bettmann/GI; Heritage Images/GI; Nastasic/GI; Culture Club/GI; Print Collector/GI; Ullstein Bild Dtl/GI; Nastasic/GI; Sepia Times/GI; Traveler1116/GI; Stock Montage/GI; Traveler1116/GI; Mikroman6/GI; Henry Guttmann Collection; Le Jeune/GI; Biblioteca Ambrosiana/GI (x2); Universal History Archive/GI; Mikroman6/GI; Maodesign/GI; Print Collector/GI; Mikroman6/GI; Ullstein Bild Dtl/GI (x2); UniversalImagesGroup/GI; **Chapter 3** Francois Xavier Marit/GI; Heritage Images/GI; Alexander Spatari/GI; UniversalImagesGroup/GI; Apic/GI; Heritage Images/GI; ICAS94/GI; Wikimedia Commons; PHAS/GI; Topical Press Agency/GI; Keystone/GI; Photo 12/GI (x2); Heritage Images/GI; Photo 12/GI; Heritage Images/GI; Universal History Archive/GI; Photo 12/GI; Topical Press Agency/GI; Ullstein Bild Dtl/GI; JHU Sheridan Libraries/Gado/GI; Keystone/GI; Wikimedia Commons; Print Collector/GI; Sovfoto/GI (x2); Universal History Archive/GI; Laski Diffusion/GI; Heritage Image Partnership Ltd/Alamy Stock Photo; TASS/GI; Ullstein Bild Dtl/GI; Heritage Images/GI; **Chapter 4** Chris Ryan/GI; Print Collector/GI; Heritage Images/GI (x2)

Key: GI = Getty Images

Index

2024 Cambridge Dedicated Teacher Awards

Our **Cambridge Dedicated Teacher Awards** are an opportunity to show appreciation for the incredible work teachers do every day.

Thank you to everyone who nominated this year; we have been inspired and moved by all of your stories. Well done to all of our nominees for your dedication to learning and for inspiring the next generation of thinkers, leaders and innovators.

Congratulations to our winners!

Global Winner
South East Asia & Pacific
Sydney Engelbert
Keningau Vocational College, Malaysia

East Asia
Pengfei Jiang
Zhuji Ronghuai Foreign Language School, China

Pakistan
Saeeda Salim
SISA - School of International Studies in Sciences & Arts, Pakistan

South Asia
Meena Mishra
Dr Sarvepalli Radhakrishnan International School, India

Middle East and North Africa
Gina Justus
Our Own English High school- Sharjah- Girls, United Arab Emirates

Sub-Saharan Africa
Tajudeen Odufeso
Isara Secondary School, Isara Remo, Nigeria

Europe
Aynur Bayazit
Menekşe Ahmet Yalçınkaya Kindergarten, Türkiye

Latin America & the Caribbean
Ramon Majé Floriano
Montessori sede San Francisco, Colombia

North America
Marisa Santos
Seminole Ridge Community High School, United States

For more information about our dedicated teachers and their stories, go to dedicatedteacher.cambridge.org

CAMBRIDGE